D1359955

The Measurement
of Personality Traits
by Scales and Inventories

Books by Allen L. Edwards

The Measurement of Personality Traits by Scales and Inventories
Experimental Design in Psychological Research, Third Edition
Statistical Methods, Second Edition
Statistical Analysis, Third Edition
Expected Values of Discrete Random Variables and Elementary Statistics
The Social Desirability Variable in Personality Assessment and Research
Techniques of Attitude Scale Construction

The Measurement
of Personality Traits
by Scales and Inventories

ALLEN L. EDWARDS

PROFESSOR OF PSYCHOLOGY

University of Washington

HOLT, RINEHART AND WINSTON, INC.

New York · Chicago · San Francisco · Atlanta
Dallas · Montreal · Toronto · London · Sydney

BF698
.5
.E4

Copyright © 1970 by Holt, Rinehart and Winston, Inc.
All rights reserved
Library of Congress Catalog Card Number: 70-101688
SBN: 03-083573-9
Printed in the United States of America
1 2 3 4 5 6 7 8 9

Preface

This book concerns the measurement of personality traits by means of scales and the interpretation of scores on such scales. The emphasis throughout is on methodological and theoretical issues. The methodology involved both in scale construction and in the interpretation of scores on scales is primarily statistical, and a knowledge of elementary statistical concepts and techniques is therefore essential for understanding most of the chapters. The first chapter provides a review of elementary statistical concepts, and every reader who understands the material in this chapter should be able to follow the discussion in subsequent ones.

A type of factor analysis called "principal-component analysis" plays a major role in many of the research studies described in the book. I have, therefore, included a nontechnical interpretation of a principal-component factor loading matrix in Chapter 6. All of the following chapters assume that the reader has a good knowledge of the contents of Chapter 6.

The material covered in this book has evolved over the years from a course I have been teaching on personality measurement for upper-division and graduate students. The students enrolled in this course come from various departments and probably no more than half of them are psychology majors. Nor are the students measurement specialists, although all have had an introductory course in statistics. Despite the technical nature of the course, the students seem able to master it and, perhaps better yet, evidence interest in it.

The instructor interested in teaching a similar course may benefit from my organization. Early in the term, before reaching Chapter 5, each student completes a number of personality inventories, the first usually being the MMPI. Sets of scoring stencils are made available and each student scores his own answer sheets and makes up his own profile on each of the inventories. The scores of the students are never seen by the instructor.

After the students have completed the MMPI, they are assigned Chapter 3, "The Basic Scales," in *An MMPI Handbook* by Dahlstrom and Welsh (1960). Manuals for the MMPI and various other inventories are read by the students after they have completed each inventory. They are also asked to read the appropriate sections in Buros' (1965) *The Sixth Mental Measurements Yearbook* regarding each of the inventories. Various journal articles are assigned as supplementary reading.

Some of the material in Chapters 7 through 16 is controversial and I assign students Block's (1965) *The Challenge of Response Sets* to read in conjunction with these chapters. They are also asked to read Jackson's (1967a) critical review of Block's monograph, Block's (1967) remarks on Jackson's review, and Jackson's rejoinder (1967b), all of which appear in *Educational and Psychological Measurement*.

In addition to completing the inventories and the readings, students are assigned simple projects that they can accomplish either cooperatively or individually. Useful materials for this purpose include the Messick and Jackson (1961a) social desir-

86163

ability scale values for the MMPI items and the Mees, Gocka, and Holloway (1964) social desirability scale values for the CPI (California Psychological Inventory) items. I am indebted to these authors for permission to reproduce the social desirability scale values of these items which are given in the appendix.

Three volumes, two by Goldberg and Rorer (1963, 1964) and one by Goldberg (1963), contain valuable item statistics for the MMPI items, the CPI items, and the EPPS (Edwards Personal Preference Schedule) items, respectively. I am indebted to these authors for permission to reproduce the proportion of male and female students answering each of the MMPI and CPI items True and the proportion of male and female students choosing the *A* statement in each of the *AB* pairs of statements in the EPPS. These values are also given in the appendix.

In addition, I have included in the appendix the social desirability scale values of the EPI (Edwards Personality Inventory) items and the proportion of male and female students answering each of these items True.

Scoring keys for some 200 MMPI scales can be found in Dahlstrom and Welsh (1960). The various issues of the *Journal of Clinical Psychology* contain scoring keys for many newly developed MMPI scales.

It is also helpful if the instructor has available for student use 100 or so completed answer sheets for each of the various inventories. These are often available in university counseling centers. Copies of the completed answer sheets can be made with all identifying information regarding the respondents blocked out.

I have been fortunate in having a number of bright and competent Ph.D. candidates, some of whom have also served as my research assistants. Although their names appear at various places throughout the book, I would like to acknowledge their assistance here also. They are, in order of service: Jerald N. Walker, Carol J. Diers, James A. Walsh, Alan J. Klockars, and Robert D. Abbott.

I am indebted to the editor of *Educational and Psychological Measurement* for permission to reproduce, with minor changes, several articles that I have published in that journal.

I should also acknowledge that almost all of the research studies with which my name is associated and which are cited in the book were supported, in part, by Research Grant 5 R01 MH04075 from the National Institute of Mental Health, United States Public Health Service.

Allen L. Edwards

Seattle, Washington
January 1970

Contents

9. SD Responding and the MMPI   123

10. Acquiescence and Social Desirability   142

Chapter 1

Personality Scales
and Elementary
Statistical Concepts

1.1 Descriptions of Personality

Personality assessment is concerned with the description of what individuals are like at any given moment in time. There are two major ways to obtain descriptions of individuals. One is to ask the individual himself to describe what he is like. The other is to ask his peers and associates or others who have studied or observed him to describe what he is like.

If an individual is asked to describe his personality or what he is like, he may describe his physical characteristics, his likes and dislikes, his interests, his motives, his goals in life, his attitudes, his feelings about various things, his typical behaviors, his skills and abilities, and so on.

It should be noted that general instructions to an individual to describe himself or his personality permit him to choose those statements he wishes to make in describing himself and also the total number of statements he may make. As a result, self-descriptions obtained under these conditions seldom permit any adequate comparisons between the self-descriptions obtained from different individuals.

Some individuals may describe themselves in terms of several hundred statements and others may describe themselves in terms of a much smaller number. If one individual describes himself by stating, "I am regarded by my friends as being very intelligent," and if another does not make this statement about himself, we have no way of knowing whether this omission is due to faulty memory, modesty, judged irrelevance of the statement, or some other reason. If an individual should fail to volunteer a particular descriptive statement about himself, it does not necessarily mean that the statement does not describe him.

An autobiography is, in part, an attempt by an individual to describe his personality, but it is also an attempt to describe his environment and those events in his life that served to shape and influence the development of his personality. Some autobiographies are complete and detailed, so that the reader may feel that he has not only a good description of the writer's personality but also some understanding of the factors that contributed to the development of his personality. At best, however, the autobiographies of two different individuals permit only a rough and crude comparison of the similarities and differences in the personalities of the two individuals.

Similar difficulties are encountered when we ask others to describe the personality of someone. In addition, descriptions obtained from others must necessarily be limited to those things that they have had an opportunity to observe. It obviously would be impossible for one individual to describe the personality of another individual if he knew nothing at all about the person he was asked to describe.

A biography is an attempt by one individual to describe in detail the personality and factors influencing the personality development of another individual. But it is the case that biographies of the same individual written by two different observers often leave the reader with the impression that not one but rather two different individuals have been described. Descriptions of the personality of a given individual by two associates or persons who presumably know him equally well often have little in common.

1.2   Standard Sets of Statements in Obtaining Personality Descriptions

If we are interested in comparing the personality of one individual with that of another and in finding out something about the way in which the two differ, we must have some common basis for the descriptions obtained of each individual. One way in which this can be accomplished is by having the individuals describe themselves in terms of personality statements. Each individual could be asked to read each statement and to mark it True if he believes it accurately describes him or to mark it False if he does not. If the same set of statements is used in obtaining the self-descriptions, then it would obviously be possible to compare similarities and differences in the self-descriptions in terms of this particular set of statements.

Similarly, if the descriptions of personality are to be obtained from peers and associates, the use of a common set of statements for obtaining the descriptions would also permit comparisons of similarities and differences among different individuals.

The adequacy of any given set of statements for obtaining descriptions of personality obviously depends both on the content of the statements and also on the number of statements in the set. The total number of possible statements that need to be used in describing an individual is unknown, but there is little doubt that the number must be very large. As the number of statements in a set increases, so also does the time required to obtain a description of an individual. And of course, the complexity of comparing the descriptions of different individuals also increases with the number of statements in the set. With k statements, there are 2^k possible different patterns of response, and this number becomes very, very large as k increases.

1.3   Qualitative Differences in Personality

Although it is accepted that individuals have different personalities, these differences are of a qualitative nature rather than quantitative. Differences in personality, in other words, cannot be measured in such a way that it is possible to say that John has X amount of personality and Jim has Y amount or that Y represents more or less personality than X. However, the fact that differences in personality may be described, but not measured, does not mean that aspects or dimensions of personality cannot be measured.

1.4   Quantitative Differences in Personality Traits

It is well recognized that individuals do differ in *degree* with respect to such variables as academic achievement, intelligence, height, weight, and so on. An individual who has an Intelligence Quotient (IQ) of 150 presumably has a greater degree of intelligence than one with an IQ of 100. An A grade in an academic course is commonly accepted as representing a greater degree of achievement or knowledge of the content of the course than a grade of C. Similarly, it is not unusual to describe some individuals as being "highly motivated to succeed in college." The implication of this descriptive statement, of course, is that there are degrees of being "motivated" and, consequently, that some individuals are more highly motivated than other individuals. Similarly, we recognize that some individuals seem to be more "anxious" than others, that some seem to be more "aggressive" in their behavior than others, that some individuals seem to have their daily life more "organized" than others, and so on.

Anxiety, motivation to succeed, and aggressiveness may thus be considered as representing dimensions or aspects of personality in terms of which there are individual differences in degree. Individual differences in variables such as these are commonly referred to as "personality traits." The term "trait" itself is a broad one which encompasses individual differences with respect to any measurable variable, such as reaction time, height, weight, intelligence, and so on. In this book we shall be concerned with those traits that are measured by means of personality scales.

1.5   Personality Scales

A *personality scale* is a limited set of descriptive statements, also called *items*, that are relevant to some common trait. If individuals describe themselves in terms of the items in a personality scale, a score on the scale can be obtained for each individual. Individual differences in the scores on a scale are interpreted as representing individual differences in the trait which the scale was designed to measure. In order to understand the essential psychometric properties of a personality scale, it is necessary to have a knowledge of some elementary statistical concepts. In this chapter we describe and develop these elementary statistical concepts.

1.6   Item Responses and Scores on Personality Scales

It is not necessary but, in general, each item in a personality scale can be answered by an individual in only one of two ways: True or False. If the individual believes that an item accurately describes him, then he is instructed to answer the item True. If he believes that the item does not accurately describe him, then he is instructed to answer the item False.

Again it is not necessary, but it is the case that in most personality scales the responses to each item are assigned a score of 0 or 1. The response assigned a score of 1 is called the *trait* or *keyed* response to the item, and the response assigned a score of 0 is called the nontrait or nonkeyed response. The trait or keyed response to some of the items in a scale may be a True response and for the other items the trait response may be a False response. An individual's score on the scale is simply the number of trait responses that he has given to the complete set of items.

If a personality scale consists of k items, then the possible scores on the scale are $0, 1, 2, \ldots, k$. We let N be the number of individuals who have described themselves on the scale and for each of the N individuals we have a score. Because the psychometric properties of a scale should be based on the responses of a relatively large number of individuals, we shall assume that N is at least 200 and preferably closer to 400. If this is true, then for all practical purposes $(N - 1)/N$ is approximately 1.00. The assumption that N is large will also simplify the notation and development of the various statistical concepts of interest.

1.7 Mean Scores on Personality Scales

The scores on a scale are values of a variable and we represent a variable by a capital letter such as X or Y. The *mean* value of a variable will be designated by $\bar{X}$ and $\bar{X}$ is defined as

$$\bar{X} = \frac{\sum X}{N} \tag{1.1}$$

The mean, in other words, is simply the sum of all of the N values of X, divided by the total number of values. The mean provides information regarding the average score on a scale.

1.8 Variability of Scores on Personality Scales

The *variance* of a variable is defined as

$$\sigma^2 = \frac{\sum (X - \bar{X})^2}{N} \tag{1.2}$$

and the *standard deviation* is defined as the square root of (1.2) or as

$$\sigma = \sqrt{\frac{\sum (X - \bar{X})^2}{N}} \tag{1.3}$$

The standard deviation provides information regarding the variability of a given set of scores. If all scores were equal to exactly the same value, then the variance and standard deviation would be equal to zero. If all of the scores fall within a relatively narrow range, then the standard deviation will be small in value. For distributions of scores that are reasonably normal in shape or form, approximately all of the scores will fall within the range $\bar{X} \pm 3\sigma$ and approximately 95 percent will fall within the range $\bar{X} \pm 2\sigma$. Even when distributions depart considerably from normality, almost all of the scores will fall within the range $\bar{X} \pm 3\sigma$.

1.9 Range of Scores on Personality Scales

Suppose that we have two scales with $k = 40$ items in each and such that for both scales we have $\bar{X} = 20.0$. If for one scale we have $\sigma = 5.0$, then, if N is large, we might expect the range of scores on the scale to be approximately $20.0 \pm (3)(5.0)$, or from 5 to 35. If for the second scale we have $\sigma = 1.0$, then we might expect the range of scores to be approximately $20.0 \pm (3)(1.0)$, or from 17 to 23. For the second scale we have a narrow range of possibly seven different scores.

In general, a desirable characteristic of a scale is that the actual observed scores for a group of N individuals fall into at least ten classes or values, and 15 classes or values would be even more desirable. We want a scale to provide a fairly wide range of scores because we want the scores to measure individual differences in a trait and the greater the range of scores, the more information the scores provide about these individual differences. If a scale results in only a narrow range of scores, then it is likely that many individuals who have the same score and are consequently believed to have the same degree of a trait will not, in fact, be very homogeneous. For example, if height were measured only to the nearest foot, then all individuals with a reported height of 6′ would be regarded as having the same height. More information would be provided about individual differences in height if the unit of measurement were the inch. The inch scale makes possible greater differentiation in measured height than a scale in which the unit of measurement is a foot. On the foot scale two individuals may both be described as being 6′ tall, whereas on the inch scale one may be described as 5′8″ and the other as 6′4″. Individual differences in height as small as 1″ are regarded by most people as being reasonably important and consequently heights are usually measured to the nearest inch.

Although personality traits cannot be measured by means of scales with the same degree of accuracy as height, we would like any given scale to result in at least ten, and preferably more, different scores. Any cruder scale of measurement may obscure important individual differences in the trait.

1.10   Skewed and Symmetrical Distributions of Scores

If we know the mean score on a scale, the number of items in the scale, and the standard deviation of the distribution of scores, we can predict something about the shape or form of the distribution of scores. If $\bar{X} = 30.0$ on a $k = 40$ item scale and if $\sigma = 5.0$, then it is a reasonable prediction that the distribution is left-skewed, or has a tail to the left or low end of the score continuum. Similarly, if $\bar{X} = 10.0$, $k = 40$, and if $\sigma = 5.0$, then the distribution of scores is likely to be right-skewed, or to have a tail to the right. For the first scale, we would expect to have a greater range of individual differences for scale scores that are below the mean of 30.0 than for scores that are above the mean. Similarly, for the second scale, we would expect to have a greater range of individual differences for scores that are above the mean of 10.0 than for scores that are below the mean. On the other hand, if we had $\sigma = 3.0$ for both scales, then we would expect the distribution of scores for both scales to be more symmetrical about the means of the distributions. In general, if the mean score, $\bar{X}$, on a scale does not deviate too much from $k/2$, the distribution of scores on a scale will tend to be fairly symmetrical.[1]

1.11 Correlation Coefficient and Covariance of Scores on Two Scales

If we have two scales, X and Y, designed to measure two different traits, then we are often interested in the degree to which scores on the two scales are linearly related. A measure of this relationship is the *product-moment correlation coefficient*,[2] which may be defined as

$$r = \frac{\sum (X - \bar{X})(Y - \bar{Y})/N}{\sigma_X \sigma_Y} \qquad (1.4)$$

The numerator of the correlation coefficient is called a *covariance*, for which we use the symbol c_{XY}. The denominator of the correlation coefficient is the product of the standard deviation of the X variable and the standard deviation of the Y variable. It is obvious that if c_{XY} is equal to zero, we must also have r equal to zero.

We have defined the covariance as

$$c_{XY} = \frac{\sum (X - \bar{X})(Y - \bar{Y})}{N} \qquad (1.5)$$

Expanding this expression and simplifying, we also have

$$c_{XY} = \frac{\sum XY}{N} - \frac{(\sum X)(\sum Y)}{N^2}$$

or

$$c_{XY} = \frac{\sum XY}{N} - \bar{X}\bar{Y} \qquad (1.6)$$

Another useful identity for the covariance is obtained by multiplying both sides of (1.4) by $\sigma_X \sigma_Y$. Then we also have

$$c_{XY} = r\sigma_X \sigma_Y \qquad (1.7)$$

[1] If $\bar{X}$ deviates considerably from $k/2$, but if k is large so that $\bar{X} + 2.5\sigma$ is less than k and $\bar{X} - 2.5\sigma$ is greater than zero, then the distribution of scores will also tend to be fairly symmetrical.

[2] A product-moment correlation coefficient will also be referred to, more briefly, as a correlation coefficient.

1.12   Range of the Correlation Coefficient
between Scores on Two Scales

If two distributions have identical shapes or forms and if both are symmetrical, then the range in the possible values of r is from -1.00 to 1.00. If the two distributions have different shapes or forms, then the range of the correlation coefficient is restricted. For example, suppose we have two scales, X and Y, and that the frequency distributions of scores on the two scales are as given below:

X	f		Y	f
25	1		10	1
24	3		9	3
23	5		8	5
22	3		7	3
21	1		6	1

These two distributions are identical in shape and both are symmetrical. Thus the values of X can be paired with the values of Y in such a way as to obtain a correlation coefficient of either 1.00 or -1.00.

Two distributions that have exactly the same shape or form in that both have the same degree of left-skewness are shown below:

X	f		Y	f
25	5		10	5
24	4		9	4
23	3		8	3
22	2		7	2
21	1		6	1

These distributions are not, however, symmetrical. For these two distributions, it is possible to pair the X and Y values in such a way that the correlation coefficient will be 1.00, but it is not possible to pair them in such a way as to obtain a correlation coefficient of -1.00. This is true because the distributions are not symmetrical. The maximum negative value of the correlation for these two distributions is -0.50.

If one distribution is right-skewed and another distribution has the same degree of left-skewness, then the correlation coefficient can be equal to -1.00, but it cannot be equal to 1.00. For the two distributions shown below, for example, the maximum positive correlation is 0.50.

X	f		Y	f
25	5		10	1
24	4		9	2
23	3		8	3
22	2		7	4
21	1		6	5

1.13   Deviation Scores on Scales

It is often convenient to express scores on scales in terms of their *deviations* from the mean score. We define a deviation of a given value of X from the mean as

$$x = X - \bar{X} \tag{1.8}$$

If scores are in deviation form, then the mean of the deviation scores will be

$$\bar{x} = \frac{\sum x}{N}$$

Because

$$\sum x = \sum (X - \bar{X}) = \sum X - N\bar{X} = 0 \tag{1.9}$$

we have

$$\bar{x} = \frac{\sum x}{N} = 0 \tag{1.10}$$

The mean of a distribution of deviation scores will always be equal to zero.
We also have

$$\sigma^2 = \frac{\sum (X - \bar{X})^2}{N} = \frac{\sum x^2}{N} \tag{1.11}$$

and

$$\sigma = \sqrt{\frac{\sum (X - \bar{X})^2}{N}} = \sqrt{\frac{\sum x^2}{N}} \tag{1.12}$$

If scores on two scales, X and Y, are both in deviation form, then for the correlation coefficient we have

$$r = \frac{\sum xy/N}{\sqrt{\dfrac{\sum x^2}{N}}\sqrt{\dfrac{\sum y^2}{N}}} \tag{1.13}$$

or

$$r = \frac{\sum xy/N}{\sigma_X \sigma_Y} \tag{1.14}$$

1.14   Standard Scores on Scales

Another convenient score is the standard score. A *standard score* is defined as

$$z = \frac{X - \bar{X}}{\sigma} \tag{1.15}$$

and the sum of a distribution of standard scores will be

$$\sum z = \frac{\sum (X - \bar{X})}{\sigma}$$

We have already shown that $\Sigma (X - \bar{X}) = 0$. Then for the mean of a distribution of standard scores we have

$$\bar{z} = 0 \tag{1.16}$$

Because the mean of a distribution of standard scores is equal to zero, the variance of a distribution of standard scores will be given by

$$\sigma_z^2 = \frac{\sum (z - \bar{z})^2}{N}$$

$$= \frac{\sum z^2}{N}$$

But

$$\sum z^2 = \frac{\sum (X - \bar{X})^2}{\sigma^2}$$

and

$$\sum (X - \bar{X})^2 = N\sigma^2$$

so that

$$\sum z^2 = \frac{N\sigma^2}{\sigma^2} = N$$

and therefore

$$\sigma_z^2 = \frac{N}{N} = 1.00 \tag{1.17}$$

We see that the variance of a distribution of standard scores will be equal to 1.00 and, because the standard deviation is equal to the square root of the variance, we also have as the standard deviation of a distribution of standard scores

$$\sigma_z = 1.00 \tag{1.18}$$

1.15   Correlation Coefficient
and Covariance for Standard Scores on Two Scales

If scores on two scales, X and Y, are both in standard score form, then we also have

$$c_{z_X z_Y} = \frac{\sum z_X z_Y}{N} \tag{1.19}$$

or

$$c_{z_X z_Y} = \left(\frac{1}{N}\right) \frac{\sum (X - \bar{X})(Y - \bar{Y})}{\sigma_X \sigma_Y} \tag{1.20}$$

and (1.20) is identical with (1.4) for the correlation coefficient. Thus, if values of X and Y are expressed in standard score form, then the covariance of the standard scores will be equal to the correlation coefficient. For this case, we have

$$c_{z_X z_Y} = r \tag{1.21}$$

1.16 Mean Score on an Item in a Scale

We have said that the trait response to an item in a personality scale is assigned a score of 1 and the nontrait response a score of 0. Then we have a variable X such that X can take only the values of $X = 1$ or $X = 0$. To find the mean score on an item, we first find $\sum X$. It is obvious that all values of $X = 0$ will contribute nothing to the sum and that $\sum X$ will simply be the number of individuals who give the trait response to the item. If we let n_1 be the number of individuals who have given the trait response, then for the item mean we have

$$\bar{X} = \frac{\sum X}{N}$$

$$= \frac{n_1}{N}$$

or

$$p = \frac{n_1}{N} \tag{1.22}$$

where p is the proportion of the total number of individuals giving the trait response.

1.17 Variance and Standard Deviation of Scores on an Item

We have defined the variance of a variable as

$$\sigma^2 = \frac{\sum (X - \bar{X})^2}{N}$$

If we expand the numerator and simplify the resulting expression, we obtain

$$\sigma^2 = \frac{\sum X^2}{N} - \frac{(\sum X)^2}{N^2} \tag{1.23}$$

For the variance of the scores on a single item, we again note that all values of $X = 0$ will contribute nothing to ΣX^2 and that for all values of $X = 1$ we also have $X^2 = 1$ and, therefore, $\Sigma X^2 = \Sigma X$. But ΣX is simply the number of individuals who have given the trait response and, therefore,

$$
\begin{aligned}
\sigma^2 &= \frac{n_1}{N} - \left(\frac{n_1}{N}\right)^2 \\
&= p - p^2 \\
&= p(1 - p)
\end{aligned}
$$

where p is the proportion of individuals giving the trait responses. If we let $q = 1 - p$ be the proportion of individuals with $X = 0$, then

$$\sigma^2 = pq \tag{1.24}$$

The variance of scores on a single item is, therefore, the product of the proportion of individuals giving the trait response and the proportion of individuals giving the nontrait response.

The standard deviation of scores on an item will, of course, be the square root of (1.24) or

$$\sigma = \sqrt{pq} \tag{1.25}$$

1.18   Covariance of Two Item Scores

Consider two items, X and Y, such that the responses to each item are scored either 1 or 0. Then we have the possible paired values of X and Y shown in Table 1.1. It is obvious that all products of X and Y are equal to

Table 1.1   Paired (X, Y) Values for Two Variables That Can Take Only the Values of 0 or 1

		X	
		0	1
Y	1	(0, 1)	(1, 1)
	0	(0, 0)	(1, 0)

zero, except for those paired values of $X = 1$ and $Y = 1$. Thus ΣXY is equal to the number of individuals who have given the trait response to both items. Then for the covariance we have

$$c_{XY} = \frac{\sum XY}{N} - p_X p_Y$$

In general, we let p_{ij} be the proportion of individuals who have given the trait response to both items, p_i be the proportion who have given the trait response to the X item, and p_j be the proportion who have given the trait response to the Y item. Then for the covariance we have

$$c_{XY} = p_{ij} - p_i p_j \qquad (1.26)$$

1.19 Correlation of Two Item Scores

If we divide the covariance by the product of the two item standard deviations, we have the correlation coefficient. Thus

$$r = \frac{p_{ij} - p_i p_j}{\sigma_i \sigma_j}$$

or

$$r = \frac{p_{ij} - p_i p_j}{\sqrt{p_i q_i} \sqrt{p_j q_j}} \qquad (1.27)$$

1.20 Range of the Correlation Coefficient for Item Scores

We have said that the correlation coefficient can take either its maximum positive value of 1.00 or its maximum negative value of -1.00 only when two distributions have the same shape and both are symmetrical. For the correlation coefficient between two items, this means that only when $p_i = p_j = 0.50$ can the correlation coefficient take either a value of 1.00 or a value of -1.00.

If $p_i = p_j \neq 0.50$, then r can be equal to 1.00, but not equal to -1.00. On the other hand, if $p_i = q_j \neq 0.50$, then r can be equal to -1.00, but cannot be equal to 1.00. If for one item $p_i = q_i = 0.50$, but for the other item $p_j \neq q_j$, then the maximum negative value of r will be equal to the maximum positive value. For example, if $p_i = q_i = 0.50$ and if $p_j = 0.80$, then the maximum positive and negative values of r are 0.50 and -0.50, respectively. In view of the limited range, -0.50 to 0.50, in the possible values of the correlation coefficient for these two items, an observed value of r equal to 0.35 would be considered a relatively high positive value. It is of some importance to remember that the maximum positive value of r in the case of two items, each scored 1 or 0, is not 1.00 whenever $p_i \neq p_j$.

1.21 Mean of a Sum of Scores

Suppose that T is a variable consisting of a sum of k other variables. For example, we define

$$T = X_1 + X_2 + \ldots + X_k$$

To obtain the mean value of T, which we designate by $\bar{T}$, we sum over all N values of T and divide the resulting sum by N. Thus

$$\bar{T} = \frac{\sum T}{N} = \frac{\sum X_1}{N} + \frac{\sum X_2}{N} + \ldots + \frac{\sum X_k}{N}$$

or

$$\bar{T} = \bar{X}_1 + \bar{X}_2 + \ldots + \bar{X}_k \tag{1.28}$$

1.22   Mean of a Sum of Item Scores

If we have a personality scale consisting of k items, with each item scored 1 or 0, then the score on the scale is the sum of the scores on each of the items. Because the mean score on each item is p, the proportion of individuals giving the trait response, we have as the mean score on the scale

$$\bar{X} = p_1 + p_2 + \ldots + p_k \tag{1.29}$$

The mean score on a personality scale, in other words, is simply the sum of the item means.

1.23   Variance of a Sum of Scores

If T is equal to the sum of scores on k variables, then the variance of T will be given by

$$\sigma_T{}^2 = \frac{\sum (T - \bar{T})^2}{N} \tag{1.30}$$

But

$$T = X_1 + X_2 + \ldots + X_k$$

and

$$\bar{T} = \bar{X}_1 + \bar{X}_2 + \ldots + \bar{X}_k$$

and, therefore,

$$\sigma_T{}^2 = \frac{\sum [(X_1 - \bar{X}_1) + (X_2 - \bar{X}_2) + \ldots + (X_k - \bar{X}_k)]^2}{N}$$

If each value of X is expressed in deviation form, then

$$\sigma_T{}^2 = \frac{\sum (x_1 + x_2 + \ldots + x_k)^2}{N} \tag{1.31}$$

where $x_1 = X_1 - \bar{X}_1$, $x_2 = X_2 - \bar{X}_2$, and $x_k = X_k - \bar{X}_k$. Expanding the numerator of (1.31), we obtain k terms of the form

$$\frac{\sum x_1^2}{N} + \frac{\sum x_2^2}{N} + \cdots + \frac{\sum x_k^2}{N}$$

and each of these k terms is simply the variance of each of the variables contributing to the sum. Thus the sum of these k terms will be equal to

$$\sum \sigma_i^2 \qquad (1.32)$$

We designate the average value of these variances by $\bar{\sigma}_i^2$. Then

$$\sum \sigma_i^2 = k\bar{\sigma}_i^2 \qquad (1.33)$$

In addition to the k values of σ_i^2 we also have, as a result of expanding (1.31), $k(k-1)$ terms of the form

$$\frac{\sum x_1 x_2}{N} + \frac{\sum x_1 x_3}{N} + \cdots + \frac{\sum x_1 x_k}{N} + \cdots + \frac{\sum x_{k-1} x_k}{N}$$

and each of the above terms is a covariance. We let c_{ij}, $i \neq j$, be a general covariance term and $\bar{c}_{ij}$ be the average of the covariance terms. Then

$$\sum c_{ij} = k(k-1)\bar{c}_{ij} \qquad (1.34)$$

Then the variance of a sum of k variables will be given by

$$\sigma_T^2 = k\bar{\sigma}_i^2 + k(k-1)\bar{c}_{ij} \qquad (1.35)$$

1.24 Variance of a Sum of Item Scores

If a personality scale consists of k items and if each item is scored 1 or 0, then the score on the scale will be the sum of the item scores. The variance of the scores on the scale will then be given by (1.35). But we know that the variance of an item that is scored 1 and 0 is $p_i q_i$ and, therefore, for the variance of the scores on the scale we have

$$\sigma_T^2 = \sum p_i q_i + k(k-1)\bar{c}_{ij} \qquad (1.36)$$

It is important to note that if the average of the item covariances is equal to zero, then the variance of the scores will be equal to the sum of the item variances.

1.25 Statistically Independent Variables

If two variables are statistically independent, then

$$c_{XY} = \frac{\sum XY}{N} - \bar{X}\bar{Y} = 0 \qquad (1.37)$$

If the covariance is equal to zero, then the correlation coefficient will also be equal to zero. In the case of two items, i and j, we have

$$c_{ij} = p_{ij} - p_i p_j$$

If each of the items in a scale measures the same common trait, then the response to each item should not be independent of the responses to the other items. In general, then, if the items in a scale measure the same common trait, we would expect the average of the item covariances, $\bar{c}_{ij}$, to be positive. In this instance the variance of scores on the scale, σ_T^2, should be large relative to the sum of the item variances, $\Sigma p_i q_i$, because

$$\sigma_T^2 = \sum p_i q_i + k(k - 1)\bar{c}_{ij}$$

Chapter 2

Internal Consistency and Reliability of Personality Scales

2.1 Domains of Personality Statements

In the previous chapter we defined a personality scale as a collection of items or statements such that each item or statement is believed to be relevant to some trait of interest. To be specific, let us assume that we have constructed a scale of k items. The k items in the scale at hand are presumably a sample of a much larger population of statements that are relevant to the trait. In fact, we shall assume that the k statements represent a random sample of the population or domain of relevant statements. A statement is *relevant* to a domain of statements if its average covariance with the other statements in the domain is positive. We let X be the score on the scale of k items, and we know that the variance of X will be given by

$$\sigma_X^2 = k\bar{\sigma}_{X_i}^2 + k(k-1)\bar{c}_{X_{ij}}$$

where

$\bar{\sigma}_{X_i}^2 = $ the average value of the k item variances

and

$\bar{c}_{X_{ij}} = $ the average value of the $k(k-1)$ item covariances

2.2 Correlation Coefficient between Scores on Two Scales with Items from the Same Domain

We are interested in the correlation of the scores X based upon the k items in the scale at hand, with the scores Y based upon another set of k items randomly selected from the same population. The correlation between X and Y would be of the form

$$r_{XY} = \frac{c_{XY}}{\sqrt{k\bar{\sigma}_{X_i}^2 + k(k-1)\bar{c}_{X_{ij}}}\sqrt{k\bar{\sigma}_{Y_i}^2 + k(k-1)\bar{c}_{Y_{ij}}}} \tag{2.1}$$

where c_{XY} is the covariance of the X and Y scores. The problem is that seldom do we have available a second random sample of k items from the same domain as the items in the first sample. Let us assume, however, that the variance of Y would be equal to the variance of X. Because the two terms in the denominator of (2.1) are $\sqrt{\sigma_X^2}$ and $\sqrt{\sigma_Y^2}$ and because we have assumed that $\sigma_X^2 = \sigma_Y^2$, we can drop the subscripts. With this assumption, then,

$$r_{XY} = \frac{c_{XY}}{k\bar{\sigma}_i^2 + k(k-1)\bar{c}_{ij}} \tag{2.2}$$

We know that if the item scores in X and the item scores in Y are expressed in deviation form, then

$$c_{XY} = \frac{1}{N}\sum (x_1 + x_2 + \ldots + x_k)(y_1 + y_2 + \ldots + y_k) \tag{2.3}$$

If we expand (2.3), sum, and divide each term by N, we will obtain a covariance term for each of the items in X with each of the items in Y. Because both scales contain k items, we will have a total of k^2 item covariances. If we let

$$\bar{c}_{X_iY_i}$$

be the average of these item covariances, then the correlation between the scores on X and Y will be given by

$$r_{XY} = \frac{k^2\bar{c}_{X_iY_i}}{k\bar{\sigma}_i^2 + k(k-1)\bar{c}_{ij}} \tag{2.4}$$

The value of $\bar{c}_{X_iY_i}$ is unknown but, because the items in X and Y have been drawn from the same domain or population, let us assume that $\bar{c}_{X_iY_i}$ will be equal to $\bar{c}_{ij}$, the average of the covariances of the k items in the scale at hand. We have

$$\sigma_X^2 = k\bar{\sigma}_i^2 + k(k-1)\bar{c}_{ij}$$

and solving for $\bar{c}_{ij}$, we obtain

$$\bar{c}_{ij} = \frac{\sigma_X^2 - k\bar{\sigma}_i^2}{k(k-1)} \tag{2.5}$$

The numerator of (2.4) is

$$k^2\bar{c}_{X_iY_i}$$

and, multiplying both sides of (2.5) by k^2, we have

$$k^2\bar{c}_{ij} = \frac{k}{k-1}(\sigma_X^2 - k\bar{\sigma}_i^2) \tag{2.6}$$

Under the assumption that the average value, $\bar{c}_{ij}$, of the item covariances in the scale at hand is equal to the average value,

$$\bar{c}_{X_iY_i}$$

of the covariances between the items in scale X and the items in scale Y, then $k^2\bar{c}_{ij}$ will be equal to

$$k^2\bar{c}_{X_iY_i}$$

or

$$k^2\bar{c}_{X_iY_i} = \frac{k}{k-1}(\sigma_X^2 - k\bar{\sigma}_i^2) \tag{2.7}$$

Substituting in (2.4) with the right side of (2.7), we have

$$r_{XY} = \frac{\dfrac{k}{k-1}(\sigma_X^2 - k\bar{\sigma}_i^2)}{k\bar{\sigma}_i^2 + k(k-1)\bar{c}_{ij}} \tag{2.8}$$

Because $\bar{\sigma}_i^2$ is the average of the item variances, $k\bar{\sigma}_i^2$ is the sum of the k item variances. But the variance of an item i that is scored 1 or 0 is simply p_iq_i and, therefore, $k\bar{\sigma}_i^2 = \Sigma p_iq_i$. The denominator of (2.8) is, of course, σ_X^2. Then (2.8) becomes

$$r_{kk} = \left(\frac{k}{k-1}\right)\frac{\sigma_X^2 - \sum p_iq_i}{\sigma_X^2} \tag{2.9}$$

We have substituted r_{kk} for r_{XY} in (2.9) to distinguish this correlation coefficient from the usual correlation coefficient between any two variables X and Y. The coefficient r_{kk} is the correlation coefficient between scores on two scales, each consisting of k randomly selected items from the same domain or population of items relevant to a common trait.

2.3   Internal Consistency of a Scale

The coefficient r_{kk}, defined by (2.9), is variously known as the Kuder-Richardson Formula 20 (K-R 20) coefficient and as coefficient alpha (α). If for a given scale of k items we have $\bar{c}_{ij} = 0$, then σ_X^2 will be equal to

$\Sigma p_i q_i$ and r_{kk} will be equal to zero. A low value of r_{kk} provides evidence that, in general, responses to the items in a scale are relatively independent or uncorrelated. The degree to which item responses are intercorrelated provides a measure of the *internal consistency* or *homogeneity* of the items in a scale. Scales which have a high degree of internal consistency or homogeneity, as measured by r_{kk}, are scales in which responses to the items tend to be positively intercorrelated so that there is reason to believe that, in general, the items are measuring some common trait.

2.4 Lower-Bound Estimate of the Internal Consistency Coefficient

A lower-bound estimate of r_{kk} can be obtained under the assumption that $\Sigma p_i q_i$ is approximately equal to $k\bar{p}_i\bar{q}_i$, where $\bar{p}_i$ is the average value of p_i and $\bar{q}_i$ is the average value of q_i. We have shown previously that $\bar{X} = \Sigma p_i$ and, therefore, $\bar{p}_i = \bar{X}/k$. Similarly, $\Sigma q_i = k - \bar{X}$ and, therefore, $\bar{q}_i = (k - \bar{X})/k$. Then, substituting with $k\bar{p}_i\bar{q}_i$ for $\Sigma p_i q_i$ in (2.9), we have

$$r_{kk} = \left(\frac{k}{k-1}\right)\frac{\sigma_X^2 - k\bar{X}(k - \bar{X})/k^2}{\sigma_X^2}$$

or

$$r_{kk} = \frac{k\sigma_X^2 - \bar{X}(k - \bar{X})}{(k-1)\sigma_X^2} \tag{2.10}$$

and r_{kk}, as defined by (2.10), is known as the Kuder-Richardson Formula 21 (*K-R* 21) estimate of internal consistency. In general, the *K-R* 21 estimate of r_{kk} will be lower than that given by *K-R* 20 and defined by (2.9).

2.5 Relationship of r_{kk} to $\bar{r}_{ij}$ and k

Suppose that scores on each item in a scale are expressed as standard scores. Then the covariance between any pair of items, i and j, will be

$$c_{z_i z_j} = \frac{\sum z_i z_j}{N} = r_{ij} \tag{2.11}$$

It is easy to understand why $c_{ij} = r_{ij}$ in the case of standard scores. In standard score form, we have $\sigma_i = \sigma_j = 1.00$ and, therefore, $c_{ij} = r_{ij}\sigma_i\sigma_j = r_{ij}$. Then, if each item is in standard score form, we have

$$k^2\bar{c}_{ij} = k^2\bar{r}_{ij} \tag{2.12}$$

and

$$\sigma_X^2 = k + k(k - 1)\bar{r}_{ij} \tag{2.13}$$

Thus, if items are in standard score form, (2.4) becomes

$$r_{kk} = \frac{k^2 \bar{r}_{ij}}{k + k(k - 1)\bar{r}_{ij}} \tag{2.14}$$

We see that the magnitude of r_{kk} is dependent on the magnitude of the average intercorrelation of the items in a scale. The magnitude is also dependent on the number of items in the scale. Table 2.1 shows the number

Table 2.1   The Number of Items in a Scale and the Corresponding Values of $\bar{r}_{ij}$ Necessary to Obtain Values of r_{kk} Equal to 0.80, 0.85, 0.90, and 0.95

Number of Items	Values of $\bar{r}_{ij}$			
10	0.286	0.362	0.474	0.655
15	0.211	0.274	0.375	0.559
20	0.167	0.221	0.310	0.487
25	0.138	0.185	0.265	0.432
30	0.118	0.159	0.231	0.388
35	0.103	0.139	0.205	0.352
40	0.091	0.124	0.184	0.322
Values of r_{kk}	0.800	0.850	0.900	0.950

of items and the value of $\bar{r}_{ij}$ necessary to obtain r_{kk} values of 0.80, 0.85, 0.90, and 0.95.

2.6   Value of $\bar{r}_{ij}$ in Terms of r_{kk} and k

It is sometimes useful to know the value of $\bar{r}_{ij}$, given the value of r_{kk} and the number of items in a scale. If we solve (2.14) for $\bar{r}_{ij}$, we obtain

$$\bar{r}_{ij} = \frac{r_{kk}}{k - (k - 1)r_{kk}} \tag{2.15}$$

Thus, if r_{kk} is equal to 0.56 for a scale containing $k = 40$ items, then we have

$$\bar{r}_{ij} = \frac{0.56}{40 - (39)(0.56)} = 0.03$$

2.7 Increasing the Number of Items in a Scale

Assume that $\bar{r}_{ij}$ remains constant and k becomes indefinitely large. Dividing both numerator and denominator of (2.14) by k^2, we have

$$r_{kk} = \frac{\bar{r}_{ij}}{\frac{1}{k} + \frac{k-1}{k}\bar{r}_{ij}} \qquad (2.16)$$

As k becomes indefinitely large, $1/k$ approaches zero and $(k-1)/k$ approaches unity. Then, in the limit, as k becomes indefinitely large, r_{kk} approaches 1.00. Of course, no one would construct a scale with an indefinitely large number of items, but a variation of (2.14) is useful as a guide in determining what value of r_{kk} might be expected with a reasonable increase in the number of items in the scale, provided $\bar{r}_{ij}$ remains the same. Dividing both numerator and denominator of (2.14) by k, we obtain

$$r_{kk} = \frac{k\bar{r}_{ij}}{1 + (k-1)\bar{r}_{ij}} \qquad (2.17)$$

Assume that for a scale consisting of $k = 10$ items, we have $\bar{r}_{ij} = 0.20$. Then for the $k = 10$ item scale we have

$$r_{kk} = \frac{(10)(0.20)}{1 + (10-1)(0.20)} = \frac{2.0}{2.8} = 0.71$$

If we double the number of items in the scale so that $k = 20$, and if $\bar{r}_{ij}$ remains the same, then for the 20-item scale we would have

$$r_{kk} = \frac{(20)(0.20)}{1 + (20-1)(0.20)} = \frac{4.0}{4.8} = 0.83$$

Because it is possible to calculate r_{kk} without the necessity of calculating $\bar{r}_{ij}$, it is convenient to know how much r_{kk} would be increased if the number of items were increased by any factor a. If n is the number of items in a scale of increased length, so that $n > k$, then $a = n/k$. In general,

$$r_{nn} = \frac{ar_{kk}}{1 + (a-1)r_{kk}} \qquad (2.18)$$

For the example discussed above, we have $k = 10$ items and we want to estimate the value of r_{nn}, where $n = 20$ items. Then $a = 20/10 = 2$. For the $k = 10$ item scale we have $r_{kk} = 0.71$. Then

$$r_{nn} = \frac{2(0.71)}{1 + (2-1)(0.71)} = \frac{1.42}{1.71} = 0.83$$

as before, provided $\bar{r}_{ij}$ remains the same.

2.8 The Test-Retest Coefficient: r_{12}

We have said that r_{kk} is an estimate of the correlation between two scales of the same length, when both scales are measures of the same common trait. In essence, the coefficient assumes that the k items in both scales are random samples from the same domain. Suppose, however, that a given scale containing k items is administered to the same individuals twice, that is, on two different occasions. Scores on the scale on the two occasions are then correlated. We designate this test-retest coefficient by r_{12}.

The test-retest correlation coefficient would be of the form

$$r_{12} = \frac{\dfrac{1}{N} \sum (x_{11} + x_{12} + \ldots + x_{1k})(x_{21} + x_{22} + \ldots + x_{2k})}{\sigma_1 \sigma_2} \tag{2.19}$$

where $x_{11}, x_{12}, \ldots, x_{1k}$ are deviation scores on the k items at the time of the first administration and $x_{21}, x_{22}, \ldots, x_{2k}$ are deviation scores of the same k items at the time of the second administration, σ_1 is the standard deviation of the scores on the first administration, and σ_2 is the standard deviation of the scores on the second administration.

For σ_1 we have

$$\sigma_1 = \sqrt{k\bar{\sigma}_i{}^2 + k(k-1)\bar{c}_{ij}}$$

Let us assume that σ_1 is equal to σ_2. Then

$$\sigma_1 \sigma_2 = k\bar{\sigma}_i{}^2 + k(k-1)\bar{c}_{ij}$$

If each of the items is in standard score form, then

$$\sigma_1 \sigma_2 = k + k(k-1)\bar{r}_{ij} \tag{2.20}$$

and

$$r_{12} = \frac{\dfrac{1}{N} \sum (z_{11} + z_{12} + \ldots + z_{1k})(z_{21} + z_{22} + \ldots + z_{2k})}{k + k(k-1)\bar{r}_{ij}} \tag{2.21}$$

We note that the numerator of (2.21) is the sum of k^2 correlation coefficients. Of these k^2 coefficients, $k(k-1)$ will be of the type r_{ij} where $i \neq j$, that is, correlation coefficients between different items. But the numerator will also involve k correlation coefficients of the type r_{ii}, that is, the correlation between responses to the same item. Then for the test-retest correlation coefficient we have

$$r_{12} = \frac{k\bar{r}_{ii} + k(k-1)\bar{r}_{ij}}{k + (k-1)\bar{r}_{ij}} \tag{2.22}$$

In general, the average value of r_{ii} may be expected to be somewhat larger than the average value of r_{ij}. Consequently, we may expect that

$$k\bar{r}_{ii} + k(k-1)\bar{r}_{ij} > k^2\bar{r}_{ij}$$

We note that the numerator for r_{kk} is $k^2\bar{r}_{ij}$, whereas the numerator for r_{12} is $k\bar{r}_{ii} + k(k-1)\bar{r}_{ij}$. Thus, under the assumptions we have made, r_{kk} will tend to underestimate r_{12}, if $\bar{r}_{ii}$ is larger than $\bar{r}_{ij}$. If r_{kk} is high, then the test-retest coefficient will also tend to be high and r_{kk} provides, under the assumptions stated, a lower-bound estimate of r_{12}. If r_{kk} should be high and r_{12} low, then this is probably so because the trait measured by the scale is not relatively stable over the time interval between the two testings.

2.9   The r_{kk} and r_{12} Values
of Scales Measuring More Than One Trait

Suppose that the items in a scale are measuring several different and independent traits. For example, assume that a scale contains $k = 10$ items and that five of the items measure one common trait, the other five items measure another common trait, and that the two traits are independent. If each of the items in the scale is in standard score form, then we can obtain the matrix of item correlations r_{ij}, $i \neq j$. There will be a total of $10(10 - 1) = 90$ values of r_{ij}, as shown in Table 2.2. We shall assume that

Table 2.2 Intercorrelations of $k = 10$ Items When $k = 5$ Items Measure One Trait and $k = 5$ Items Measure Another Trait and the Two Traits Are Independent

		Trait 1					Trait 2				
	Items	1	2	3	4	5	6	7	8	9	10
Trait 1	1	1.00									
	2		1.00								
	3			1.00							
	4	$\bar{r}_{ij} = 0.20$			1.00		$\bar{r}_{ij} = 0.00$				
	5					1.00					
Trait 2	6						1.00				
	7							1.00			
	8								1.00		
	9	$\bar{r}_{ij} = 0.00$					$\bar{r}_{ij} = 0.20$			1.00	
	10										1.00

the average intercorrelation of the five items measuring Trait 1 is 0.20. Because there are $5(5 - 1) = 20$ of these correlation coefficients, as shown in Table 2.2, the sum of the coefficients will be $20(0.20) = 4.0$. Similarly, we assume that the average intercorrelation of the five items measuring Trait 2 is also 0.20 and the sum of these correlation coefficients will also be $(20)(0.20) = 4.0$. Thus the sum of 40 of the 90 correlation coefficients will be $4.0 + 4.0 = 8.0$. The 50 remaining correlation coefficients, as shown in Table 2.2, involve the correlations between the five items measuring Trait 1 and the five items measuring Trait 2.

If Trait 1 and Trait 2 are independent traits, then we may assume that the average value of these 50 correlations is zero. The sum of all $k(k - 1) = 10(10 - 1) = 90$ correlations or values of r_{ij}, $i \neq j$, will then be

$$\sum r_{ij} = 5(5 - 1)(0.20) + 5(5 - 1)(0.20) + 5^2(0.00) + 5^2(0.00)$$
$$= 8.0$$

and the average value of $\bar{r}_{ij}$ will be $8.0/90 = 0.089$. There will be $k = 10$ values of $\sigma_i{}^2$ and, in standard score form, each of these will be equal to 1.0. Then the total variance of the scores on the scale will be

$$\sigma_1{}^2 = k + k(k - 1)\bar{r}_{ij}$$

or

$$\sigma_1{}^2 = 10 + 10(10 - 1)(0.089)$$
$$= 18.0$$

The value of r_{kk} will then be

$$r_{kk} = \frac{k^2 \bar{r}_{ij}}{k + (k - 1)\bar{r}_{ij}}$$
$$= \frac{100(0.089)}{18.0}$$
$$= 0.49$$

and this scale would have a relatively low degree of internal consistency.

We assume that if the scale is administered to the same individuals a second time, the variance of the scores on the second administration will be equal to the variance of the scores obtained on the first administration. If the items are in standard score form, then the covariance between the scores on the first and second administrations will be

$$\frac{1}{N} \sum (z_{11} + z_{12} + \ldots + z_{1k})(z_{21} + z_{22} + \ldots + z_{2k})$$

There will be k values of the form

$$r_{ii} = \frac{\sum z_{1i} z_{2i}}{N}$$

LUTHER THEOLOGICAL SEMINARY
LIBRARY
ST. PAUL, MINNESOTA

and these will be not variances but correlations between responses to identical items. Although these k correlations will not be equal to 1.00, it seems reasonable to believe that the average value of r_{ii} will be considerably higher than the average value of the $k(k - 1)$ correlations of the form

$$r_{ij} = \frac{\sum z_{1i} z_{2j}}{N}$$

Let us assume that the average value of r_{ii} is equal to 0.90 and that the average value of r_{ij} is 0.089 as before. Then, the sum of all $k^2 = 100$ correlation coefficients will be

$$k\bar{r}_{ii} + k(k - 1)\bar{r}_{ij} = 10(0.90) + 10(10 - 1)(0.089)$$
$$= 17.01$$

Then for the correlation between scores on the first and second administrations we have

$$r_{12} = \frac{17.01}{18.00} = 0.94$$

and $r_{12} = 0.94$ is considerably higher than $r_{kk} = 0.49$. It is also obvious that r_{12} is considerably larger than r_{kk} because the $k = 10$ values of r_{ii} have served to almost double the estimate of $\bar{r}_{ij}$ based on the intercorrelations of the k items obtained at the time of the first administration.

In essence, this scale is not one in which the items are all measuring the same common trait, but instead is one in which the items are measuring two independent traits. If r_{kk} is high, then we have some assurance that the items in a scale are measuring a common trait or variable and that the relative ordering of the individuals in terms of their scores on the scale represents individual differences in a common trait. The mere fact that r_{12} is high offers no assurance that the items in a scale are measuring the same common trait.

Even when r_{kk} is equal to zero, it is still possible for r_{12} to be relatively high. This is so because the numerator of the test-retest coefficient will involve the k correlations of each item with itself. Assuming that individuals tend to be fairly consistent in their responses to the same item on two different occasions, these k correlations may be sufficiently high to result in a substantial value of r_{12}. In other words, a high value of r_{12} offers no evidence with regard to whether r_{kk} is either high or low. A low value of r_{12}, however, indicates that either r_{kk} is low or that the trait measured by the scale is not stable over time.

2.10   Predicted Values and Errors of Estimate

Assume that the same scale is administered on two occasions and that the scores for both administrations are in standard score form. If r_{12} were to be equal to 1.00, then we would have $z_1 = z_2$ for each of the paired scores. In other words, if the z_2 values were plotted against their paired z_1 values, then each of the paired (z_1, z_2) values would fall on a straight line and the slope of this line would be equal to r_{12} or 1.00. If r_{12} is not equal to 1.00, but if the relationship between z_1 and z_2 can be assumed to be linear, that is, if the trend of the plotted (z_1, z_2) values can be represented by a straight line, then the best predicted value of z_2 corresponding to any given value of z_1 is

$$\bar{z}_2 = r_{12}z_1 \tag{2.23}$$

This is the best predicted value in that the sum of the squared errors of prediction is at a minimum. That is, if we define an error of prediction as

$$e = z_2 - \bar{z}_2 \tag{2.24}$$

then

$$\sum e^2 = \sum (z_2 - \bar{z}_2)^2$$

is at a minimum.

We consider now some properties of $\bar{z}_2$. First of all, we note that

$$\sum \bar{z}_2 = r_{12} \sum z_1 = 0 \tag{2.25}$$

Because $\Sigma z_1 = 0$, the mean or average value of $\bar{z}_2$ will be equal to zero. The variance of $\bar{z}_2$ will then be

$$\frac{\sum \bar{z}_2{}^2}{N} = r_{12}{}^2 \frac{\sum z_1{}^2}{N}$$

and because $\Sigma z_1{}^2 / N = 1.00$, the variance of $\bar{z}_2$ will be

$$\sigma_{\bar{z}_2}{}^2 = r_{12}{}^2 \tag{2.26}$$

The correlation between $\bar{z}_2$ and z_1 will be

$$r_{\bar{z}_2 z_1} = \frac{\sum \bar{z}_2 z_1}{N} = \frac{\sum r_{12} z_1 z_1}{N} = \frac{r_{12} \sum z_1{}^2}{N} = r_{12} \tag{2.27}$$

or the same as the correlation between z_2 and z_1.

To determine the variance of the errors of prediction, we substitute $r_{12}z_1$ for $\bar{z}_2$ in (2.24), square, sum, and divide by N to obtain

$$\frac{\sum e^2}{N} = \frac{\sum (z_2 - r_{12}z_1)^2}{N}$$

$$= \frac{\sum z_2{}^2 - 2r_{12} \sum z_2 z_1 + r_{12}{}^2 \sum z_1{}^2}{N}$$

$$= 1 - 2r_{12}{}^2 + r_{12}{}^2$$

or

$$\sigma_e{}^2 = 1 - r_{12}{}^2 \tag{2.28}$$

and

$$\sigma_e = \sqrt{1 - r_{12}^2} \qquad (2.29)$$

The standard deviation defined by (2.29) is called the *standard error of estimate* when scores on both variables are expressed in standard score form.

If X_1 and X_2 are not in standard score form, then the variance of the errors of prediction will be

$$\sigma_e^2 = \sigma_2^2(1 - r_{12}^2) \qquad (2.30)$$

and the standard error of estimate will be

$$\sigma_e = \sigma_2\sqrt{1 - r_{12}^2} \qquad (2.31)$$

Because r_{kk} is a lower-bound estimate of r_{12} and because it can be obtained from a single administration of a scale, we can substitute r_{kk} for r_{12} in (2.30) and (2.31) to obtain estimates of σ_e^2 and σ_e. Of course if the scale has a low degree of internal consistency, as measured by r_{kk}, it may still have a relatively high test-retest coefficient. Thus, if r_{kk} considerably underestimates the value of r_{12}, its use in (2.30) and (2.31) will result in estimates of σ_e^2 and σ_e that will be larger than those obtained with the use of r_{12}.

Chapter 3

Rational Scales

3.1 Introduction

There are two major types of personality scales: *rational* and *empirical*. The strategy involved in developing a rational scale and the strategy involved in developing an empirical scale are quite different. In addition, the two types of scales differ in their measurement objectives. In this chapter we discuss rational scales and in the next, empirical scales.

3.2 Objectives of a Rational Scale

The primary objective in developing a rational personality scale is to be able to measure accurately individual differences with respect to some common trait or attribute that is of theoretical or scientific interest and is not adequately measured by any existing technique. Presumably, no one would undertake to develop a new rational scale to measure a trait if there already existed some reliable method for measuring the individual differences of interest.

3.3 Defining a Construct

If a scale is to be developed to measure a common trait, the scale must contain items. And before the items can be written, the trait or construct that the items will presumably measure must be defined. It is necessary, in other words, to make explicit the nature of the trait or construct that we hope to measure. If the construct or trait can be defined, then we can ask in what way individuals who have a high degree of the trait would differ from those who have a low degree of the trait. To be specific, we might consider two individuals, A and B, who are well known to us. We believe A possesses to a high degree the trait of interest and B does not. How do A and B differ? What actions or behaviors on the part of A lead us to believe that he has a high degree of the trait? As we continue to enumerate these differences and to describe them, we are in essence making statements that describe A, and not B, or that describe B, and not A. These statements form the initial pool of items for a rationally developed personality scale. We may, of course, seek assistance from others in obtaining statements we believe to be relevant to the trait.

Assume that eventually we have 60 or more statements. The next step is to decide whether the True or the False response to each statement is to be the keyed or trait response, that is, the response that is more likely to be given by those with a high degree of the trait than those with a low degree of the trait. If the trait or construct has been well-defined, there should be no difficulty in determining the trait response to each item. Again, we may wish to check our initial judgments of the trait responses with others who are knowledgeable about the nature of the trait.

3.4   Variance and Mean on a Rational Scale

The statements or items are then presented to a large number of individuals, who are asked to describe themselves by answering each item True or False. As we have indicated earlier, the number of individuals describing themselves should be at least 200 and preferably closer to 400. The responses of each of these individuals to the items are then scored according to the trait scoring of the items. For each trait response the individual receives a score of 1 and for each nontrait response a score of 0. We then sum the item scores for each individual to obtain his score on the scale. The variance of the scores on the tentative scale can then be obtained by calculating

$$\sigma_X{}^2 = \frac{\sum (X - \bar{X})^2}{N}$$

For each item, we can then find p_i, the proportion of individuals who have given the trait response to the item. Each item variance will be given by

$$\sigma_i{}^2 = p_i q_i$$

Because we wish to know the value of the sum of the item variances, or $\Sigma \sigma_i^2 = \Sigma p_i q_i$, we note that

$$\sigma_i^2 = p_i q_i$$
$$= p_i(1 - p_i)$$
$$= p_i - p_i^2$$

and

$$\sum \sigma_i^2 = \sum p_i - \sum p_i^2 \qquad (3.1)$$

The sum of the item variances can be found by means of (3.1) quite easily with a desk calculator or, of course, very rapidly with a high-speed electronic computer. We note also that the mean score on the scale can be obtained from Σp_i because

$$\bar{X} = p_1 + p_2 + \ldots + p_k = \sum p_i$$

3.5 Internal Consistency of a Rational Scale

We then calculate

$$r_{kk} = \left(\frac{k}{k-1}\right)\frac{\sigma_X^2 - \sum p_i q_i}{\sigma_X^2} \qquad (3.2)$$

for the scale. If r_{kk} is reasonably high, say 0.80 or larger, then we can examine the mean score on the scale in relation to the number of items in the scale. Hopefully, the mean score will not deviate too greatly from $k/2$ or $1/2$ the number of items in the scale. Next we should look at the range of $\bar{X} \pm 2\sigma$ or $\bar{X} \pm 3\sigma$. If $\bar{X} - 2\sigma$ is less than zero, then we know that the scale will not discriminate individual differences in the trait among those individuals with scores below the mean as well as it will among those individuals with scores above the mean. For similar reasons, we would like $\bar{X} + 2\sigma$ to be less than k, the number of items in the scale. All of the statements we have made, however, other than the one about the scale having a high value of r_{kk}, may be considered as suggesting desirable properties of a rational scale, but by no means essential properties. The main thing is that the scale have a high value of r_{kk} and that the values of the scores fall into at least ten or more different classes.

3.6 Increasing the Value of r_{kk}

If we have 60 or more items in a scale and r_{kk} is low, say less than 0.80, this indicates that some of the items in the scale have a very low average covariance with the other items in the scale. To determine which items are contributing the least to $\bar{c}_{ij}$, we could find the average covariance of each item in the scale with all of the other items. A simpler procedure, however, is simply to calculate the covariance between each item and total scores on the scale.

Let X be the score on an item and Y be the total score on the scale. For all values of $X = 0$, we have $XY = 0$. For all values of $X = 1$, we have $XY = Y$. Then ΣXY will simply be the sum of the Y values for those individuals with scores of 1 on the item. We designate this sum as ΣY_1. Then for the covariance of X and Y, we have

$$c_{XY} = \frac{\sum Y_1}{N} - p_i \bar{Y} \tag{3.3}$$

We also know that

$$c_{XY} = r_{XY}\sigma_X\sigma_Y$$

The correlation coefficient r_{XY} is the correlation between scores on an item X and total scores on the scale Y. This coefficient is called the *point biserial coefficient* and is designated by r_{pb}. If we are interested in the value of r_{pb}, we can calculate this by finding

$$r_{pb} = \frac{c_{XY}}{\sigma_X\sigma_Y} \tag{3.4}$$

or

$$r_{pb} = \frac{\dfrac{\sum Y_1}{N} - p_i\bar{Y}}{\sigma_Y\sqrt{p_iq_i}} \tag{3.5}$$

If we eliminate from a scale those items for which c_{XY} is low, then the value of $\bar{c}_{ij}$ for the items retained in the scale should be greater than the value of $\bar{c}_{ij}$ for the original set of items. The reason for this is that c_{XY} is the sum of the covariances of item X with itself and with each of the other $k - 1$ items in the scale. For example, if all items in the scale were expressed in deviation form, then

$$c_{XY} = \frac{1}{N}\sum x(y_1 + y_2 + \ldots + y_k)$$

or

$$c_{XY} = c_{xy_1} + c_{xy_2} + \ldots + c_{xy_k} \tag{3.6}$$

Thus, by eliminating those items for which the covariance of the item score with total scores is low, an increased value of r_{kk} may be obtained for the shortened scale.

If r_{kk} is low and the original number of items is small, say 20 or less, then adding additional items to the scale should result in an increased value of r_{kk}. Formula (2.18) can be used to gain some indication of the value of r_{nn} to be expected for a scale of n items when n is greater than k.

The importance of having a high value for r_{kk} in a rational scale is that a high value offers some assurance that the responses to all possible pairs of items in the scale are not, in general, independent. We recall that the covariance between any two items, i and j, is

$$c_{ij} = p_{ij} - p_i p_j$$

and if c_{ij} is equal to zero, then the responses to these two items are independent and r_{ij} will also be equal to zero. But if two items are measuring the same common trait, then responses to the two items should not be independent but positively correlated, and this can be true only if c_{ij} is positive. Similarly, if a given item has a positive covariance with each of the other items in a scale, this offers some assurance that the item is measuring something in common with each of the other items. It is only when r_{kk} is relatively high that we may have some confidence that total scores on a scale represent individual differences with respect to a common trait or variable.

3.7   The Value of r_{kk} in Terms of $\bar{r}_{ij}$ and k

We have shown that if each of the items in a scale is in standard score form, then

$$r_{kk} = \frac{k\bar{r}_{ij}}{1 + (k - 1)\bar{r}_{ij}}$$

and it is obvious that for any finite number of items r_{kk} can be equal to 1.00 only if $\bar{r}_{ij}$ is equal to 1.00. But $\bar{r}_{ij}$ can be equal to 1.00 only if each item correlates 1.00 with every other item in the scale. We have pointed out previously that r_{ij}, the correlation between two items, can be equal to 1.00 only if $p_i = p_j$. Thus, only if p_i, the proportion of individuals giving the keyed response to an item, is the same for all items could all of the values of r_{ij} be equal to 1.00. But under these restrictive conditions, total scores on the scale could take only two possible values, 0 and k, where k is the number of items in the scale. Thus, even if it were possible to construct a rational scale for which $\bar{r}_{ij}$ was equal to 1.00, the total scores on the scale would provide no more information about individual differences in the trait than would the score on any single item in the scale.

It is also true that for any fixed value of $\bar{r}_{ij}$, r_{kk} will approach a value of 1.00 as k, the number of items in the scale, increases without limit. Thus, if k is sufficiently large, r_{kk} will approach a value of 1.00, even though $\bar{r}_{ij}$ is relatively low. For example, if $\bar{r}_{ij}$ is equal to 0.01 for $k = 891$ items, then r_{kk} will be equal to 0.90.

If $\bar{r}_{ij}$ should be close to zero for any very large set of items, the most reasonable explanation of this result is that within the large set of items there are subsets of items that tend to be positively intercorrelated with each other but negatively correlated with the items in other subsets. The large set may also include some items that have very low or zero correlations with the other items.

If a rational scale with a reasonably high value of r_{kk} cannot be constructed with 50 or fewer items, this is probably so because the trait is not well-defined or because the items used in developing the scale are not relevant to a common trait.

3.8 Importance of the Original Item Pool

The importance of initially developing a good item pool cannot be overemphasized. The statements in the original pool should map adequately the domain or trait of interest. If the trait of interest is not a highly specific one, then it should not be too difficult to write or construct a substantial number of items, each of which is relevant to the trait. Developing a representative set of statements is not a task to be taken lightly and surely not one that can be completed in an afternoon of armchair theorizing. It is helpful if one can think of two or three individuals who have the trait of interest and to consider how these individuals characteristically manifest the trait in their behavior, feelings, or in other ways. The initial item pool should include more items than we contemplate including in the scale, so that those items which have a high covariance with total scores can be selected for the scale and those with low covariances eliminated.

3.9 Cross-Validating the Value of r_{kk}

If items are selected for retention in a rational scale because they have relatively high covariances with total scores, then to some degree this selection process capitalizes on chance factors that tend to inflate the average interitem correlation and consequently the value of r_{kk}. It is necessary, therefore, to administer the scale to a new sample of individuals and to recalculate the value of r_{kk} for this new sample. If the value of r_{kk} obtained with the new sample is substantially the same as the value obtained with the original sample, we have some assurance that it is a stable value and not simply the result of chance factors involved in the item selection process.

3.10   Rational Scales and Criterion Measures

As was stated previously, the primary objective in developing a rational personality scale is to be able to measure accurately individual differences in some common trait of theoretical and scientific interest. It was also pointed out that it would be of no value to develop a rational scale to measure a trait if there already existed some method of obtaining adequate measures of the trait. A rational scale, in other words, should be a scale that measures accurately a trait that cannot be assessed accurately in any other way.

Suppose, for example, that a trait of interest is "anxiety." Statements are written that are believed to be relevant to this trait and a rational scale is developed that has a satisfactory value of r_{kk}. How can we be sure that the scale is really measuring a trait of anxiety? If some criterion measure of anxiety were available, then the scale might be validated by demonstrating that scores on the scale are correlated with the criterion measure. The difficulty, however, is that any measure or index of anxiety external to scores on the scale may not itself be an adequate criterion of the trait the scale was designed to measure. If the scale correlates low with another purported index of anxiety, the fault may not be with the scale but rather with the other index. The essential point is that a rational scale can never be validated by correlating scores on the scale with a criterion measure, because a rational scale is ordinarily developed to measure a trait for which there is no acceptable criterion measure. If there were, there would be no need for the rational scale.

On the other hand, we should not make the mistake of concluding that simply because a trait name is assigned to a rational scale the scores on the scale are, therefore, measures of the trait named by the scale. If the scale has a satisfactory value of r_{kk}, it is a reliable measure of something, but the scientific and theoretical nature of the "something" can be determined only by further research. It is entirely possible for two different investigators to develop rational scales with the same trait name and such that each scale has a high r_{kk} value. Yet the correlation between scores on the two scales may be quite low. The failure of two rational scales with the same trait name to correlate highly with each other simply means that the investigators developing the scales had different conceptions of the nature of the trait.

3.11   Construct Validity of Rational Scales

If rational scales cannot be validated by correlating scores on the scales with a criterion measure, how can the validity of the scales be demonstrated? Or, perhaps better, how can one determine what interpretation should be given to scores on a rational scale? Rational scales are most often developed by scientists and research workers who wish to use the scales in experimentation and research to test various theories and hypotheses about the nature of the trait that the scale was designed to measure. For example, a scientist may postulate that there are individual differences with respect to some trait, such as anxiety, for which there is no adequate criterion measure. He may also hypothesize that individuals who have a high degree of anxiety are more likely to respond in some specific manner in a given experimental situation than individuals with a low degree of anxiety. In order to investigate experimentally his hypothesis, he must find some way of classifying or measuring the anxiety levels of individuals. In the absence of any criterion measure for level of anxiety, he sets out to develop a rational scale to measure this trait. If he is successful in developing a rational scale and if he is satisfied that the items in the scale map the trait of anxiety as he conceives it, he can use scores on the scale to classify individuals according to their level of anxiety. He can then test these individuals in the experimental situation and attempt to confirm his hypothesis regarding the difference in behavior between individuals with high and low levels of anxiety.

If the scientist has given considerable thought to the nature of the trait of anxiety, he may have many different hypotheses that he wishes to test. Each hypothesis that he investigates and confirms provides additional support for his interpretation of the scores on the scale as measuring anxiety. In essence, a rational scale is validated as a result of hypothesis testing and experimentation. This type of validity has been called *construct validity*. Construct validity studies are directed toward clarifying the nature of the trait measured by a scale. In investigating the construct validity of a scale, one attempts to demonstrate that the scores on the scale are correlated with other variables which, in terms of theory, should be correlated with the trait. It is also equally important, however, to demonstrate that scores on the scale have low correlations with variables which, in terms of theoretical considerations, should not be correlated with the trait.

Suppose that a rational scale is developed to measure a given trait and it is then found, contrary to expectation, that scores on the scale are correlated with scores on another scale that has been assigned a different trait name. For example, a rational scale designed to measure Trait X may be constructed and it may then be found that scores on this scale are correlated with scores on another scale with a different trait name Y. If the correlation coefficient is sufficiently high, then obviously one of the two scales is redundant in that the rank ordering of individuals on both scales would be much the same.

Assume that the scientist who has developed Scale X is convinced that scores on Scale Y should be interpreted as measuring Trait X, whereas the scientist who has developed Scale Y is convinced that scores on Scale X should be interpreted as measuring Trait Y. Such differences in the interpretation of scores on rational scales that are highly correlated can and do occur. They can be resolved only by hypothesis testing and research directed toward clarifying the nature of the trait measured by the two scales. If it is assumed that the two scales are both measures of Trait X, then it should be possible to formulate various hypotheses regarding the relationship between scores on the scales and various other situations in which individual differences in Trait X should be manifested. If these hypotheses are confirmed, this would support the interpretation of scores on the scales as measuring Trait X. Similarly, if the two scales are both measures of Trait Y, then a different set of hypotheses may be developed and tested. If it can be demonstrated that interpreting the scores as measuring Trait Y results in predictions regarding the correlations between scores and other variables that cannot be made by interpreting the scores as measuring Trait X, and if these predictions are empirically confirmed, this would support the interpretation of the scales as measuring Trait Y.

3.12   Predictive Validity of Rational Scales

Simply because a rational scale is seldom developed with the purpose of predicting some criterion measure, it does not mean that a rational scale may not be found to have some degree of predictive validity. Criterion measures or variables most often have either social or practical significance and seldom represent individual differences with respect to a single trait or ability. To consider an example, grades in school and college have often been regarded as criterion measures and to be able to predict grades may have both social and practical significance.

It is well established, however, that school grades are not simply a function of academic aptitude or of ability. The correlation between scores on aptitude or ability tests and grades is seldom any greater than 0.60 and this means that only about 36 percent of the variance in grades can be accounted for by individual differences in aptitude. Obviously, then, factors or traits other than aptitude must be related to grades. Furthermore, it has been clearly demonstrated that, although there may be a substantial correlation between aptitude and freshman grades in college, aptitude test scores correlate only about 0.16 with senior grades in college (Humphreys, 1968). Thus, if senior grades reflect, in part, differences in personality traits, rational scales devised to measure these traits may be correlated with these criterion measures, even though they were not originally constructed for this purpose.

Chapter 4

Empirical Scales

4.1 Criterion and Control Groups

Empirical scales are most often constructed because it is hoped that scores on the scale will be correlated with some criterion measure of interest. Often, but not necessarily, the criterion measure is a dichotomous variable such that individuals can be said to belong to one of two classes. One of the two classes represents those individuals who possess some trait, attribute, characteristic, or property in common, and this group is called the *criterion* group. The other class represents those individuals who do not possess the trait, attribute, characteristic, or property, and this group is called the *control* group.

Presumably, a reasonably accurate classification of an individual as a member of the criterion group is possible. It is not always the case, however, that a reasonably accurate classification occurs with respect to those individuals assigned to the control group. For example, if the criterion group consists of alcoholics, then those individuals undergoing treatment for alcoholism are undoubtedly accurately classified as members of the criterion group. If an individual is assigned to a control group of non-alcoholics simply because there is no record that he is being treated for alcoholism, it is possible that he is erroneously classified.

Similarly, individuals who are in mental institutions, and who have been diagnosed as schizophrenics, may be reasonably accurately classified as members of a criterion group. The words "reasonably accurately" are necessary, in this instance, because the diagnosis of schizophrenia is made by a psychiatrist, and it is well known that different psychiatrists may and do disagree upon the diagnosis of a mental patient. If an individual is classified as a member of the control, or nonschizophrenic, group simply because he is not in a mental institution, he may or may not be erroneously classified. There are undoubtedly many individuals who are not in mental institutions, but who would be diagnosed as schizophrenic by a psychiatrist if they ever came to the attention of the psychiatrist. The control group may, in this instance, also include individuals who should properly be classified in the criterion group.

The criterion and control groups may, of course, represent the two extremes of an ordered variable. Students in a university with high grade-point averages may be a criterion group of high achievers, and those with low grade-point averages may constitute a control group of low achievers.

The number of scales that can be developed by the empirical approach is limited only by the number of ways in which any large group of individuals can be classified into a criterion and a control group. The following are some examples of criterion groups that have been used in the development of empirical scales: juvenile delinquents, major league baseball players, actors, psychopaths, social workers, engineers, psychologists, and various other occupational classifications, individuals complaining of low back pain, members of sororities, and so on.

4.2 Selection of Items in Empirical Scales

The first and most important consideration in the empirical approach to scale development is that there exist some basis for establishing membership in the criterion and control groups. It would then be possible for the individual using the empirical approach to attempt to write statements and items that he believes would differentiate between the members of the criterion and control groups, but, in general, much less attention is given to this problem than in the rational approach to scale development. The reason for this is that the empiricist regards item content as more or less irrelevant. It does not matter what the item says; the only relevant aspect of an item is that it differentiates between members of the criterion and control groups. Any item that does this is considered a good item to include in an empirical scale.

Furthermore, the difference between the members of a criterion and a control group is most often not with respect to a single dimension or trait but rather with respect to several. If a relatively large and heterogeneous collection of items is given to both groups, then it may be found that some items differentiate between the groups with respect to one trait and others may differentiate between the two groups with respect to some other trait. The empiricist ordinarily begins his scale construction, therefore, not by attempting to map a single trait or domain but rather with a relatively large collection of heterogeneous items. It is then a matter of empirical test to discover those items that do and those that do not differentiate between the two groups.

If a large number of items are given to both the criterion and control groups, the number of individuals giving the True response to each item can be obtained. Let n_1 be the number in the criterion group giving the True response to an item and let N_1 be the total number of individuals in the criterion group. Then $p_1 = n_1/N_1$ will be the proportion in the criterion group giving the True response to the item. Similarly, if n_2 is the number in the control group responding True to the item and N_2 is the total number of individuals in the control group, then $p_2 = n_2/N_2$.

Under the assumption that both samples have been drawn from a common binomial population, the best estimate of P, the proportion in the population responding True to the item, will be

$$P = \frac{n_1 + n_2}{N_1 + N_2} \tag{4.1}$$

Assume, for example, that a criterion group consists of $N_1 = 100$ individuals and a control group consists of $N_2 = 100$ individuals. If $n_1 = 84$ and $n_2 = 66$, then

$$P = \frac{84 + 66}{100 + 100} = 0.75$$

and $Q = 1 - P = 0.25$ is an estimate of the proportion in the population responding False to the item.

Under the assumption that p_1 and p_2 are approximately normally distributed, then

$$Z = \frac{p_1 - p_2}{\sqrt{PQ\left(\dfrac{1}{N_1} + \dfrac{1}{N_2}\right)}} \tag{4.2}$$

will be a *standard normal deviate* and can be evaluated in terms of the table of the standard normal distribution.

If it is the case that P_1, the population proportion in the criterion group responding True to the item, is equal to P_2, the population proportion in the control group responding True to the item, then values of $Z \geq 2.0$ or values of $Z \leq -2.0$ have a probability of approximately 0.05. Therefore, a value of $Z \geq 2.0$ or a value of $Z \leq -2.0$ may be regarded as indicating that in the population $P_1 \neq P_2$. Because we are searching for items that differentiate between the criterion and control groups, all items for which $Z \geq 2.0$ or for which $Z \leq -2.0$ may be considered for inclusion in an empirical scale.

Substituting in (4.2) we have, for the item under discussion,

$$Z = \frac{0.84 - 0.66}{\sqrt{(0.75)(0.25)\left(\dfrac{1}{100} + \dfrac{1}{100}\right)}} = 3.0$$

and this item might be included in the scale and keyed True, because $Z > 2.0$. If the value of p_1 had been 0.66 and p_2 had been 0.84, then Z would be equal to -3.0 and this item might be included in the scale and keyed False.

In the first instance, with $p_1 > p_2$, the item would be keyed True because individuals who possess the attribute of interest, that is, who are members of the criterion group, are more likely to answer the item True than members of the control group. A True response, in other words, would be a sign or indication that an individual is more likely to belong to the criterion group than the control group. Similarly, in the second instance, with $p_1 < p_2$, the item would be keyed False because members of the criterion group are more likely to give this response than members of the control group. The keyed response to an item is always the one that is more likely to characterize members of the criterion group than members of the control group.

We have said that if $Z \geq 2.0$ or if $Z \leq -2.0$, then the item might be included in the scale. If an extremely large number of items have been administered to the two groups, then a large number of items might be found for which $Z \geq 2.0$ or $Z \leq -2.0$. In this case only the 40 or so items with the largest positive or negative values of Z might be retained for the scale and the other items discarded, even though the Z values for these items meet the standards suggested. Similarly, if an insufficient number of items with Z values greater than 2.0 or less than -2.0 are found, then the standards might be lowered to include items with Z values greater than 1.5 or less than -1.5 in the scale.

4.3   Correlation of an Empirical Scale with the Criterion

What are the characteristics of a scale constructed by the empirical approach? It is often claimed that an empirical scale will have predictive validity of the criterion because the scores on the scale should be substantially and positively correlated with the criterion used in selecting the items in the scale. If scores on the criterion variable are in standard score form and if each of the items in the scale is also in standard score form, then the correlation between the criterion variable (C) and scores on the scale (X) would be of the form

$$r_{CX} = \frac{\frac{1}{N} \sum z_C(z_1 + z_2 + \ldots + z_k)}{\sigma_C \sigma_X} \tag{4.3}$$

where r_{CX} is the correlation between the criterion variable and scores on the scale, z_C represents standard scores on the criterion variable, and $z_1, z_2, \ldots,$ z_k represent standard scores on the k items in the scale. The numerator of (4.3) is simply the sum of the correlations of the criterion variable with each of the k items in the scale. If we let the average value of these correlations be $\bar{r}_{Ck}$, then the sum of the k correlations will be $k\bar{r}_{Ck}$. Because the criterion variable is in standard score form, we have $\sigma_C = 1.0$ and, because the items on the scale are also in standard score form, we also have

$$\sigma_X = \sqrt{k + k(k - 1)\bar{r}_{ij}}$$

The correlation between the criterion and score on the scale will then be

$$r_{CX} = \frac{k\bar{r}_{Ck}}{\sqrt{k + k(k - 1)\bar{r}_{ij}}} \tag{4.4}$$

If the criterion is a dichotomous variable, then each of the correlations in the numerator of (4.3) will be a correlation between two variables, each scored 0 or 1. If the criterion is an ordered variable that can take a number of different values, than each of the correlation coefficients in the numerator will be a point biserial coefficient.

It is obvious from (4.4) that if r_{CX} is to be high, then not only should each of the items in the scale correlate positively with the criterion, but also the average of the $k(k - 1)$ values of r_{ij}, that is, the average of the correlations among the items in the scale, should be low. For any fixed value of k and $\bar{r}_{Ck}$, in other words, r_{CX} will increase as $\bar{r}_{ij}$ decreases.

If $\bar{r}_{ij}$ were negative this would, of course, result in a decrease in the value of the denominator of (4.4). The limiting maximum negative value of $\bar{r}_{ij}$ is $-1/(k - 1)$. Thus, if $\bar{r}_{ij}$ takes its limiting maximum negative value, and if each of the items is in standard score form, we would have

$$\sigma_X = \sqrt{k + k(k - 1)\frac{-1}{(k - 1)}} = 0.0 \tag{4.5}$$

But if σ_X is equal to zero, then all scores on the scale must be equal to each other and, consequently, scores on the scale could not possibly be correlated with the criterion. As a matter of fact, the correlation coefficient between two variables is not defined if the variance for either variable is equal to zero.

We note that as k increases, $-1/(k - 1)$ becomes a very small negative number. With $k = 51$ items, the maximum negative value of $\bar{r}_{ij}$ is -0.02 and, in this instance, σ_X would be equal to zero. Thus, if a scale contains a relatively large number of items, a very small negative value of $\bar{r}_{ij}$ may result in a variance and standard deviation that is close to zero.

The above discussion has assumed that each of the items in the scale is in standard score form. If the items are not in standard score form, then

$$\sigma_X^2 = \sum p_i q_i + k(k-1)\bar{c}_{ij}$$

Thus, if σ_X^2 is equal to zero, the average item covariance must be negative, and the sum of the item covariances must be negative and equal to the sum of the item variances.

The most desirable scale, for purposes of predicting a criterion, would appear to be one in which $\bar{r}_{ij}$ is equal to zero, so that σ_X^2 would be equal to k. If this were the case and if the items are in standard score form, then

$$r_{CX} = \frac{k\bar{r}_{Ck}}{\sqrt{k}} \tag{4.6}$$

We note, however, that if $\bar{r}_{ij}$ is equal to zero, then the internal consistency of the scale, as measured by r_{kk}, would be equal to zero also. In this case, the scale could not be regarded as measuring individual differences with respect to a single common trait. If, at the same time, each of the items in the scale is positively correlated with the criterion measure, this would indicate that the criterion itself is complex and does not represent individual differences with respect to a single common variable.

When r_{ij}, the correlation between two items, i and j, is equal to zero, the two items have no variance in common; the only thing that can be said about the two items is that whatever is being measured by one item is independent or uncorrelated with whatever is being measured by the other item. Similarly, if for all possible pairs of items in a scale it is true that r_{ij} is equal to zero, then each item would be measuring something that is independent or uncorrelated with whatever each of the other items is measuring. Even though scores on a scale of this kind may be correlated with a criterion measure, there is no basis for interpreting individual differences in scores as representing differences in degree of any meaningful trait or characteristic.

It is informative to examine the limiting value of $\bar{r}_{Ck}$ for any value of $\bar{r}_{ij}$ as k becomes indefinitely large. If we divide both numerator and denominator of (4.4) by k, then we have

$$r_{CX} = \frac{\bar{r}_{Ck}}{\sqrt{\dfrac{1}{k} + \dfrac{(k-1)}{k}\bar{r}_{ij}}} \tag{4.7}$$

If $\bar{r}_{ij}$ is equal to zero, then the limiting value of $\bar{r}_{Ck}$ is $\sqrt{1/k}$, because r_{CX}

cannot be greater than 1.00. If $\bar{r}_{ij}$ is greater than zero, then as k becomes indefinitely large, $1/k$ will approach zero as a limit and $(k - 1)/k$ will approach 1.00 as a limit. In this instance, we have

$$r_{CX} = \frac{\bar{r}_{Ck}}{\sqrt{\bar{r}_{ij}}} \qquad (4.8)$$

If $\bar{r}_{ij}$ is equal to 0.10, for example, and if this value remains unchanged as k becomes indefinitely large, then the limiting value of $\bar{r}_{Ck}$ will be $\sqrt{0.10}$, or 0.316. Similarly, if $\bar{r}_{ij}$ is equal to 0.16 and remains unchanged as k becomes indefinitely large, then the limiting value of $\bar{r}_{Ck}$ will be $\sqrt{0.16}$, or 0.40.

We can use (4.7) to illustrate what happens if the number of items in a scale is increased and if, at the same time, the values of $\bar{r}_{Ck}$ and $\bar{r}_{ij}$ remain unchanged by the additional items. Suppose, for example, that $\bar{r}_{Ck}$ is 0.20 and that $\bar{r}_{ij}$ is 0.10. For a scale of $k = 10$ items, r_{CX} will be approximately 0.46. If we add ten additional items, such that $\bar{r}_{Ck}$ and $\bar{r}_{ij}$ remain unchanged, then r_{CX} will be approximately 0.52 for the scale of $k = 20$ items. If we add 40 additional items, with $\bar{r}_{Ck}$ and $\bar{r}_{ij}$ remaining unchanged then, for the $k = 50$ item scale, r_{CX} will be approximately 0.58. If k becomes indefinitely large, and $\bar{r}_{Ck}$ and $\bar{r}_{ij}$ remain fixed, then in the limit

$$r_{CX} = \frac{0.20}{\sqrt{0.10}} = \frac{0.20}{0.316} = 0.63$$

It is apparent that the most efficient way of increasing the value of r_{CX} would be to add items that will increase the value of $\bar{r}_{Ck}$ and, at the same time, will not increase the value of $\bar{r}_{ij}$. A good item, in the present example, would be one which correlates greater than 0.20 with the criterion and such that its average correlation with the other items in the scale is equal to or less than 0.10.

4.4   The Point Biserial Coefficient as a Measure of Validity

When a scale is constructed by the empirical approach, it should be cross-validated by showing that scores on the scale are related to the criterion variable in a new sample of subjects. The sample used in deriving the items included in the scale will be referred to as the *standardization* sample and the new sample will be referred to as the *cross-validation* sample.

If the scale is scored for the standardization sample, a distribution of scores can be obtained for both the criterion and the control groups. Suppose, for example, that these two distributions are as shown in Table 4.1 for a $k = 15$ item scale. Because the items were selected on the basis of their ability to differentiate between the criterion and control groups, we

Table 4.1   Frequency Distribution of Scores on a
Scale for a Control Group and for a
Criterion Group

	Control	Criterion
Scores	f	f
15		1
14		3
13		6
12		6
11	1	8
10	1	16
9	2	16
8	7	16
7	12	11
6	20	12
5	25	3
4	20	1
3	5	1
2	4	
1	2	
0	1	

should expect the mean score on the scale to be higher for the criterion
group than for the control group. This is, in fact, the case. The mean score
for the criterion group is 8.98 and the mean score for the control group is
5.29.

We can regard the classification of the individuals as members of the
control or criterion group as a variable Y which takes a value of 1 for each
criterion group member and a value of 0 for each control group member.
Then the correlation between Y and scores on the scale (X) will be a point
biserial coefficient, as defined by (3.5), or

$$r_{pb} = \frac{\dfrac{\sum X_1}{N} - p_i \overline{X}}{\sigma_X \sqrt{p_i q_i}}$$

The sum of scores on the scale for the criterion group is 898 and the mean
score on the scale for both groups combined is 7.135. The standard deviation of the distribution of scores for both groups combined is 2.84 and the
proportion of the total number of individuals in the criterion group is
0.50. Then substituting with these values, we have

$$r_{pb} = \frac{(898/200) - (0.50)(7.135)}{2.84\sqrt{(0.50)(0.50)}}$$

$$= 0.65$$

The value of the point biserial coefficient obtained with the standardization sample is only suggestive and should, of course, be cross-validated with a new sample.

4.5   The Phi Coefficient as a Measure of Validity

An empirical scale will seldom differentiate completely between a criterion and a control group. In general, some degree of overlap between the two distributions of scores is to be expected. Figure 4.1 shows the frequency polygons for the two distributions and the overlap between

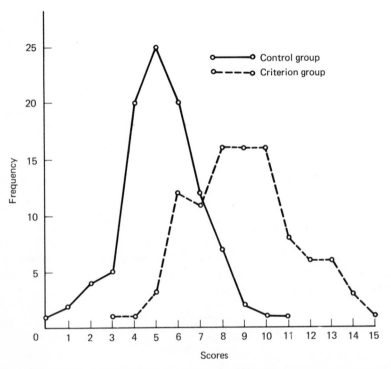

Figure 4.1   Distributions of scores for a control group and a criterion group on a scale.

the two distributions for the standardization sample. The point at which the two frequency polygons intersect is sometimes taken as a cutting point on the scale of scores. If an individual has a score above the cutting point, he is classified as a member of the criterion group. If below the cutting point, he is classified as a member of the control group. If the cutting point is set at 7.00 on the scale of scores, then we have the 2×2 classification of the individuals as shown in Table 4.2. We note that if the

Table 4.2   Number of Individuals in a Control and Criterion Group with Scores Greater Than 7.0 or Equal to or Less Than 7.0 on a Scale

	Control	Criterion	Total
$Y > 7.0$	11	72	83
$Y \leq 7.0$	89	28	117
Total	100	100	200

cutting point is set at 7.00, then 72 percent of the criterion group members and 89 percent of the control group members will be correctly classified. These percentages, based on the standardization sample, are only suggestive and need to be cross-validated with a new sample.

Each individual with a scale score above the cutting point may be assigned a value of $X = 1$ and each individual below the cutting point, a value of $X = 0$. Similarly, each individual who is actually a member of the criterion group is assigned a value of $Y = 1$ and each member of the control group, a value of $Y = 0$. Because both the X and Y variables can take values of 1 or 0, the correlation coefficient for the data of Table 4.2 would be

$$r_{XY} = \frac{p_{ij} - p_i p_j}{\sqrt{p_i q_i} \sqrt{p_j q_j}}$$

Table 4.3   Schematic Representation of the 2×2 Table

	Control	Criterion	Total
$Y > 7.0$	a	b	$a + b$
$Y \leq 7.0$	c	d	$c + d$
Total	$a + c$	$b + d$	N

Table 4.3 shows a schematic representation of the cell frequencies for the 2×2 table. In terms of this schematic representation, we have

$$r_{XY} = \frac{\dfrac{b}{N} - \left(\dfrac{a + b}{N}\right)\left(\dfrac{b + d}{N}\right)}{\sqrt{\left(\dfrac{a + b}{N}\right)\left(\dfrac{c + d}{N}\right)\left(\dfrac{b + d}{N}\right)\left(\dfrac{a + c}{N}\right)}}$$

which simplifies to

$$r_{XY} = \frac{bc - ad}{\sqrt{(a + b)(c + d)(b + d)(a + c)}} \qquad (4.9)$$

The correlation coefficient defined by (4.9) is commonly referred to as a *phi coefficient* and is frequently designated by r_ϕ. For Table 4.2 we have

$$r_\phi = \frac{(72)(89) - (11)(28)}{\sqrt{(83)(117)(100)(100)}} = 0.62$$

The value of the phi coefficient for the standardization sample, like the value of the point biserial coefficient, must be regarded as suggestive and should be cross-validated with a new sample.

4.6   Concurrent Validity of an Empirical Scale

As we have emphasized, when a scale is constructed by the empirical approach, it should be cross-validated by showing that scores on the scale are related to the criterion variable in a new sample of individuals. If scores on an empirical scale are found on cross-validation to be related to the criterion variable, this finding may be interpreted as indicating that the scale has some degree of *concurrent* validity. Concurrent validity refers to the relationship between a criterion variable and a scale when measures on both variables are available at the same moment in time. Because the classification of the individuals on the criterion variable is known at the same time as the scale scores are obtained, the correlation coefficient indicates something about the degree of concurrent validity of the scale.

If a criterion variable Y is an ordered variable, so that Y can take any one of a number of different values, then evidence regarding the concurrent validity of the scale can be obtained by taking a new or cross-validation sample and correlating the values of X and Y. Suppose, for example, that individuals are administered the Thematic Apperception Test (TAT) and that the stories they give to each of the pictures are analyzed. A rating is assigned to each individual that presumably indicates the degree to which his stories reflect his "need for achievement." These ratings, made on a nine-point scale, represent the criterion variable. The same subjects are given a large collection of items and the responses to each item are correlated with the criterion ratings. The resulting correlation coefficients would be point biserial coefficients and the k items with the highest point biserial coefficients are selected for the scale.

A cross-validation sample is then obtained and for this sample the criterion ratings are made. These criterion ratings may then be correlated with the scores on the scale. The degree to which the scores on the scale are correlated with the criterion ratings provides evidence with respect to the concurrent validity of the scale.

If the values of a criterion variable are available at the same time as scale scores, why would anyone have any interest in the concurrent validity of a scale? The major reason is a practical one. The values of the criterion variables may be relatively difficult and time consuming to obtain. For example, to obtain ratings of need for achievement using the TAT requires that each subject respond to each of a number of pictures and to make up a story about each one. These stories must then be read and rated by experienced individuals in order to obtain the ratings on the criterion variable. If it could be demonstrated that scores on a scale are highly correlated with the criterion ratings, then they could be regarded as a convenient and easily obtained substitute for the criterion ratings. This is the major purpose in demonstrating that a scale has a high degree of concurrent validity.

4.7 Difference between Predictive and Concurrent Validity

Simply because a scale has been demonstrated to have some degree of concurrent validity offers no assurance that the scale will also have some degree of *predictive* validity. The predictive validity of a scale is measured by the degree to which scores on the scale, available at the present time, are related to values of a criterion variable that are not immediately available but can only be obtained at some time in the future. For example, an academic aptitude test may be administered to entering students at a university. If scores on the aptitude test can be used to predict with some degree of success the grade points of the students at the end of their first year of college, the test would be said to have some degree of predictive validity. The difference between predictive and concurrent validity is primarily a difference in the time at which the values of the criterion variable are available. The first-year grade points of the college students are not known at the time the aptitude test is given to the students, because at this moment in time the students have not yet taken any college courses.

If scores on the aptitude test for entering college students were correlated with their high school grade points, this would be an instance of concurrent, not predictive, validity. It is interesting to note that, although aptitude test scores for entering college students are substantially correlated with their freshman grades, they have a very low correlation with grades earned during the senior year. Thus, in discussing the predictive validity of a scale, we must be concerned with the time interval between the administration of the scale and the obtaining of the criterion measures.

If an empirical scale designed to differentiate between alcoholics and nonalcoholics is developed, it may be found to have some degree of concurrent validity upon cross-validation. To demonstrate that the scale has predictive validity with respect to alcoholism and nonalcoholism is a much more difficult problem. To do so would require that the scale be administered to a large number of individuals who are not, at the time the scale is administered, designated as alcoholics. These same individuals would have to be studied at some time in the future to determine which had become alcoholics and which had not. If it could be shown that scores on the scale could be used to predict with some degree of success those individuals who did become alcoholics at some time in the future, the scale could be said to have some degree of predictive validity.

4.8   Importance of Cross-Validating an Empirical Scale

In studies of either concurrent or predictive validity of an empirical scale, the groups used in deriving the scale should not be used in assessing the validity of the scale. If the correlation between scores on the scale and the criterion variable is found for the standardization sample, then it is almost certain this value will be higher than that obtained with a cross-validation sample. Evidence regarding the concurrent or predictive validity of a scale becomes available only when the scale is cross-validated with a new sample not used in deriving the scale.

4.9   Practical and Social Significance of Predictive Validity

When a scale is developed with the primary objective of demonstrating that it has predictive validity, the criterion variable is almost always one that has some practical or social significance. Alcoholics, schizophrenics, juvenile delinquents, student dropouts, and so on represent criterion groups of social significance. There would obviously be practical implications if a scale could be developed which could successfully predict, on the basis of current scores, potential future membership in these various criterion groups. For example, if it were possible to determine at this moment in time which individuals not now so classified would be most likely to become alcoholics, or juvenile delinquents, or schizophrenics at some time in the future, then it might be possible to provide treatment and assistance now that would tend to lessen the chances of an individual becoming a social deviant in the future. Similarly, it is of practical value to know which students at the time of entering college are most likely to have difficulties with their school work in the future. They may then be given advice and remedial instruction that may lessen the chance that they will have difficulty in their subsequent school work.

If a scale can be shown to have some degree of predictive validity with respect to a criterion measure of success at a trade, skill, or profession, it may be used for selection purposes, just as performance on aptitude tests is often used as a basis for selecting students to be admitted to a college or university. As we have pointed out, however, although scores on aptitude tests are correlated with college grades during the first few semesters, they have very little predictive validity of grades earned during the junior and senior years. As Humphreys (1968) states, senior grades are not predicted with sufficient accuracy from scores available at the time of college entrance for one to be at all content with current college admission practices.

Similarly, when scales or tests are used to select individuals for employment or for training and when the criterion measure of success is not available until after a period of several years, it is of the greatest importance to demonstrate that the scales or tests have predictive validity of future performance and not just concurrent validity.

Chapter 5

Personality Inventories

5.1 Introduction

In this chapter we describe briefly some standard personality inventories. A *personality inventory* is simply a collection of items that may be scored for more than one trait. It is not intended to provide a complete description of each of the inventories discussed. To do so would involve repeating material that can be found in the manuals for the various inventories. For each of the inventories that is briefly described, it is suggested that the manual also be read. Not only should the manual for each inventory be studied, but a copy of the inventory itself should be consulted so that the nature of the items in each of the scales scored in the inventory can be examined. Trait names assigned to scales are often abstract and occasionally esoteric. A better understanding of the trait that a scale is designed to measure can be obtained only by a careful examination of the items included in the scale. This is particularly true with respect to rational scales and perhaps less so with respect to empirical scales. Item content is relatively unimportant in empirical scales.

Critical reviews and evaluations of personality inventories can be found in the *Sixth Mental Measurements Yearbook* (Buros, 1965). As stated above, the inventories that have been selected for brief discussion do not, by any means, exhaust the list of all published inventories. Descriptions of all inventories published prior to 1965 can be found in the *Sixth Mental Measurements Yearbook*.

5.2   The MMPI

There are various forms of the Minnesota Multiphasic Personality Inventory (MMPI), but probably the most widely used form is the booklet consisting of 550 items plus 16 duplicate items which are included for ease in machine scoring the MMPI. As originally published, the MMPI provided for the scoring of several rational scales and a number of empirical scales. The empirical scales were developed by comparing the responses of the members of a criterion group with those of a control group and selecting those items which differentiated between the two groups. In general, the criterion groups consisted of neuropsychiatric patients who could, in turn, be classified into one of several diagnostic categories. Patients within each diagnostic category presumably had similar symptoms and personality disorders.

One of the diagnostic groups, for example, consisted of hypochondriacs (individuals whose major problems consisted of undue concern over health and bodily symptoms). The responses of the hypochondriacs to the items in the MMPI were compared with those of the control group and those items which clearly differentiated between the two groups were selected for inclusion in a scale labelled Hypochondriasis (*Hs*). Thus, individuals who obtain high scores on *Hs* are those who tend to give responses to the items in the scale that are similar to those given by the original diagnostic group. In other words, the trait keyed response to each item in *Hs* is the response that was given significantly more often by the members of the diagnostic group than by the control group.

The original item pool used in developing the MMPI scales was obtained by selecting statements describing various symptoms, complaints, and aspects of personality disorders such as can be found in textbooks of psychiatry and clinical psychology. Case histories, medical and psychiatric examination forms, and various other sources were also used to obtain items. Most of the items developed from these sources tend to be relevant to the general domain of psychopathology. In addition, however, the MMPI item pool included some items selected from various other scales designed to measure personal and social attitudes and personality traits.

In its ordinary clinical use, the MMPI is scored for 14 scales. The first four scales are usually referred to as "validity" or "control" scales. High scores on any of the control scales are regarded as possibly invalidating the scores on the ten clinical scales.

5.3   The ? Scale

Scores on one of the control scales consist of the number of items that an individual has failed to answer either True or False, but instead has answered with a "?". High scores on this scale are commonly interpreted as indicating that the individual is evasive, defensive and/or indecisive. Obviously, if the ? score is high, then scores on the various other MMPI scales must inevitably be lowered because all of the other scales are scored either for True or False responses to the items.

5.4   The *L* Scale

The Lie (*L*) scale is a rational scale and consists of items to which very few individuals could, in honesty, consistently give the keyed response. For example, almost all individuals, if honest, would respond True to the statement: "I do not like everyone I know." A False response to this item, therefore, might be interpreted as a sign that the individual has not answered the item truthfully. One item, of course, does not make a scale, and there are undoubtedly some individuals who could give the trait and False response to this item without necessarily being dishonest. However, almost all individuals who take the MMPI obtain relatively low scores on the *L* scale, and the exceptional high score is regarded as revealing something about an individual's tendency not to be frank.

5.5   The *F* Scale

The *F* scale is a rational scale and consists of items to which less than 10 percent of the members of the control group gave the keyed response. All of the items in the *F* scale are keyed for improbable responses, that is, responses that are ordinarily given by less than 10 percent of so-called normals. Because the mean score on a scale is simply the sum of the proportions of a group giving the keyed response to each of the items in the scale, and because these proportions are less than 0.10 for the 64 items in the *F* scale, the mean score on this scale for a normal group would be expected to be less than 6.4. High scores by individuals may be obtained if they answer the items in the MMPI without reading them carefully or by those individuals who intentionally wish to call attention to themselves by giving many unusual and improbable responses.

5.6 The K Scale

The K scale is an empirical scale. The criterion group consisted of individuals who were known to belong to a diagnostic group but whose scores on certain of the diagnostic scales were relatively low. The objective of the K scale was to provide a correction for scores on certain of the diagnostic scales. Presumably, individuals with high scores on the K scale have been somewhat defensive in answering the items in the MMPI and consequently have failed to obtain as high a score on some of the diagnostic scales as they would have obtained if they had been less defensive. For example, the K corrected score on the Hs scale is obtained by adding $0.5K$, or one-half of the score on the K scale, to the original score on Hs.

5.7 The Clinical Scales

The ten MMPI scales described briefly below are often referred to as the "clinical" scales. The clinical scales are all empirical scales developed by selecting items which differentiated between two groups. The criterion groups for all but two of the scales consisted of individuals with some type of personality disorder. The trait names assigned to these scales are those that correspond to the psychiatric diagnosis of the individuals in the criterion groups. In all cases the items in the clinical scales are keyed for the responses that were given more often by the criterion group. Thus, a high score on Sc means that the individual has answered the item in this scale in the same way as the members of the criterion group used in developing the scale.

A brief and incomplete description of each criterion group is given after each of the clinical scales. The ten clinical scales are as follows:

Scale 1 (*Hs*). *Hypochondriasis:* individuals with undue concern about health and bodily symptoms.

Scale 2 (*D*). *Depression:* individuals with depressed states and feelings of hopelessness.

Scale 3 (*Hy*). *Hysteria:* individuals with multiple physical symptoms of various sorts and for which, in general, there was no known physical basis for the symptoms.

Scale 4 (*Pd*). *Psychopathic deviate:* individuals in trouble because of delinquency, habitual lying, stealing, etc.

Scale 5 (*Mf*). *Masculinity-femininity:* the items in this scale were selected to differentiate between males and females.

Scale 6 (*Pa*). *Paranoia:* individuals described as having paranoid personalities and characterized as being suspicious and jealous of others.

Scale 7 (*Pt*). *Psychasthenia:* individuals with obsessive thoughts, fears, feelings of guilt and anxiety.

Scale 8 (*Sc*). *Schizophrenia:* individuals characterized as having marked distortions of reality, bizarre thoughts, and tending to be withdrawn.

Scale 9 (*Ma*). *Hypomania:* individuals characterized as being overactive, excitable, and irritable.

Scale 10 (*Si*). *Social introversion:* the items in this scale were selected to differentiate between individuals with high and low scores on another scale designed to measure introversion-extroversion.

Because the items in each of the MMPI clinical scales were selected solely because they differentiated between the criterion and control groups, the various MMPI scales contain items that are also scored in other MMPI scales. Details regarding the item overlap in the MMPI scales can be found in Dahlstrom and Welsh (1960), along with the scoring keys for the MMPI scales.

5.8   Additional MMPI Scales

The empirical method of developing personality scales by finding those items that differentiate between a criterion and a control group has had considerable appeal to many investigators and the MMPI has provided a convenient source of items for this purpose. All that is needed is some basis for classifying individuals into criterion and control groups. If some individuals can be classified as complaining of low back pain and others as not so complaining and if the MMPI is administered to both groups, it is a simple matter to compare the responses of the two groups on each of the 550 MMPI items. If a sufficient number of items can be found which differentiate between the two groups, the result is a low back-pain "scale."

The exact number of scales that can be scored with the MMPI items is not known, but the number is undoubtedly quite large. Dahlstrom and Welsh (1960) provide scoring keys for approximately 200 MMPI scales, although not all of these scales were developed by empirical methods; some are rational scales. In addition, some of the MMPI scales described by Dahlstrom and Welsh simply consist of shorter forms or variations of other MMPI scales.

Although it would appear to be obvious that the original MMPI scales were designed primarily to be of interest to clinical psychologists and psychiatrists concerned with the diagnosis and treatment of psychopathology, the MMPI has been administered to hundreds of thousands of normal adults, college, and high school students. Because of the pathological content of many of the MMPI items, it is reasonable that many individuals consider it offensive to be asked to answer True or False to some of the items.

5.9   The CPI

In another inventory, the California Psychological Inventory (CPI), which is modeled after the MMPI, an attempt was made to eliminate the more offensive items in the MMPI. Approximately 200 of the items from the MMPI appear in the CPI along with 280 additional items. Like the MMPI, most of the scales in the CPI were developed by the empirical approach. But, unlike the MMPI, the criterion groups for the CPI scales were not based on psychiatric diagnoses. Instead, the criterion groups used in developing the CPI scales were, in some cases, established through the use of ratings. For example, individuals might be asked to select, nominate, or rate other individuals known to them in terms of leadership potential, or responsibility, or some other trait. Those individuals with high ratings on each of the traits may be regarded as the criterion group and those with low ratings as the control group. In other cases criterion and control groups were formed on the basis of grades in courses or social class membership.[1]

The CPI provides scoring keys for 18 scales. The trait names assigned to the scales are: Dominance (*Do*), Capacity for Status (*Cs*), Sociability (*Sy*), Social Presence (*Sp*), Self-acceptance (*Sa*), Sense of Well-being (*Wb*), Responsibility (*Re*), Socialization (*So*), Self-control (*Sc*), Tolerance (*To*), Good Impression (*Gi*), Communality (*Cm*), Achievement via Conformance (*Ac*), Achievement via Independence (*Ai*), Intellectual Efficiency (*Ie*), Psychological Mindedness (*Py*), Flexibility (*Fx*), and Femininity (*Fe*). Because the CPI has a considerable number of items in common with the MMPI, some of the CPI scales can also be scored, in briefer form, in the MMPI.

5.10   The 16 PF

The Sixteen Personality Factor Questionnaire (16 PF) provides measures on 16 traits. The 16 PF comes in various forms. Form A consists of 187 items, with from 10 to 13 items comprising each scale. The 16 PF scales were developed by factor-analytic techniques that result in oblique or correlated factors rather than orthogonal or uncorrelated factors.[2] Con-

---

[1]The CPI also includes a number of rationally developed scales. For a more complete discussion of the CPI scales, see Gough (1968).

[2]Orthogonal and oblique factors are discussed in Chapter 6.

sequently, the scores on the 16 PF scales are not independent, but instead correlated.

The trait names assigned to the scales are: Reserved versus Outgoing (A), Less Intelligent versus More Intelligent (B), Affected by Feelings versus Emotionally Stable (C), Humble versus Assertive (E), Sober versus Happy-go-lucky (F), Expedient versus Conscientious (G), Shy versus Venturesome (H), Tough-minded versus Tender-minded (I), Trusting versus Suspicious (L), Practical versus Imaginative (M), Forthright versus Shrewd (N), Placid versus Apprehensive (O), Conservative versus Experimenting (Q_1), Group-dependent versus Self-sufficient (Q_2), Undisciplined versus Controlled (Q_3), and Relaxed versus Tense (Q_4).

5.11   The GZTS

The Guilford-Zimmerman Temperament Survey (GZTS) consists of 300 items and provides scores on ten scales. The original item pool used in developing the GZST consisted primarily of items that had previously been used in a variety of scales. An attempt was made to put together in a single scale those items that had relatively high correlations with all other items included in the scale. Scores on the ten GZST scales, however, are not uncorrelated.

The trait names assigned to the ten scales are the following: General Activity (G), Restraint (R), Ascendance (A), Sociability (S), Emotional Stability (E), Objectivity (O), Friendliness (F), Thoughtfulness (T), Personal Relations (P), and Masculinity (M).

5.12   The MPI

The Maudsley Personality Inventory (MPI) consists of 48 items and provides scores on two traits: neuroticism and extroversion-introversion. Although the two scales in the MPI were also developed by attempting to include in each scale items that were correlated with the other items in the scales, the two scales are not uncorrelated with each other when scores are obtained from college students in the United States.

5.13   The EPI

The Edwards Personality Inventory (EPI) was designed to measure a large number of personality traits in which normal individuals vary. The EPI consists of five booklets: IA, IB, II, III, and IV. Each booklet contains

300 items, although a few items in some of the booklets are not scored. All items are in the True-False format. Booklets IA and IB were intended as comparable forms and provide scores on the same 14 scales. Booklets II, III, and IV provide scores on 11, 15, and 13 scales, respectively. The complete EPI thus provides scores on 53 personality traits. A list of the trait names of the scales in the EPI is given in Table 5.1.

Table 5.1   The Scales of the EPI

Booklets IA and IB	Booklet III
A. Plans and Organizes Things	A. Motivated to Succeed
B. Intellectually Oriented	B. Impressed by Status
C. Persistent	C. Desires Recognition
D. Self-Confident	D. Plans Work Efficiently
E. Has Cultural Interests	E. Cooperative
F. Enjoys Being the Center of Attention	F. Competitive
G. Carefree	G. Articulate
H. Conforms	H. Feels Superior
I. Is a Leader	I. Logical
J. Kind to Others	J. Assumes Responsibility
K. Worries About Making a Good Impression on Others	K. Self-Centered
L. Seeks New Experiences	L. Makes Friends Easily
M. Likes to Be Alone	M. Independent in His Opinions
N. Interested in the Behavior of Others	N. Is a Hard Worker
	O. Neat in Dress

Booklet II	Booklet IV
A. Anxious About His Performance	A. Self-Critical
B. Avoids Facing Problems	B. Critical of Others
C. Is a Perfectionist	C. Active
D. Absentminded	D. Talks About Himself
E. Sensitive to Criticism	E. Becomes Angry
F. Likes a Set Routine	F. Helps Others
G. Wants Sympathy	G. Careful About His Possessions
H. Avoids Arguments	H. Understands Himself
I. Conceals His Feelings	I. Considerate
J. Easily Influenced	J. Dependent
K. Feels Misunderstood	K. Shy
	L. Informed About Current Affairs
	M. Virtuous

The EPI differs from some other personality inventories in a number of ways. For example, almost all items that might be regarded as offensive have been eliminated. There are no items in the EPI inquiring into the individual's religious and political beliefs. There are no items that ask about the individual's health or body functions.

Another way in which the EPI differs from a number of other personality inventories is in the point of view that the individual is asked to take in answering the items. Instead of asking the individual to respond to the items in terms of whether he personally believes them to be True or False of himself, he is asked to judge whether he believes those individuals who know him best would answer the item True or False if *they* were asked to describe him. In other words, the individual is asked to try to stand off and take an objective look at himself in terms of how he believes other individuals would describe him.

In some inventories a considerable number of items are scored in more than one scale. When a substantial number of items are scored in two or more scales, the resulting correlations between the scales are spurious because of item overlap. In the EPI, no item is scored in more than one scale.

The items in the EPI were developed from three major sources: (1) interviews in which individuals were asked informally about the personality of someone well known to them; (2) published biographies and autobiographies; and (3) statements written specifically to represent a given personality trait. The original item pool consisted of 2824 statements. Items from this pool have been used in a number of research studies on social desirability and response sets (Edwards, 1963; Edwards, 1966b; Edwards and Diers, 1963; Edwards and Walsh, 1963b; Edwards and Walsh, 1964a; and Edwards and Walsh, 1964b).

The EPI scales are rational scales and were not developed by comparing the responses of a criterion group with those of a control group. Although the EPI scales were developed by means of factor analytic techniques, scores on the scales are not uncorrelated.

5.14   The EPPS

The Edwards Personal Preference Schedule (Edwards, 1959) is a forced-choice inventory. In this inventory, items are paired and the individual is asked to choose that member of each pair that he believes is more descriptive of himself. There are 210 different pairs of statements in the EPPS and scores are provided on 15 scales. The EPPS scales are: Achievement (*ach*), Deference (*def*), Order (*ord*), Exhibition (*exh*), Autonomy (*aut*), Affiliation (*aff*), Intraception (*int*), Succorance (*suc*), Dominance (*dom*), Abasement (*aba*), Nurturance (*nur*), Change (*chg*), Endurance (*end*), Heterosexuality (*het*), and Agression (*agg*).

Scores on the complete set of EPPS scales are ipsative. This formidable sounding term simply means that if the sum of the 15 scores is obtained for each individual, these sums are all equal to the same number, 210.

This, in turn, means that scores on one of the 15 scales are completely determined by the scores on the other 14 scales. For example, if we sum the scores on any 14 scales for a given individual, then his score on the remaining scale is fixed and can be determined by subtracting the sum of the 14 scores from 210.

5.15   The PRF

The Personality Research Form (PRF) is a rational inventory. Forms A and B are intended as comparable forms. Each form contains 300 items and provides scores on the same 15 traits. The traits measured by these forms are: Achievement (*Ac*), Affiliation (*Af*), Aggression (*Ag*) Autonomy (*Au*), Dominance (*Do*), Endurance (*En*), Exhibition (*Ex*), Harm-avoidance (*Ha*), Impulsivity (*Im*), Nurturance (*Nu*), Order (*Or*), Play (*Pl*), Social Recognition (*Sr*), Understanding (*Un*), and Infrequency (*In*). The latter scale is intended as a validity scale to check random or nonpurposeful responding.

Forms AA and BB each consist of 440 items. They include the same scales as in Forms A and B and, in addition, seven other scales. The additional scales are called: Abasement (*Ab*), Change (*Ch*), Cognitive Structure (*Cs*), Defendence (*De*), Sentience (*Se*), Succorance (*Su*), and Desirability (*Dy*). The latter scale is intended as a measure of individual differences in the tendency to give desirable responses.

Chapter 6

An Introduction
to Principal-Component
Factor Analysis

6.1 Coefficients of Determination and Nondetermination

Suppose we have two scales, X and Y, and that scores on both scales are expressed in deviation form, that is, $x = X - \bar{X}$ and $y = Y - \bar{Y}$. If scores on the scales are correlated, then

$$\hat{y} = bx \tag{6.1}$$

is an estimate of y, and $b = \Sigma xy / \Sigma x^2$ is the *regression coefficient of Y on X*. The discrepancy between the observed value of y and the estimated value of $\hat{y}$ will be

$$y - \hat{y} = y - bx \tag{6.2}$$

The sum of the squared errors of estimate will then be given by

$$\begin{aligned}
\sum (y - \hat{y})^2 &= \sum (y - bx)^2 \\
&= \sum y^2 - 2b \sum xy + b^2 \sum x^2 \\
&= \sum y^2 - \frac{(\sum xy)^2}{\sum x^2}
\end{aligned} \tag{6.3}$$

Multiplying both numerator and denominator of the last term on the right by Σy^2, we have

$$\begin{aligned}
\sum (y - \hat{y})^2 &= \sum y^2 - r^2 \sum y^2 \\
&= \sum y^2 (1 - r^2)
\end{aligned}$$

We also have

$$\sum y^2 = \sum (y - \bar{y})^2 + r^2 \sum y^2$$

and because

$$\sum (y - \bar{y})^2 = \sum y^2(1 - r^2)$$

then

$$\sum y^2 = \sum y^2(1 - r^2) + r^2 \sum y^2 \qquad (6.4)$$

Dividing both sides of (6.4) by N, we see that

$$\sigma_Y^2 = \sigma_Y^2(1 - r^2) + r^2\sigma_Y^2 \qquad (6.5)$$

The value of $1 - r^2$ is called the *coefficient of nondetermination* and indicates the proportion of the total variance σ_Y^2 that is independent of variation in X. Similarly, the coefficient r^2 is called the *coefficient of determination* and indicates the proportion of the total variance σ_Y^2 that is associated with variation in X. Because $r_{XY} = r_{YX}$ we also have

$$\sigma_X^2 = \sigma_X^2(1 - r^2) + r^2\sigma_X^2$$

Thus the proportion of the total variance σ_X^2 associated with variation in Y is equal to r^2 and the proportion of the total variance that is independent of variation in Y is $1 - r^2$. In other words, r^2 may be interpreted as the proportion of common variance in X and Y and $1 - r^2$ as the proportion of variance in X and Y that is independent. It is obvious that if X and Y have all of their variance in common, that is, if $r = 1.00$, then it would be possible to predict perfectly, or without error, values of X from values of Y or vice versa. If two scales have no variance in common, that is, if r is equal to zero, then the two scales can be said to measure independent or uncorrelated traits.

6.2   Prediction of One Variable from Two Uncorrelated Variables

Consider now the case of three scales. Suppose that the correlation between Scale 1 and 2 is $r_{12} = 0.80$, the correlation between Scale 1 and 3 is $r_{13} = 0.60$, and the correlation between Scale 2 and 3 is $r_{23} = 0.00$. Then the proportion of variance in Scale 1 that can be accounted for by Scale 2 is $r^2 = (0.80)^2 = 0.64$ and the proportion of variance in Scale 1 that can be accounted for by Scale 3 is $r_{13}^2 = (0.60)^2 = 0.36$. Scales 2 and 3 share no common variance because $r_{23} = 0.00$. Thus the variance in Scale 1 accounted for by Scale 2 must be independent of the variance accounted for by Scale 3. Furthermore, because $r_{12}^2 + r_{13}^2 = (0.80)^2 + (0.60)^2 = 1.00$, this suggests that it should be possible to account for all of the variance in the scores on Scale 1, that is, to predict these scores perfectly, from some linear combination of the scores on Scales 2 and 3. Because a larger percentage of the variance in Scale 1 is associated with Scale 2 than with Scale 3, it may also seem reasonable that, in the linear combination, scores on Scale 2 be given more weight than scores on Scale 3.

To simplify things, suppose that scores on all three scales are in standard score form. We have defined the regression coefficient of Y on X as

$$b = \frac{\sum xy}{\sum x^2}$$

Multiplying both the numerator and the denominator of the right side of the above expression $\sqrt{\Sigma x^2}\sqrt{\Sigma y^2}$, we have

$$b = r\frac{\sqrt{\sum x^2}\sqrt{\sum y^2}}{\sum x^2}$$

and dividing both numerator and denominator of the right side by N, we obtain

$$b = r\frac{\sigma_Y}{\sigma_X}$$

We see, therefore, that if two variables have equal standard deviations, then the regression coefficient is equal to the correlation coefficient. If all three scales are in standard score form, then each variable will have a standard deviation equal to 1.00, and the regression coefficient of Scale 1 on Scale 2 will be equal to r_{12} and the regression coefficient of Scale 1 on Scale 3 will be equal to r_{13}. Then, as an estimate of the observed standard score on Scale 1, we might try the following weighted linear combination of the standard scores on Scales 2 and 3:

$$\bar{z}_1 = r_{12}z_2 + r_{13}z_3 \qquad (6.6)$$

The variable represented on the left side of (6.6) and which we are trying to predict is called the *dependent* variable. The variables on the right side of (6.6) which are used in predicting the dependent variable are called the *independent* variables. In the example cited, Variable 1 is the dependent variable and Variables 2 and 3 are the independent variables.

To show that $\bar{z}_1$, as defined by (6.6), is in fact in standard score form, we must prove that the mean of the $\bar{z}_1$ values is equal to zero and that the variance of the $\bar{z}_1$ values is equal to 1.00. The mean of the $\bar{z}_1$ values will be

$$\frac{\sum \bar{z}_1}{N} = r_{12}\frac{\sum z_2}{N} + r_{13}\frac{\sum z_3}{N} = 0$$

because both $\Sigma z_2/N$ and $\Sigma z_3/N$ are equal to zero. The variance of $\bar{z}_1$ will then be

$$\frac{\sum \bar{z}_1^2}{N} = r_{12}{}^2\frac{\sum z_2^2}{N} + r_{13}{}^2\frac{\sum z_3^2}{N} + 2r_{12}r_{13}\frac{\sum z_2z_3}{N}$$

and because $\Sigma z_2 z_3 / N = r_{23} = 0.00$ the last term is equal to zero. Because $\Sigma z_2^2 / N$ and $\Sigma z_3^2 / N$ are both variances of a set of standard scores, they are both equal to 1.00. Then, in this example,

$$\sigma_{\tilde{z}_1}^2 = \frac{\sum \tilde{z}_1^2}{N} = r_{12}^2 + r_{13}^2 = (0.80)^2 + (0.60)^2 = 1.00$$

Therefore, $\tilde{z}_1$ is, in this example, in standard score form.

In the example described, the errors of estimate will be given by

$$z_1 - \tilde{z}_1 = z_1 - (r_{12}z_2 + r_{13}z_3) \tag{6.7}$$

and squaring and summing the errors of estimate, we have

$$\sum (z_1 - \tilde{z}_1)^2 = \sum z_1^2 - 2(r_{12} \sum z_1 z_2 + r_{13} \sum z_1 z_3) + \sum (r_{12}z_2 + r_{13}z_3)^2$$

Dividing both sides of the above expression by N, we obtain

$$\frac{\sum (z_1 - \tilde{z}_1)^2}{N} = 1.00 - 2r_{12}^2 - 2r_{13}^2 + \frac{1}{N} \sum (r_{12}z_2 + r_{13}z_3)^2 \tag{6.8}$$

Expanding the last term on the right in (6.8), we have

$$\frac{1}{N} \sum (r_{12}z_2 + r_{13}z_3)^2 = \frac{1}{N} \sum (r_{12}^2 z_2^2 + 2r_{12}r_{13}z_2 z_3 + r_{13}^2 z_3^2)$$

$$= r_{12}^2 + 2r_{12}r_{13}r_{23} + r_{13}^2$$

$$= r_{12}^2 + r_{13}^2$$

because $r_{23} = 0.00$. Then (6.8) becomes

$$\frac{\sum (z_1 - \tilde{z}_1)^2}{N} = 1.00 - 2r_{12}^2 - 2r_{13}^2 + r_{12}^2 + r_{13}^2$$

$$= 1.00 - r_{12}^2 - r_{13}^2$$

$$= 0.00$$

because $r_{12} = 0.80$ and $r_{13} = 0.60$.

In the present example then, all errors of estimate, that is, all values of $z_1 - \tilde{z}_1$, must be equal to zero and the weighted linear combination of z_2 and z_3 must be perfectly correlated with the values of z_1.

6.3 The Multiple Correlation Coefficient: $R_{1\cdot23}$

We designate the square of the correlation coefficient between any one variable and an appropriately weighted linear sum of any two other variables as $R^2_{1\cdot23}$. $R_{1\cdot23}$ is called a *multiple correlation coefficient* and $R^2_{1\cdot23}$ is simply the square of the multiple correlation coefficient. In general,

$$R^2_{1.23} = \frac{r_{12}^2 + r_{13}^2 - 2r_{12}r_{13}r_{23}}{1 - r_{23}^2} \tag{6.9}$$

In the example described, we have $r_{12} = 0.80$, $r_{13} = 0.60$, and $r_{23} = 0.00$. Then, for this example,

$$R^2_{1 \cdot 23} = \frac{(0.80)^2 + (0.60)^2}{1 - (0.00)^2} = 1.00$$

and

$$R_{1 \cdot 23} = \sqrt{1.00} = 1.00$$

The multiple correlation coefficient, $R_{1 \cdot 23}$, may be interpreted in much the same manner as any other correlation coefficient. It can never be greater than 1.00 and $R^2_{1 \cdot 23}$ is the proportion of variance in one variable, Variable 1, that can be accounted for by a weighted linear combination of two other variables, Variables 2 and 3. $R_{1 \cdot 23}$ is, in fact, the correlation between z_1 and $\bar{z}_1$. For example,

$$r_{z_1 \bar{z}_1} = \frac{\dfrac{1}{N} \sum z_1 (r_{12} z_2 + r_{13} z_3)}{\sigma_{z_1} \sigma_{\bar{z}_1}}$$

Because in this example $\sigma_{z_1} = \sigma_{\bar{z}_1} = 1.00$, we have

$$r_{z_1 \bar{z}_1} = r_{12} \frac{\sum z_1 z_2}{N} + r_{13} \frac{\sum z_1 z_3}{N}$$

$$= r_{12}^2 + r_{13}^2$$

and

$$r_{z_1 \bar{z}_1}$$

is equal to $R_{1 \cdot 23}$.

If Scales 2 and 3 have part of their variance in common, as would be the case if $r_{23} = 0.50$, then we would have

$$R^2_{1 \cdot 23} = \frac{(0.80)^2 + (0.60)^2 - 2(0.80)(0.60)(0.50)}{1 - (0.50)^2}$$

$$= \frac{1.00 - 0.48}{0.75}$$

$$= 0.6933$$

and

$$R_{1 \cdot 23} = \sqrt{0.6933} = 0.83$$

6.4 Prediction of One Variable from Any Number of Uncorrelated Variables

Although the multiple correlation coefficient is applicable to the case where one variable is being correlated with the weighted sum of a number of other variables that are correlated with each other, our primary interest is in the case where each of the variables contributing to the sum has a zero correlation with every other variable. If the intercorrelations of these variables are all equal to zero, then we can define

$$\bar{y}_1 = r_{12}z_2 + r_{13}z_3 + \ldots + r_{1k}z_k \tag{6.10}$$

and the correlation between $\bar{y}_1$, as defined by (6.10), and y_1 will be equal to the multiple correlation coefficient, $R_{1 \cdot 234 \ldots k}$.

It is important to note that the predicted value $\bar{y}_1$, defined by (6.10), has a mean equal to zero, but it is not necessarily true that the variance of $\bar{y}_1$ is equal to 1.00. If we sum both sides of (6.10) and divide by N to obtain the mean of the $\bar{y}_1$ values, we note that each of the terms on the right side will involve the mean of a set of standard scores and that these means are all equal to zero. Thus the mean of the $\bar{y}_1$ values is also equal to zero.

The variance of the $\bar{y}_1$ values will then be

$$\frac{\sum \bar{y}_1^2}{N} = \frac{1}{N} \sum (r_{12}z_2 + r_{13}z_3 + \ldots + r_{1k}z_k)^2 \tag{6.11}$$

All of the cross-product terms in the square of the expression on the right in (6.11) disappear when summed and divided by N because each one involves a correlation between two of the independent variables and these correlations are all, by definition, equal to zero. Then the variance of $\bar{y}_1$ will be

$$\frac{\sum \bar{y}_1^2}{N} = r_{12}^2 + r_{13}^2 + \ldots + r_{1k}^2 \tag{6.12}$$

and $\sigma_{\bar{y}_1}^2$ will be equal to 1.00 if and only if the squares of the correlations sum to 1.00. In the example considered previously, we had only two correlations on the right side, r_{12} and r_{13}, and because $r_{12}^2 + r_{13}^2 = (0.80)^2 + (0.60)^2 = 1.00$, we could say that the predicted value was in standard score form.

Because the mean of the $\bar{y}_1$ values is equal to zero, we can translate $\bar{y}_1$ into a standard score by dividing each of the $\bar{y}_1$ values by the standard deviation of the $\bar{y}_1$ values. Thus

$$\bar{z}_1 = \bar{y}_1 / \sigma_{\bar{y}_1} \tag{6.13}$$

and because

$$\sigma_{\bar{y}_1} = \sqrt{r_{12}^2 + r_{13}^2 + \ldots + r_{1k}^2} \tag{6.14}$$

then

$$\bar{z}_1 = \bar{y}_1 / \sqrt{r_{12}^2 + r_{13}^2 + \ldots + r_{1k}^2} \tag{6.15}$$

and $\bar{z}_1$, as defined by (6.15), will be in standard score form.

With both z_1 and $\bar{z}_1$ in standard score form, we have as the variance of the errors of estimate

$$\frac{\sum (z_1 - \bar{z}_1)^2}{N} = \sigma_{z_1}^2 - 2r_{z_1\bar{z}_1} + \sigma_{\bar{z}_1}^2 \qquad (6.16)$$

and both $\sigma_{z_1}^2$ and $\sigma_{\bar{z}_1}^2$ will be equal to 1.00. As we shall show later

$$r_{z_1\bar{z}_1} = R_{1\cdot23\ldots k} = \sqrt{r_{12}^2 + r_{13}^2 + \ldots + r_{1k}^2}$$

Thus, if all of the observed values of z_1 are exactly equal to the corresponding predicted values $\bar{z}_1$, then it will also be true that

$$R_{1\cdot23\ldots k} = \sqrt{r_{12}^2 + r_{13}^2 + \ldots + r_{1k}^2} = 1.00$$

To determine the value of $R_{1\cdot23\ldots k}$, we could derive the correlation between z_1 and $\bar{z}_1$. However, if each value of a variable is divided by a constant, this will have no influence on the correlation of that variable with another variable. Therefore, because

$$\bar{z}_1 = \bar{y}_1/\sigma_{\bar{y}_1},$$

we have

$$r_{z_1\bar{z}_1} = r_{z_1\bar{y}_1} = R_{1\cdot23\ldots k}$$

Then

$$r_{z_1\bar{y}_1} = \frac{\dfrac{1}{N}\sum z_1(r_{12}z_2 + r_{13}z_3 + \ldots + r_{1k}z_k)}{\sigma_{z_1}\sigma_{\bar{y}_1}}$$

$$= \frac{r_{12}^2 + r_{13}^2 + \ldots + r_{1k}^2}{\sigma_{z_1}\sigma_{\bar{y}_1}}$$

Because z_1 is in standard score form, we have $\sigma_{z_1} = 1.00$. The value of $\sigma_{\bar{y}_1}$ is given by (6.14) and is equal to $\sqrt{r_{12}^2 + r_{13}^2 + \ldots + r_{1k}^2}$. Therefore,

$$r_{z_1\bar{y}_1} = \frac{r_{12}^2 + r_{13}^2 + \ldots + r_{1k}^2}{\sqrt{r_{12}^2 + r_{13}^2 + \ldots + r_{1k}^2}}$$

$$= \sqrt{r_{12}^2 + r_{13}^2 + \ldots + r_{1k}^2} \qquad (6.17)$$

and (6.17) will be equal to the multiple correlation, $R_{1\cdot23\ldots k}$. We also have

$$R^2_{1\cdot23\ldots k} = r_{12}^2 + r_{13}^2 + \ldots + r_{1k}^2 \qquad (6.18)$$

Thus we see that if all of the variables contributing to the weighted linear sum defined by (6.10) have zero correlation with each other, the multiple correlation squared will simply be the sum of the squares of the correlations.

The weights assigned to the independent variables in standard score form in (6.10) are the correlation coefficients of the independent variables with the dependent variable. These weights are the best, or optimal, weights that could be assigned to each of the independent variables. They are optimal in that they minimize the sum of the squared errors of estimate and in doing so they maximize the value of $R_{1 \cdot 23 \ldots k}$. This is to say, no other set of weights could be assigned to the independent variables which would result in a smaller sum of squared errors of estimate or a larger value of $R_{1 \cdot 23 \ldots k}$.

6.5 A Principal-Component Factor Loading Matrix

The preceding discussion regarding multiple correlation provides an elementary introduction to some of the properties of an orthogonal factor loading matrix obtained by a type of factor analysis called a *principal-component analysis*.[1] Assume that we have $k = 10$ scales and that scores on each scale are available for N individuals. We can arrange the scores in a matrix or table, with the columns corresponding to the scales and the rows to the individuals. Scores on each scale may then be standardized so that each scale has a mean equal to zero and a variance equal to 1.00. If we intercorrelate the scores on the scales, then we obtain a correlation matrix. Table 6.1 gives the correlation matrix for 10 scales based on a

Table 6.1 Intercorrelations of $k = 10$ Scales Based on a Sample of $N = 150$

Scale	1	2	3	4	5	6	7	8	9	10
1. A	1.00	0.82	0.13	−0.70	0.05	−0.21	0.81	−0.30	−0.79	−0.14
2. Dy	0.82	1.00	0.06	−0.68	−0.01	−0.29	0.72	−0.25	−0.79	−0.14
3. Hy	0.13	0.06	1.00	0.26	−0.07	0.36	0.16	0.30	−0.12	−0.18
4. K	−0.70	−0.68	0.26	1.00	−0.14	0.39	−0.63	0.44	0.67	0.12
5. Ma-S	0.05	−0.01	−0.07	−0.14	1.00	0.27	0.01	−0.35	0.02	0.28
6. Pd-S	−0.21	−0.29	0.36	0.39	0.27	1.00	−0.16	0.16	0.23	0.03
7. Pt	0.81	0.72	0.16	−0.63	0.01	−0.16	1.00	−0.19	−0.76	−0.18
8. R	−0.30	−0.25	0.30	0.44	−0.35	0.16	−0.19	1.00	0.18	−0.16
9. SD	−0.79	−0.79	−0.12	0.67	0.02	0.23	−0.76	0.18	1.00	0.12
10. Sd	−0.14	−0.14	−0.18	0.12	0.28	0.03	−0.18	−0.16	0.12	1.00

sample of $N = 150$ individuals. The numbers in the upper-left to lower-right diagonal of the table are the variances of the scales in standard score form and the off-diagonal elements are the correlations between the scales. It is

[1]There are other methods of factor analysis in addition to a principal-component analysis. The various methods are described by Horst (1965). We shall, however, be concerned only with the method of principal components. Almost all computer centers have standard programs for a principal-component analysis and the nature of the calculations involved will not be discussed.

obvious that Scales 1, 2, 4, 7, and 9 all tend to have fairly substantial correlations with each other and they must, therefore, share some variance in common.

The correlation matrix given in Table 6.1 was factor-analyzed by the method of principal components. The results of this factor analysis are shown in Table 6.2. Table 6.2 is called an *orthogonal principal-component*

Table 6.2 **Principal-Component Factor Loadings for the Correlation Matrix Given in Table 6.1**

Scale	I	II	III	IV	V	VI	VII	VIII	IX	X
					Factors					
1. *A*	0.92	0.11	0.14	0.05	−0.04	−0.04	0.03	0.14	0.09	−0.30
2. *Dy*	0.90	0.09	0.01	0.10	0.02	−0.02	−0.25	0.28	0.05	0.17
3. *Hy*	−0.01	0.75	0.44	0.11	−0.35	0.29	−0.04	−0.12	0.09	0.03
4. *K*	−0.85	0.27	0.09	0.15	−0.15	0.02	0.05	0.28	−0.26	−0.04
5. *Ma-S*	0.04	−0.49	0.72	−0.20	−0.27	0.36	0.00	0.05	−0.06	−0.01
6. *Pd-S*	−0.37	0.28	0.73	−0.18	0.12	−0.45	−0.05	−0.01	0.04	0.01
7. *Pt*	0.86	0.21	0.13	0.05	0.05	−0.05	0.41	0.03	−0.04	0.13
8. *R*	−0.38	0.66	−0.19	0.28	0.53	0.10	0.00	0.01	0.07	−0.03
9. *SD*	−0.88	−0.17	−0.06	−0.16	−0.08	0.05	0.15	0.20	0.30	0.03
10. *Sd*	−0.17	−0.54	0.31	0.76	−0.05	−0.08	0.02	−0.04	0.06	0.01
Eigenvalue	4.20	1.77	1.42	0.80	0.53	0.44	0.26	0.24	0.19	0.14

factor loading matrix. We now wish to point out some of the important properties of this matrix.

The columns of Table 6.2 represent factors and the elements in the cells of the table are called *factor loadings.* Note that the sum of the squared factor loadings in each row of the table is equal to 1.00, within rounding errors. For example, for Scale 1 we have

$$(0.92)^2 + (0.11)^2 + \ldots + (-0.30)^2 = 1.00$$

Note also that the sum of cross products between the elements or loadings in any two columns of the table is, within rounding errors, equal to zero. For example, the sum of the cross products of the loadings for Factors I and II is

$$(0.92)(0.11) + (0.90)(0.09) + \ldots + (-0.17)(-0.54) = -0.01$$

The sum of the squared loadings in each column is called an *eigenvalue* or *latent root.* For the first factor, the eigenvalue is

$$(0.92)^2 + (0.90)^2 + \ldots + (-0.17)^2 = 4.20$$

The eigenvalue or latent root represents the amount of the total variance that can be accounted for by a given factor. The total variance is always equal to the number of scales (in this instance ten) and we note that the sum of the eigenvalues is, within rounding errors, also equal to ten. Thus the ten factors account for all of the variance in the ten scales. If the sum of squared factor loadings in a given column is divided by the number of scales, then this gives the proportion of the total variance accounted for by the factor. The eigenvalue for the first factor, for example, is 4.20 and the first factor accounts for $4.20/10 = 0.420$ of the total variance. The fourth factor accounts for 0.080 of the variance and together the first four factors account for 0.819 of the total variance.

If the sum of cross products of any two rows of the factor loading matrix is obtained, the result will be the correlation between the two scales represented by the two rows in the matrix. For example, if we multiply the loadings in rows 1 and 2, we have

$$(0.92)(0.90) + (0.11)(0.09) + \ldots + (-0.30)(0.17) = 0.83$$

and this value is, within rounding errors, equal to the correlation $r_{12} = 0.82$, between Scales 1 and 2, as shown in Table 6.1.

6.6 Factors and Factor Scores

We have said that the columns of the factor loading matrix represent factors. By means to be described later, it is possible to obtain for each individual a standardized score on each of the ten factors. For example, a factor score can be obtained for each individual on Factor I such that the mean of the factor scores is equal to zero and the standard deviation of the factor scores is equal to 1.00. If standardized factor scores are obtained for each individual on each of the ten factors, it would then be possible to find the intercorrelations of the scores on each pair of factors. If this were done, it would be found that all of the intercorrelations of the factor scores are equal to zero. The ten factors thus represent a set of variables that are independent or uncorrelated with each other.

When we said that the entries in the factor loading matrix are the correlations of each scale with each of the ten factors, we meant that the loadings are the correlations of scores on the original scales with scores on the corresponding factor scales. For example, if we obtained factor scores for each individual on Factor I, and then correlated scores on Scale 1 with these factor scores, the resulting correlation coefficient would be 0.92. Thus Scale 1, because it has a high loading on Factor I (i.e., a high correlation with the factor scores on Factor I) can be said to be a very good measure of Factor I.

If we square the loading of Scale 1 on Factor I, we have $(0.92)^2 = 0.85$ and because the factor loading is the correlation of Scale 1 with scores on Factor I, the square of the loading represents the proportion of variance that scores on Scale 1 have in common with scores on Factor I.

6.7 Multiple Correlation in Terms of Factors

If it is true that the factor loadings in each row of the factor loading matrix are the correlations of a given scale with scores on each of the corresponding factors, and if these factors are in turn uncorrelated with each other, then the squared multiple correlation of the scale with the factors will be the same as that given by (6.18). Thus, for Scale 1, we have[2]

$$R^2_{1 \cdot 123\ldots10} = (0.92)^2 + (0.11)^2 + \ldots + (-0.30)^2 = 1.00$$

For each of the scales, we see that the squared multiple correlation is equal to 1.00. This will always be the case when the number of factors is equal to the number of scales.

There is no reason, however, why we should base the multiple correlations on all ten factors. It may be possible, for example, to obtain a satisfactorily high value for the multiple correlation if we use only a limited number of factors. Obviously, if we are to use a limited number of factors, we should use those that account for the greatest proportion of the variance in the scales. It is one of the characteristics of a principal-component factor analysis that the first factor accounts for the largest proportion of the total variance, the second factor for the next largest proportion, and so on. As we noted previously, the first four factors account for 0.819 of the total variance and we might see just how well we could do in predicting scores on the ten scales using only the first four factors.

Table 6.3 gives the loadings of the ten scales on the first four principal-component factors. At the right of the table, we have the sum of the squared loadings of each scale on the first four factors. These values are called *communalities* and are usually designated by h^2, but it is also true that they are the squared multiple correlations of each scale with the four factors. We note that the smallest squared multiple correlation is that for Scale 8, which is equal to 0.69. Thus, 0.69 of the variance in Scale 8 can be accounted for by a weighted linear combination of the factor scores on the first four factors. We note that the multiple correlation will be $\sqrt{0.69}$ and is approximately equal to 0.83. For all of the other scales, the squared multiple correlations are greater than 0.69 and, therefore, all of the other multiple correlations are greater than 0.83.

---

[2] In $R^2_{1 \cdot 123\ldots10}$ the subscripts following the first dot refer to the scores on the ten factors.

Table 6.3   Factor Loadings of $k = 10$ Scales on the First Four Principal Components

Scales	Factor Loadings				
	I	II	III	IV	h^2
1. A	0.92	0.11	0.14	0.05	0.88
2. Dy	0.90	0.09	0.01	0.10	0.83
3. Hy	−0.01	0.75	0.44	0.11	0.77
4. K	−0.85	0.27	0.09	0.15	0.83
5. Ma-S	0.04	−0.49	0.72	−0.20	0.80
6. Pd-S	−0.37	0.28	0.73	−0.18	0.78
7. Pt	0.86	0.21	0.13	0.05	0.80
8. R	−0.38	0.66	−0.19	0.28	0.69
9. SD	−0.88	−0.17	−0.06	−0.16	0.83
10. Sd	−0.17	−0.54	0.31	0.76	0.99
Proportion of Variance	0.420	0.177	0.142	0.080	

6.8   Normalized Factor Loadings

In general, the number of principal-component factors will be equal to k, the number of scales or tests. Because the principal-component factors are extracted in such a way that the first factor accounts for the largest proportion of the total variance, the second the next largest, and so on, the later factors will often account for a very small proportion of the total variance. In the example in Table 6.2, we see that the first four factors account for 82 percent of the total variance and that each of the remaining factors accounts for a relatively small percentage of the total variance.

When all of the principal-component factors are extracted, the sum of the squared loadings in each row will always be equal to 1.00. If we are concerned only with the first k' factors where $k' < k$, then, in general, the sum of squared loadings in each row will be less than 1.00 and will simply be the proportion of the total variance in the scale that can be accounted for by the first k' factors. In other words, the sum of squared loadings in a given row will be the proportion of variance that a scale has in common with the k' factors and, as we have pointed out, is called the communality of the scale and is designated by h^2.

It is often of interest to determine how the common variance in each scale is distributed over the k' factors, that is, to determine what proportion of h^2 can be accounted for by each of the k' factors. This is accomplished by normalizing the loadings of the scale on the k' factors. Any set of numbers can be normalized by dividing each one by the square root of the sum of their squares. A *normalized* set of numbers when squared will sum to 1.00. Thus, to normalize the numbers 1, 2, and 3, we would divide each one by $\sqrt{1^2 + 2^2 + 3^2} = \sqrt{14}$. Then

$$\left(\frac{1}{\sqrt{14}}\right)^2 + \left(\frac{2}{\sqrt{14}}\right)^2 + \left(\frac{3}{\sqrt{14}}\right)^2 = 1.00$$

To normalize the loadings of a scale on k' factors, therefore, we divide each of the original loadings by $\sqrt{h^2}$, the square root of the proportion of the variance accounted for by the k' factors. In Table 6.3, we have $k' = 4$ factors. For Scale 1, we have h^2 equal to 0.88. Then the normalized loadings of Scale 1 on the $k' = 4$ factors will be

$$\frac{0.92}{\sqrt{0.88}}, \quad \frac{0.11}{\sqrt{0.88}}, \quad \frac{0.14}{\sqrt{0.88}}, \text{ and } \frac{0.05}{\sqrt{0.88}}$$

or

$$0.98, \quad 0.12, \quad 0.15, \text{ and } \quad 0.05$$

The normalized loadings of the other scales on the four factors can be obtained in the same manner. The normalized loadings of the ten scales on the four factors are shown in Table 6.4. If the normalized factor loadings

Table 6.4   Normalized Factor Loadings of $k = 10$ Personality Scales on the First Four Principal Components

Scales	Factor Loadings			
	I	II	III	IV
1. A	0.98	0.12	0.15	0.05
2. Dy	0.99	0.10	0.01	0.11
3. Hy	−0.01	0.85	0.50	0.13
4. K	−0.93	0.30	0.10	0.16
5. Ma-S	0.04	−0.55	0.81	−0.22
6. Pd-S	−0.42	0.32	0.83	−0.20
7. Pt	0.96	0.23	0.15	0.06
8. R	−0.46	0.79	−0.23	0.34
9. SD	−0.97	−0.19	−0.07	−0.18
10. Sd	−0.17	−0.54	0.31	−0.76

of a scale are squared and summed, they will sum to 1.00, within rounding errors. For example, if we square and sum the normalized loadings of Scale 1 on the $k' = 4$ factors, we have

$$(0.98)^2 + (0.12)^2 + (0.15)^2 + (0.05)^2 = 1.00$$

The squares of normalized factor loadings simply indicate the proportion of the common variance, h^2, of a scale that can be accounted for by each of the k' factors.

When all k principal-component factors are extracted, then the squared loadings in each row of the factor loading matrix will always sum to 1.00, and in this instance, the factor loadings will always be in normalized form. Factor loadings need to be normalized only if we are concerned with the first $k' < k$ factors and if we wish to determine how the variance, h^2, that a scale has in common with the k' factors is distributed over the k' factors. If factor loadings are reported as normalized loadings and we want to determine the *denormalized* loadings, then the normalized loadings may be multiplied by $\sqrt{h^2}$. The result will be the denormalized loadings.

6.9 Interpretation of Factors

If each scale involved in a factor analysis has a high loading on only one factor and if the factors are different for each scale, then obviously no two scales could have very much variance in common. A factor loading matrix of this kind is most apt to be obtained when all of the scales have relatively low correlations with each other. In this case, the factor scores on each factor would be substantially correlated with a single scale, the scale with a high loading on the factor. Whatever it is that each scale measures would be relatively independent of whatever it is that the other scales are measuring.

In the present example, however, we note that Scales 1, 2, 4, 7, and 9 have loadings of 0.92, 0.90, -0.85, 0.86, and -0.88, respectively, on Factor I. It is reasonable to believe that these scales, regardless of the trait names assigned to the scales, are all quite good measures of whatever it is that is being measured by factor scores on Factor I. Thus, despite the fact that high scores on Scales 1, 2, 4, 7, and 9 have been interpreted, by those who developed the scales, as measuring: "anxiety," "dependency," "defensiveness," "psychasthenia," and "the tendency to give socially desirable responses," respectively, the scores on these scales could all be estimated quite accurately in terms of the factor scores on Factor I.

It would be possible to obtain the factor scores on Factor I for each individual. Each of the items in the scales with large loadings on Factor I could then be correlated with the factor scores, and the k items with the highest correlations with the factor scores could be selected. These items would comprise a scale that should be a very good measure of Factor I. If this scale were developed, what trait name should be assigned to it? Should we choose as a trait name one of the five traits measured by the five scales with high loadings on the factor? If so, how could we justify the choice? Why would "anxiety," for example, be any more appropriate than one of the other trait names? The problem of interpreting what it is that is being measured by a factor is not an easy one to solve. We shall see later that different investigators quite often give different interpretations to the same set of factor loadings, with each one attempting to justify his choice of a trait name or his interpretation of a given factor.

As we have emphasized previously, one way in which to "validate" the interpretation of the trait being measured by a scale is by means of studies of construct validity. The testing of hypotheses about the trait that a scale is designed to measure is of value in clarifying what a scale is measuring. The situation is very similar with respect to the meaning of a factor. If various interpretations of a factor result in different hypotheses and if these can be tested by research and experimentation, the results of such investigations should be of assistance in clarifying the nature of the factor.

6.10   Calculation of Factor Scores: Unrotated Factors

We now show how factor scores can be obtained. In the interest of simplicity, we show in Table 6.5 the standard scores on $k = 6$ scales for

Table 6.5   Standard Scores for $N = 12$ Individuals on $k = 6$ Scales

Individuals	Scales					
	1	2	3	4	5	6
1	0.44	0.63	1.75	2.97	0.97	0.62
2	2.65	2.56	−1.34	−1.02	0.90	0.98
3	−0.10	−0.16	0.51	−0.38	2.22	2.38
4	−0.97	−1.22	−0.08	−0.38	0.29	0.31
5	−1.16	−1.06	−1.88	−0.02	−1.48	0.19
6	−0.96	−1.12	−1.28	−0.78	0.45	−1.57
7	0.20	−0.24	0.02	0.53	−0.58	−1.24
8	−0.04	−0.49	−0.01	−0.89	−1.42	−0.71
9	−1.05	0.79	0.10	−0.35	−0.30	−0.38
10	0.30	0.20	0.56	0.25	−0.28	−0.24
11	0.57	0.37	0.81	−0.01	−0.25	0.08
12	0.12	−0.26	0.84	0.08	−0.51	−0.42

each of $N = 12$ individuals. The intercorrelation matrix of these scales is given in Table 6.6 and the loadings of the scales on the first four principal components are given in Table 6.7. The first three principal components account for 86 percent of the total variance, and we shall obtain the factor scores only for the first three factors. The procedures described would be

Table 6.6   Intercorrelations of the $k = 6$ Scales for the Data of Table 6.5

Scales	1	2	3	4	5	6
1	1.00	0.83	0.11	0.03	0.30	0.31
2	0.83	1.00	0.12	0.06	0.32	0.34
3	0.11	0.12	1.00	0.64	0.25	0.18
4	0.03	0.06	0.64	1.00	0.14	0.09
5	0.30	0.32	0.25	0.14	1.00	0.66
6	0.31	0.34	0.18	0.09	0.66	1.00

Table 6.7   Principal Component Factor Loadings for the Correlation Matrix Given in Table 6.6

Scales	Factors			
	I	II	III	IV
1	0.74	−0.41	0.45	−0.03
2	0.76	−0.39	0.42	0.03
3	0.47	0.76	0.14	−0.39
4	0.36	0.81	0.22	0.39
5	0.73	0.00	−0.55	−0.15
6	0.71	−0.09	−0.56	0.20
Eigenvalue	2.52	1.55	1.07	0.36
Proportion of Variance	0.42	0.26	0.18	0.06

exactly the same if we had decided to obtain factor scores on the first four factors or on only the first two factors.

The necessary calculations can be shown most simply in terms of matrix multiplication and can also be easily programmed and accomplished very rapidly on an electronic computer. The nature of matrix multiplication is illustrated below, where one matrix, B, is to be multiplied by another matrix, A, to obtain the product matrix, C. Thus

$$A \quad \times \quad B \quad = \quad C$$

or

$$\begin{bmatrix} a_{11} & a_{12} \\ a_{21} & a_{22} \\ a_{31} & a_{32} \end{bmatrix} \times \begin{bmatrix} b_{11} & b_{12} \\ b_{21} & b_{22} \end{bmatrix} = \begin{bmatrix} c_{11} & c_{12} \\ c_{21} & c_{22} \\ c_{31} & c_{32} \end{bmatrix}$$

The cell entries in C are given by:

$$c_{11} = a_{11}b_{11} + a_{12}b_{21}$$

$$c_{12} = a_{11}b_{12} + a_{12}b_{22}$$

$$c_{21} = a_{21}b_{11} + a_{22}b_{21}$$

$$c_{22} = a_{21}b_{12} + a_{22}b_{22}$$

$$c_{31} = a_{31}b_{11} + a_{32}b_{21}$$

$$c_{32} = a_{31}b_{12} + a_{32}b_{22}$$

If one matrix B is to be multiplied by another matrix A, then the two matrices must be *conformable*. The two matrices A and B are conformable if the number of rows in B is equal to the number of columns in A. The product matrix, C, will have the same number of rows as A and the same number of columns as B.

In order to calculate factor scores, the first matrix equation required is

$$F\delta^{-1} = Y \qquad (6.19)$$

F is the matrix of factor loadings and, in our example, will have six rows, one for each scale, and three columns, one for each factor. The matrix δ^{-1} will be a square matrix in which all of the elements are equal to zero except those in the upper-left to lower-right, or *principal diagonal* of the matrix. The principal-diagonal elements are the reciprocals of the eigenvalues or latent roots of the factors. Because we are using only the first three factors, the upper-left to lower-right diagonal elements of δ^{-1} will be the reciprocals of 2.52, 1.55, and 1.07, the latent roots for Factors I, II, and III, respectively. Matrix Y will have six rows, one for each scale, and three columns, one for each factor. The calculations defined by (6.19) are shown in Table 6.8.

Table 6.8   Calculation of the Y Matrix Defined by Formula (6.19)

$$
\begin{bmatrix}
0.74 & -0.41 & 0.45 \\
0.76 & -0.39 & 0.42 \\
0.47 & 0.76 & 0.14 \\
0.36 & 0.81 & 0.22 \\
0.73 & 0.00 & -0.55 \\
0.71 & -0.09 & -0.56
\end{bmatrix}
\times
\begin{bmatrix}
0.40 & 0.00 & 0.00 \\
0.00 & 0.64 & 0.00 \\
0.00 & 0.00 & 0.94
\end{bmatrix}
=
\begin{bmatrix}
0.29 & -0.26 & 0.42 \\
0.30 & -0.25 & 0.40 \\
0.19 & 0.49 & 0.13 \\
0.14 & 0.52 & 0.20 \\
0.29 & 0.00 & -0.52 \\
0.28 & -0.06 & -0.53
\end{bmatrix}
$$

$$\qquad\qquad F \qquad\qquad\qquad\qquad \delta^{-1} \qquad\qquad\qquad\qquad Y$$

After Y has been obtained, we then calculate

$$ZY = B \qquad (6.20)$$

where Z is a matrix of the standard scores of the individuals on the original six scales. In our example, this matrix will have 12 rows, one for each individual, and six columns, one for each scale. The product of Z and Y gives the matrix B and B will be the matrix of standardized factor scores. In our example, B will have 12 rows, one for each individual, and three columns, one for each of the first three factors. The calculations defined by (6.20) are shown in Table 6.9.

If we intercorrelate the factor scores we obtain Table 6.10. We see that the intercorrelations of the factor scores are, within rounding errors, approximately equal to zero and that the variance of each of the factor scores is equal to 1.00, again within rounding errors.

Table 6.9   Calculation of the B Matrix Defined by Formula (6.20). The Elements of B are the Factor Scores of the $N = 12$ Individuals on the First Three Principal Components

$$
\begin{matrix}
Z & & & & & & & & Y \\
\end{matrix}
$$

$$
\begin{bmatrix}
0.44 & 0.63 & 1.75 & 2.97 & 0.97 & 0.62 \\
2.65 & 2.56 & -1.34 & -1.02 & 0.90 & 0.98 \\
-0.10 & -0.16 & 0.51 & -0.38 & 2.22 & 2.38 \\
-0.97 & -1.22 & -0.08 & -0.38 & 0.29 & 0.31 \\
-1.16 & -1.06 & -1.88 & -0.02 & -1.48 & 0.19 \\
-0.96 & -1.12 & -1.28 & -0.78 & 0.45 & -1.57 \\
0.20 & -0.24 & 0.02 & 0.53 & -0.58 & -1.24 \\
-0.04 & -0.49 & -0.01 & -0.89 & -1.42 & -0.71 \\
-1.05 & 0.79 & 0.10 & -0.35 & -0.30 & -0.38 \\
0.30 & 0.20 & 0.56 & 0.25 & -0.28 & -0.24 \\
0.57 & 0.37 & 0.81 & -0.01 & -0.25 & 0.08 \\
0.12 & -0.26 & 0.84 & 0.08 & -0.51 & -0.42 \\
\end{bmatrix}
\times
\begin{bmatrix}
0.29 & -0.26 & 0.42 \\
0.30 & -0.25 & 0.40 \\
0.19 & 0.49 & 0.13 \\
0.14 & 0.52 & 0.20 \\
0.29 & 0.00 & -0.52 \\
0.28 & -0.06 & -0.53 \\
\end{bmatrix}
$$

$$
B
$$

$$
=
\begin{bmatrix}
1.53 & 2.09 & 0.44 \\
1.69 & -2.58 & 0.79 \\
1.28 & -0.03 & -2.51 \\
-0.55 & 0.30 & -1.29 \\
-1.39 & -0.37 & -0.49 \\
-1.29 & -0.41 & -0.58 \\
-0.46 & 0.37 & 1.05 \\
-0.90 & -0.30 & 0.71 \\
-0.29 & -0.03 & 0.16 \\
0.14 & 0.29 & 0.60 \\
0.38 & 0.15 & 0.58 \\
-0.14 & 0.51 & 0.56 \\
\end{bmatrix}
$$

Table 6.10   Intercorrelations of the Factor Scores
Given in Table 6.9

	I	II	III
I	1.00	0.01	0.00
II	0.01	1.00	0.02
III	0.00	0.02	1.00

6.11   Rotation of a Factor Loading Matrix

Given any factor loading matrix it is always possible to rotate the matrix by means of an orthogonal transformation matrix. Any such orthogonally rotated factor matrix will result in a new set of factors that are also independent or uncorrelated.[3] The usual objective in rotating a factor matrix is to attempt to approximate what Thurstone (1947) has described as a *simple-structure* factor loading matrix. If a factor loading matrix can be rotated to approximate a simple-structure matrix, then the simple-structure matrix may be of value in the interpretation of the factors. In essence, a simple-structure matrix is one in which:

(1) There are one or more zero loadings in each row and preferably more than one.

(2) Each column of factor loadings will have some variables with high loadings and others with low or zero loadings.

(3) For any given pair of factors, some variables will have low loadings on both factors.

(4) For any given pair of factors, it will be the case that for both factors there are some variables with high loadings on one factor but not on the other factor.

If a simple-structure matrix can be approximated by means of a rotation, then we can rule out those scales or variables that have low or zero loadings on a factor and concentrate on the interpretation of those scales that have relatively high loadings on the factor. Similarly, if we are attempting to interpret how two factors differ, we can rule out those scales that have low loadings on both factors and concentrate on interpreting those scales that have high loadings on only one of the two factors.

A number of different analytical procedures have been developed for

---

[3]It is also possible to make an oblique rotation of a factor loading matrix. Factor scores on oblique factors, unlike scores on orthogonal factors, will be correlated with each other and are not independent.

attempting to rotate a factor loading matrix to approximate a simple-structure matrix. In this book, the only analytic rotation we shall be concerned with is Kaiser's Varimax orthogonal rotation; judging from published research, this procedure appears to be the one in most common use.[4]

Table 6.11 shows the results of a Varimax rotation of the first four principal component factors of the factor loading matrix given in Table 6.2. Each column sum of squared loadings, when divided by the number

Table 6.11   Varimax Rotated Factor Loadings of $k = 10$ Scales on the First Four Principal Components

	Rotated Factors				
Scales	I′	II′	III′	IV′	h^2
1. A	0.93	−0.01	0.10	−0.05	0.88
2. Dy	0.90	−0.11	0.01	−0.03	0.82
3. Hy	0.18	0.82	−0.26	−0.05	0.77
4. K	−0.74	0.41	−0.29	0.14	0.82
5. Ma-S	0.00	0.20	0.85	0.19	0.80
6. Pd-S	−0.26	0.79	0.30	−0.02	0.78
7. Pt	0.89	0.07	0.02	−0.08	0.80
8. R	−0.24	0.38	−0.71	−0.01	0.71
9. SD	−0.91	0.02	0.04	−0.02	0.83
10. Sd	−0.12	−0.08	0.18	0.97	0.99
Proportion of Variance	0.40	0.17	0.15	0.10	

of scales, gives the proportion of the total variance accounted for by each of the rotated factors.[5] We see that the four rotated factors together account for

$$0.40 + 0.17 + 0.15 + 0.10 = 0.82$$

of the total variance. The proportion of the total variance accounted for by the four rotated factors is equal to the proportion of the total variance accounted for by the four unrotated factors.

[4]The nature of the Varimax rotation is described by Kaiser (1958). Almost all computer centers have a standard program for a Varimax rotation. See Kaiser (1959) for a description of the program.

[5]We shall here, and elsewhere, indicate rotated factors with a prime sign.

The values given at the right of the table are the sums of the squared loadings in each row of the rotated factor loading matrix. These communalities are, within rounding errors, equal to the communalities of the scales on the first four unrotated factors, as shown in Table 6.3. Thus the four rotated factors account for the same proportion of the total variance in each scale as the four unrotated factors within, of course, the limits of rounding errors.

6.12   Factor Scores on Rotated Principal-Component Factors

The Varimax rotated factor loading matrix can be regarded in much the same manner as the unrotated factor loading matrix. For example, it would be possible to obtain factor scores on the rotated factors in much the same manner as factor scores are obtained with the unrotated factors. To obtain factor scores on the *unrotated* principal-component factors, we calculated

$$ZY = B$$

or, because $Y = F\delta^{-1}$,

$$ZF\delta^{-1} = B$$

and B is the matrix of standardized factor scores on unrotated principal component factors.

In the case of an orthogonally *rotated* factor loading matrix, however, one additional matrix multiplication is involved. Factor scores on the *rotated* factors will be given by

$$ZF\delta^{-1}T = B \qquad (6.21)$$

The matrix T is the transformation matrix used to obtain the rotated factor loading. When a principal-component factor loading matrix is rotated by the Varimax program, the program calculates the transformation matrix and the computer will print out the elements of T. The T matrix will

Table 6.12   Elements of the Transformation Matrix T Used in Obtaining the Rotated Factor Loadings Shown in Table 6.11[a]

$$
\begin{bmatrix}
0.97 & -0.20 & 0.12 & -0.09 \\
0.17 & 0.65 & -0.64 & -0.36 \\
0.10 & 0.73 & 0.61 & 0.28 \\
0.14 & 0.02 & -0.44 & 0.89
\end{bmatrix}
$$

[a]The values reported have been rounded from eight to two decimal places.

be a square matrix with rows and columns equal to the number of factors rotated. Table 6.12 gives the transformation matrix used in obtaining the rotated factor loadings shown in Table 6.11.

6.13   Number of Factors to Extract

In general, when a correlation matrix is factor analyzed by the method of principal components, there is little value in calculating all of the principal components necessary to account for the total variance in the scales. The problem then becomes one of determining how many factors to extract. One general principle is to decide what proportion of the total variance one wants to account for by the factors and to stop factoring when this proportion is reached.[6] In the example described, if we had decided that we wanted to account for approximately 82 percent of the total variance, the factoring would have stopped after the first four principal components had been extracted.

Another principle that is often followed is to extract factors until a factor is obtained which has an eigenvalue less than 1.00. If this principle had been followed in the example cited, then the factoring would also have stopped after four factors had been extracted.

The principles relating to the number of principal-component factors to be extracted also apply, in general, to the number of factors to be rotated. It is fairly common practice not to include in a rotation those factors with eigenvalues less than 1.00. However, in some cases, the inclusion of one or two factors with eigenvalues slightly less than 1.00 in a rotation may be helpful in clarifying the factorial structure.

6.14   Calculation of Factor Scores: Rotated Factors

In order to illustrate the calculation of factor scores on Varimax rotated factors, we use, in the interest of simplicity, the same example considered previously in which we had $k = 6$ scales and $N = 12$ individuals. In this example, only the first $k' = 3$ factors have eigenvalues greater than 1.00. If the first $k' = 3$ factors are rotated by the Varimax program, we obtain the transformation matrix T shown in Table 6.13. We have already calculated $F\delta^{-1} = Y$ for the first $k' = 3$ factors and the results of these calculations are given in Table 6.8 and are reproduced in Table 6.13.

---

[6]We are almost never interested in accounting for the total variance of a scale but rather in accounting for the *reliable* variance. Any variance in excess of the reliable variance is *error* variance, and it would be meaningless to attempt to account for the error or unreliable variance of a scale.

Table 6.13   Calculation of $F\delta^{-1}T$

$$
\begin{array}{ccc}
F\delta^{-1} & T & F\delta^{-1}T
\end{array}
$$

$$
\begin{bmatrix}
0.29 & -0.26 & 0.42 \\
0.30 & -0.25 & 0.40 \\
0.19 & 0.49 & 0.13 \\
0.14 & 0.52 & 0.20 \\
0.29 & -0.00 & -0.52 \\
0.28 & -0.06 & -0.53
\end{bmatrix}
\times
\begin{bmatrix}
0.67 & 0.38 & -0.64 \\
-0.44 & 0.89 & 0.07 \\
0.59 & 0.24 & 0.77
\end{bmatrix}
=
\begin{bmatrix}
0.56 & -0.02 & 0.12 \\
0.55 & -0.01 & 0.10 \\
-0.02 & 0.54 & 0.01 \\
-0.02 & 0.57 & 0.10 \\
-0.11 & -0.02 & -0.58 \\
-0.10 & -0.07 & -0.59
\end{bmatrix}
$$

The product of $F\delta^{-1}$ and T is shown at the right in Table 6.13. Then, if we multiply $F\delta^{-1}T$ by the original standard score matrix Z, as given in Table 6.5, we obtain $ZF\delta^{-1}T$ or the standard scores of the $N = 12$ individuals on the first three rotated factors. The results of this matrix multiplication are given in Table 6.14. If the standard scores on the rotated factors are

Table 6.14   The Elements of $ZF\delta^{-1}T$ Are the Factor Scores of the $N = 12$ Individuals on the First Three Varimax Rotated Factors

$$ZF\delta^{-1}T$$

$$
\begin{bmatrix}
0.35 & 2.55 & -0.49 \\
2.75 & -1.47 & -0.64 \\
-0.62 & -0.14 & -2.74 \\
-1.27 & -0.25 & -0.62 \\
-1.06 & -0.98 & 0.48 \\
-1.02 & -0.99 & 0.34 \\
0.15 & 0.41 & 1.12 \\
-0.05 & -0.44 & 1.10 \\
-0.09 & -0.10 & 0.31 \\
0.32 & 0.46 & 0.39 \\
0.53 & 0.41 & 0.21 \\
0.01 & 0.53 & 0.55
\end{bmatrix}
$$

intercorrelated, it will be found that, within rounding errors, the inter-correlations are equal to zero.

Note that if the factors are *unrotated*, then the columns of the matrix $F\delta^{-1}$ provide the weights to be assigned to each scale in determining the standard scores on each factor. For example, Scales 1, 2, 5, and 6 are all weighted about equally, the weights being 0.29, 0.30, 0.29, and 0.28, respectively, in determining the scores on unrotated Factor I. If you look back at the unrotated factor loading matrix, in Table 6.7, you will see that Scales 1, 2, 5, and 6 have unrotated loadings of 0.74, 0.76, 0.73, and 0.71, respectively, on Factor I.

Now examine the weights assigned to the scales in obtaining the factor scores on rotated Factor I'. These are given by the first column of matrix $F\delta^{-1}T$. We see that Scales 1 and 2 have weights of 0.56 and 0.55, respectively, and that the weights for Scales 5 and 6 are now -0.11 and -0.10, respectively. This indicates that Scales 1 and 2 have higher loadings on rotated Factor I' and that Scales 5 and 6 have lower loadings on rotated Factor I' than they do on the unrotated first factor.

6.15   Factor Loadings of the k = 6 Scales on the Varimax Rotated Factors

The factor loadings of the scales on the rotated factors are shown in Table 6.15. The rotated factor loadings are obtained by multiplying the

Table 6.15   Varimax Rotated Factor Loadings of k = 6 Scales on the First Three Principal Components

Scales	Rotated Factors		
	I'	II'	III'
1	0.94	0.03	−0.15
2	0.94	0.05	−0.19
3	0.06	0.89	−0.15
4	0.01	0.91	−0.01
5	0.16	0.14	−0.89
6	0.19	0.06	−0.89

factor loadings on the first three unrotated factors by the transformation matrix. Thus the rotated factor loadings are given by FT, where F is a matrix of factor loadings on the k' factors being rotated. We see that after a Varimax rotation, Scales 1 and 2 have high loadings on Factor I' and low loadings on the other two factors, Scales 3 and 4 have high loadings on Factor II' and low loadings on the other two factors, and Scales 5 and 6 have high loadings on Factor III' and low loadings on the other two factors.

If you compare the loadings of the scales on the rotated factors with the loadings of the scales on the unrotated factors, you will note that the rotated factor loading matrix is almost an ideal case of a simple structure matrix, whereas this is not true of the unrotated factor loading matrix. As we stated previously, the primary objective in rotating a factor loading matrix is to attempt to approximate a simple structure matrix. In the present example, the Varimax rotation has accomplished this objective very well.

6.16   Reflection of Factor Loadings for a Given Factor

In the principal-component factor analysis reported in Table 6.2, the SD scale has a loading of -0.88 on the first factor. In other factor analyses described in later chapters, it will sometimes be the case that the SD scale has a relatively high *positive* loading on the first principal-component factor and in other factor analyses a relatively high *negative* loading. It is important to understand that it is always possible to multiply the factor loadings in any given column of the factor loading matrix by -1.00 without changing any of the essential properties of the factor.

We know, for example, that scores on the SD scale will correlate -0.88 with factor scores on Factor I, when the factor scores are based on the signed loadings given in Table 6.1. The A scale has a loading of 0.92 on the first factor and scores on this scale would correlate 0.92 with the same factor scores. If we were now to reflect or reverse the signs of all of the loadings on Factor I and obtain factor scores on the reflected factor, these factor scores would correlate -1.00 with the factor scores based on the unreflected factor loadings. The SD scale would then correlate 0.88 with the reflected factor scores and the A scale would correlate -0.92 with the reflected factor scores.

Reversing the signs of the factor loadings in a given column merely reverses the signs of the factor scores on the factor and, consequently, reverses the signs of the correlations of the scales with the factor scores. The absolute magnitudes of the correlations of the scales with the original and reflected factor scores remain the same.

In some studies to be described later, the correlations between the proportion of items keyed True and first factor loadings of scales are reported. In one study the obtained correlation is positive, and in another study the obtained correlation is negative. The absolute magnitude of the two correlation coefficients is much the same in both studies. There is nothing contradictory about these results. A reflection of the factor loadings in either one of the two studies would result in correlations that have the same sign.

6.17   Ipsative Scales

We have said that whenever the number of principal-component factors is equal to the number of scales, then all of the variance in each scale can be accounted for in terms of the factors and the squared multiple correlation of the scale with the factor scores on the factors will be equal to 1.00. Suppose, however, that scores on one scale are linearly dependent on scores on one or more other scales. For example, scores on one scale might simply be equal to two times the score on some other scale. In this case the correlation between the two scales would be equal to one, and the number of principal-component factors could not be greater than $k - 1$, where k is the number of scales included in the factor analysis. In general, the number of principal-component factors can never exceed the number of linearly independent scales.

In certain inventories, to be discussed later, scores on the scales are ipsative, that is, the sum of the scores on the k scales results in exactly the same sum for each individual. As a result, scores on one of the k scales must correlate -1.00 with the sum of the scores on the other $k - 1$ scales. In this case, the number of principal-component factors cannot be greater than $k - 1$.

Chapter 7

The Social Desirability
Scale Values (SDSVs)
of Personality Statements

7.1 Obtaining the SDSVs of Personality Statements

Given any set of personality statements, it is possible to obtain for each one a *social desirability scale value* or SDSV. Any of the available psychological scaling methods can be used to obtain the SDSVs of personality statements. These methods are described by Edwards (1957b), Guilford (1954), Green (1954), and Torgerson (1958). The various psychological scaling methods result in SDSVs that are highly correlated with one another and it will, therefore, be sufficient to describe only one of these methods.

To obtain the SDSVs, personality statements are presented, one at a time, to a group of judges who are asked to rate each statement on a 9-point rating scale ranging from extremely desirable, through neutral, to extremely undesirable. In Table 7.1 a 9-point rating scale that has been used in a large number of studies is shown along with the instructions given to the judges for making their ratings of social desirability. For each statement a distribution of ratings is obtained and it is then possible to find the mean rating assigned to a statement. This mean rating is called *the SDSV of the statement*. If a large and representative set of personality statements is rated for social desirability, it will be found that on the average, some statements are judged as being extremely desirable, others as extremely undesirable, and still others as falling somewhere between these two extremes.

Figure 7.1 shows the distribution of SDSVs for 2824 personality state-

Table 7.1   Instructions Used in Obtaining Judgments of Social Desirability for Personality Statements

---

Trait Rating Schedule

DIRECTIONS: Below are four statements which might be used in describing another person.

Rating	*Statement*
——————	1. He likes to punish his enemies.
——————	2. He likes to read science fiction.
——————	3. He sometimes makes excuses for his friends.
——————	4. He is considered to be an honest person.

Please rate each of the four statements as to how socially desirable or socially undesirable you consider it to be when used to describe *other* people. *We are not interested in whether the statement does or does not describe you.* Just rate it according to how socially desirable or undesirable you consider it to be if applied to other people in general. Use the rating scale shown below in making your ratings.

Rating	*Meaning of Rating*
1	Extremely Undesirable
2	Strongly Undesirable
3	Moderately Undesirable
4	Mildly Undesirable
5	NEUTRAL
6	Mildly Desirable
7	Moderately Desirable
8	Strongly Desirable
9	Extremely Desirable

Your task is to read and rate the social desirability of each of the statements in the test booklet using the rating scale shown above. Remember that you are to judge the statements in terms of whether you consider them to be socially desirable or undesirable *when applied to other people*. We are not interested in whether a statement does or does not describe you. Be sure to make a judgment about each statement.

---

ments as reported by Edwards (1966a). These statements were rated by 47 male and 48 female judges, and the distribution of SDSVs is based on the ratings of the combined group of 95 judges. The SDSVs of another large set of 1647 personality statements have been obtained by Cruse (1965), and the distribution of the SDSVs for these 1647 statements is similar in form to that shown in Figure 7.1.

The SDSV of a personality statement represents an *average* value as determined by a group of raters. Within any large group of raters, individual differences in the ratings assigned to a given statement are to be expected. For example, some individuals may rate a statement as mildly desirable, while others may rate the same statement as neutral, as moderately desirable,

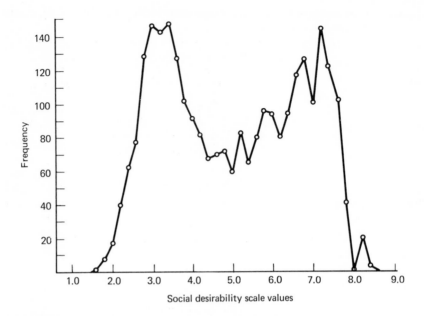

Figure 7.1   Distribution of social desirability scale values of 2824 personality statements. From Edwards (1966a).

or as strongly desirable. If the average rating assigned to a statement is regarded as the SDSV of the statement, then the standard deviation of the distribution of ratings provides an index of the degree of agreement among the judges as to the location of the statement on the social desirability rating scale or continuum. Two statements, for example, may have the same SDSV, but the standard deviation of the ratings assigned to one statement may be considerably larger than the standard deviation of the ratings assigned to the other statement. This simply means that there is greater variability in the judgments of social desirability for the statement with the larger standard deviation than for the statement with the smaller standard deviation. In other words, the larger the standard deviation, the less the agreement among the judges as to the location of the statement on the social desirability continuum.

7.2   Correlations between SDSVs
Based on the Judgments of Different Groups

There is considerable evidence to show that the SDSVs of personality statements based on the judgments of one group of college students are highly correlated with the SDSVs of the same statements based on the judgments of another group of college students. Edwards (1966a), Cruse (1965), Messick and Jackson (1961a), and Mees, Gocka, and Holloway (1964), using different sets of statements, all report correlations of 0.95 or higher between the SDSVs of statements when judged by different groups of college students.

Similarly, the evidence is quite clear that the SDSVs obtained from female judges are highly correlated with the SDSVs obtained from male judges. Edwards (1966a) and Cowen (1961), using different sets of statements, both report correlations of 0.99 between male and female SDSVs for college students in the United States. It has also been shown that SDSVs of male and female French students (Cowen and Frankel, 1964) and male and female Japanese students (Iwawaki, Okuno, and Cowen, 1965) are highly correlated. For French students a correlation of 0.99 was obtained and for Japanese students a correlation of 0.95.

Klieger and Walsh (1967) developed a pictorial social desirability rating scale for use with young children. A series of nine line drawings of a stylized female face were prepared. A very frowning, angry face was equated with a rating of 1, a neutral face with a rating of 5, and a brightly smiling and approving face with a rating of 9. When children age 3 to 4 years were asked to rate personality statements using the pictorial scale, it was found that the SDSVs based on their judgments correlated 0.56 with those of adults. With 4- to 5-year-old children, the SDSVs correlated 0.89 with those of adults, and with 5- to 6-year-old children the correlation was 0.96. Klieger and Walsh also found that the pictorial ratings correlated 0.90 with the ratings on the usual verbal rating scale for two groups of fifth graders. For two adult groups, the correlation between SDSVs using the pictorial rating scale and the verbal rating form was 0.96.

To complete the age cycle, it has been shown that SDSVs based on the judgments of adolescents (Klett, 1957a; Stiller, Schwartz, and Cowen, 1965) and those based on the judgments of geriatric groups (Cowen, Davol, Reimanis, and Stiller, 1962) are also highly correlated with the SDSVs based on the judgments of college students.

If one considers various diverse groups within a given culture, it is also found that the SDSVs based on the judgments of these groups are all highly intercorrelated and that they are also highly correlated with the SDSVs based on the judgments of college students. For example, the evidence is quite clear that SDSVs based on the judgments of neurotics (Edwards, 1957a), schizophrenics (Taylor, 1959; Cowen, Staiman, and Wolitzky, 1961), sex offenders (Cowen and Stricker, 1963), mental defectives with an average IQ of 68 (Heineman and Cowen, 1965), alcoholics (Zax, Cowen, Budin, and Biggs, 1962; Edwards, 1957a), psychotics (Klett, 1957b), novice nuns (Zax, Cowen, and Peter, 1963), and Nisei (Fujita, 1957), are all highly correlated with the SDSVs based on the judgments of college students.

There is also evidence that the SDSVs of personality statements tend to be much the same for groups from different cultures. For example, SDSVs based on the judgments of Norwegian (Lövaas, 1958), Japanese (Iwawaki and Cowen, 1964), and French (Cowen and Frankel, 1964) students are highly correlated with those based on the judgments of United States students, as are also the SDSVs based on the judgments of students at the American University of Beirut in Lebanon (Klett and Yaukey, 1959).

The various studies cited above are not intended to be complete, but they are representative of those that have appeared in psychological literature. In all cases, where a fairly large and representative sample of statements has been judged for social desirability by various groups, it has been found that the SDSVs tend to be highly correlated.

7.3 Correlations between Individual Ratings and the SDSVs of Personality Statements

The correlations reported above between the SDSVs of personality statements, as based on the ratings of two independent groups of judges, are correlations between two sets of averages. Of interest also is the degree to which each individual judge's ratings of social desirability are correlated with the average ratings and with the ratings of other judges.

It would appear to be obvious that if the social desirability ratings assigned to personality statements by different judges were random or idiosyncratic, the resulting SDSVs of the statements would all have approximately the same value and that any variation in the SDSVs could be attributed to chance or random variation. If a statement has a relatively low SDSV, then most of the judges must agree that it should be rated low. If each judge simply selected at random a number from 1 to 9 to assign to the statement, then the expected SDSV or average rating of the statement would be 5. In the extreme case, of an item with an SDSV equal to 1, all judges must of necessity assign a value of 1 to the statement. Thus, the fact that the SDSVs of any large or representative set of statements have been found to vary along the complete social desirability continuum is evidence that, in general, the judges show some degree of agreement in their ratings of individual items.

Even so, within any large group of judges, there may be some who tend to disagree with the others in their ratings of social desirability. We now consider the evidence regarding the degree to which individual judges agree with each other and with the average ratings assigned to a set of personality statements.

The SDSVs of a serial sample of 176 statements drawn from a larger set of 2824 statements were obtained by Edwards and Walsh (1963b). The frequency distribution of the SDSVs of these 176 statements based on the ratings of 95 judges (47 males and 48 females), as reported by Edwards (1965a), is shown in Table 7.2. It may be noted that the distribution of

Table 7.2   Frequency Distribution of the SDSVs of a Serial Sample of 176 Personality Statements Drawn from a Larger Set of 2824 Statements[a]

SDSVs	Frequency
7.5–7.9	5
7.0–7.4	25
6.5–6.9	13
6.0–6.4	14
5.5–5.9	11
5.0–5.4	12
4.5–4.9	8
4.0–4.4	14
3.5–3.9	25
3.0–3.4	29
2.5–2.9	17
2.0–2.4	3

[a]From Edwards (1965a).

SDSVs is bimodal and that only 20 of the statements have scale values in the neutral interval, 4.5 to 5.5, on the 9-point rating scale. The shape of the distribution of the SDSVs for this serial sample of 176 statements is quite similar to that shown earlier for the complete set of 2824 statements.

In another study (Edwards, 1965a), the 176 statements were given to an independent group of 103 female and 105 male students. The students were asked to rate the items for social desirability on a 9-point rating scale. For each student a rating was obtained for each of the 176 statements, and these individual ratings of social desirability may be designated by IRSD to distinguish them from the average ratings or SDSVs of the same statements based on the independent group of 95 judges.

The IRSDs for each student were then correlated with the normative SDSVs. The distribution of these correlation coefficients is shown in Figure 7.2. The average correlation between the IRSDs and SDSVs for the female students was 0.82, with a standard deviation of 0.07. For males the average correlation between the IRSDs and SDSVs was 0.79, with a standard deviation of 0.10. It is obvious that, with but few exceptions, the

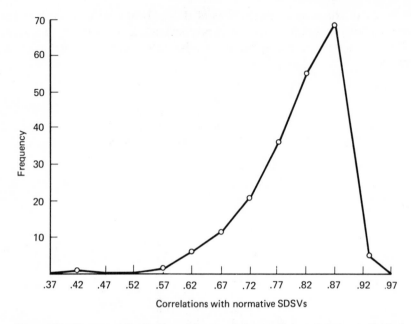

Figure 7.2 Frequency distribution of the correlation coefficients between individual ratings of social desirability of 176 personality statements and the normative SDSVs of the same statements for a combined group of 105 males and 103 females. From Edwards (1965a).

IRSDs tend to be substantially and positively correlated with the normative SDSVs.

7.4 Factor Analysis of the Correlations between Judges

To determine the degree to which ratings of social desirability obtained from different individuals are correlated, the intercorrelations of the ratings of the 103 females and the intercorrelations of the ratings for the 105 males for the first 150 items in the serial sample of 176 items were obtained.[1] Included in the two correlation matrices were the SDSVs of the 150 statements as determined from the ratings of the independent group of 95 judges. The SDSVs of the 150 statements, in other words, were treated as another individual judge, so that one correlation matrix of order 104×104 was obtained for the females and another of order 106×106 was

[1] The last 26 items in the serial sample of 176 items had to be eliminated because of restrictions in the computer program.

obtained for the males. These two correlation matrices were then factor analyzed by the method of principal components.

Figure 7.3 shows the distribution of the loadings on the first principal-component factor separately for males and females. The vector of SDSVs

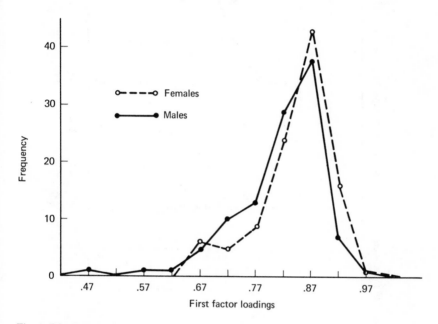

Figure 7.3   Frequency distribution of the first factor loadings of 105 males and 103 females. The last point on the right is the loading of the vector of normative SDSVs. From Edwards (1965a).

had the highest loading in both analyses, the obtained values being 0.98 for both males and females. The SDSVs, in other words, are an excellent measure of the first factor, as might be expected. It is also obvious that the IRSDs, with but few exceptions, also have relatively high positive loadings or correlations with the first factor. As a matter of fact, the first principal-component factor accounts for 71 percent of the total variance for the females and 67 percent of the total variance for the males. The second principal-component factor accounts for only 1.77 percent of the total variance for the female ratings and 2.19 percent of the total variance for the male ratings. These results are reassuring. They are reassuring in that we may have some confidence that individual ratings of social desirability are not, in general, idiosyncratic or random, but

Table 7.3 Individual Ratings of Social Desirability for a Sample of 15 Personality Statements by a Sample of 15 Judges

Judges	Items															Mean
	1	2	3	4	5	6	7	8	9	10	11	12	13	14	15	
1	5	5	2	5	7	3	4	5	3	8	2	4	3	6	6	4.53
2	6	8	2	7	8	4	4	6	7	8	3	3	3	7	8	5.60
3	4	4	2	5	7	3	3	5	5	8	3	3	3	7	7	4.60
4	5	6	2	7	7	6	6	5	4	7	2	4	5	7	7	5.33
5	7	8	2	7	9	3	2	4	6	8	3	4	8	8	8	5.80
6	4	4	2	6	7	6	3	6	4	8	3	1	3	7	7	4.73
7	5	6	3	6	8	5	4	5	4	7	3	4	2	7	8	5.13
8	5	5	3	6	6	4	4	5	5	7	4	4	4	6	6	4.93
9	7	7	2	8	7	5	4	5	5	9	3	5	1	8	8	5.60
10	5	5	1	8	7	4	3	4	4	8	1	4	4	6	7	4.73
11	6	5	1	7	7	3	2	4	3	8	1	4	3	7	7	4.53
12	4	6	2	7	8	4	4	6	3	6	4	4	3	8	7	5.07
13	4	4	1	8	8	4	2	5	4	5	3	2	2	7	8	4.47
14	7	7	1	6	8	3	1	3	7	8	1	2	3	9	8	4.93
15	5	5	2	4	6	5	3	4	5	8	1	3	3	6	6	4.40
Mean	5.27	5.67	1.87	6.47	7.33	4.13	3.27	4.80	4.60	7.53	2.47	3.40	3.33	7.07	7.20	

Table 7.4 Intercorrelations between the 15 Judges. Original Data Given in Table 7.3

Judges	1	2	3	4	5	6	7	8	9	10	11	12	13	14	15
1	1.00	0.81	0.89	0.80	0.70	0.76	0.87	0.90	0.85	0.87	0.92	0.80	0.71	0.78	0.85
2	0.81	1.00	0.86	0.74	0.76	0.77	0.86	0.90	0.87	0.82	0.83	0.75	0.81	0.92	0.84
3	0.89	0.86	1.00	0.71	0.72	0.87	0.86	0.95	0.80	0.82	0.86	0.79	0.82	0.86	0.85
4	0.80	0.74	0.71	1.00	0.64	0.77	0.80	0.77	0.75	0.88	0.82	0.80	0.74	0.68	0.78
5	0.70	0.76	0.72	0.64	1.00	0.57	0.62	0.77	0.61	0.80	0.82	0.67	0.66	0.84	0.70
6	0.76	0.77	0.87	0.77	0.57	1.00	0.83	0.85	0.90	0.77	0.76	0.78	0.84	0.73	0.81
7	0.87	0.86	0.86	0.80	0.62	0.83	1.00	0.85	0.90	0.82	0.87	0.84	0.87	0.84	0.82
8	0.90	0.90	0.95	0.77	0.77	0.85	0.85	1.00	0.89	0.91	0.92	0.82	0.84	0.87	0.84
9	0.85	0.87	0.80	0.75	0.61	0.74	0.90	0.89	1.00	0.86	0.90	0.76	0.79	0.85	0.82
10	0.87	0.82	0.82	0.88	0.80	0.77	0.82	0.91	0.86	1.00	0.96	0.79	0.82	0.81	0.82
11	0.92	0.83	0.86	0.82	0.82	0.76	0.87	0.92	0.90	0.96	1.00	0.82	0.81	0.87	0.84
12	0.80	0.75	0.79	0.80	0.67	0.78	0.84	0.82	0.76	0.79	0.82	1.00	0.88	0.69	0.60
13	0.71	0.81	0.82	0.74	0.66	0.84	0.87	0.84	0.79	0.82	0.81	0.88	1.00	0.79	0.64
14	0.78	0.92	0.86	0.68	0.84	0.73	0.84	0.87	0.85	0.81	0.87	0.69	0.79	1.00	0.87
15	0.85	0.84	0.85	0.78	0.70	0.81	0.82	0.84	0.82	0.82	0.84	0.60	0.64	0.87	1.00

rather that they tend to agree with each other and with the normative SDSVs.[2]

To illustrate the points made above, Table 7.3 shows the IRSDs for a small sample of 15 statements drawn from the serial sample of 176 statements, but does not include the normative SDSVs for the statements.[3] The 15 individual judges in this sample were selected at random from the larger group of individuals used in the study described above. Table 7.4 gives the intercorrelations of the IRSDs, and it may be noted that these correlations are all positive and relatively high. A matrix of intercorrelations of this kind suggests that, because all of the variables share common variance, the first principal-component factor will account for a relatively large proportion of the total variance. Table 7.5 gives the factor loadings

Table 7.5 Factor Loadings on the First Six Principal Components when Correlations between Judges Are Factor-Analyzed

	Factors					
Judges	I	II	III	IV	V	VI
1	0.92	0.01	−0.09	0.20	−0.08	−0.25
2	0.92	0.12	−0.08	−0.18	−0.04	0.14
3	0.93	0.00	−0.11	−0.15	0.14	−0.24
4	0.86	−0.16	0.11	0.39	0.10	0.21
5	0.80	0.46	0.35	−0.04	0.12	0.00
6	0.87	−0.28	−0.14	−0.07	0.33	0.00
7	0.93	−0.18	−0.11	−0.06	−0.14	0.08
8	0.97	0.04	−0.03	−0.06	0.02	−0.16
9	0.91	−0.04	−0.18	0.00	−0.32	0.06
10	0.94	0.06	0.13	0.21	−0.03	0.02
11	0.96	0.09	0.08	0.12	−0.14	−0.08
12	0.87	−0.30	0.32	−0.03	−0.05	−0.09
13	0.88	−0.27	0.20	−0.26	0.01	0.11
14	0.91	0.28	−0.06	−0.21	−0.03	0.14
15	0.89	0.19	−0.33	0.14	0.16	0.08
Eigenvalue	12.31	0.65	0.50	0.45	0.34	0.27
Proportion of Variance	0.82	0.04	0.03	0.03	0.02	0.02

[2]The study described has since been replicated by Boe, Gocka, and Kogan (1966) using MMPI items. They obtained results comparable to those reported in this and the next section.

[3]The fifteen items are listed at the end of the chapter.

on the first six principal-component factors. Again it may be noted that, for this relatively small sample of both individuals and statements, the first principal component accounts for approximately 82 percent of the total variance and the second factor for only approximately 4 percent of the total variance. As a matter of fact, each of the individuals has his highest loading on the first factor. The lowest loading on Factor I is 0.80 for Judge 5, and the next to lowest loading is 0.86 for Judge 4. It is obvious that the ratings for almost all of these judges could be predicted quite accurately in terms of the first factor. It may also be noted that only the first factor has an eigenvalue greater than 1.00.

7.5   Factor Analysis of the Correlations between Items

Suppose that instead of finding the correlations between each individual's ratings of social desirability, that is, the correlations between each of the rows of Table 7.3, we had calculated the correlations between the ratings assigned to each pair of items. In this case we would find the intercorrelations between the columns of Table 7.3, and these are given in Table 7.6. It may be noted that the correlations between items are considerably lower than those between individuals.

In our earlier discussion of principal-component factor analysis, it was pointed out that if the intercorrelations between a set of variables are relatively low, then a factor analysis of the intercorrelations would, in general, result in a factor loading matrix in which the variables tend to have high loadings on a number of different factors. Thus, if we factor-analyze the correlations given in Table 7.6, we should expect to find a number of different factors, each with one or more high loadings.

Table 7.7 gives the factor loadings of the items on the first six principal components when the item correlations of Table 7.6 are factor-analyzed. We note now that the first principal component accounts for only 31 percent of the total variance, whereas when we factor-analyzed the correlations between judges the first principal component accounted for 82 percent of the total variance. In order to account for the same proportion of the total variance in the present analysis, we must take into account the first five principal factors. We also note that each of these factors has an eigenvalue greater than 1.00.

The results cited above are in accord with a similar study by Messick (1960), in which he also correlated the ratings of social desirability between pairs of items and then factor-analyzed the resulting correlation matrix. It seems reasonable to believe, therefore, that the correlation matrix factor analyzed by Messick also consisted primarily of relatively low positive and negative correlations.

Table 7.6 Intercorrelations between the 15 Items. Original Data Given in Table 7.3

Items	1	2	3	4	5	6	7	8	9	10	11	12	13	14	15
1	1.00	0.79	-0.15	0.23	0.48	-0.28	-0.27	-0.54	0.58	0.58	-0.30	0.33	0.11	0.50	0.44
2	0.79	1.00	0.11	0.28	0.57	-0.12	0.06	-0.12	0.61	0.30	0.07	0.35	0.28	0.56	0.55
3	-0.15	0.11	1.00	-0.38	-0.29	0.34	0.60	0.47	0.02	0.01	0.62	0.30	0.11	-0.24	-0.23
4	0.23	0.28	-0.38	1.00	0.31	0.06	0.01	0.10	-0.06	-0.23	0.16	0.24	0.06	0.31	0.59
5	0.48	0.57	-0.29	0.31	1.00	-0.35	-0.48	-0.28	0.49	-0.05	-0.02	-0.23	0.16	0.69	0.82
6	-0.28	-0.12	0.34	0.06	-0.35	1.00	0.58	0.42	-0.17	-0.07	0.13	-0.12	-0.15	-0.16	-0.04
7	-0.27	0.06	0.60	0.01	-0.48	0.58	1.00	0.60	-0.29	0.34	0.34	0.46	0.06	-0.35	-0.29
8	-0.54	-0.12	0.47	0.10	-0.28	0.42	0.60	1.00	-0.27	-0.28	0.74	-0.06	-0.10	-0.17	-0.04
9	0.58	0.61	0.02	-0.06	0.49	-0.17	-0.29	-0.27	1.00	0.34	-0.01	-0.24	0.07	0.40	-0.44
10	0.58	0.30	0.01	-0.23	-0.05	-0.07	0.34	-0.28	0.34	1.00	-0.39	0.19	-0.03	0.04	-0.06
11	-0.30	0.07	0.62	0.16	-0.02	0.13	0.34	0.74	-0.01	-0.39	1.00	0.08	0.11	0.12	0.14
12	0.33	0.35	0.30	0.24	-0.23	-0.12	0.46	-0.06	-0.24	0.19	0.08	1.00	0.21	-0.11	-0.10
13	0.11	0.28	0.11	0.06	0.16	-0.15	0.06	-0.10	0.07	-0.03	0.11	0.21	1.00	-0.02	-0.11
14	0.50	0.56	-0.24	0.31	0.69	-0.16	-0.35	-0.17	0.40	0.04	0.12	-0.11	-0.02	1.00	0.71
15	0.44	0.55	-0.23	0.59	0.82	-0.04	-0.29	-0.04	-0.44	-0.06	0.14	-0.10	-0.11	0.71	1.00

Table 7.7   Factor Loadings on the First Six Principal Components When the Correlations between Items are Factor-Analyzed

	Factors					
Items	I	II	III	IV	V	VI
1	0.82	0.13	0.49	−0.04	0.14	−0.06
2	0.69	0.57	0.33	0.01	−0.01	0.07
3	−0.45	0.61	0.34	0.36	−0.24	−0.12
4	0.34	0.37	−0.37	−0.62	0.32	0.08
5	0.83	0.16	−0.33	0.05	−0.18	0.08
6	−0.44	0.35	−0.06	0.22	0.58	0.47
7	−0.59	0.60	0.29	−0.10	0.23	0.13
8	−0.56	0.60	−0.32	0.15	0.05	−0.08
9	0.65	0.16	0.16	0.55	−0.10	0.12
10	0.30	−0.13	0.71	0.26	0.28	−0.06
11	−0.28	0.75	−0.31	0.13	−0.34	−0.25
12	−0.04	0.38	0.60	−0.61	0.03	−0.29
13	0.10	0.20	0.25	−0.31	−0.64	0.58
14	0.74	0.28	−0.28	0.09	0.04	−0.11
15	0.73	0.39	−0.43	0.01	0.22	−0.03
Eigenvalue	4.69	2.74	2.22	1.47	1.27	0.80
Proportion of Variance	0.31	0.18	0.15	0.10	0.08	0.05

7.6   Average Intercorrelation between Judges and between Items

In the limiting case, if each judge assigned exactly the same ratings to the various items as every other judge, then the correlations between all pairs of judges would be equal to 1.00 and the correlations between all pairs of items would be equal to zero. For example, consider the ratings assigned to five items by each of ten judges, as shown in Table 7.8. In this case, each judge has assigned exactly the same ratings to the items, and the correlations between judges are all equal to 1.00, whereas the correlations between items are all equal to zero. For the data of Table 7.8, all of the variation in the ratings can be accounted for by differences in the SDSVs of the items, and none of the variation can be attributed to differences among the judges.

In general, when the average intercorrelation between judges is positive and high, this indicates that a substantial proportion of the variance in the ratings is primarily the result of systematic differences in the SDSVs of the items rated. On the other hand, when the average intercorrelation between

Table 7.8 A Matrix of Item Ratings Where Each Judge Has Assigned the Same Rating to an Item as Every Other Judge

	Items				
Judges	1	2	3	4	5
1	2	4	9	6	3
2	2	4	9	6	3
3	2	4	9	6	3
4	2	4	9	6	3
5	2	4	9	6	3
6	2	4	9	6	3
7	2	4	9	6	3
8	2	4	9	6	3
9	2	4	9	6	3
10	2	4	9	6	3

items is positive and high, this indicates that a substantial proportion of the variance in the ratings can be attributed to systematic differences in the judges themselves. In other words, some judges may consistently tend to overrate the items and others may consistently tend to underrate the items.

7.7 Analysis of Variance of Ratings of Social Desirability

If any large representative or random set of items is rated for social desirability by a large group of judges, then the SDSVs of the items can be obtained as can also the mean ratings assigned to the set of items by each judge. If the variance of the SDSVs of the items is large relative to the variance of the mean ratings of the judges, it will also be true that the correlations between judges will tend to be high and positive relative to the correlations between items. These points can be illustrated with the data of Table 7.3.

In Table 7.3 we have $k = 15$ items and we also have $n = 15$ judges or raters. We let X_{kn} be a general symbol for any rating in the table, with the understanding that k and n when used as subscripts represent variables. For example, in Table 7.3, k can take any value from 1 to 15, because there are 15 items, and n can take any value from 1 to 15, because there are 15 judges. When k and n are used alone or as coefficients of other terms, they will always represent constants.

The sum of all kn ratings will be represented by $\Sigma X..$, where the dots that replace the subscripts kn indicate that we have summed all kn values of X_{kn}. Similarly, we let $\bar{X}..$ be the mean of all kn ratings. The sums of ratings for the individual items can be represented by $\Sigma X_{1.}$, $\Sigma X_{2.}$, ..., $\Sigma X_{15.}$, where the dot that has replaced the subscript n means that we have summed over the n judges for a given item. Then $\Sigma X_{k.}$ will be a general symbol for any item sum and $\bar{X}_{k.}$ will be a general symbol for any item mean (which is, of course, the SDSV of the item). Similarly, the sums of the ratings for the judges can be represented by $\Sigma X_{.1}$, $\Sigma X_{.2}$, ..., $\Sigma X_{.15}$, where the dot that has replaced the subscript k means that we have summed the k ratings for a given judge. Then $\Sigma X_{.n}$ will be a general symbol for the sum of ratings for any given judge and $\bar{X}_{.n}$ will be a general symbol for the mean rating for any given judge. With this notation we can now write the following identity:

$$X_{kn} - \bar{X}.. = (\bar{X}_{k.} - \bar{X}..) + (\bar{X}_{.n} - \bar{X}..) + (X_{kn} - \bar{X}_{k.} - \bar{X}_{.n} + \bar{X}..) \qquad (7.1)$$

which states that the deviation of any given value of X_{kn} from the overall mean can be expressed as a sum of the three component parts on the right. If we square both sides of this expression and sum over all kn observations, we find that all products between terms on the right sum to zero. Therefore,

$$\sum_1^{kn} (X_{kn} - \bar{X}..)^2 = n \sum_1^{k} (\bar{X}_{k.} - \bar{X}..)^2 + k \sum_1^{n} (\bar{X}_{.n} - \bar{X}..)^2$$

$$+ \sum_1^{kn} (X_{kn} - \bar{X}_{k.} - \bar{X}_{.n} + \bar{X}..)^2 \qquad (7.2)$$

The term on the left in the above expression is the total sum of squared deviations. The first term on the right is the item sum of squares, and the second term is the judge sum of squares. The last term is commonly called the *error sum of squares*. To calculate these sums of squares, we have for the total sum of squares

$$\sum_1^{kn} (X_{kn} - \bar{X}..)^2 = \sum_1^{kn} X_{kn}^2 - \frac{\left(\sum X..\right)^2}{kn} \qquad (7.3)$$

and for the data of Table 7.3 we have

$$\sum_1^{kn} (X_{kn} - \bar{X}..)^2 = (5)^2 + (6)^2 + \ldots + (6)^2 - \frac{(1116)^2}{225}$$

$$= 988.639$$

The sum of squares for items will be given by

$$n \sum_1^{k} (\bar{X}_{k.} - \bar{X}..)^2 = \sum_1^{k} \frac{\left(\sum X_{k.}\right)^2}{n} - \frac{\left(\sum X..\right)^2}{kn} \qquad (7.4)$$

and for the data of Table 7.3, we have

$$n \sum_1^k (\bar{X}_{k.} - \bar{X}_{..})^2 = \frac{(79)^2}{15} + \frac{(85)^2}{15} + \ldots + \frac{(108)^2}{15} - \frac{(1116)^2}{225}$$

$$= 737.173$$

To obtain the sum of squares for judges, we have

$$k \sum_1^n (\bar{X}_{.n} - \bar{X}_{..})^2 = \sum_1^n \frac{(\sum X_{.n})^2}{k} - \frac{(\sum X_{..})^2}{kn} \qquad (7.5)$$

and for the data of Table 7.3

$$k \sum_1^n (\bar{X}_{.n} - \bar{X}_{..})^2 = \frac{(68)^2}{15} + \frac{(84)^2}{15} + \ldots + \frac{(66)^2}{15} - \frac{(1116)^2}{225}$$

$$= 42.906$$

The error sum of squares can then be obtained by subtraction. Thus

$$\text{Total} - \text{judges} - \text{items} = \text{error} \qquad (7.6)$$

and

$$988.639 - 42.906 - 737.173 = 208.560$$

The results of the analysis of variance are summarized in Table 7.9. The test of significance of the mean square for items results in an F ratio of 49.488 with 14 and 196 degrees of freedom, and this is a highly significant

Table 7.9   Analysis of Variance of the Ratings Given in Table 7.3

Source of variation	d.f.	Sum of squares	Mean square	F
Judges	14	42.906	3.065	2.881
Items	14	737.173	52.655	49.488
Error	196	208.560	1.064	
Total	224	988.639		

value. The test of the significance of the judge mean square results in an F ratio of 2.881 with 14 and 196 degrees of freedom, and this also is a significant value. Of greater interest, however, is the fact that the variation in the mean ratings of the judges accounts for only $42.906/988.639 = 4$ percent of the total sum of squares, whereas the variation in the item means or SDSVs accounts for $737.173/988.639 = 75$ percent of the total sum of squares.

An examination of the means of the judges and the means (SDSVs) of the items, as given in Table 7.3, shows that there is considerably greater variation in the SDSVs of the items compared with the variation in the means of the judges.

7.8   The Content of the Fifteen Items

The fifteen items for which ratings of social desirability are given in Table 7.3 are as follows:

1. He admires people who have made a great deal of money.
2. He works best when he has a planned routine to follow.
3. He will use other people in any way he can to obtain his goals.
4. He lets others know how much he likes them.
5. He understands what he reads.
6. He is much concerned about matters of status and prestige.
7. He seldom stays with a task long enough to complete it.
8. He loses interest in a game if he wins too easily.
9. He always wants things to be done immediately.
10. He can express his thoughts well in talking to others.
11. He allows prejudice and bias to enter into his judgments of others.
12. He says things that have no relevance to the topic under discussion.
13. He has difficulty in making an important decision without help from others.
14. He has a great deal of energy.
15. He is at ease in a social situation with those of the opposite sex.

Chapter 8

Individual Differences
in Rates
of SD Responding

8.1 The Relationship between P(T) and SDSV

Suppose that a given set of personality statements has been rated for social desirability and that the SDSVs of the statements are available. If this same set of statements is given to another independent group of individuals and they are asked to describe themselves by responding True or False to each statement, then it is possible to obtain the proportion of True responses, P(T), given to each statement. P(T) is called the *probability of item endorsement*. Then for each item we have a value of P(T) and a value of SDSV. If P(T) is plotted against SDSV for any random or representative set of personality statements, it will be found that P(T) increases linearly with SDSV. In other words, statements with low or socially undesirable scale values have a low probability of being answered True and statements with high or socially desirable scale values have a high probability of being answered True.

Figure 8.1 shows the relationship between P(T) and SDSV for a set of 140 personality statements, as reported by Edwards (1953). It is important to note that the SDSVs of the 140 items were obtained by a scaling method known as the *method of successive intervals* and that the range of the SDSVs is not on a scale from 1 to 9, but rather on a scale ranging from approximately 0.5 to 4.5. The correlation between P(T) and SDSV for the 140 statements is 0.87.

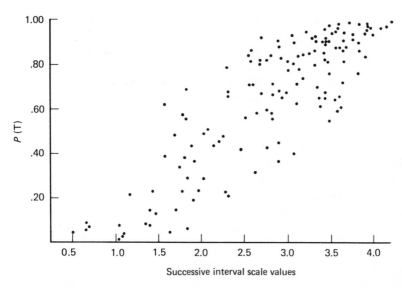

Figure 8.1   The relationship between $P(T)$ and SDSV for a set of 140 personality statements. From Edwards (1953).

Various other studies have also shown that $P(T)$ is linearly related to SDSV (Cowen and Tongas, 1959; Edwards, 1957c; Edwards and Walsh, 1963b; Hanley, 1956; Iwawaki, Fukuhara, and Hidano, 1966; Kenny, 1956; Sperber and Spanner, 1962; Taylor, 1959). In one large scale study involving 2824 statements, Edwards (1966a) found a correlation of 0.89 between $P(T)$ and SDSV. In still another large scale study involving 1647 statements, Cruse (1965) obtained a correlation of 0.90 between $P(T)$ and SDSV. These correlations between $P(T)$ and SDSV are typical of those reported by other investigators using smaller representative sets of personality statements.

The linear relationship between $P(T)$ and SDSV is found not only for college students and adults, but also when young children are asked to describe themselves. For example, the correlation between $P(T)$ and SDSV has been reported by Cruse (1966) to increase from 0.61 for children age 3, to 0.71 for children age 4, to 0.74 for children age 5, and to 0.88 for children age 6. For Grades 1 through 11, Cruse (1963) reports correlations between $P(T)$ and SDSV ranging from 0.91 to 0.96.

8.2   Socially Desirable (SD) Responses to Personality Statements

When the SDSV of a personality statement is known, it is possible to define a socially desirable (SD) response to the statement (Edwards, 1957a). An SD response may be defined as a True response to an item with a socially desirable scale value or as a False response to an item with a socially undesirable scale value. In other words, if the SDSV of the statement has been located on a 9-point rating scale with 5 as the neutral point then, if the SDSV of the statement is greater than 5, the SD response to the statement is defined as a True response. If the SDSV of the statement is less than 5, then the SD response to the statement is defined as a False response. A socially undesirable (SUD) response to a statement is, of course, just the opposite of an SD response.

When an individual gives an SD response to an item, he is either attributing to himself a characteristic that is judged by the average person as desirable or he is denying a characteristic that is judged by the average person as undesirable. Similarly, when an individual gives an SUD response to an item, he is either denying a characteristic that the average person considers desirable or attributing to himself a characteristic that the average person considers undesirable.

8.3 Relationship between $P(SD)$ and SDSV

If individuals have been asked to describe themselves by responding True or False to a given set of personality statements, then it is possible to find the proportion of SD responses, $P(SD)$, to each statement. $P(SD)$ is called the *probability of an item eliciting an SD response*. Because the relationship between $P(T)$ and SDSV is linear, the relationship between $P(SD)$ and SDSV is V-shaped. In other words, if $P(SD)$ is plotted against SDSV, $P(SD)$ decreases with SDSVs from 1 to 5 and then increases with SDSVs from 5 to 9, as shown in Figure 8.2.

The relationship between $P(SD)$ and SDSV, as shown in Figure 8.2, is based on a serial sample of 176 statements drawn from a larger set of 2824 statements. If we consider only those 96 items with SDSVs from 1 to 5, then the correlation between $P(SD)$ and SDSV is -0.610 and the regression coefficient of $P(SD)$ on SDSV is -0.165. The mean probability of a False *and* SD response to these items is 0.787. For those 80 items with SDSVs from 5 to 9, the correlation between $P(SD)$ and SDSV is 0.669 and the regression coefficient of $P(SD)$ on SDSV is 0.155. The mean probability of a True *and* SD response to these 80 items is 0.750.

8.4 Rates of SD Responding and *SD* Scales

If, for any given set of statements, the SDSVs of the statements are known and if individuals are asked to describe themselves by answering the statements True or False, then it is also possible to find for each individual

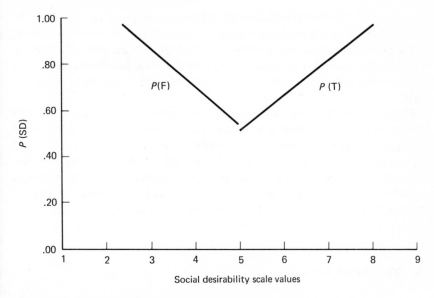

Figure 8.2   The relationship between *P*(SD) and SDSV. From Edwards (1967b).

the number of SD responses that he has given in self-description. If the number of SD responses is divided by the total number of items, then we can obtain an estimate of the *rate* of SD responding for each individual.

Thus any set of statements might be regarded as a Social Desirability (*SD*) scale measuring individual differences in the tendency to give SD responses in self-description. If a set of items is regarded as an *SD* scale, then the trait keyed response to each item, regardless of the content of the item, is the SD response to the item. All items with SDSVs greater than 5 would be keyed True for SD responses and all items with SDSVs less than 5 would be keyed False for SD responses.

We have said that any set of items keyed for SD responses may be regarded as an *SD* scale. We have observed, however, that the relationship between *P*(SD) and SDSV is V-shaped. Items with extremely low or socially undesirable scale values will tend to elicit an extremely large proportion of False *and* SD responses, and items with extremely high or socially desirable scale values will also tend to elicit an extremely large proportion of True *and* SD responses. Items with SDSVs in the neutral section of the social desirability continuum tend to elicit the smallest proportion of SD responses. Thus, if the items in a given set all have extreme, either high or low, SDSVs the mean score on this *SD* scale will tend to be close to the number of items in the scale because

$$\bar{X} = p_1 + p_2 + \ldots + p_k$$

where the p's are the proportion of SD responses given to the items. In other words, if the items have extreme scale values, the mean rate of SD responding to the set of items will tend to be high and the score distribution considerably skewed. The mean score on an SD scale can be decreased and the skewness reduced if items with a range of SDSVs are selected for the scale.

There is also evidence to indicate that items with relatively neutral SDSVs, that is, items with scale values in the central section of the social desirability continuum, are not as sensitive to individual differences in SD tendencies as items outside the neutral area (Edwards, 1963; 1964b). Consequently, if we should set out to build a rational SD scale, we might consider including in the scale only those items that fall outside the neutral interval, 4.5 to 5.5, on the social desirability continuum.

8.5   The MMPI SD Scale

Figure 8.3 shows the relationship between P(T) and SDSV for a 39-item SD scale composed of items from the Minnesota Multiphasic Personality Inventory (MMPI). It may be noted that none of the items in this SD scale falls within the neutral interval and that the items have a range of SDSVs. There are 9 items with SDSVs > 5 and these items are keyed for True responses. The 30 items with SDSVs < 5 are keyed for False responses. The 39-item SD scale was a very early attempt (Edwards, 1957a) to measure individual differences in the tendency to give socially desirable responses in self-description and has been used in a large number of investigations.[1] More recently developed SD scales will be described later.

It should be made clear that individual differences in rates of SD responding can be altered by altering the SDSVs of the items included in the scale. In general, if the SD scale contains only items with extreme SDSVs, then individual rates of SD responding will all tend to be higher than if rates of SD responding are measured by SD scales in which the items have a wider range of SDSVs. As we shall see later, however, individual differences in rates of SD responding, as measured by different SD scales, all tend to be highly correlated.

---

[1]Because the MMPI SD scale will be referred to frequently, we give here the MMPI Booklet Numbers of the items in this scale. The nine items keyed True are 7, 18, 54, 107, 163, 169, 247, 371, and 528. The 30 items keyed False are 32, 40, 42, 43, 138, 148, 156, 158, 171, 186, 218, 241, 245, 247, 252, 263, 267, 269, 286, 301, 321, 335, 337, 352, 383, 424, 431, 439, 549, and 555.

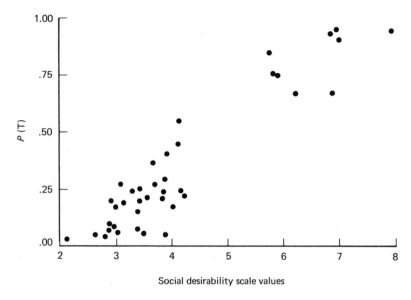

Figure 8.3   The relationship between P(T) and SDSV for the 39 items in the MMPI *SD* scale.

8.6   Factor Analysis of *SD* and Other Personality Scales

Given a large set of items with known SDSVs, it is possible to construct any number of different *SD* scales and this has been done using a pool of 2824 items (Edwards and Walsh, 1964b). The SDSVs of the 2824 items were keypunched on IBM cards which could then be sorted according to the SDSVs of the items. It is also to be emphasized that in constructing the *SD* scales the content of the items was not considered. The items for each *SD* scale were selected only on the basis of the SDSVs of the items and no attention was given to the content of the items.

From the pool of 2824 items, 240 items were selected to form six *SD* scales. Scales 1–6 each consisted of 40 items. All of the items in these scales were keyed for SD responses. In Scales 1–4 there was a balance in the True-False keying of the items with each scale consisting of 20 items with SDSVs > 5 and keyed True and 20 items with SDSVs < 5 and keyed False. Scale 5 consisted of 40 items in which all of the items had SDSVs < 5 and, consequently, all of the items in this scale were keyed False. Scale 6 consisted of 40 items in which all of the items had SDSVs > 5 and, consequently, all of the items in this scale were keyed True. Scale 7 was the previously developed 39-item *SD* scale consisting of items from the MMPI

and in which 9 items are keyed True and 30 are keyed False. These seven
SD scales were administered along with 24 other scales to 95 female and 35
male students. Table 8.1 lists the 31 scales involved in this study. The table also gives
the True-False keying of the items in the scales, the mean probability of a
keyed or trait response to the items in each scale, the mean scores on the
scales, and the standard deviation of the scores on each scale. The last

Table 8.1   Mean Probabilities of a Keyed Response, $P(K)$, Means, Standard Deviations, and K-R 21 Values for 31 Personality Scales[a]

	Keying					
Scales	T	F	$P(K)$	$\bar{X}$	σ	K-R 21
1. Ex. *SD*	20	20	0.82	32.98	5.68	0.84
2. Ex. *SD*	20	20	0.74	29.61	6.52	0.84
3. Ex. *SD*	20	20	0.84	33.60	5.76	0.86
4. Ex. *SD*	20	20	0.81	32.32	6.35	0.87
5. Ex. *SD*		40	0.71	28.58	7.32	0.87
6. Ex. *SD*	40		0.74	29.62	7.10	0.87
7. MMPI *SD*	9	30	0.74	28.77	6.23	0.83
8. Ex. High Neutral	50		0.64	32.00	5.29	0.60
9. Ex. Middle Neutral	46		0.48	21.94	5.65	0.65
10. Ex. Low Neutral	50		0.28	13.79	5.10	0.63
11. MMPI Neutral		18	0.58	10.45	2.95	0.53
12. MMPI *Lie*		11	0.16	1.81	2.14	0.74
13. Marlowe-Crowne *MC*	18	15	0.45	14.99	5.77	0.78
14. Ex.-*MC*	17	16	0.46	15.18	6.10	0.80
15. Block's MMPI Factor I	19	20	0.52	20.35	5.92	0.74
16. Nichols-Schnell CPI Factor I	5	34	0.64	24.83	6.83	0.83
17. Nichols-Schnell CPI Factor II	10	5	0.72	10.78	3.05	0.72
18. Buss-Durkee Hostility Factor I	24	3	0.31	8.39	5.80	0.86
19. Buss-Durkee Hostility Factor II	31	12	0.44	18.95	7.13	0.81
20. Schultz's Hostility	22	22	0.52	22.84	6.04	0.71
21. Eysenck's *N*	24			23.68	10.58	
22. Eysenck's *E*	16	8		27.98	9.94	
23. Ex. "I like" scale	40		0.75	30.18	5.72	0.79
24. Ex. Controversial	38		0.50	19.02	4.52	0.55
25. Ex. Deviant True	40		0.27	10.98	4.56	0.63
26. Bass's *SA*	56		0.57	31.84	8.42	0.82
27. Couch-Keniston	30		0.74	22.28	4.61	0.76
28. California *F* Scale	27		0.35	9.45	4.34	0.70
29. Ex. Edwards-Diers *B-1*	40		0.62	24.82	4.74	0.60
30. Ex. Edwards-Diers *B-2*	40		0.57	22.91	4.25	0.47
31. Ex. *SD* Deviant True	40		0.39	15.75	6.05	0.76

[a]From Edwards and Walsh (1964b).

column gives the K–R 21 value of each scale, with the exception of the MPI scales of neuroticism (N) and extroversion (E). A more complete description of the 31 scales can be found in Edwards and Walsh (1964b).

Scores on the 31 scales were intercorrelated and factor-analyzed by the method of principal components. The first six principal-component factors accounted for 33.12, 16.12, 10.51, 6.01, 3.95, and 3.09 percent of the total variance, respectively. The six factors together accounted for approximately 73 percent of the total variance. The six factors were rotated orthogonally by means of Kasier's normal Varimax rotation. Of primary interest are the factor loadings of the seven *SD* scales on the first principal component. All of the *SD* scales have their highest loading on this factor. The factor loadings of the scales are shown in Table 8.2.

The factor loadings given in Table 8.2 are normalized factor loadings so that the sum of the squared loadings in any given row is equal to 1.00, within rounding errors. As we pointed out previously, the square of a normalized factor loading is simply the proportion of the common variance of a scale, h^2, that is accounted for by a given factor. Thus, for *SD* Scale 1 we have $h^2 = 0.79$ and this is the proportion of the total variance of the scale that can be accounted for by the six factors. It is, in other words, the variance that the scale has in common with the six factors. Because *SD* Scale 1 has a loading of 0.99 on Factor I, it is obvious that almost all of the common variance, $h^2 = 0.79$, in this scale is accounted for by Factor I.

If we wish to determine the proportion of the total variance of *SD* Scale 1 that is accounted for by the first factor, then the normalized factor loading must be multiplied by $\sqrt{0.79}$. The denormalized loading of Scale 1 on Factor I would then be $\sqrt{0.79}\ (0.99) = 0.88$. If each of the normalized loadings of Scale 1 is multiplied by $\sqrt{0.79}$, the denormalized loadings of the scale on the factors will be obtained and the sum of these squared denormalized factor loadings will, within rounding errors, be equal to the communality of the scale or 0.79.

The denormalized loadings of the various *SD* scales on Factor I are 0.88, 0.91, 0.91, 0.91, 0.76, 0.77, and 0.76, respectively. Thus, all of the *SD* scales have substantial correlations with Factor I. Furthermore, each of the *SD* scales has a relatively high degree of internal consistency, as measured by the Kuder-Richardson Formula 21 lower-bound estimate of r_{kk}. For the *SD* scales, these values are 0.84, 0.84, 0.86, 0.87, 0.87, and 0.83, respectively.

The total number of items in the seven *SD* scales is 279. The fact that each of the *SD* scales has a relatively high lower-bound estimate of r_{kk} and also a relatively high loading on a common factor strongly suggests that they are all measuring the same common trait. We emphasize again that the items in these scales were not selected in terms of their content but solely on the basis of their SDSVs. It is difficult to believe, therefore, that the

Table 8.2 Orthogonally Rotated and Normalized Factor Loadings of 31 Personality Scales and Communalities of the Scales[a]

		Factors					
Scales	I'	II'	III'	IV'	V'	VI'	h^2
1. Ex. SD	−0.99	0.04	0.03	0.12	−0.08	0.07	0.79
2. Ex. SD	−0.99	−0.02	0.12	0.03	−0.08	0.00	0.85
3. Ex. SD	−0.99	0.01	−0.13	−0.05	0.03	0.07	0.85
4. Ex. SD	−0.98	0.05	−0.05	−0.07	−0.04	0.19	0.86
5. Ex. SD	−0.88	−0.17	−0.31	0.28	−0.05	−0.13	0.75
6. Ex. SD	−0.87	0.35	−0.14	−0.26	0.17	−0.02	0.78
7. MMPI SD	−0.85	−0.19	−0.31	0.03	0.11	−0.35	0.80
8. Ex. High Neutral	0.10	0.05	0.35	−0.92	0.10	−0.11	0.63
9. Ex. Middle Neutral	0.60	0.37	0.37	−0.57	−0.01	0.20	0.56
10. Ex. Low Neutral	0.39	0.63	0.05	−0.61	−0.17	0.21	0.70
11. MMPI Neutral	−0.39	−0.61	0.17	0.30	−0.50	−0.33	0.68
12. MMPI Lie	0.03	0.03	−0.99	−0.04	0.08	0.09	0.82
13. Marlowe-Crowne MC	−0.43	0.24	−0.83	−0.13	−0.20	0.13	0.81
14. Ex.-MC	−0.56	0.16	−0.77	−0.11	0.23	0.08	0.79
15. Block's MMPI Factor I	−0.45	−0.24	−0.52	0.07	−0.23	−0.64	0.72
16. Nichols-Schnell CPI Factor I	−0.72	−0.34	−0.04	0.12	−0.54	−0.25	0.76
17. Nichols-Schnell CPI Factor II	−0.80	0.09	0.28	−0.26	0.01	−0.46	0.73
18. Buss-Durkee Hostility Factor I	0.68	0.48	−0.15	0.01	0.37	0.38	0.82
19. Buss-Durkee Hostility Factor II	0.49	0.02	0.15	−0.12	0.85	0.06	0.80
20. Schultz's Hostility	0.10	−0.20	0.21	−0.29	0.90	−0.14	0.75
21. Eysenck's N	0.60	0.10	0.72	−0.02	0.12	0.31	0.64
22. Eysenck's E	−0.60	0.26	0.08	−0.31	0.11	−0.68	0.69
23. Ex. "I like" Scale	−0.69	0.66	0.15	0.02	0.11	−0.23	0.65
24. Ex. Controversial	0.30	0.38	0.79	−0.37	0.11	0.01	0.68
25. Ex. Deviant True	0.78	0.26	0.43	−0.36	0.09	0.06	0.69
26. Bass's SA	−0.01	0.98	−0.05	0.17	−0.05	0.03	0.72
27. Couch-Keniston	−0.20	0.86	−0.46	0.00	0.13	−0.02	0.67
28. California F Scale	0.25	0.95	−0.12	0.13	−0.08	0.07	0.66
29. Ex. Edwards-Diers B-1	−0.46	0.74	0.06	−0.28	0.30	−0.26	0.63
30. Ex. Edwards-Diers B-2	−0.41	0.69	0.03	−0.43	−0.40	0.03	0.60
31. Ex. SD Deviant True	−0.53	0.55	−0.14	−0.63	0.01	0.09	0.68

[a]From Edwards and Walsh (1964b).

r_{kk} values are a result of homogeneity of item content within each scale. We shall show later that scales in which items of heterogeneous content are consistently keyed for SD responses tend to have relatively high r_{kk} values. This fact alone can account for the r_{kk} values of the present scales. Furthermore, in view of the manner in which the scales were constructed, it is not unreasonable to believe that the common trait being measured by the scales is the tendency to give SD responses in self-description.

8.7 Another Factor Analysis of *SD* and Personality Scales

In another study (Edwards, 1963), four scales in which all of the items were keyed for SUD responses were constructed from the pool of 2824 items. Items in each of these scales had SDSVs < 5 and, consequently, the items in each of the scales were keyed for True *and* SUD responses. In addition, two *SD* scales were constructed in which all of the items had SDSVs > 5 and in which, consequently, all of the items were keyed for True and SD responses. The 39-item MMPI *SD* scale was also included in the analysis along with 12 other scales. Table 8.3 describes the nature of the *SUD* and *SD* scales and the True-False keying of the items in the other scales.

Table 8.3   Mean Probabilities of a Keyed Response, $P(\text{K})$, Means, Standard Deviations, and K-R 21 Values for 19 Personality Scales[a]

Scales and Keying	Scale Values	$P(\text{K})$	$\bar{X}$	σ	K-R 21
1. *SUD*: 75 True	2.5–3.0	0.11	8.57	9.69	0.93
2. *SUD*: 67 True	3.0–3.5	0.19	12.51	10.47	0.92
3. *SUD*: 23 True	2.0–3.0	0.26	6.04	4.28	0.79
4. *SUD*: 54 True	3.0–4.0	0.45	24.30	9.85	0.88
5. Low Neutral: 50 True	4.5–5.5	0.25	12.36	4.35	0.52
6. Neutral: 46 True	4.5–5.5	0.49	22.62	5.69	0.66
7. High Neutral: 50 True	4.5–5.5	0.65	32.60	6.04	0.70
8. *SD*: 75 True	7.0–7.5	0.80	59.95	9.19	0.87
9. *SD*: 51 True	7.5–8.0	0.91	46.45	4.75	0.83
10. *SD* Deviant: 55 True	≥6.0	0.36	19.76	7.47	0.80
11. *SD* Doubtful: 51 True	4.0–8.0	0.65	33.30	7.42	0.81
12. MMPI *SD*: 9 True, 30 False		0.83	32.39	5.20	0.82
13. M-C *SD*: 18 True, 15 False		0.44	14.39	5.62	0.77
14. Wiggins' *Sd*: 31 True, 9 False		0.36	13.09	3.82	0.41
15. Couch-Keniston *HM*: 35 True		0.81	28.49	4.31	0.74
16. Couch-Keniston *MM*: 40 True		0.52	20.73	4.70	0.56
17. Total number ? responses		0.16	393.73	308.19	0.93[b]
18. P(T/?) on Scale 17			.60	.14	0.73[b]
19. Consistency: 176 repeated items		0.85	149.19	9.42	0.75

[a]From Edwards (1963).

[b]These two coefficients are split-half coefficients. The two scores for each subject are based on blocks of 1200 items each.

Table 8.4 Orthogonally Rotated and Normalized Factor Loadings of 19 Personality Scales and Communalities of the Scales[a]

Scales	I'	II'	III'	IV'	V'	VI'	VII'	VIII'	IX'	X'	h^2
1. *SUD*	−0.98	0.11	−0.01	−0.09	0.05	−0.03	0.01	0.00	0.09	−0.06	0.89
2. *SUD*	−0.99	0.04	0.08	0.02	0.05	0.03	−0.02	0.04	0.01	−0.01	0.88
3. *SUD*	−0.91	−0.04	−0.11	0.17	−0.21	0.13	−0.03	−0.07	−0.01	0.25	0.80
4. *SUD*	−0.85	0.05	−0.02	0.16	−0.34	0.19	0.06	−0.11	−0.16	0.23	0.89
5. Low Neutral	−0.17	0.28	0.02	0.03	0.22	0.32	−0.86	0.00	0.01	−0.01	0.94
6. Neutral	−0.54	0.52	−0.15	0.11	−0.29	0.36	−0.34	−0.20	−0.13	0.12	0.83
7. High Neutral	−0.46	0.36	0.05	0.33	−0.21	0.18	0.11	−0.04	−0.64	0.21	0.83
8. *SD*	0.72	0.51	−0.12	0.04	0.02	0.40	0.06	−0.18	−0.04	0.05	0.80
9. *SD*	0.82	0.42	0.04	0.19	−0.09	0.07	−0.07	−0.20	−0.16	0.18	0.82
10. *SD* Deviant	0.25	0.95	0.07	−0.03	0.09	−0.04	−0.02	0.10	−0.08	−0.09	0.84
11. *SD* Doubtful	0.51	0.82	−0.12	0.07	−0.06	0.00	0.05	−0.09	0.16	0.13	0.87
12. MMPI *SD*	0.86	0.04	−0.21	0.03	0.06	0.09	0.19	0.04	0.24	0.32	0.76
13. M-C *SD*	0.38	0.18	0.04	−0.03	0.91	−0.02	−0.01	−0.01	0.01	0.00	0.92
14. Wiggins' *Sd*	0.31	0.35	−0.01	−0.09	0.39	0.78	0.05	0.04	−0.05	0.06	0.90
15. Couch-Keniston	0.14	0.27	−0.13	0.94	−0.01	−0.03	0.00	0.00	0.00	0.06	0.95
16. Couch-Keniston	−0.16	0.39	−0.10	0.45	0.07	0.41	−0.06	−0.11	0.13	−0.63	0.96
17. Total ?	−0.12	0.04	−0.08	−0.04	−0.23	0.13	0.07	0.95	0.01	0.00	0.98
18. P(T/?)	0.18	0.09	−0.98	0.01	−0.01	0.01	0.00	0.00	0.00	0.00	0.98
19. Consistency	0.57	−0.02	−0.13	−0.12	−0.04	−0.37	0.20	−0.08	−0.64	−0.19	0.88

[a]From Edwards (1963).

Scores on the 19 scales were intercorrelated and factor-analyzed by the method of principal components. Ten factors were extracted which accounted for 88 percent of the total variance. The normalized and Varimax rotated factor loadings of the scales are given in Table 8.4. The communalities of the scales are given in the column headed h^2. The denormalized loading of each scale on Factor I can be obtained by multiplying the normalized loading in each row by the corresponding value of $\sqrt{h^2}$. Again, we find that the various SD and SUD scales have relatively high loadings on the first principal component and, as shown in Table 8.3, that all of these scales have relatively high Kuder-Richardson Formula 21 lower-bound estimates of r_{kk}. As would be expected, the SUD scales have loadings with signs opposite to those of the SD scales. This simply means that factor scores on Factor I would correlate positively with the SD scales and negatively with the SUD scales. If the signs of the factor loadings were reflected, then the SD scales would correlate negatively with the reflected factor scores and the SUD scales positively.

8.8   Individual and Mean Rates of SD Responding

The evidence presented above indicates that a variety of different scales in which all of the items are keyed for either SD or SUD responses will tend to be intercorrelated and to have loadings on a common factor. Scores on SD scales, if divided by the number of items in the scales, can be interpreted as measuring individual differences in rates of SD responding. If individual rates of SD responding are averaged, the resulting value is the mean rate of SD responding. As was pointed out previously, because the relationship between $P(SD)$ and SDSV is V-shaped, it should not be surprising that the mean rate of SD responding can be made to vary by the appropriate selection of sets of items with differing distributions of SDSVs. For a bimodal distribution of SDSVs with many items at both extremes of the social desirability continuum and relatively few in the neutral section, the mean rate of SD responding would be higher than the mean rate based on a set of items with a normal distribution of SDSVs. A set of items with a normal distribution of SDSVs would have many items in the neutral section and relatively few items at the two extremes of the social desirability continuum.

Neutral items have relatively low probabilities of eliciting SD responses compared with items with more extreme SDSVs. Thus, one might say that the mean rate of SD responding to items with a normal distribution is low compared with the mean rate of SD responding to a set of items with a bimodal distribution of SDSVs. Because SD responses to neutral items tend not to be highly correlated with SD responses to items outside the neutral range, an *SD* scale in which many of the items are relatively neutral with respect to SDSV could also be expected to have a relatively low internal consistency coefficient as measured by r_{kk}.

8.9   Point Biserial Coefficient as a Measure of SD Responding

There are other methods by which one might attempt to measure individual differences in SD responding. One of these methods would involve calculating a point biserial coefficient between the True and False responses of a given individual to a set of items and the SDSVs of the items. We can let X be a variable corresponding to the response to an item and if the response is True, then $X = 1$, and if the response is False, then $X = 0$. The Y variable would be the SDSVs of the items. If an individual tends primarily to respond True to those items with high SDSVs and False to those items with low SDSVs, the point biserial coefficient between his True and False responses and the SDSVs of the items should be positive. If an individual shows no consistent tendency to respond True to items with high SDSVs and False to items with low SDSVs, then the point biserial coefficient should be low. Both the point biserial coefficient and rate of SD responding, as measured by an *SD* scale, should presumably reflect individual differences in the tendency to give SD responses. These two measures should, therefore, be positively correlated.

In one study (Edwards, 1965a), rates of SD responding were obtained for each individual for the serial sample of 176 items discussed previously. Using the normative SDSVs of these items, a point biserial coefficient was calculated for each of 103 females and 105 males. The point biserial coefficients for each individual were then correlated with their rates of SD responding. For females the correlation between these two measures was 0.98 and for males, 0.96. Similar results have been obtained by Block (1965) using items from the MMPI.[2]

The same individuals in the above study had, on another occasion, rated each of the 176 items for social desirability on a 9-point scale. Thus, instead of using the normative SDSVs of the items, it is possible to calculate for each individual the point biserial coefficient between his True and False responses to the items and his own individual ratings of the social desirability of the items. When these point biserial coefficients were calculated and then correlated with rates of SD responding, the correlation for the females was 0.91 and for males the correlation was 0.80. Interestingly enough, when the

---

[2]For five samples consisting of 100 males, 95 males, 45 males, 110 females, and 49 males, Block (1965, p. 79) reports correlations between the point biserial coefficients and scores on the *SD* scale of 0.82, 0.75, 0.78, 0.90, and 0.90, respectively.

point biserial coefficients are based on the individual ratings of social desirability, they correlate lower with rates of SD responding than do the point biserial coefficients based on the same constant set of SDSVs.

The correlations between the point biserial coefficients using the SDSVs and the point biserial coefficients using the individual ratings were 0.92 for females and 0.86 for males.

It is obvious that individual differences in the tendency to give SD responses as measured by the point biserial coefficient and by rates of SD responding on *SD* scales are sufficiently high that either measure could be substituted for the other. An individual's rate of SD responding, however, is relatively simple to obtain in contrast to the more elaborate calculations required in obtaining the point biserial coefficient. Other things being equal, then, the preferred measure is the simpler measure, namely, rate of SD responding as measured by *SD* scales.

8.10   Range and Average Value of the Point Biserial Coefficient

As was pointed out earlier, rates of SD responding can be altered by selecting items with differing distributions of SDSVs. With respect to point biserial coefficients as measures of individual differences in SD responding, precisely the same considerations apply as in the case of rates of SD responding. The range of the point biserial coefficient is not from −1.00 to 1.00, because the coefficient is based on the correlation of a dichotomous variable and a continuous or multivalued variable. As has been emphasized before, a correlation coefficient can attain its maximum positive value of 1.00 only when the distributions of both variables have the same shape or form. With one variable continuous and the other dichotomous, this is obviously an impossible condition.

In a study by Boe and Kogan (1963) a set of 100 items from the MMPI was selected with an approximately normal distribution of SDSVs. For this particular distribution it can be shown that if an individual gave the SD response to every one of the 100 items, the point biserial coefficient would only be approximately 0.81. This is the highest possible positive point biserial coefficient for this particular distribution of SDSVs. In the set of 100 items, 54 had SDSVs in the neutral interval on the social desirability continuum. If one assumes that within this interval the probability of an SD response is the same as the probability of an SUD response and if it also assumed that all of the remaining 46 responses are SD responses, then the maximum positive value of the point biserial coefficient is approximately 0.62. The highest individual point biserial coefficient reported by Boe and Kogan was 0.61 and the mean value was 0.27.

In the study described earlier (Edwards, 1965a) the highest point biserial coefficient was 0.84 for both males and females. The mean point biserial coefficient for males was 0.50 and that for females was 0.52. That these values differ from the corresponding values reported by Boe and Kogan can undoubtedly be attributed to the fact that they are based on a bimodal distribution of SDSVs rather than a normal distribution of SDSVs. For example, when the complete set of MMPI items is used to determine the point biserial coefficients, the average value is 0.57, as reported by Block (1965). The distribution of SDSVs for the complete set of MMPI items is bimodal, not normal.

When $P(T)$ is based on the proportion or percentage of a group of individuals answering an item True, the correlation between $P(T)$ and SDSV is typically about 0.90. In a sense, the point biserial coefficient may be regarded as the correlation between $P(T)$ and SDSV for the individual case, the difference being that $P(T)$ for the individual case can take only a value of 1 or 0. The average point biserial coefficient will generally be considerably lower than 0.90. That the average point biserial coefficient, in at least two studies (Taylor, 1959; Boe and Kogan, 1963), was found to be approximately 0.30 has been misinterpreted as indicating that for the individual case, the tendency to give SD responses is relatively unimportant. We have already pointed out that the maximum positive value of the point biserial coefficient is limited by the shape of the distribution of SDSVs. Even with a bimodal distribution, the maximum possible positive value will seldom be greater than 0.85. Positive values of the point biserial coefficient cannot, therefore, be interpreted as having a potential range from 0.00 to 1.00.

Furthermore, it would not matter even if the *average* point biserial coefficient were equal to zero, provided that there are individual differences in the values of the point biserial coefficients and that these individual differences are, in turn, highly and positively correlated with rates of SD responding. One would not conclude, for example, that simply because the average IQ is 100, intelligence is a relatively unimportant trait in answering items correctly on an intelligence test. Similarly, even if the average point biserial coefficient were equal to zero, this would not indicate that individual differences in rates of SD responding are unimportant in answering items on personality scales.

The average point biserial coefficient corresponds to the average rate of SD responding as measured by *SD* scales. As long as there are reliable individual differences in rates of SD responding and in point biserial coefficients, and as long as these two measures are highly correlated, it makes no difference whether the average point biserial is regarded as "high" or "low." It is the individual differences in a trait that are of importance, not the mean value on a measure of the trait.

8.11   Rates of SD Responding and Correlations
between IRSD and the SDSVs of Personality Statements

In the previous chapter we showed that when individual ratings of social desirability (IRSDs) were correlated with the normative or SDSVs of personality statements, the average correlation for females was 0.82 and the average correlation for males was 0.79. Despite these high average values, there are still individual differences in the magnitudes of the correlation coefficients. It might be argued therefore that individuals with high rates of SD responding are simply those whose ratings of social desirability are in close agreement with the normative values. This is not, however, the case.

For each individual the correlation coefficient between his ratings of social desirability and the SDSVs of personality statements may be regarded as a score. For females the correlations between these scores and rates of SD responding as measured by an *SD* scale consisting of 176 items, the 39-item MMPI *SD* scale, and point biserial coefficients, were 0.21, 0.11, and 0.21, respectively. The corresponding correlation coefficients for males were 0.12, 0.06, and 0.09, respectively.

The evidence seems quite clear, therefore, that one cannot account for individual differences in rates of SD responding simply in terms of the degree to which individuals rate items for social desirability in accord with the normative ratings of SDSVs of the items.

8.12   Mean Rates of SD and SUD Responding

Because $P(SD)$ is a V-shaped function of SDSV, for almost any item that falls outside the neutral interval on the social desirability continuum it will be found that $P(SD)$ is almost always greater than $P(SUD)$; that is, $P(SD)$ will usually be greater than 0.50. There are some exceptions to this general principle. For example, there are some items with relatively high SDSVs for which $P(SD)$ is less than 0.50. It is much more difficult, however, to find items with relatively low SDSVs for which $P(SD)$ is less than 0.50. It is also the case that for those items with SDSVs close to the neutral point of 5 on the 9-point rating scale, items can be found for which $P(SD)$ may be less than 0.50.

Because $P(SD)$ is almost always greater than 0.50, it follows that for any *SD* scale composed of items with SDSVs outside the neutral interval, the mean rate of SD responding will tend to be greater than 0.50. *SD* scales that have different mean rates of SD responding can, of course, be constructed. For the 39-item MMPI *SD* scale the mean score for different groups of college students tends to range from about 29.0 to 32.0. The mean rate of SD responding on this scale, therefore, tends to range from about 0.74 to 0.83. The serial sample of 176 statements, discussed earlier, is more representative of a large population of personality statements, including those with SDSVs in the neutral interval. The mean rate of SD responding to the items in this sample has been found to range from about 0.73 to 0.76 for both males and females.

Chapter 9

SD Responding
and the MMPI

9.1 Introduction

In the previous chapter we described the nature of *SD* and *SUD* scales.
We also found that various *SD* and *SUD* scales constructed without regard
to the content of the items in the scales were highly intercorrelated and
that they all had loadings on a common factor with the 39-item MMPI
SD scale. Because the items in these various *SD* and *SUD* scales were
selected from a large set of 2824 items solely on the basis of their SDSVs, we
have some basis for believing that the tendency to give SD responses in
self-description is not limited or confined to a single *SD* scale or to obviously
homogeneous sets of items. In other words, we may entertain the hypothesis
that individual differences in rates of SD responding represent a general and
reliable personality trait and that this trait is operative whenever an individual is asked to describe himself in terms of any given set of personality
statements. In this chapter we examine some of the implications of this
hypothesis.

9.2 Confounding of Trait and SD Responses

The trait or keyed response to the items in a personality scale is the
response that is supposed to be indicative of the trait the scale was designed
to measure. In an anxiety scale, for example, each of the items would be

keyed for the response that indicates the presence of the trait. Suppose that the items in the anxiety scale are rated for social desirability and the SDSV of each of the items is obtained. In examining the trait responses to the items, it is then discovered that each trait response is also an SUD response. In this instance, we can say that the trait and the SUD responses to the items are completely confounded. Scores on the scale may be measuring individual differences in anxiety or they may simply reflect individual differences in the more general trait that we have called "the tendency to give SD responses in self-description."

If the anxiety scale is a rational scale, then presumably the content of each of the items is considered to be relevant to anxiety or from the domain of all anxiety items. If anxiety is a specific trait and unrelated to the tendency to give SD responses in self-description, then we might expect scores on the anxiety scale to be relatively independent of rates of SD respondng. On the other hand, if scores on the anxiety scale reflect individual differences in rates of SD responding, then individuals with high rates of SD responding should obtain low scores on the anxiety scale and individuals with low rates of SD responding should obtain high scores. In this instance, scores on the anxiety scale should be negatively correlated with scores on various *SD* scales.

Consider another scale, designed to measure the trait of dominance. The items in this scale are also rated for social desirability and the SDSV of each of the items is obtained. Upon further examination of the trait keying of the items in the dominance scale, it is found that each of the trait responses is also an SD response. In this instance, the trait responses to the items and the SD responses to the items are completely confounded. High scores on the scale may be measuring individual differences in dominance or they may reflect individual differences in rates of SD responding. If individual differences in rates of SD responding are operative, then individuals with high rates should obtain high scores on the dominance scale and individuals with low rates should obtain low scores. We would thus expect scores on the dominance scale to be positively correlated with scores on various *SD* scales. Furthermore, because the dominance items are all keyed for SD responses, and because the anxiety items are all keyed for SUD responses, we would expect scores on the dominance and anxiety scales to be negatively correlated.

Consider still a third scale, one designed to measure repression. The items in this scale are also rated for social desirability and the SDSVs of the items obtained. When the trait-keying of the items is examined, it is found that for half of the items the trait response is also an SD response and for the other half of the items the trait response is also an SUD response. If individual differences in rates of SD responding are operating, then individuals with high rates should obtain high scores on the items keyed for SD responses and individuals with low rates should obtain low scores. On the items keyed for SUD responses, just the reverse should happen. Thus scores on half the items might be expected to correlate positively with rates of SD responding and scores on the other half negatively. In this case, the total scores on the scale might be expected to have a relatively low correlation with rates of SD responding.

In general, then, we might expect scores on various personality scales to be correlated with rates of SD responding, to the degree that there is an imbalance in the number of SD and SUD trait-keyed responses. Scales in which all or a large proportion of the trait-keyed responses are SD responses might be expected to correlate positively with rates of SD responding. Scales in which a small proportion of trait responses are SD responses (and which, therefore, have a large proportion of trait-keyed SUD responses) might be expected to have negative correlations with rates of SD responding. As the number of trait-keyed SD and trait-keyed SUD responses approaches a balance, the correlation of scores on the scale with rates of SD responding might be expected to decrease and approach zero.

9.3   The *A* and *R* Factor Scales of the MMPI

Two scales, *A* and *R*, were developed by Welsh (1956) as marker variables for the first and second factors obtained when MMPI scales are inter-correlated and factor-analyzed. The *A* scale in every factor analysis of MMPI scales in which it has been included has a high loading on the first principal component. The *R* scale tends to have a relatively low loading on the first principal component and a high loading on the second principal component. The *A* scale consists of 39 items, all but one of which are keyed True. The *R* scale consists of 40 items, all of which are keyed False.

Figure 9.1 shows the relationship between *P*(T) and SDSV for the 39 items in the *A* scale. Note that most of the items have socially undesirable scale values. Because all but one of the items in the *A* scale are keyed True, almost all of the items are also keyed for SUD responses. The correlation between scores on the *A* scale and the *SD* scale should, therefore, be negative, and it is. For various samples of individuals, the *A* scale typically correlates from −0.81 to −0.91 with the *SD* scale.

Figure 9.2 shows the relationship between *P*(T) and SDSV for the 40 items in the *R* or second-factor scale. Note that the SDSVs of these items are fairly well distributed over the social desirability continuum and that a considerable number of items are close to the neutral point. Because all of the items in the *R* scale are keyed False, there is a degree of balance in the SD-SUD keying of the items in the scale. This scale would therefore be predicted to have a relatively low correlation with the *SD* scale, and it

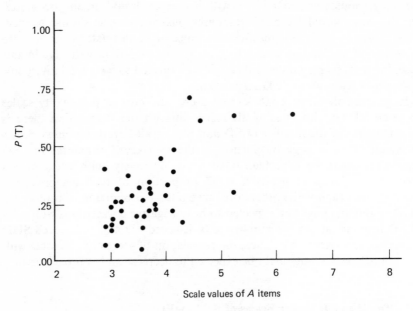

Figure 9.1 The relationship between *P*(T) and SDSV for the 39 items in the *A* scale of the MMPI. From Edwards (1964b).

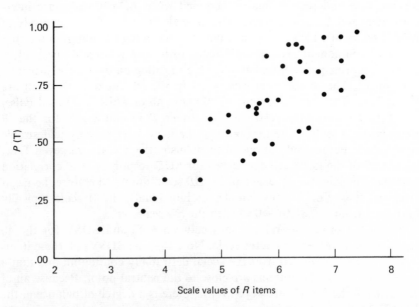

Figure 9.2 The relationship between *P*(T) and SDSV for the items in the *R* scale of the MMPI. From Edwards (1964b).

does. The typical correlation between scores on the R and the SD scale ranges from about 0.15 to 0.25 in various samples.

Note also that the correlation between $P(T)$ and SDSV would be considerably higher for the R items than for the A items. This is because there is a restriction in range of the SDSVs of the items in the A scale, with most of the items falling to the left of the neutral point on the social desirability continuum. At the same time, scores on the A scale are highly correlated with scores on the SD scale, whereas scores on the R scale have only a negligible correlation with scores on the SD scale.

It is important to distinguish between the degree to which $P(T)$ is related to SDSV and the degree to which scores on a scale will be correlated with individual differences in the tendency to give SD responses in self-description, as measured by an SD scale. The distinction is important because it has sometimes been erroneously assumed that if there is a high correlation between $P(T)$ and SDSV for the items in a scale, then scores on the scale must also be highly correlated with scores on a measure of the tendency to give SD responses. Figure 9.2 shows that this is not necessarily the case. The correlation of a scale with the SD scale depends primarily on the degree to which the items in a scale are consistently keyed for either SD or SUD responses and on the intensity of the SD-SUD keying of the items, and not on the magnitude of the correlation between $P(T)$ and SDSV.

9.4   MMPI Trait Scales

The prediction that correlations between trait scores on various personality scales and rates of SD responding should be related to the proportion of items in the scales keyed for SD responses does not take into account other factors or conditions that may influence the correlations. Some of these conditions will be discussed later. What is important is that the prediction is one that can easily be submitted to empirical test, provided we have available a large number of trait scales for which the SDSVs of the items are known and a scale that can be used as a measure of individual differences in rates of SD responding. One readily available source for a large number of trait scales is the MMPI. Although the MMPI when first published provided scoring keys for a limited number of scales, the inventory has been widely used by hundreds of investigators to develop various other scales. Some of the scales that can be scored in the MMPI are rational scales and others are empirical scales. Dahlstrom and Welsh (1960) provide scoring keys for approximately 200 MMPI scales and there are still other MMPI scales for which the scoring keys are available in various psychological journals.

In addition, the SDSVs of the MMPI items on a 5-point rating scale have been obtained by Heineman (1960) and on a 9-point rating scale by Messick and Jackson (1961a). Because the SDSVs of the MMPI items are known, it is possible to find the proportion of SD keyed-trait responses for any of the various MMPI scales. Furthermore, scores on the 39-item *SD* scale consisting of MMPI items can be used to obtain estimates of individual differences in rates of SD responding.

The discussion above does not imply that the MMPI is the ideal instrument for testing the prediction that the correlations of scales with rates of SD responding should be related to the proportion of items in the scales keyed for SD responses. The reason for this is that the 39-item *SD* scale, designed to measure individual differences in rates of SD responding, also consists of MMPI items. Consequently, some of the items in the *SD* scale must inevitably overlap with items in various other MMPI scales. If an MMPI trait scale and the *SD* scale contain items in common and if in both scales the items are keyed for SD responses, these common items will contribute to a positive correlation between scores on the two scales. If the common items are keyed for SUD responses in the trait scale, these items will contribute to a negative correlation between scores on the scale and scores on the *SD* scale. The problem of item overlap between the *SD* scale and various other MMPI scales will be considered later.

9.5   Correlations of MMPI Scales with the *SD* Scale in Relation to the Proportion of Items Keyed for SD Responses

A total of 43 MMPI trait scales was used as an early test of the prediction that the correlations between various MMPI trait scales and rates of SD responding would be related to the proportion of items in the trait scales keyed for SD responses (Edwards, 1961). For each of the 43 trait scales the correlation with the *SD* scale was obtained. These correlations were then plotted against the proportion of items in the scales keyed for SD responses. The resulting plot was linear and the correlation coefficient between the proportion of items keyed for SD responses and the correlations of the scales with the *SD* scale was 0.92.

The study described above was subsequently replicated by Edwards, Diers, and Walker (1962) with a new sample of individuals and 57 MMPI trait scales. The correlation between the proportion of items in the trait scales keyed for SD responses and the correlations of the trait scales with the *SD* scale was 0.90. The evidence seems quite clear that, at least for MMPI scales, the correlations of these scales with rates of SD responding is directly related to the proportion of items in the scales keyed for SD responses.

9.6   First Factor Loadings of MMPI Scales
   and the Proportion of Items Keyed for SD Responses

We have previously shown that, when *SD* and/or *SUD* scales with no overlapping items are included in a principal-component factor analysis along with various other scales, the *SD* and/or *SUD* scales have their highest loadings on a common factor. This finding may be attributed to the fact that they were all designed to measure the same common trait, namely, individual differences in rates of SD responding.

When MMPI scales were originally developed, it seems reasonable to believe that they were not constructed to measure individual differences in rates of SD responding but rather other personality traits of interest. Thus, if MMPI scales are included in a factor analysis along with *one SD* scale, and the *SD* scale along with other MMPI scales are found to have high loadings on a common factor, this result cannot be accounted for by the intentional inclusion in the factor analysis of a large number of scales specifically designed to measure individual differences in rates of SD responding. We can only conclude that if MMPI trait scales are found to have high loadings on a factor in common with the *SD* scale, then these MMPI scales are, along with the *SD* scale, measuring the same common trait.

A principal-component factor analysis of 58 MMPI scales, including the *SD* scale, and three other scales, was done by Edwards, Diers, and Walker (1962). Ten factors were extracted which accounted for 75 percent of the total variance. The ten factors were rotated orthogonally by means of a Varimax rotation. We are concerned primarily with the first rotated factor on which the *SD* scale has its highest loading. The first rotated principal-component factor accounted for 38 percent of the total variance and 43 percent of the common variance.

The *SD* scale had a loading of 0.97 on the first rotated factor. A considerable number of the MMPI scales also had high (negative or positive) loadings on this same factor. Table 9.1 shows the frequency distribution of the *absolute* values of the first factor loadings of the 58 MMPI scales.

If the factor loadings of the MMPI scales are plotted against the proportion of items in the scales keyed for SD responses, the resulting plot is linear. The correlation between the proportion of items keyed for SD responses and the factor loadings of the scales is 0.90. Thus the factor loadings can be predicted quite accurately from knowledge of the proportion of items in the scales keyed for SD responses. If a scale has a large proportion of items keyed for SD responses it also has a high loading, with the same sign as the loading of the *SD* scale. If it has a large proportion

Table 9.1 Frequency Distribution of
the Absolute Values of the
First Principal-Component
Factor Loadings of 58
MMPI Scales[a]

Absolute Values	Frequency
0.90–0.99	10
0.80–0.89	9
0.70–0.79	6
0.60–0.69	7
0.50–0.59	6
0.40–0.49	6
0.30–0.39	7
0.20–0.29	2
0.10–0.19	3
0.00–0.09	2

[a]From Edwards, Diers, and Walker (1962).

of items keyed for SUD responses and, consequently, a small proportion keyed for SD responses, the scale has a high loading with the opposite sign of the loading of the *SD* scale.

In other words, the more nearly the MMPI scale resembles an *SD* or an *SUD* scale, the higher is its loading on a factor in common with the *SD* scale. It does not seem unreasonable, therefore, to interpret the factor as measuring individual differences in rates of SD responding. Of course, other interpretations of the factor are possible. One might choose to interpret the factor as "leadership" because the *Lp* or Leadership scale of the MMPI also has a high loading of 0.93 on the factor. Anxiety with a loading of −0.93 might also be chosen, or Schizophrenia with a loading of −0.89, or any one of the various other scales with high loadings might be selected for interpreting the factor. It is difficult to believe, however, that the constructs of Anxiety and Schizophrenia are much the same and that both simply represent the opposite of Leadership.

The interpretation of the factor as measuring individual differences in rates of SD responding provides an objective basis for predicting the loadings of the scales on the factor in terms of the proportion of items in the scales keyed for SD responses. An SD response is operationally defined and the proportion of items keyed for SD responses in a scale can be objectively determined. It is doubtful whether any other interpretation of the factor lends itself to the prediction of the loadings of the scales on the factor.

9.7 Average Interitem Correlation of a Scale and the SD-SUD Keying of the Scale

If all of the items in a scale are keyed for responses in such a way that the keyed responses are believed to measure a common personality trait, then the average interitem correlation of the keyed responses should be positive. Consider a scale in which all of the items are keyed not only for trait but also for SD responses. In a scale of this kind, the tendency to give the trait response is completely confounded with the tendency to give the SD response, and we should expect to find not only that the average interitem correlation is positive but also that scores on the scale are positively correlated with scores on an *SD* scale.

If the trait-keying of the items in a scale is the same as the SUD keying of the items, then the tendency to give the trait response is confounded with the tendency to give the SUD response, and we should expect to find that the average interitem correlation is positive and that scores on the scale are negatively correlated with scores on an *SD* scale.

Suppose, however, that the trait-keying of some of the items is the same as the SD response, and the trait-keying for the remaining items is the same as the SUD response. If the trait itself is the only important determiner of responses to the items, then the average interitem correlation should still be positive. To the degree to which the tendency to give SD responses is operating, we should expect to find that the average interitem correlation for those items keyed for both trait *and* SD responses is positive. Similarly, we should expect to find that the average interitem correlation of those items keyed for both trait *and* SUD responses is positive. However, the correlations between those items in the set keyed for trait *and* SD responses and those items in the set keyed for trait *and* SUD responses should be decreased.

To be specific, consider two items such that for one item the trait response is an SD response and for the other item the trait response is an SUD response. If the trait is the only determiner of responses to these two items, then those individuals who give the trait response to one item should also tend to give the trait response to the other item, and the correlation between the trait responses to the two items should be positive. If SD tendencies are operating, however, then individuals with high rates of SD responding might be expected to give the SD and trait response to the first item and the SD and nontrait response to the second item. The SD tendency should, in other words, lower the correlation between the trait responses to the two items. The number of item correlations of the kind described is at a maximum when a scale contains an equal number of SD keyed-trait responses and SUD keyed-trait responses.

9.8   K-R 21 Values of Scales and the SD-SUD Keying of the Scales

As an index of the imbalance between the SD and SUD keying of the trait responses in a scale, Edwards, Walsh, and Diers (1963) defined

$$I\text{-SD} = |P(\text{SD}) - 0.50| \tag{9.1}$$

where $P(\text{SD})$ is the proportion of items keyed for SD responses in the scale. Thus, when I-SD is equal to 0.50, it means either that all of the items in a scale are keyed for SD responses or that all of the items are keyed for SUD responses. When I-SD is equal to 0.00, then it means that the scale contains an equal number of items keyed for SD and for SUD responses.

As a measure of the degree of internal consistency of a scale, Edwards, Walsh, and Diers used the Kuder-Richardson Formula 21 lower-bound estimate of r_{kk}. Other things being equal, the K-R 21 value of a scale provides an index of the degree to which the items in a scale tend to be positively intercorrelated and therefore a measure of the degree to which the items in the scale are being responded to in terms of a common trait. If responses to the items in personality scales are influenced not only by the traits which the scales were designed to measure but also by the tendency to give SD responses, then we should expect to find that the K-R 21 values of the scales are related to the nature of the SD-SUD keying of the items in the scales. Trait scales in which all of the items are consistently keyed for either SD or SUD responses should have higher K-R 21 values than scales which are more balanced in their SD-SUD keying.

Scores were obtained for 151 male students on 58 MMPI scales. For each scale the imbalance in the SD-SUD keying, as defined by (9.1), was obtained. The K-R 21 values of each of the scales were also calculated. The correlation between I-SD and the K-R 21 values of the 58 scales was 0.62. Thus we have evidence to demonstrate that when an MMPI trait scale contains either a large proportion of items keyed for SD responses or a large proportion of items keyed for SUD responses, so that I-SD is large, then it also tends to have a relatively high index of internal consistency as measured by K-R 21. Scales in which there is a balance in the SD-SUD keying, so that I-SD is low, tend also to have low K-R 21 values. This result is consistent with the hypothesis that the internal consistency of scales should be related to the imbalance in the SD-SUD keying of the items in the scales.

9.9   K-R 21 Values and Correlations of MMPI Scales with the *SD* Scale

It also follows that those MMPI scales with high positive or negative correlations with individual differences in rates of SD responding, as measured by the *SD* scale, should also tend to have higher K-R 21 values than those scales with low positive or negative correlations with the *SD* scale, because the correlations of MMPI scales with the *SD* scale are also related to the imbalance in the SD-SUD keying of the scales. Taking the absolute values of the correlations of the 57 MMPI scales with the *SD* scale, the K-R 21 values correlated 0.65 with these correlations.

That the results cited above apply, in general, to all MMPI scales is shown in Table 9.2, which gives the frequency distribution of the absolute

Table 9.2   Frequency Distribution of the Absolute Values of the Correlations of 200 MMPI Scales with the *SD* Scale and Mean K-R 21 Values of the Scales[a]

$|r|$	Frequency	Mean K-R 21
0.90–0.99	12	0.92
0.80–0.89	41	0.84
0.70–0.79	50	0.74
0.60–0.69	27	0.70
0.50–0.59	17	0.55
0.40–0.49	15	0.49
0.30–0.39	10	0.43
0.20–0.29	7	0.21
0.10–0.19	18	0.31
0.00–0.09	3	0.38

[a]The correlations and K-R 21 values of the scales were calculated by Edward F. Gocka, and I am indebted to him for making the values available to me.

values of the correlations of 200 MMPI scales with the *SD* scale. It may be noted that over half of these 200 MMPI scales have absolute correlations of 0.70 or greater with the *SD* scale. The average K-R 21 value is shown in the column at the right of the table for those scales with absolute correlations with the *SD* scale falling within the class interval on the left. For example, the 12 MMPI scales that have absolute correlations of 0.90 or greater with the *SD* scale also have a very high average K-R 21 value of 0.92. As the absolute correlations of the scales with the *SD* scale decrease, so also does the average K-R 21 value of the scales. In other words, scales that have relatively low positive or negative correlations with the *SD* scale tend, in turn, to have a relatively low K-R 21 value. As we have pointed out earlier, when a scale has a relatively low K-R 20 or K-R 21 value, the indication is that not all of the items in a scale are measuring the same common trait.

Thus, in general, if an MMPI scale has a high K-R 21 value, so that it can be described as one in which all of the items are measuring the same common trait, then scores on this scale will also tend to be highly correlated with individual differences in rates of SD responding. And because the correlations of MMPI scales with the SD scale are linearly related to the proportion of items keyed for SD responses in the scale, MMPI scales with high K-R 21 values will also tend to be those in which the items are consistently keyed for either SD or SUD responses.

9.10   K-R 21 Values and First Factor Loadings of MMPI Scales

We have previously shown that scales that have an extreme imbalance in their SD-SUD keying tend to have high positive or negative loadings on a common factor with the SD scale. Thus scales with such high positive or negative loadings should also tend to have higher K-R 21 values than those scales with low positive or negative loadings on the factor. In other words, the K-R 21 values of scales should be positively correlated with the absolute values of their factor loadings on the factor on which the SD scale has its highest loading. In one study, Edwards (1966b) reports that the unrotated absolute loadings of 57 MMPI scales on the first principal-component factor (the factor on which the SD scale had its highest loading) correlated 0.66 with the K-R 21 values of the scales.

9.11   K-R 21 Values and the Proportion of Neutral Items in a Scale

It has been pointed out that the probability of an SD response decreases as the SDSVs of items become more neutral. If responses to the items in a scale are primarily determined by the trait which the scale is supposedly measuring, then the presence of a large number of neutral items in the scale should have little or no influence on the interitem correlations. If anything, because the tendency to give SD responses is minimal for neutral items, we might expect trait responses to be more dominant to these items. In other words, if all of the items in a scale have neutral SDSVs, then we might expect all responses to the items to be trait determined and uninfluenced by SD tendencies. If this is the case, then the proportion of neutral items in a scale should be correlated positively with the K-R 21 value of the scale.

On the other hand, if SD tendencies contribute to the internal consistency of a scale and if these tendencies are minimized, as we might expect them to be with respect to neutral items, then scales that contain a large proportion of neutral items should have lower K-R 21 values than scales that contain a small proportion of neutral items. In this case, the proportion of neutral items in a scale should be correlated negatively with the K-R 21 value of the scale.

To test the above hypotheses, Edwards, Walsh, and Diers (1963) found for each of 58 MMPI scales the proportion of items with scale values between 2.5 and 3.5 on a 5-point social desirability continuum. These proportions correlated −0.46 with the K-R 21 values of the scales. Thus there is some tendency for those scales with a relatively large proportion of neutral items to have lower K-R 21 values than scales with a small proportion of neutral items.

9.12   Intensity of the SD-SUD Keying of Scales

In determining the number of items keyed for SD responses in a scale, it has been the practice to regard all items with SDSVs above the neutral point which are keyed True, and all items with SDSVs below the neutral point which are keyed False, as being keyed for SD responses. This index, however, does not differentiate between two scales that have the same proportion of items keyed for SD responses. Even though the two scales may have the same proportion of items keyed for SD responses, the intensity of the SD keying may be different for the two scales. For example, the items in one scale may all have SDSVs close to the extremes of the social desirability continuum, whereas the items in the other scale may all have SDSVs close to the neutral point. It is to be expected that, in general, a scale that contains items with more extreme SDSVs which are keyed consistently for either SD or SUD responses would tend to be more highly correlated with individual differences in rates of SD responding than a scale that contains items with less extreme SDSVs.

To test the above hypothesis, the MMPI was administered to 150 male college students (Edwards and Walsh, 1963a). Three additional scales were also administered to the same students: The Couch and Keniston (1960) Agreement Response Set (*ARS*), the Crowne and Marlowe (1960) *MC* scale, and a Forced Choice *SD* scale (*FC–SD*) described by Edwards, Diers, and Walker (1962). On the basis of SDSVs for MMPI items as given by Messick and Jackson (1961a), 20 MMPI scales were selected which met the criterion of having five or more items keyed for SD responses and also five or more items keyed for SUD responses. Two scores were obtained for each individual on these 20 scales, one score being based on those items in each scale keyed for SD responses and the other being based on those items keyed for SUD responses. The sum of these two-part scores results in the usual total score for each of the 20 scales.

Five additional MMPI scales were scored for each individual. These scales were *Ca, Hs, Sc, A,* and the 39-item *SD* scale. *Hs* is consistently keyed for SUD responses and *SD* is consistently keyed for SD responses. *Ca* has one item, *Sc* has two items, and *A* has two items keyed for SD responses, but all of the remaining items in these scales are keyed for SUD responses.

Thus 48 scores were obtained for each individual, all of which, but for the slight exceptions noted above and the *ARS* and *MC* scales, are consistently keyed for either SD or SUD responses. Scores on these scales were inter-correlated and factor-analyzed by the method of principal components. The first principal component accounted for 34 percent of the total variance.

To determine the intensity of the SD and SUD keying of each scale, the SDSVs of False keyed items were reflected. For example, in the *SD* scales, if an item is keyed False it must have an SDSV less than 5. If the SDSV of the item was 2.8, then after reflection the SDSV would be regarded as 7.2. In the *SUD* scales, if an item is keyed False it must have an SDSV greater than 5. If the SDSV of the item was 6.0, then after reflection the SDSV would be regarded as 4.0. The sum of the reflected and unreflected SDSVs was then obtained for each scale and divided by the number of items in the scale to obtain an index of the intensity of the SD or SUD keying of the scale. All *SUD* scales must of necessity have an intensity index less than 5 and all *SD* scales must of necessity have an intensity index greater than 5. The average intensity index for all of the scales was 4.89.

The intensity index for each scale was then correlated with the factor loading of the scale on the first unrotated principal component. The resulting correlation coefficient was 0.88. With but a few exceptions, the *SD* scales had positive loadings on the first factor and the *SUD* scales had negative loadings. It was also found that the intensity index of the scales correlated 0.86 with the correlations of the scales with the 39-item *SD* scale, which has been used in other studies to obtain estimates of individual differences in rates of SD responding.

It is to be emphasized that the part scores on each of the 20 MMPI scales, when added together, result in the usual total score on the scale. The items in each MMPI scale were merely separated into two sets: those items in the scale keyed for trait *and* SD responses, and those items in the scale keyed for trait *and* SUD responses. With but few exceptions for each of the MMPI scales, the SD part of the scale had a positive loading on the first factor and the SUD part of the scale had a negative loading. If scores on the various part scales were correlated with factor scores on the first factor, one part of the scale would have a positive correlation with the factor scores and the other a negative correlation.

If the items in an MMPI scale can be divided into two sets, those keyed for SD and those keyed for SUD responses, and if the number of items in one set is relatively small compared to the number of items in the other set, then the complete scale might still have a relatively large loading on a factor in common with the *SD* scale. For example, if the total number of items in a scale is 50 and if only five of these are keyed for SD responses and the other 45 are keyed for SUD responses, then total scores on the scale would be determined primarily by the 45 items keyed for SUD responses. This scale might, therefore, be expected to have a loading on a common factor with the *SD* scale but with an opposite sign.

This same scale might also be expected to have a relatively high K-R 21 value, because the item correlations between the 45 items keyed for trait *and* SUD responses greatly outnumber the correlations between the set of five items keyed for SD responses and the set of 45 items keyed for SUD responses. Still, it is of interest to examine the average K-R 21 value of total scores on the 20 scales which were divided into two parts. The average K-R 21 value for the 20 scales was 0.49 with a standard deviation of 0.25. The range of the K-R 21 values was from 0.03 to 0.83. On the average, then, these 20 scales have lower K-R 21 values than would be expected if all of the items in each scale were measuring the same common trait.

9.13   Mean Scores on MMPI Scales as Related to Mean Rates of SD Responding

Consider an MMPI trait scale in which all of the trait-keyed responses are also SD responses. If the mean rate of SD responding to the items in the trait scale is approximately the same as that estimated by the 39-item *SD* scale, then the mean score on the trait scale should be approximately equal to

$$\bar{X} = k\bar{P} \tag{9.2}$$

where k is the number of items in the scale and $\bar{P}$ is an estimate of the mean rate of SD responding provided by the 39-item *SD* scale. For example, if the mean score on the *SD* scale for a group of individuals is 31.0, then the mean rate of SD responding for the group will be estimated as

$$\bar{P} = 31/39 = 0.79$$

If a trait scale consists of $k = 60$ items keyed for trait and SD responses and if the same mean rate of SD responding applies to the 60 items in the trait scale, then the expected mean score on the trait scale will be

$$\bar{X} = 60(0.79) = 47.4$$

If all of the keyed responses in a trait scale are also SUD responses, then the mean trait score on the scale would be predicted to be

$$\bar{X} = k(1 - \bar{P}) \tag{9.3}$$

Thus, if the same group of individuals were administered a 60-item trait scale in which all of the trait responses were SUD responses, then on the basis of their estimated mean rate of SD responding, as given by the *SD* scale, the predicted trait mean score would be

$$\bar{X} = 60(1 - 0.79) = 12.6$$

For trait scales that have some degree of balance in their SD-SUD keying, the mean score on the trait scales would be estimated to be

$$\bar{X} = k_1\bar{P} + k_2(1 - \bar{P}) \tag{9.4}$$

where k_1 and k_2 are the number of items keyed for SD and SUD responses, respectively. Thus, for a 60-item trait scale with 40 items keyed for SD responses and 20 keyed for SUD responses, the estimated mean score on the trait scale, for the same group of individuals, would be

$$\bar{X} = 40(0.79) + 20(1 - 0.79) = 35.8$$

In general, mean rate of SD responding, as measured by the *SD* scale, has been found to be a fairly good predictor of mean rate of SD responding on a variety of MMPI trait scales. In two independent studies, predictions concerning mean scores on MMPI trait scales, based on the assumption that the mean rates of SD responding to the items in these scales would be approximately the same as the mean rate of SD responding on the *SD* scale, were found to be, in general, fairly accurate (Edwards, 1962, 1964a).

Table 9.3 shows the predicted and observed means on 57 MMPI trait scales based on the responses of a sample of 150 male college students. The mean score on the *SD* scale for this group of students was 30.81 and consequently the mean rate of SD responding was

$$\bar{P} = 30.81/39 = 0.79$$

This is the value of $\bar{P}$ that was used to obtain the predicted means on the MMPI trait scales for the same group of students.

It is obvious from the values of the differences between the predicted and observed means shown in Table 9.3 that there are cases where the predicted trait mean score over- or underestimates the observed trait mean score. An example is the F scale of the MMPI. All but one of the items in the F scale are keyed for SUD responses. Because $\bar{P} = 0.79$ for this group of individuals, the predicted mean on the F scale is

$$\bar{X} = 1(0.79) + 63(1 - 0.79) = 14.02$$

whereas the observed mean is 5.71.

We can better understand why the F scale mean is overestimated if we look at the relationship between the probability of a trait response and SDSV for the 64 items in the F scale, as shown in Figure 9.3. The SDSVs of

Table 9.3   Actual Means, $\overline{X}_A$, Predicted Means, $\overline{X}_P$, and Differences Between the Two Means[a]

Scale	$\overline{X}_A$	$\overline{X}_P$	D	Scale	$\overline{X}_A$	$\overline{X}_P$	D
Ai	10.89	10.32	0.57	Ma-O	7.09	5.99	1.10
A	13.42	9.35	4.07	Ma-S	11.27	12.37	−1.10
Ac	12.85	13.64	−0.79	Mf	26.86	28.84	−1.98
Ad	5.82	6.72	−0.90	Mp	11.60	22.59	−10.99
MA	17.28	11.08	6.20	Ne	5.52	6.30	−0.78
B	25.73	25.41	0.32	No	5.52	3.78	1.74
Ca	11.93	8.72	3.21	Nu	12.75	9.83	2.92
Cn	27.57	25.00	2.57	Or	13.89	11.05	2.84
D	19.54	20.72	−1.18	Pa	9.55	14.20	−4.65
Dn	15.19	17.64	−2.45	Pa-O	1.87	4.83	−2.96
Do	17.04	16.90	0.14	Pa-S	7.53	9.37	−1.84
D-O	9.77	8.77	1.00	Pd	17.58	15.14	2.44
D-S	10.55	11.16	−0.61	Pd-O	6.82	6.46	0.36
Dy	20.15	17.68	2.45	Pd-S	10.60	8.68	1.92
Eo	11.79	10.05	1.74	Pn	13.37	8.67	4.70
Es	48.68	45.02	3.66	Pr	8.44	8.46	−0.02
F	5.71	14.02	−8.31	Pt	13.30	10.66	2.64
Fm	14.09	16.10	−2.01	Pv	15.70	16.88	−1.18
Ho	18.05	13.40	4.65	R	15.74	14.20	1.54
Hs	5.08	6.93	−1.85	Re	20.34	19.48	0.86
Hy	21.51	24.78	−3.27	Rp	20.58	21.80	−1.22
Hy-O	6.23	6.72	−0.49	Sc	12.87	17.54	−4.67
Hy-S	15.70	18.06	−2.36	Si	26.46	17.60	8.86
Ie	31.21	28.49	2.72	Sp	17.80	19.17	−1.37
Im	8.79	7.31	1.48	St	21.40	22.22	−0.82
K	14.93	19.64	−4.71	To	21.77	21.96	−0.19
L	3.56	7.21	−3.65	Tt	12.67	19.38	−6.71
Lp	32.25	36.02	−3.77	Sd	13.22	27.54	−14.32
Ma	18.40	18.36	0.04				

[a]From Edwards (1964a).

the items in the F scale are based on the values reported by Messick and Jackson (1961a) and the probabilities of a keyed or trait response are based on the values reported by Goldberg and Rorer (1963). As Figure 9.3 shows, the SDSVs of the items in the F scale are, in general, extreme so that they have relatively high probabilities of eliciting SD responses and, consequently, low probabilities of eliciting keyed and SUD responses. The mean rate of SD responding to these items is approximately 0.91 rather than 0.79, as estimated by the SD scale. As a result, the predicted mean trait score of 14.02 overestimates considerably the observed mean of 5.71. But this discrepancy between the predicted mean and the observed mean is not unexpected when one considers the fact that the items in the *F* scale were originally selected in such a way that less than ten percent of the normal subjects in the MMPI standardization group gave the trait response to the items.

The trait means on *Mp* and *Sd* are both underestimated by assuming that the mean rate of SD responding to the items in these scales will also be approximately 0.79. Both *Mp* and *Sd* are dissimulation scales constructed by asking individuals to role play in taking the MMPI.

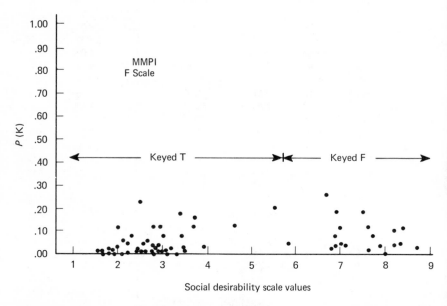

Figure 9.3 The relationship between the probability of a trait or keyed response to each of the items in the *F* scale of the MMPI and the SDSVs of the items. From Edwards (1967b).

For example, the items in the *Sd* scale were selected by finding those items that differentiated between individuals taking the MMPI under standard instructions and those taking it under instructions to give SD responses to the items. When MMPI items have relatively extreme SDSVs, we know that under standard instructions the proportion of individuals giving the SD response to the items will be relatively large. For items of this kind under instructions to give SD responses, the proportion giving the SD response cannot be very much larger than the proportion giving the SD response under standard instructions.

When items have relatively neutral SDSVs, the proportion of SD responses under standard instructions tends to be minimal and these items are, in general, ones for which large differences in the proportion giving the SD response under specific instructions to do so and under standard instructions might be found. As a matter of fact, of the 33 items in the *Mp* scale, 11 have SDSVs falling within the neutral interval on the social desirability continuum and of the 40 items in the *Sd* scale, 16 have SDSVs falling within the neutral interval. Quite a few of the items included in the *Sd* scale are of the kind: "I would like to be a singer; I would like to be a nurse; I would like to be a soldier; I would like to be a private secretary," and so on. Items with content of this kind tend to have relatively neutral SDSVs. It must be emphasized that the mean score on a trait scale will be accurately predicted only insofar as the mean rate of SD responding to the items in the scale is approximately the same as the mean rate of SD responding to the items in the 39-item *SD* scale, and this will not be true for scales that have either a relatively large proportion of items with relatively neutral SDSVs, or for those scales that have a relatively large proportion of items with extreme SDSVs.

If we divide the observed mean score on a trait scale by the number of items in the scale, we obtain an index of the average probability of a trait response to the items in the scale. If SD tendencies are operating, then this index should vary directly with the proportion of items in the scale keyed for SD responses. In another study (Edwards, Walsh, and Diers, 1963), it was found that the correlation of this index with the proportion of items keyed for SD responses was 0.83 in 61 personality scales.

Chapter 10

Acquiescence
and Social Desirability[1]

10.1 Acquiescent Tendencies

Scores on personality scales have been regarded as being susceptible to the influence of *acquiescent* tendencies to the degree to which there is an imbalance in the True-False keying of the items in the scale (Couch and Keniston, 1960; Fricke, 1956; Jackson and Messick, 1958, 1961; Messick and Jackson, 1961b; Wiggins, 1959). For example, if there are reliable individual differences in the tendency to answer personality items True, regardless of the content of the items, then individuals with high rates of True responding could be expected to obtain high scores on scales where all trait responses are True responses, whereas individuals with low rates of True responding could be expected to obtain low scores on these scales. Thus scores on two scales in which all of the items are keyed True might be expected to have some degree of positive correlation simply because of individual differences in acquiescent tendencies. For the same reason, scores on two scales in which all of the items are keyed False might be expected to have some degree of positive correlation, and scores on a scale

[1]The first part of this chapter is substantially the same as a previously published article by Edwards and Diers (1962b).

142

in which all of the items are keyed True and one in which all of the items are keyed False might be expected to have some degree of negative correlation.

10.2   Correlations of First Factor Loadings of MMPI Scales with the Proportion of Items Keyed True in the Scales

MMPI scales vary in the proportion of items keyed for True responses, and it is possible that the correlations between various MMPI scales reflect, in part, individual differences in acquiescent tendencies. Thus, if MMPI scales are intercorrelated and factor-analyzed, a factor may be obtained on which the loadings of the scales are correlated with the proportion of items keyed for True responses in the scales. Evidence regarding this point has been summarized by Messick and Jackson (1961b). They reviewed eight early factor analyses of MMPI scales. For each factor analysis, they calculated rank order correlations between the proportion of items keyed True in each scale and the loadings of the scale on the factor that accounted for the largest proportion of the total variance. The rank order correlations ranged in magnitude from approximately 0.52 to 0.91, and Messick and Jackson (p. 300) state: "These strikingly consistent findings indicate that in most of these studies the largest factor on the MMPI is interpretable in terms of acquiescence."

Six of the eight studies reviewed by Messick and Jackson involved a limited number, 11 to 15, of the MMPI scales. Only two studies, one an unpublished study by Slater (1958) and one by Kassebaum, Couch, and Slater (1959), involved a substantial number of MMPI scales. Slater's factor analysis was based upon 43 scales and the Kassebaum, Couch, and Slater analysis upon 32 scales. For these two studies, the rank order correlations between the first factor loadings and the proportion of items keyed True were 0.72 and 0.62, respectively.[2]

We thus have an alternative interpretation of the first factor loadings of MMPI scales which, at least on the surface, appears to oppose the SD interpretation. Evidence for the interpretation of the first factor loadings in terms of acquiescence is based on the correlation between an index of acquiescence, the proportion of items keyed True in a scale, and the factor loadings. Evidence for the interpretation of the first factor loadings in terms of SD is based on the correlation between an index of SD, the proportion of items keyed for SD responses in a scale, and the factor loadings.

[2]Edwards and Heathers (1962) report a correlation of -0.93 between the first factor loadings of the MMPI scales obtained by Kassebaum, Couch, and Slater and the proportion of items keyed for SD responses in the scales.

10.3   Confounding of the Index of Acquiescence and the Index of SD

Both Hanley (1961) and Edwards (1961) have pointed out that the index of acquiescence and the index of SD are often confounded. For example, if a majority of the items in a scale are keyed True and if, at the same time, these items have socially desirable (or undesirable) scale values, then there is no way to isolate the influence of the tendency to acquiesce from that of the tendency to give SD (or SUD) responses. Similar considerations apply to scales in which a majority of the items are keyed False and when these items also have socially desirable (or undesirable) scale values. Within the framework of MMPI scales, as we shall see, it is generally the case that when an MMPI scale has a large proportion of items keyed True, the scale will also have a small proportion of items keyed for SD responses. Thus, one possible explanation of the Messick and Jackson correlations is that they are partially or wholly the result of the confounding of the acquiescence keying of the MMPI scales with the SD keying rather than the result of acquiescence *per se*.

Let us assume that scores on MMPI scales under Standard (S) test conditions are influenced by both SD and acquiescent tendencies and that these tendencies are reflected in the first factor loadings of the scales so that the loadings are correlated with both the index of social desirability and the index of acquiescence. Now suppose that the MMPI is administered under instructions to give SD responses. If the individuals accept the instructions, then they should respond True or False to an item primarily in terms of its judged SDSV; that is, if the item is judged to have a socially desirable scale value, they should respond True, whereas if the item is judged to have a socially undesirable scale value, they should respond False. Since there are individual differences in judgments of SDSVs, we may still expect some variation in the scores on the various MMPI scales under SD instructions. It seems reasonable to believe, however, that under these instructions acquiescent tendencies will be minimized. Similarly, if the MMPI is administered under instructions to give SUD responses, then it seems reasonable to believe that acquiescent tendencies under these instructions will be minimized also.

If the first factor loadings under S instructions are interpretable in terms of acquiescence, then there should be little or no relationship between the index of acquiescence and the factor loadings under SD and SUD instructions. On the other hand, if the relationship between the factor loadings and the index of acquiescence under S instructions is the result of the confounding between the acquiescence keying and the SD keying, then we should expect little or no change in the relationship under SD and SUD instructions.

10.4   Correlations of First Factor Loadings of MMPI Scales under Three Sets of Instructions with the Proportion of Items Keyed for True and for SD Responses in the Scales

To test the above hypothesis, Edwards and Diers (1962b) administered the MMPI to 150 male students under S instructions. Approximately one week later 120 of the original members of the S group were administered the MMPI under SD instructions. Another independent group of 150 males was administered the MMPI under SUD instructions.

For each of the three sets of instructions, MMPI scores were obtained on 58 MMPI scales. Intercorrelations of the scales were then obtained separately for each set of instructions, and the three resulting correlation matrices were factor-analyzed by the method of principal components. The factor loadings of the scales on the first unrotated principal component are of primary interest, because it is this factor that has been interpreted in terms of acquiescence and social desirability. The proportion of the total variance accounted for by the first factor under S, SD, and SUD instructions was 0.38, 0.46, and 0.42, respectively. The proportion of the total variance accounted for by the second principal component under S, SD, and SUD instructions was 0.10, 0.10, and 0.14, respectively. No subsequent factor, under any of the sets of instructions, accounted for more than 0.08 of the total variance.

Using Heineman's SDSVs for the MMPI items, as given by Dahlstrom and Welsh (1960), the proportion of items keyed for SD responses in each of the scales was obtained. This proportion was used as an index of the degree to which scores on the scale might by influenced by individual differences in rates of SD responding. Similarly, for each scale the proportion of items keyed for True responses was obtained and this proportion, following Messick and Jackson, was used as an index of the degree to which scores on the scale might be influenced by acquiescent tendencies.

Table 10.1 gives the product-moment correlations of the two indices

Table 10.1   Correlations of the Proportion of Items Keyed for SD Responses (SDR) and the Proportion Keyed for True Responses (TR) with the First Factor Loadings under Three Sets of Instructions[a]

Instructions	SDR	TR
Standard	0.89	−0.73
Socially desirable	0.92	−0.69
Socially undesirable	0.94	−0.66

[a]From Edwards and Diers (1962b).

with the loadings of the scales on the first factor under each set of instructions. Under S instructions the proportion of items keyed True correlates -0.73 with the first factor loadings of the 58 MMPI scales. Messick and Jackson obtained a correlation of 0.72 between this same index of acquiescence and the (reflected) first factor loadings for 43 MMPI scales under S instructions. We note, however, that the relationship between the acquiescence index and the first factor loadings changes very little under SD ($r = -0.69$) and SUD ($r = -0.66$) instructions. It may be argued that under SD and SUD instructions, acquiescent tendencies should be minimized and that, therefore, the proportion of items keyed True should have a relatively low correlation with the factor loadings under these instructions. The fact that the correlation remains relatively unchanged under SD and SUD instructions would appear to be the result of the fact that the acquiescence index is confounded with the SD index.

Under all three sets of instructions the proportion of items keyed for SD responses correlates highly and positively with the first factor loadings. These correlations show that the first factor loadings can be interpreted in terms of social desirability considerations, regardless of the conditions under which the MMPI is administered. That the first factor loadings of the MMPI scales are quite stable under different instructions is shown by the fact that the loadings under SD and SUD instructions both correlate 0.97 with the loadings under S instructions. The correlation between the SD and SUD loadings is 0.99.

Further evidence that the first factor loadings can be interpreted in terms of SD tendencies is available from the correlations of the loadings of the scales on the first factor with the correlations of the scales with the 39-item SD scale. Scores on the SD scale were correlated with scores on each of the other MMPI scales under each set of instructions. These correlations were then correlated with the loadings of the scales on the first factor. The correlations are shown in Table 10.2.

Table 10.2   Correlations between the First Factor Loadings of MMPI Scales and the Correlations of the Scales with the SD Scale under Three Sets of Instructions[a]

	Instructions		
	S	SD	SUD
r_S	0.99	0.96	0.96
r_{SD}	0.97	1.00	0.99
r_{SUD}	0.96	0.97	0.99

[a]From Edwards and Diers (1962b).

As Table 10.2 shows, the correlations of the MMPI scales with the *SD* scale under any of the three sets of instructions are highly related to the first factor loadings of the scales under any of the three sets of instructions. The correlations of the *SD* scale with the other MMPI scales are themselves highly related over the three sets of instructions. The correlations under S instructions correlated 0.96 and 0.97 with the those obtained under SD and SUD instructions. The correlations under SD instructions correlated 0.98 with those under SUD instructions.

The evidence presented shows that the first factor loadings of the MMPI scales can be predicted quite accurately from either the proportion of items keyed for SD responses or from the correlations of the scales with the 39-item *SD* scale. The relationships hold regardless of whether the MMPI is administered under S, SD, or SUD instructions. These results support the interpretation of the first factor loadings of the MMPI scales in terms of social desirability rather than in terms of acquiescence.

10.5   Correlations of Mean Scores on MMPI Scales
under Three Sets of Instructions with the Number of Items
Keyed for True, False, SD, and SUD Responses in the Scales

It might be argued, however, that the instructions to the subjects to give SD and SUD responses were relatively ineffective and that they were responding in terms of acquiescent tendencies, despite the instructions given them. If this were actually the case, then the relationship between the proportion of items keyed True and the first factor loadings should be (as was found) much the same for all three sets of instructions. This argument can easily be discounted in view of other evidence.

For each MMPI scale, the number of items keyed True, the number keyed False, and the number keyed for SD and SUD responses was obtained. If the individuals accepted the instructions to give SD responses then, within the limits of error of judgment of the SDSVs of the items, the mean score on each of the MMPI scales under SD instructions should approach the number of items in the scale keyed for SD responses. On the other hand, if they failed to accept the instructions and were responding on the basis of acquiescent tendencies, then the mean score should approach the number of items keyed for True responses. Similarly, under SUD instructions the mean should approach the number of items keyed for SUD responses. Table 10.3 shows the correlations of the number of items keyed for True, False, SD, and SUD responses with the means of the scales for each set of instructions.

The correlations shown in Table 10.3 clearly support the belief that the individuals did, in fact, respond to the items in accordance with the instruc-

Table 10.3   Correlations of the Number of Items Keyed T, F, SD, and SUD with MMPI
Means under Three Sets of Instructions[a]

	Instructions		
	S	SD	SUD
No. items keyed T	0.17	−0.11	0.78
No. items keyed F	0.53	0.53	0.00
No. items keyed SD	0.82	0.98	−0.43
No. items keyed SUD	−0.12	−0.47	0.98

[a]From Edwards and Diers (1962b).

tions given them and not in terms of acquiescent tendencies. The correlation of 0.78 between the number of items keyed True and the means under SUD instructions can be accounted for in terms of the relatively high correlation of 0.74 between the number of keyed True items in the scales and the number keyed for SUD responses in these 58 scales. Similarly, the correlation of 0.53 between the number of items keyed False and the means under S and SD instructions can be accounted for by the fact that the number of items keyed False correlates 0.48 with the number keyed for SD responses in the 58 scales. Of interest is the fact that the number of items keyed for SD responses also correlates quite highly with the means of the scales under S instructions.

10.6   Correlations of First Factor Loadings of MMPI Scales under Three Sets of Instructions with the Proportion of Neutral Items in the Scales

It has been suggested by Hanley (1961) and Edwards (1957a) that if a scale contains a large proportion of items with neutral SDSVs, then scores on the scale are less likely to be influenced by SD tendencies. With SD tendencies minimized, we might expect acquiescent tendencies to become more dominant. Thus, if a scale contains a large proportion of neutral items, acquiescent tendencies may be of greater importance than SD tendencies. This point tends to be accepted by Messick and Jackson in their review. The point is also relevant to the interpretation of the first factor loadings in terms of social desirability.

If the first factor loadings involve primarily acquiescent tendencies and if these tendencies are most operative when scales have a large proportion of neutral items, then the proportion of neutral items in the scales should correlate positively with the absolute values of the first factor loadings. On the other hand, if the first factor loadings involve primarily SD tendencies, then the proportion of neutral items in the scales should correlate negatively with the absolute values of the first factor loadings.

For each of the MMPI scales, the proportion of items falling in the neutral interval on the social desirability continuum was obtained and this index was then correlated with the absolute values of the factor loadings under all three sets of instructions. These correlations for S, SD, and SUD instructions are -0.42, -0.46, and -0.44, respectively. The fact that these correlations are all negative is consistent with the interpretation of the first factor loadings in terms of social desirability.

10.7   First Factor Loadings of Full-Length MMPI Scales

It has been shown in principal-component factor analyses of MMPI scales that the 39-item SD scale has a high loading at one pole of the first MMPI factor. MMPI scales which have a large proportion of items keyed for SD responses also tend to have a relatively high loading at the same pole of the first factor as the SD scale. MMPI scales which have a small proportion of items keyed for SD responses and, consequently, a large proportion of items keyed for SUD responses tend to have relatively high loadings at the opposite pole of the first factor. MMPI scales that have a fair degree of balance in their social desirability keying tend to have relatively low loadings on the first factor. The proportion of items keyed for SD responses in the MMPI scales has been shown to be substantially correlated with the first factor loadings of the scales.

10.8   First Factor Loadings of SD and SUD Keyed Parts
of MMPI Scales as Related to the Intensity Index

There are some MMPI scales which have an imbalance in their SD-SUD keying but which, at the same time, contain a sufficient number of items so that it is possible to divide the items in the scales into two sets: those keyed for trait *and* SD responses and those keyed for trait *and* SUD responses. When scores on these part scales were intercorrelated and factor-analyzed, along with other scales which had an extreme imbalance in their social desirability keying, it was found that, in general, the part scales keyed for SD responses had loadings with one sign on the first factor and the part scales keyed for SUD responses had loadings of the opposite sign on the first factor. An index of the intensity of the social desirability keying of the part scales was found to correlate 0.88 with the first factor loadings of the scales.

10.9   A Factor Analysis of True and False Keyed Parts of MMPI Scales

Jackson and Messick (1962) also divided MMPI scales into two parts and factor-analyzed the intercorrelations of the part scales. In their case, the two part scales consisted of those items keyed for trait *and* True responses and those items keyed for trait *and* False responses. They found that, in general, the True keyed scales had loadings of the same sign and the False keyed scales had loadings of the opposite sign on a common factor. They suggested, therefore, that the common factor could be interpreted as an acquiescence factor.

We have shown, however, that in MMPI scales the number of items keyed for True responses is negatively correlated with the number keyed for SD responses, and that the number keyed for False responses is positively correlated with the number keyed for SD responses. The possibility exists, therefore, that when MMPI scales are split into two parts (those items keyed for True responses and those keyed for False responses) the two parts are such that the True keyed items also tend to be keyed for SUD responses and the False keyed items also tend to be keyed for SD responses. Thus the False keyed part scales and the True keyed part scales might be expected to have loadings of opposite signs on a common factor—not because of acquiescent tendencies but rather because of SD tendencies.

10.10   A Factor Analysis of MMPI Scales
Balanced in Their True and False Keying

Block (1965) also divided a selected set of MMPI scales into two parts: those items keyed for True responses and those items keyed for False responses. If a scale contained more True keyed items than False keyed items, he discarded a sufficient number of the True keyed items to obtain a scale which had an equal number of items keyed for True and False responses. He argued that the total scores on these shortened scales would measure the same traits as the original full-length scales, but with less reliability. By factor-analyzing separately the intercorrelations of the original scales and of the shortened scales, and by showing that the factor loadings of both the original and shortened scales were fairly comparable on the first two factors, he hoped to demonstrate that an acquiescence interpretation of the MMPI first or second factor was untenable.

If, however, the first MMPI factor is a social desirability factor and if an original full-length MMPI scale has an imbalance in its SD-SUD keying, then simply discarding an excess of either True or False keyed items does not, of course, offer any assurance that the shortened scale is balanced in its SD-SUD keying or in the intensity of the SD keying of the two parts. Thus, if the same kind of imbalance in the SD-SUD keying of the shortened scales is present as in the original scales, the first factor loadings of the balanced True-False scales might be expected to be comparable to the first factor loadings of the original scales.

10.11   Equating SD and SUD Parts of MMPI Scales in Terms of the Intensity Index

There are some MMPI scales which have either a balance or an im-balance in their SD-SUD keying but such that when the items are divided into two parts, those keyed for SD responses and those keyed for SUD responses, the intensity index of the two part scales is not comparable. For some of these scales, however, it is possible to discard items from the part scales in such a way as to obtain an equal number of items in the two parts and such that they have an approximately equal intensity index. These two part scales can then be combined so as to yield a total score for a scale which has an equal number of items keyed for SD and for SUD responses and in which the intensity index is approximately the same for the items keyed for SD and for SUD responses.

If Block's argument that the shortened forms of MMPI scales, balanced for True-False keying, measure the same traits as the full-length original scales is correct, then it should also apply to shortened forms of MMPI scales balanced for their SD-SUD keying. Thus, according to Block, the first factor loadings of MMPI scales balanced for SD-SUD keying should remain much the same as the factor loadings of the same scales in their original and imbalanced form.

To investigate these two opposing hypotheses with respect to the first MMPI factor, 21 MMPI scales were selected.[3] The scales can be arranged according to the degree of imbalance in their SD-SUD keying. The index of imbalance in the social desirability keying for each scale was the same as that used in an earlier study, namely

$$I\text{-SD} = |P(\text{SD}) - 0.50|$$

where $P(\text{SD})$ is the proportion of items in the scale keyed for SD responses. Thus, when all of the items in a scale are keyed for either SD or for SUD

[3]The study described is from an unpublished paper by Edwards and Klockars (1968).

responses, then I-SD $= 0.50$. When a scale contains an equal number of items keyed for SD and for SUD responses, then I-SD $= 0.00$. Table 10.4 lists the 21 MMPI scales and gives the number of items in each of the original full-length scales. The table also gives the degree of imbalance in the SD-SUD keying of the scales.

Table 10.4   The Number of Items in 21 Full-Length MMPI Scales and in Scales 9–20 when They Are Shortened so as to Have a Balance in Their Social Desirability Keying. I-SD Is a Measure of the Degree of Imbalance in the Social Desirability Keying of the Scales[a]

	Full-Length		Shortened	
Scales	No. Items	I-SD	No. Items	I-SD
1. SD	39	0.50	39	0.50
2. Pa-O	23	0.50	23	0.50
3. Ne	30	0.50	30	0.50
4. Hs	33	0.50	33	0.50
5. No	18	0.50	18	0.50
6. A	39	0.45	39	0.45
7. Ca	36	0.44	36	0.44
8. Dn	26	0.31	26	0.31
9. Dy	57	0.32	18	0.00
10. Pv	50	0.28	22	0.00
11. Es	68	0.28	28	0.00
12. K	30	0.27	14	0.00
13. D	60	0.27	26	0.00
14. Do	28	0.18	14	0.00
15. Hy	60	0.15	32	0.00
16. Eo	23	0.11	16	0.00
17. Or	25	0.10	14	0.00
18. Ma-S	23	0.06	18	0.00
19. Mf	60	0.02	30	0.00
20. Cn	50	0.02	26	0.00
21. ER-S	40	0.00	40	0.00

[a]From an unpublished study by Edwards and Klockers (1968).

The items in Scales 9–20 were divided into two sets: those keyed for SD responses and those keyed for SUD responses. For each scale the set containing the larger number of items was used in an attempt to match each of the items in the set with the smaller number with respect to intensity of social desirability keying. In some cases it was necessary to discard items in the smaller set because no good match for the items could be found in the larger set. At the same time, some moderate discrepancies were permitted in order to keep the number of items in the smaller set as large as possible. Table 10.4 shows the number of items in each of the shortened MMPI scales. Each of these scales contains exactly the same number of items keyed for SD and for SUD responses, and the mean intensity of the items keyed for SD responses is approximately the same as the mean intensity of the items keyed for SUD responses.

10.12   First Factor Loadings of the Full-Length and Shortened Scales

Scores on the full-length 21 MMPI scales were based on the records of 150 male students. These scores were intercorrelated, and the correlation matrix was factor-analyzed by the method of principal components. Five

Table 10.5   Rotated Factor Loadings of 21 Full-Length MMPI Scales[a]

			Rotated Factors			
Scales	I′	II′	III′	IV′	V′	h^2
1. SD	−0.82	−0.34	−0.20	0.13	−0.03	0.84
2. Pa-O	0.68	0.17	0.20	−0.01	0.07	0.53
3. Ne	0.63	0.34	0.55	−0.18	−0.00	0.85
4. Hs	0.53	0.32	0.59	−0.17	0.02	0.75
5. No	0.46	0.09	0.09	−0.60	0.24	0.65
6. A	0.85	0.37	0.17	−0.02	0.10	0.91
7. Ca	0.78	0.31	0.24	−0.21	0.12	0.82
8. Dn	−0.65	−0.49	0.41	0.20	0.15	0.90
9. Dy	0.87	0.22	0.06	−0.06	0.19	0.84
10. Pv	0.91	0.01	−0.10	0.06	0.04	0.84
11. Es	−0.74	0.10	−0.35	0.19	−0.01	0.71
12. K	−0.70	−0.56	0.22	0.01	0.08	0.86
13. D	0.47	0.04	0.55	−0.41	0.14	0.72
14. Do	−0.72	0.03	−0.13	0.07	0.30	0.62
15. Hy	−0.05	−0.12	0.94	0.01	0.17	0.94
16. Eo	−0.14	−0.60	0.07	−0.44	−0.06	0.59
17. Or	−0.61	−0.05	0.08	−0.31	0.44	0.68
18. Ma-S	0.09	0.12	−0.08	0.83	0.01	0.71
19. Mf	0.15	0.09	0.18	−0.07	0.90	0.88
20. Cn	0.16	0.89	0.12	0.02	0.09	0.84
21. ER-S	−0.78	−0.19	−0.02	−0.10	−0.16	0.68
Percent total variance	39.04	11.67	11.67	8.24	6.35	76.97
Percent common variance	50.72	15.17	15.16	10.70	8.25	

[a]From an unpublished study by Edwards and Klockars (1968).

factors were extracted and rotated by means of an orthogonal Varimax rotation.

The MMPI records of the 150 students were then scored on the short forms of Scales 9–20. Scores on these scales were intercorrelated along with the scores on the other full-length scales and the resulting correlation matrix was factor-analyzed by the method of principal components. Five factors were extracted and rotated by means of an orthogonal Varimax rotation.

Table 10.5 gives the rotated and denormalized factor loadings of the 21 full-length MMPI scales. The percentage of the total and common variance accounted for by each factor is given in the last two rows of the table, and the communalities are given in the extreme right column. Table 10.6 gives the corresponding values for the factor analysis involving

Table 10.6   Rotated Factor Loadings of 21 MMPI Scales when Scales 9–20 Are Shortened so as to Have a Balance in Their SD-SUD Keying[a]

Scales	Rotated Factors					
	I′	II′	III′	IV′	V′	h^2
1. SD	−0.82	0.27	0.26	−0.09	−0.07	0.83
2. Pa-O	0.70	−0.20	−0.14	0.11	−0.05	0.56
3. Ne	0.92	−0.09	0.05	0.05	0.02	0.85
4. Hs	0.85	−0.06	0.10	−0.01	−0.02	0.74
5. No	0.58	−0.08	−0.17	−0.48	0.22	0.65
6. A	0.82	−0.31	−0.25	0.18	0.12	0.88
7. Ca	0.84	−0.23	−0.20	−0.02	0.12	0.82
8. Dn	−0.52	0.12	0.75	−0.02	0.03	0.85
9. Dy	0.23	−0.74	−0.17	0.19	0.28	0.74
10. Pv	0.33	−0.69	−0.32	0.05	−0.07	0.69
11. Es	−0.06	0.69	−0.20	0.20	0.03	0.57
12. K	−0.35	0.08	0.52	−0.46	−0.01	0.62
13. D	0.17	−0.08	0.53	−0.40	0.06	0.49
14. Do	−0.22	0.54	−0.13	−0.10	0.51	0.63
15. Hy	−0.12	0.12	0.90	−0.01	0.06	0.84
16. Eo	−0.20	0.06	0.12	−0.64	−0.10	0.48
17. Or	−0.39	0.60	0.31	−0.18	0.01	0.63
18. Ma-S	−0.03	−0.09	−0.07	0.71	−0.14	0.55
19. Mf	0.16	−0.10	0.16	−0.03	0.84	0.78
20. Cn	0.44	0.42	−0.09	0.47	0.26	0.67
21. ER-S	−0.57	0.51	0.23	−0.18	−0.16	0.69
Percent total variance	27.71	13.94	12.12	9.39	6.07	69.22
Percent common variance	40.03	20.13	17.51	13.56	8.77	

[a]From an unpublished study by Edwards and Klockars (1968).

the balanced scales. In this second factor analysis, the scores on Scales
1–8 and on the *ER-S* remained exactly the same as in the first analysis.
The first factor loadings obtained in the second analysis are differentiated
from those obtained in the first analysis by means of an asterisk in the
discussion that follows.

The first factor loadings of the nine scales for which the scores remained
exactly the same in both analyses are

		I'	$I'*$
1.	*SD*	−0.82	−0.82
2.	*Pa–O*	0.68	0.70
3.	*Ne*	0.63	0.92
4.	*Hs*	0.53	0.85
5.	*No*	0.46	0.58
6.	*A*	0.85	0.82
7.	*Ca*	0.78	0.84
8.	*Dn*	−0.65	−0.52
21.	*ER-S*	−0.78	−0.57

In both analyses the proportion of variance accounted for by the five
factors with respect to these scales remains much the same.

The *SD* scale, which was developed as a rational measure of the tendency
to give SD responses in self-description, has the same loading of −0.82 on
the first factor in both factor analyses. Scales 2–7 have first factor loadings
which either remain much the same in both analyses or have a higher
loading when analyzed with the balanced scales. *Dn*, with 21 out of 26
items keyed for SD responses, and *ER-S*, with 20 out of 40 items keyed for
SD responses, both have lower loadings on the first factor in the second
analysis than they do in the first.

Scales 9–14, in their full-length form, have an imbalance in their SD-SUD
keying. For the second factor analysis these scales were shortened so that
each one had a balance in its SD-SUD keying. The first factor loadings of
these scales in the two analyses are:

		I'	$I'*$
9.	*Dy*	0.87	0.23
10.	*Pv*	0.91	0.33
11.	*Es*	−0.74	−0.06
12.	*K*	−0.70	−0.35
13.	*D*	0.47	0.17
14.	*Do*	−0.72	−0.22

With but one exception, *Do*, the proportion of variance accounted for in
these scales by the five factors is greater for the full-length scales than for
the scales in their balanced form. In all cases, the scales have lower loadings
on the first factor in their balanced form than in their full length and

imbalanced form. If these scales are considered to be measures of the first MMPI factor in their full-length and imbalanced form, then it seems obvious that they cannot be so described when they are shortened so as to have a balance in their SD-SUD keying.

Why should these balanced scales have lower loadings on the first factor in the second analysis than they do in their imbalanced form in the first analysis? If one regards the first MMPI factor as measuring the tendency to give SD responses, then a reasonable explanation for the lower first factor loadings of the balanced scales is that scores on scales which have a balance in their SD-SUD keying are less influenced by the tendency to give SD responses than scales which have an imbalance in their SD-SUD keying.

10.13   Acquiescence and the MMPI *SD* Scale

In the 39-item MMPI *SD* scale, 9 items are keyed True and 30 items are keyed False. This *SD* scale has a degree of imbalance in its True-False keying and the possibility exists that scores on the scale reflect in some degree individual differences in rates of True responding. We have described earlier, however, a factor analysis that included a number of experimental *SD* scales along with the 39-item MMPI *SD* Scale (Edwards and Walsh, 1964b). Four of the experimental *SD* scales in this study had a balance in their True-False keying with 20 items keyed True and 20 items keyed False. Another experimental *SD* scale had 40 items all keyed for False responses and still another had 40 items all keyed for True responses. All of these *SD* scales and the 39-item MMPI *SD* scale had relatively high loadings on a common factor. If scores on the 39-item MMPI *SD* scale are at all influenced by individual differences in the tendency to respond True to items, then it is evident that this influence must be fairly minimal.

Additional evidence on this point is provided by the factor analyses reported by Block (1965). It will be recalled that Block shortened various MMPI scales, including the *SD* scale, by discarding items from the scales so as to obtain a balance in the True-False keying of the items in the scales. In other words, in each of the scales the number of items keyed for True responses was equal to the number keyed for False responses. The loadings of the balanced True-False form of the *SD* scale on the first principal component in five different factor analyses were: 0.82, 0.82, 0.71, 0.83, and 0.89. Thus, the first factor loadings of this shortened form of the *SD* scale, consisting of only 18 items, are not considerably different from the first factor loadings of the full-length 39-item *SD* scale.

10.14 Attempts to Develop Acquiescence Scales

There have been various attempts to develop scales to measure acquiescent tendencies (Fricke, 1957; Jackson and Messick, 1961; Wiggins, 1962; Couch and Keniston, 1960; Edwards, 1963; Edwards and Diers, 1963; Crowder, 1962; Diers, 1964). Fricke (1957) developed a response bias (B) scale using MMPI items of high controversiality (i.e., items for which the probability of a True response is approximately equal to the probability of a False response) as a measure of acquiescence. However, in a study by Edwards (1961), the B scale was found to correlate -0.59 with the 39-item SD scale and, in a factor analysis of MMPI scales, Edwards, Diers, and Walker (1962) found that the B scale had a loading of -0.56 on the first principal component. These are not unexpected results, since the B scale has an imbalance in its SD-SUD keying with more items keyed for SUD responses than for SD responses.

It has been suggested (Hanley, 1961; Edwards, 1957a) that scales containing items with neutral SDSVs might be relatively independent of the influence of SD tendencies and therefore more susceptible to the influence of acquiescent tendencies. In a study by Edwards (1963), a number of proposed measures of acquiescence were investigated, including three scales in which all of the items in each scale had SDSVs in the neutral interval, 4.5 to 5.5, on a 9-point rating scale. One scale consisted of 50 items such that all of the items had a relatively low probability of being answered True, the average probability being 0.25. This scale may be referred to as a Low Neutral (LN) scale. Another consisted of 46 items, each of which had a probability between 0.47 and 0.53 of being answered True and may be referred to as a Neutral (N) scale. The third consisted of 50 items, each of which had a probability equal to or greater than 0.58 of being answered True, the average probability being 0.65. This scale may be referred to as a High Neutral (HN) scale. The items in each of these three neutral scales were keyed for True responses.

In addition to the three scales consisting of neutral items, two additional scales that might measure acquiescent tendencies were investigated. These two scales were based on the 360 items used by Couch and Keniston (1960) in their study of acquiescence. A substantial number of the items in these two scales are not typical of those found in personality scales but rather resemble the kinds of items found in attitude and opinion questionnaires. These items relate to relatively broad and general beliefs and values. Typical of the items in these two scales are the following:

There are days when one awakes from sleep without a care in the world, full of zest and eagerness for what lies ahead.
The world is teeming with opportunities and promises of success for anyone with sufficient imagination to perceive them.
Happiness is one of the primary goals of life.
The vast majority of men are truthful and dependable.

One of the two scales consisted of 35 items of the kind described above and all of the items were keyed True. The items in this scale are those that Couch and Keniston found to have a mean agreement rating on a 7-point Disagree-Agree rating scale between 5.0 and 5.9 and can be described as a High Mean (*HM*) scale. The second scale consisted of 40 items of the kind described above. The items in this scale differed from those in the first scale in that the mean agreement rating on the 7-point Disagree-Agree rating scale for each item was between 3.8 and 4.2. This second scale may be described as a Middle Mean (*MM*) scale. The items in this scale were also keyed for True responses.

Still another proposed measure of acquiescence was investigated. It has been suggested by Cronbach (1946) that acquiescent tendencies are most likely to be elicited by achievement items when an individual does not know or is in doubt as to the correct response to an item. In the present study, each individual had been permitted to respond to an item with a ? if he was in doubt as to whether the item accurately described him. He was then instructed to give his best guess as to the correct response. For each of 2400 items, the number of items answered with a ? was found for each individual. Within this subset of items, the number of items answered True was obtained and this number was then divided by the total number of items answered with a ?. Thus we have a highly personalized measure for each individual of his tendency to answer True to items when he is initially in doubt as to the correct response.

When these six proposed measures of acquiescence were intercorrelated and factor-analyzed along with 13 other scales, it was found that each of the proposed measures had its highest loading on a different factor. As Edwards states:

In view of these results, it would appear that considerable attention needs to be given to the problem of the meaning of acquiescence and how to measure it, before one can conclude that it is a general response set influencing scores on all personality scales to the degree to which there is an imbalance in the True-False keying of the scales (1963, pp. 315–316).

In addition to the study cited above, McGee (1962) has also reported relatively low correlations between other proposed measures of acquiescent tendencies.

10.15   Acquiescence and the *R* Scale

As we have stated previously, the *R* scale of the MMPI was developed by Welsh (1956) as a marker variable for the second MMPI factor. The *R* scale consists of 40 items and all of the items are keyed for False responses. Consequently, scores on the *R* scale have been interpreted as possibly reflecting acquiescent tendencies. For example, individuals with high rates of True responding would obtain low scores on the *R* scale, and individuals with low rates of True responding would obtain high scores.

We have shown previously the relationship between *P*(T) and SDSV for the 40 items in the *R* scale. The SDSVs of the items are fairly well distributed over the social desirability continuum and the scale has a fair degree of balance in its SD-SUD keying. The *R* scale tends to have a low correlation with the *SD* scale, a low loading on the first MMPI factor, and a high loading on the second factor. Furthermore, as Edwards, Diers, and Walker (1962) have shown, the factor loadings of MMPI scales on the *second* principal component are substantially correlated ($r = 0.82$) with the proportion of items keyed True in the scales, whereas the correlation between the second factor loadings and the proportion of items keyed for SD responses is relatively low ($r = -0.38$). It is possible, therefore, that the second principal component may, in part, reflect acquiescent tendencies.

Assume that scores on the *R* scale do in fact measure individual differences in rates of True responding to personality items, regardless of the content of the items. If this is the case, then those individuals with low scores on the *R* scale should be more likely to respond True to personality items, in general, than individuals with high scores. Thus, if a group of low scorers on the *R* scale and a group of high scorers were selected and the responses of these two groups to another set of personality items were obtained, we should find that, in general, the *P*(T)s for the two groups on the various items differ.

Suppose that for this new set of statements we find the regression line of *P*(T) on SDSV for each group. We know that the relationship between *P*(T) and SDSV is linear for any representative or random set of statements with a range of SDSVs. If we have effectively separated individuals into two groups on the basis of their scores on the *R* scale, one group consisting of individuals with low rates of True responding and the other group consisting of individuals with high rates of True responding, regardless of item content, then the regression lines of *P*(T) on SDSV for these two groups should not intersect. In other words, the high acquiescers should, in general, have a higher probability of a True response to each personality item, regardless of the SDSV of the item, than the low acquiescers.

To investigate the above hypothesis with respect to the *R* scale, two groups of individuals were selected from a larger group of 150 male students.[4] One group consisted of 20 individuals with the highest scores, from 21 to 27, on the *R* scale and will be referred to as a group with a relatively *low* rate of True responding. The other group consisted of the 20 individuals with the lowest scores, from 6 to 11, on the *R* scale and will be referred to as a group with a relatively *high* rate of True responding.

Eliminating the duplicate items and the items in the *R* scale, the remaining 510 items in the MMPI were arranged in rank order in terms of their SDSVs. The 20 items with the lowest SDSVs were then selected to form Scale 1, the next 20 to form Scale 2, and so on. The last scale consisted of the ten MMPI items with the highest SDSVs. For each of these 26 scales the mean probability of a True response for each group of subjects was obtained. For each of the 26 scales, the average SDSV of the items in the scale was also obtained. The regression lines of the mean probability of a True response on the mean SDSV of the 26 scales were then found separately for the group of high acquiescers and the group of low acquiescers.

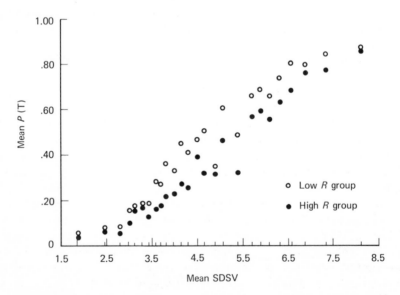

Figure 10.1   Mean probabilities of a True response on 26 scales for a high-and a low-scoring group on the *R* scale of the MMPI. From Edwards and Abbott (1969).

[4]The study described in this section was unpublished at the time the chapter was written. It was subsequently published by Edwards and Abbott (1969).

Figure 10.1 shows the plot of the mean $P(T)$s on mean SDSVs of the 26 scales for the two groups of subjects. It may be noted that in every case the high-acquiescent group has a higher mean probability of a True response than the low-acquiescent group. The differences are not large, in some cases, but they are consistent.

Table 10.7 gives the mean probability of a True response over all 26 scales, the standard deviation of the mean $P(T)$s, the correlation coefficient between $P(T)$ and SDSV, and the regression coefficient of $P(T)$ on SDSV

Table 10.7 Mean Probability of a True Response, $P(T)$, Standard Deviation of the $P(T)$s, the Correlation between $P(T)$ and Mean SDSV, and the Regression Coefficient of $P(T)$ on SDSV for Low- and High-Acquiescent Groups on 26 Scales[a]

	Low Group	High Group
$P(T)$	0.355	0.441
σ	0.239	0.250
r	0.977	0.974
b	0.149	0.155
N	20	20

[a]From Edwards and Abbott (1969).

for the two groups. For the low-acquiescent group the regression coefficient is 0.149 and for the high-acquiescent group the regression coefficient is 0.155. In other words, the slopes of the two regression lines are approximately equal and the two lines are approximately parallel. The average difference between the mean $P(T)$s for the high- and low-acquiescent groups is $0.441 - 0.395 = 0.086$.

The results cited above were sufficiently striking and unusual that the study was replicated with three additional samples. One sample consisted of 163 male students, another of 155 male students who had taken the MMPI at a counseling center, and the third consisted of 164 female students. In all three samples the same criterion used in the first study was applied to select high- and low-scoring groups on the R scale. The data analysis for each of these three samples was the same as in the first study. The results are shown in Table 10.8. In none of the samples do the regression lines for the high and low groups intersect within the range of the SDSVs investigated. For both of the male samples, the mean $P(T)$ for the high-acquiescent group was larger than the mean $P(T)$ for the low-acquiescent

Table 10.8   Mean Probability of a True Response, $P(T)$, Standard Deviation of the $P(T)$s, the Correlation between $P(T)$ and Mean SDSV, and the Regression Coefficient of $P(T)$ on SDSV for Low- and High-Acquiescent Groups on 26 Scales[a]

		Low Group	High Group
Sample 1:	$P(T)$	0.354	0.464
	σ	0.251	0.253
	r	0.981	0.973
	b	0.157	0.157
	N	22	35
Sample 2:	$P(T)$	0.357	0.446
	σ	0.244	0.247
	r	0.967	0.980
	b	0.150	0.154
	N	15	30
Sample 3:	$P(T)$	0.389	0.453
	σ	0.228	0.257
	r	0.987	0.983
	b	0.143	0.161
	N	18	16

[a]From Edwards and Abbott (1969).

group on each of the 26 scales. For the female sample there were five scales on which the mean $P(T)$ for the low-acquiescent group was greater than that for the high-acquiescent group. These differences, which are opposite to those predicted, were quite small and were found on the scales with the lowest mean SDSVs. On the remaining 21 scales, the mean $P(T)$ for the high-acquiescent group was larger than the corresponding mean for the low-acquiescent group.

The results obtained in the first study and replicated in three additional samples provide a rather convincing demonstration that, in general, low scorers on the R scale tend, on the average, to have a higher rate of True responding to MMPI items, regardless of the SDSVs of the items, than high scorers. The extreme groups in all of the samples, however, consisted of those individuals with scores on the R scale that were approximately one or more standard deviations above the mean, or one or more standard deviations below the mean, and it is possible that the acquiescence effect holds only for these two extreme groups. As an additional test, therefore, scores on the R scale for the combined sample of 468 males were correlated with the number of True responses on each of the 26 scales. Table 10.9 gives the values of these correlation coefficients and also the mean SDSV of the items in each of the 26 scales.

All 26 of the correlation coefficients are negative in sign. This finding is consistent with the notion that low scorers on the *R* scale tend to be more acquiescent than high scorers. We note also that the correlations tend

Table 10.9   Correlations of the *R* Scale with 26 True Keyed MMPI Scales in Which the Mean SDSV of the Items Increases from Scale to Scale

Scales	Mean SDSV	*r*	Scales	Mean SDSV	*r*
1	1.85	−0.10	14	4.50	−0.31
2	2.47	−0.13	15	4.65	−0.38
3	2.80	−0.13	16	4.87	−0.33
4	2.97	−0.15	17	5.13	−0.45
5	3.12	−0.12	18	5.37	−0.37
6	3.30	−0.08	19	5.67	−0.24
7	3.46	−0.18	20	5.87	−0.30
8	3.59	−0.23	21	6.09	−0.40
9	3.68	−0.20	22	6.32	−0.21
10	3.81	−0.32	23	6.57	−0.26
11	3.96	−0.21	24	6.89	−0.12
12	4.14	−0.34	25	7.35	−0.14
13	4.30	−0.29	26	8.12	−0.09

to be larger for those scales consisting of items with SDSVs in the middle range of the social desirability continuum than for those scales consisting of items with SDSVs toward the two extremes of the continuum. Apparently acquiescent tendencies, as measured by the *R* scale, are most dominant when items have relatively neutral SDSVs and, as we have shown, it is with respect to these items that SD tendencies are, in turn, less dominant. For example, we would expect scores on the *SD* scale to be less highly correlated with scales consisting of items with SDSVs in the middle range of the social desirability continuum and in which the items are keyed True, than with scales consisting of True keyed items with SDSVs toward the two extremes.

To illustrate the point made above, the 39 items in the *SD* scale and the 16 duplicate items were eliminated, leaving a total of 511 items which do not appear in the *SD* scale. These items were then sorted according to their SDSVs and 26 scales constructed. Scale 1 consisted of the 20 items with the lowest SDSVs, Scale 2 of the next 20 items, and so on, Scale 26 consisting of the 11 items with the highest SDSVs. Scores on the *SD* scale were then correlated with the number of True responses on each of the 26 scales using the sample of 468 males. Table 10.10 gives the resulting correlation coefficients and also the mean SDSV of the items in each scale. As expected, those scales in which the items are keyed for True *and* SUD responses and in which the items have low SDSVs have relatively high negative correlations with the *SD* scale. The three lowest correlations are

Table 10.10 Correlations of the 39-Item *SD* Scale with 26 True Keyed MMPI Scales in Which the Mean SDSV of the Items Increases from Scale to Scale

Scales	Mean SDSV	r	Scales	Mean SDSV	r
1	1.78	−0.63	14	4.66	−0.35
2	2.46	−0.70	15	4.87	−0.18
3	2.84	−0.70	16	5.12	−0.17
4	3.02	−0.77	17	5.34	−0.10
5	3.20	−0.82	18	5.59	0.25
6	3.40	−0.78	19	5.79	0.31
7	3.56	−0.81	20	5.98	0.52
8	3.66	−0.66	21	6.18	0.37
9	3.79	−0.61	22	6.38	0.55
10	3.94	−0.70	23	6.60	0.42
11	4.14	−0.60	24	6.90	0.65
12	4.33	−0.48	25	7.34	0.53
13	4.52	−0.41	26	8.11	0.44

those of Scales 15, 16, and 17 in which the mean SDSV of the items is 4.87, 5.12, and 5.34, respectively. Scale 18, consisting of items with a mean SDSV of 5.59, has a positive correlation with the *SD* scale, as do all of the other scales keyed for True *and* SD responses.

The mean SDSVs of the 26 scales listed in Tables 10.9 and 10.10 are not greatly different. If one plots the value of the correlation of each of the 26 scales with the *R* scale against the corresponding absolute value of the correlation of each of the 26 scales with the *SD* scale, he will observe that the trend of the plotted points is downward. In other words, the larger the absolute correlation of a True keyed scale with the *SD* scale, the smaller the correlation of the scale with the *R* scale.

The results cited above, and the fact that the *R* scale has been found consistently to have a relatively low loading on the first principal component of the MMPI and a high loading on the second principal component, and that the second factor loadings of MMPI scales have been found to correlate 0.82 with the proportion of items keyed True in the scales, strongly suggest that the second MMPI factor is in some degree measuring individual differences in rates of True responding.

10.16   Acquiescence and the *SD* Scale: Further Evidence

The correlation between scores on the 39-item *SD* scale and scores on the *R* scale for the sample of 468 males is 0.12. If the *R* scale is accepted as measuring in some degree acquiescent tendencies, then scores on the *SD* scale may also be reflecting in a minor degree acquiescent tendencies. One possible explanation of the small positive correlation between scores on the *R* scale and scores on the *SD* scale is the fact that the number of False keyed items (30) in the *SD* scale is considerably larger than the number of True keyed items (9) and that all of the 40 items in the *R* scale are keyed for False responses. Any common tendency to acquiesce with respect to the False keyed items in the two scales would influence scores on the two scales in the same direction.

Acquiescent tendencies on the False keyed items in the *SD* scale would also tend to lower scores on the scale and consequently to enhance the *negative* correlations between the *SD* scale and scales keyed for True *and* SUD responses. On the other hand, acquiescent tendencies should serve to lower the positive correlations found between scores on the *SD* scale and scores on scales keyed for True *and* SD responses. If the correlations between the *SD* scale and the 26 True keyed scales given in Table 10.10 are examined, it will be noted that, in general, the negative correlations between the *SD* scale and scales keyed for True *and* SUD responses tend to be greater in absolute value than the corresponding correlations between the *SD* scale and scales keyed for True *and* SD responses.

Presumably, an *SD* scale with a balance in its True and False keying would have *slightly smaller negative* correlations with True *and* SUD keyed scales and *slightly higher positive* correlations with True *and* SD keyed scales than those obtained with the 39-item *SD* scale. An *SD* scale balanced in its True and False keying would also presumably have a correlation smaller than 0.12 with the *R* scale.

To test the above hypotheses, the 39-item *SD* scale was reduced to 18 items by eliminating 21 of the 30 False keyed items. In choosing which of the False keyed items to eliminate, an effort was made to keep the mean rate of SD responding on the 18-item scale approximately the same as the mean rate of SD responding on the 39-item scale. The resulting 18-item *SD* scale consisted of nine items keyed for False responses and nine keyed for True responses.[5] For the sample of 468 males the mean rate of SD responding on the 18-item *SD* scale was $14.35/18 = 0.80$ and is equivalent to the mean rate of SD responding, $31.12/39 = 0.80$, on the 39-item *SD* scale.

---

[5]The nine False keyed items retained in the 18-item *SD* scale have the following MMPI Booklet Numbers: 138, 156, 171, 186, 252, 267, 352, 439, and 555.

When scores on the 18-item SD scale were correlated with scores on the R scale, a correlation coefficient of 0.02 was obtained. The 18-item SD scale can thus be considered as almost completely free of acquiescent tendencies as measured by the R scale.

The correlations between scores on the 18-item SD scale and the 26 True keyed scales of MMPI items are given in Table 10.11. Note that with

Table 10.11   Correlations of the 18-Item SD Scale with 26 True Keyed MMPI Scales in Which the Mean SDSV of the Items Increases from Scale to Scale

Scales	Mean SDSV	r	Scales	Mean SDSV	r
1	1.78	−0.67	14	4.66	−0.21
2	2.46	−0.73	15	4.87	−0.01
3	2.84	−0.72	16	5.12	−0.02
4	3.02	−0.68	17	5.34	−0.01
5	3.20	−0.77	18	5.59	0.38
6	3.40	−0.68	19	5.79	0.43
7	3.56	−0.73	20	5.98	0.61
8	3.66	−0.56	21	6.18	0.49
9	3.79	−0.52	22	6.38	0.60
10	3.94	−0.61	23	6.60	0.52
11	4.14	−0.45	24	6.90	0.73
12	4.33	−0.31	25	7.34	0.64
13	4.52	−0.31	26	8.11	0.53

the exception of Scales 1, 2, and 3, the negative correlations between the 18-item SD scale are in all other cases *lower* than those obtained with the 39-item SD scale. Similarly, in all cases where the 39-item SD scale correlates positively with the True keyed scales, the correlations of the 18-item SD scale with the same scales are *higher*. These results indicate that minor acquiescent tendencies with respect to the 39-item SD scale may operate in such a way as to increase slightly the negative correlations between the SD scale and other scales keyed for True *and* SUD responses. At the same time, the positive correlations between the SD scale and other scales keyed for True *and* SD responses may be decreased slightly by acquiescent tendencies.

Chapter 11

A Comparison of 57 MMPI Scales
and 57 Experimental Scales
Matched with the MMPI Scales
in Terms of Item SDSVs and P(T)s[1]

11.1 Introduction

If the tendency to give SD responses operates with respect to personality items in general, then scores on trait scales which have a large proportion of items keyed for SD responses should be positively correlated with rates of SD responding as measured by an *SD* scale. Similar considerations apply to trait scales that have a small proportion of items keyed for SD responses and, consequently, a large proportion keyed for SUD responses. If the tendency to give SD responses is operating, then in this instance scores on the scale should be negatively correlated with rates of SD responding. The fact that both the correlations of MMPI scales with the MMPI *SD* scale and the first factor loadings of MMPI scales have been found to be highly correlated with the proportion of items in the scales keyed for SD responses, offers fairly convincing evidence that responses to items in MMPI scales are influenced by social desirability tendencies.

11.2 Problem of Item Overlap in MMPI Scales

We have pointed out that some of the items in the MMPI *SD* scale are also scored in other MMPI trait scales and that the item overlap will influence the correlation between the MMPI trait scale and the *SD* scale.

[1]The material in this chapter is substantially the same as that in a previously published article by Edwards (1966b).

As an extreme example, suppose that an MMPI scale consists of 39 items and that the trait keying of each of the items is also an SD response. If the 39 items in this trait scale are the same as those that are in the 39-item *SD* scale, then the correlation between the two scales must be equal to 1.00, simply because both consist of the same common items. In addition, the MMPI trait scale would have 100 percent of its items keyed for SD responses. Similarly, if an MMPI trait scale consists of the same 39 items that are included in the *SD* scale and if these items in the trait scale are all keyed for SUD responses, then the correlation between the trait scale and the *SD* scale must be equal to −1.00. In addition, this MMPI trait scale would have zero percent of its items keyed for SD responses.

Although the two scales described above are extreme examples, they serve to emphasize the fact that to the degree to which an MMPI trait scale has items in common with the *SD* scale, and such that the items are consistently keyed for either SD or SUD responses, then both the proportion of items keyed for SD responses and the correlation of the scale with the *SD* scale may be influenced in the same manner by the overlapping items. Thus the relationship between the proportion of items keyed for SD responses and the correlations of MMPI trait scales with the *SD* scale may be spuriously inflated, simply because of item overlap. This is one of the problems to be considered in this chapter.

11.3 Constructing an Experimental MMPI

It is also important to determine whether the relationship observed between the proportion of items keyed for SD responses in MMPI scales and the correlations of these scales with the *SD* scale is restricted to scales composed of MMPI items. More specifically, if we build experimental scales consisting of non-MMPI items but such that each experimental scale has certain structural properties in common with a corresponding MMPI scale, will the correlations of the experimental scales with the *SD* scale be proportional to the correlations of the corresponding MMPI scales with the *SD* scale? Furthermore, will the internal consistency of the experimental scales be proportional to the internal consistency of the corresponding MMPI scales? And will the correlation between the experimental scale and the corresponding MMPI scale be related to the proportion of items keyed for SD responses in the two scales?

Messick and Jackson (1961a) have provided SDSVs, based on the ratings of college students, for each of the 566 items in the MMPI. Goldberg and Rorer (1963) give the values of $P(T)$ for each of the MMPI items, based on the responses of college students. The 2824 items described previously were sorted according to their SDSVs. Using the SDSV of each item in the MMPI, a corresponding item was selected from the 2824 items with approximately the same SDSV and P(T) as the MMPI item. The items were selected from the pool of 2824 items without regard to the content of the items. For example, the first three items in the MMPI are (1) I like mechanics magazines, (2) I have a good appetite, and (3) I wake up fresh and rested most mornings. The corresponding items in the Experimental Minnesota Multiphasic Personality Inventory (EMMPI) are (1) I value logic above personal feelings, (2) I am not resistant to new ideas, and (3) I will keep at a problem long after others have given it up as hopeless. The SDSVs and P(T)s of these paired items are given as follows:

	MMPI		EMMPI	
	SDSV	P(T)	SDSV	P(T)
1.	5.48	0.65	5.60	0.58
2.	6.78	0.96	6.78	0.96
3.	7.75	0.46	7.65	0.46

MMPI scales were developed by a variety of techniques. Some of the scales are rational scales and others are empirical scales. Presumably, each MMPI scale was developed to measure some trait of interest and, presumably, each scale has some degree of predictive, concurrent, or construct validity. If the scoring stencils for MMPI scales are applied to the items in the EMMPI, scores can also be obtained for EMMPI "scales." These EMMPI scales, however, cannot be said to possess any validity of any kind in any degree. The basis for this statement is that the EMMPI scales were never scored before and the items in the scales were not selected on the basis of content, or by means of internal consistency analysis, or in terms of the degree to which the items would differentiate between a control and an experimental group.

The EMMPI scales, however, do have some structural properties in common with the MMPI scales. First of all, for each MMPI scale there is a corresponding EMMPI scale scored by the same scoring stencil as the MMPI scale. The corresponding MMPI and EMMPI scales have the following properties in common:

(1) Each scale contains the same number of items.
(2) The location of the items in the EMMPI scale in a set of 566 items is the same as the location of the items in the MMPI scale in a set of 566 items.
(3) The corresponding items in the EMMPI scale and the MMPI scale have approximately the same SDSVs and also approximately the same P(T)s.
(4) The keying of the items in the EMMPI scale is exactly the same as the *trait* keying of the items in the MMPI scale.

Thus it follows that each MMPI scale and its EMMPI counterpart have the same proportion of items keyed for SD responses.

11.4   The Experimental Study

The MMPI was administered to a group of male college students. Approximately one week later the EMMPI was administered to the same students. Test records for both the MMPI and the EMMPI were obtained from 138 students. Using the scoring stencils for each of 57 MMPI scales, scores on the 57 MMPI scales were obtained for each student, based on his responses to the MMPI items. The same scoring stencils were then applied to the student's EMMPI answer sheet to obtain corresponding scores on the 57 EMMPI scales, based on his responses to the EMMPI items. Scores on the 114 scales were intercorrelated and factor-analyzed by the method of principal components. Two factors were extracted. The first principal component accounted for 37 percent of the total variance and the second factor for 10 percent of the total variance. These percentages are comparable to those obtained when only the MMPI scales are factor-analyzed. Of primary interest are the first factor loadings of the scales, since it is the first factor of the MMPI which has been interpreted as an SD factor.

The original SD scale, consisting of 39 items from the MMPI, will be referred to as SD_1. The corresponding 39-item SD scale as scored in the EMMPI will be referred to as SD_2. The correlations of the MMPI scales with scores on both SD_1 and SD_2 were obtained. The correlations between the MMPI scales and SD_2 cannot be attributed to item overlap because SD_2 contains no items in common with any of the MMPI scales. The correlations between the 57 EMMPI scales with SD_1 and SD_2 were also obtained. In this instance, the correlations between the EMMPI scales and SD_1 cannot be attributed to item overlap because SD_1 contains no items in common with any of the EMMPI scales.

11.5   Dependent and Independent Variables of Interest

The first factor loadings of each of the EMMPI and MMPI scales and the correlations of each of the scales with SD_1 and SD_2 represent dependent variables of interest. A common property of each of the corresponding EMMPI and MMPI scales is the proportion of items keyed for SD responses and this is an independent variable of interest. The data can be arranged in a matrix with 57 rows, corresponding to the 57 scales, and 7 columns, corresponding to the first factor loadings of MMPI scales, the first factor loadings of EMMPI scales, the correlations of the MMPI scales with SD_1 and with SD_2, the correlations of the EMMPI scales with SD_1 and SD_2, and the proportion of items in the scales keyed for socially desirable responses. Correlations were then obtained between each of the column variables.

All of the variables described above, with the exception of the proportion of items keyed for SD responses in the scales, are *signed variables*, that is, the first factor loading of both EMMPI and MMPI scales are in some cases positive and in other cases negative. This is true also of the correlations of the scales with SD_1 and SD_2. All of these dependent signed variables should be linearly related to one another and to the proportion of items keyed for SD responses. There are other variables of interest, however, which should be nonlinearly related to the signed first factor loadings and signed correlations of the scales with the two SD scales, but which should be linearly related to the absolute values of these variables. For example, if we obtain K-R 21 values for each of the scales and plot these values against (1) the signed first factor loadings, (2) the signed correlations of the scales with the two SD scales, or (3) the proportion of items keyed for SD responses, we should expect to find higher K-R 21 values for scales which have values at both extremes of these three variables than for scales which have values in between the two extremes. Scales with middle values are scales that have (1) low loadings on the first factor, (2) low correlations with the SD scales, and (3) a balance in their SD keying. Scales with any of these properties should have relatively lower K-R 21 values than scales which do not have these properties.

Similar considerations apply to the correlations between corresponding EMMPI and MMPI scales. All of these correlations are predicted to be positive in sign. But high values of the correlations should be associated with scales which have either a large or a small proportion of items keyed for SD responses and low values should be associated with scales which have a better balance in their SD-SUD keying. Thus, it follows that high correlations between the EMMPI and MMPI scales should also be associated with scales which have either high positive or high negative first factor loadings and which have either high positive or high negative correlations with the SD scale.

For the reasons cited above, intercorrelations were also obtained between the K-R 21 values of the MMPI and EMMPI scales, the absolute values of the first factor loadings of the EMMPI and MMPI scales, the absolute values of the correlations of the scales with the two SD scales, the product of the first factor loadings of corresponding EMMPI and MMPI scales, and the correlations between the corresponding EMMPI and MMPI scales.

Table 11.1 gives the intercorrelations between the signed first factor loadings of the EMMPI and MMPI scales, the signed correlations of the EMMPI and MMPI scales with the two SD scales, and the proportion of items keyed for SD responses in the scales. It is obvious that the first factor

Table 11.1   Intercorrelations between the First Factor Loadings of 57 MMPI Scales (I), the First Factor Loadings of 57 EMMPI Scales (I'), the Correlations of the MMPI and EMMPI Scales with Two SD Scales (SD_1 and SD_2), and the Proportion of Items Keyed for SD Responses in the Scales, $P(SD)$. Means and Standard Deviations Are Given in the Last Two Rows[a]

	MMPI I	EMMPI I'	MMPI SD_1	EMMPI SD_1	MMPI SD_2	EMMPI SD_2	$P(SD)$
MMPI I	—	0.98	0.99	0.97	0.99	0.93	0.90
EMMPI I'		—	0.98	0.99	0.97	0.94	0.90
MMPI SD_1			—	0.97	0.99	0.92	0.91
EMMPI SD_1				—	0.96	0.94	0.90
MMPI SD_2					—	0.92	0.93
EMMPI SD_2						—	0.87
$\bar{X}$	−0.12	−0.13	−0.13	−0.11	−0.11	−0.12	0.39
σ	0.63	0.58	0.58	0.44	0.50	0.54	0.33

[a]From Edwards (1966b).

loadings of the MMPI scales could be predicted quite accurately ($r = 0.98$) from the factor loadings of the EMMPI scales.[2] It is also clear that the correlations of the EMMPI scales with SD_1 are proportional to the corresponding correlations of MMPI scales with SD_1, despite the fact that SD_1 contains no items in common with any of the EMMPI scales. Similarly, the correlations of the MMPI scales with SD_2 are proportional to the corresponding correlations of EMMPI scales with SD_2, despite the fact that SD_2 contains no items in common with any of the MMPI scales. Of interest also is the fact that the SD_1 correlations with the EMMPI scales are proportional to the SD_2 correlations with the MMPI scales.

The last column of Table 11.1 gives the correlations between the proportion of items keyed for SD responses in the EMMPI and MMPI scales and the other dependent variables. No matter whether we look at the first factor loadings of the MMPI and EMMPI scales or the correlations of the MMPI and EMMPI scales with either of the two SD scales, the proportion of items keyed for SD responses in the scales is a fairly accurate predictor of the factor loadings and of the correlations of the scales with the SD scales.

The most parsimonious explanation of the correlations given in Table 11.1 would appear to be in terms of the fact that corresponding MMPI and EMMPI scales have exactly the same proportion of items keyed for

[2]The second factor loadings of the MMPI scales correlated 0.67 with the second factor loadings of the EMMPI scales.

SD responses. When this proportion is large in an MMPI scale and, consequently, in an EMMPI scale, then high scorers on the SD scales also tend to obtain high scores on the EMMPI and MMPI scales and, as a result, the correlations of *both* the EMMPI and MMPI scales tend to be positively correlated with the SD scales. When the proportion of items keyed for SD responses in an MMPI scale is small, then high scorers on the SD scales tend to obtain low scores on both the MMPI and EMMPI scales and the correlations of the MMPI and EMMPI scales with the SD scale *both* tend to be negative. The correlations given in Table 11.1 can thus be accounted for in terms of a common trait, the tendency to give SD responses in self-description, and by the fact that some MMPI and corresponding EMMPI scales are better measures of this trait than other MMPI and corresponding EMMPI scales by virtue of the imbalance in the SD keying of the items in the scales.

11.6   Correlations between the Paired EMMPI and MMPI Scales

Table 11.2 shows the frequency distribution of the correlation coefficients between the paired MMPI and EMMPI scales. Test-retest reliability coefficients were available for each of the 57 MMPI scales based upon the responses of another sample of 95 male college students.[3] Test-retest

Table 11.2   Frequency Distribution of the Correlation Coefficients between 57 Paired MMPI and EMMPI Scales (*f*) and the Correlations Corrected for Attenuation (*f'*)[a]

Correlations	*f*	*f'*
0.90–0.99		2
0.80–0.89		4
0.70–0.79	5	9
0.60–0.69	6	11
0.50–0.59	13	6
0.40–0.49	8	8
0.30–0.39	11	8
0.20–0.29	7	5
0.10–0.19	7	4

[a]From Edwards (1966b).

[3]I am indebted to Lewis R. Goldberg and Leonard G. Rorer of the Oregon Research Institute for calculating and making available to me the test-retest coefficients of the MMPI scales.

reliability coefficients were not available for the 57 EMMPI scales. However, assuming that the coefficients for the MMPI scales represent upperbounds for the corresponding EMMPI scales, the correlations between the paired MMPI and EMMPI scales were corrected for attenuation using the reliability coefficients for the MMPI scales. The frequency distribution of the corrected correlations is given in the last column of Table 11.2.

We are interested in accounting for the variation in the magnitude of the correlation coefficients between paired MMPI and EMMPI scales. That is, we would like to understand why some pairs of MMPI and EMMPI scales have relatively high correlations and other pairs have relatively low correlations. Table 11.3 shows the degree to which the correlations between the paired MMPI and EMMPI scales are related to the K-R 21 values of the MMPI and EMMPI scales, the absolute values of the first factor loadings of the MMPI and EMMPI scales, the absolute values of the correlations of the MMPI and EMMPI scales with the *SD* scales, and the product of the signed first factor loadings of the paired MMPI and EMMPI scales. Table 11.3 also gives the intercorrelations of these variables.

It has already been shown in Table 11.1 that the first factor loadings of MMPI and EMMPI scales are highly correlated. Thus, when an MMPI scale has a high positive loading on the first factor, so also does the corresponding EMMPI scale and the product of the factor loadings is also high and positive. Similarly, when an MMPI scale has a high negative loading on the first factor, so also does the corresponding EMMPI scale and the product of their first factor loadings is also high and positive. Table 11.3 shows that the products of the first factor loadings of corresponding MMPI and EMMPI scales correlate 0.85 with the observed correlations between the corresponding MMPI and EMMPI scales. The table also shows that the higher the absolute value of the correlation of an MMPI scale with the *SD* scales, the higher the correlation of the MMPI scale with the corresponding EMMPI scale. In other words, when an MMPI scale has either a high positive or a high negative correlation with the *SD* scales it, in turn, tends to have a relatively high positive correlation with its EMMPI counterpart.

It has also been shown that the first factor loadings of both MMPI and EMMPI scales are related to the proportion of items keyed for SD responses in the scales. MMPI scales which have high positive correlations with the *SD* scales are those which also have a large proportion of items keyed for SD responses. MMPI scales which have high negative correlations with the *SD* scales are those which also have a large proportion of items keyed for SUD responses. Thus, the magnitude of the correlation between paired EMMPI and MMPI scales is related to the imbalance in the SD-SUD keying of the scales. MMPI scales which have either a large proportion of items keyed for SD responses or a large proportion of items keyed for SUD responses tend to have higher correlations with their EMMPI counter-

Table 11.3 Intercorrelations of the K-R 21 Values of 57 MMPI and 57 EMMPI Scales, the Absolute Values of the First Factor Loadings of the Scales, the Absolute Values of the Correlations of the Scales with Two SD Scales, the Product of the Signed First Factor Loadings of the Scales, and the Correlations between Corresponding MMPI and EMMPI Scales[a]

	MMPI K-R 21	EMMPI K-R 21	MMPI I	EMMPI I'	MMPI SD_1	EMMPI SD_1	MMPI SD_2	EMMPI SD_2	$I \times I'$	$r_{\text{EMMPI-MMPI}}$
MMPI K-R 21	—	0.78	0.66	0.72	0.65	0.71	0.62	0.70	0.75	0.73
EMMPI K-R 21		—	0.71	0.74	0.75	0.74	0.70	0.72	0.80	0.82
MMPI I			—	0.87	0.96	0.82	0.95	0.83	0.94	0.75
EMMPI I'				—	0.84	0.98	0.82	0.95	0.95	0.79
MMPI SD_1					—	0.82	0.95	0.84	0.91	0.71
EMMPI SD_1						—	0.78	0.82	0.92	0.75
MMPI SD_2							—	0.84	0.90	0.74
EMMPI SD_2								—	0.91	0.74
$I \times I'$									—	0.85

[a]From Edwards (1966b).

parts than MMPI scales which have a better balance in their SD-SUD keying.

Reasons have been presented previously to show why, if the tendency to give SD responses is operating, a higher degree of internal consistency is obtained for personality scales in which the trait-keyed responses are also consistently SD or consistently SUD responses than for scales which are more balanced in their SD-SUD keying. The results reported in Table 11.3 are in accord with this prediction, both with respect to the MMPI and EMMPI scales. Both MMPI and EMMPI scales, which have high absolute correlations with either of the two *SD* scales, tend to have a higher degree of internal consistency, as measured by the K-R 21 values of the scales, than scales which have low correlations with the *SD* scales. Since the important characteristic of corresponding MMPI and EMMPI scales which have high absolute correlations with the *SD* scales is that they have either a large proportion of items keyed for SD responses or a large proportion of items keyed for SUD responses, it follows that the internal consistency of the scales is related to the imbalance in the SD-SUD keying of the items in the scales. It may also be noted that the K-R 21 values of the EMMPI scales are related to the K-R 21 values of the corresponding MMPI scales, the correlation between the paired K-R 21 values being 0.78, and that, in general, the higher the K-R 21 value of an MMPI scale, the higher its correlation with the corresponding EMMPI scale.

11.7　Summary

The relationships found in this study between the correlations of EMMPI scales with the *SD* scale, the first factor loadings of the MMPI scales, the K-R 21 values of the MMPI scales, and the proportion of items keyed for SD responses in the MMPI scales, are in accord with the results of studies reported previously. Of greater significance, however, is the fact that essentially the same relationships between these variables are obtained when the scales involved are the EMMPI scales consisting of non-MMPI items. In view of the fact that each of the items in the EMMPI was selected solely on the basis of the SDSV and *P*(T) of a corresponding item in the MMPI, it does not seem reasonable to believe that the items in each of the 57 EMMPI scales are similar in content to the content of the items in each of the corresponding 57 MMPI scales. If corresponding EMMPI and MMPI scales do not have a common content, they do have in common the same intensity of SD or SUD keying and the same proportion of items keyed for SD responses. The latter variable has been shown to be a quite accurate predictor of the relationship between the correlations of MMPI and EMMPI scales with the *SD* scales and the first factor loadings of the MMPI and EMMPI scales.

Chapter 12

Revised and New
MMPI Scales

12.1 Introduction

There have been various attempts either to modify the standard clinical scales of the MMPI or to develop shorter versions of the clinical scales. In addition, there have been attempts to develop scales which would measure the first two principal-component factors of the MMPI. There have also been at least two major attempts to regroup the items in the MMPI into a set of new scales. In this chapter we consider some of these attempts to revise and to develop new MMPI scales.

12.2 Revised Depression Scale

The Depression (D) scale of the MMPI is one of the standard clinical scales. An examination of the 60 items in the D scale shows that 14 are keyed for SD responses and 46 are keyed for SUD responses. The D scale typically correlates about -0.59 with the SD scale, has a loading of approximately -0.57 on the first principal component when MMPI scales are factor-analyzed, and a K-R 21 value of approximately 0.50 when scores are based on the responses of male students.

Dempsey (1964) proposed a revision of the D scale designed to improve its internal consistency. In developing his revision, he used the major dimension underlying responses to the 60 items in the D scale to select those items which related in the same direction to the major dimension in a number of different samples. A total of 30 items met his criterion and the resulting D_{30} scale he described as a "unidimensional" depression scale.

Because 46 of the 60 items are keyed for SUD responses in the D scale, it seems reasonable to believe that the major dimension is represented by items for which the trait response is an SUD response. If this is the case, then trait responses to the 14 items keyed for SD responses should not, in general, be in the same direction as the trait response to the major dimension represented by the 46 items keyed for SUD responses.

An examination of the SDSVs of the items in the D_{30} scale shows that all 14 of the items originally keyed for SD responses have been eliminated. Thus, in contrast to the original D scale, all of the trait responses to the items in the D_{30} scale are SUD responses. The trait keying of the items in the D_{30} scale and the SD keying are, in other words, completely confounded.

Because the items in the D_{30} scale are consistently keyed for SUD responses we would expect, for reasons discussed previously, that scores on the D_{30} scale should have a higher negative correlation with scores on the SD scale than the original D scale and also that the K-R 21 value of the D_{30} scale should be higher than that for the D scale. These predictions were tested by Edwards (1965b) with three different samples, and the results are shown in Table 12.1.

Table 12.1 Means, Standard Deviations, K-R 21 Values, and Correlations of the Depression (D) and Revised Depression (D_{30}) Scales with the SD Scale[a]

	Scale	$\overline{X}$	σ	K-R 21	r_{SD}
Sample 1:	D	19.55	5.01	0.48	−0.57
$N = 155$ males	D_{30}	7.33	4.59	0.76	−0.80
Sample 2:	D	20.15	5.19	0.51	−0.63
$N = 150$ males	D_{30}	7.57	4.94	0.79	−0.82
Sample 3:	D	20.70	4.41	0.31	−0.63
$N = 163$ females	D_{30}	7.33	4.49	0.73	−0.83

[a]From Edwards (1965b).

In all three samples, the D_{30} scale has a higher negative correlation with the SD scale than the D scale and in all three samples the K-R 21 value of the D_{30} scale is higher than the K-R 21 value of the D scale. The D_{30} scale thus is more internally consistent than the D scale, but this increase in internal consistency is accompanied by a higher negative correlation of the D_{30}

scale with the *SD* scale than was true of the original *D* scale. This result suggests that if the D_{30} scale replaced the *D* scale in a factor analysis of MMPI scales, the D_{30} scale would have a relatively high loading on the first principal component.

12.3   Subtle and Obvious Scales

Weiner (1948) sorted MMPI items into two sets, those to which a response indicating an emotional disturbance was relatively easy to judge and those to which a response indicating an emotional disturbance was more difficult to judge. The first group of items he refers to as "obvious" items and the second as "subtle." For five of the clinical scales of the MMPI a sufficient number of both subtle and obvious items were obtained to make possible the splitting of the scale into two part scales, one consisting of subtle items and the other of obvious items. The five scales were *D*, *Hy*, *Pd*, *Pa*, and *Ma*.

12.4   Correlations between Subtle and Obvious Scores on a Scale

Table 12.2 shows the number of items in each of the subtle and obvious scales and the correlations between the subtle and obvious scores for each scale, as given by Weiner (1948). The correlations between the subtle and obvious scores on each scale, as reported by Gocka, Holloway, and Bigger (1962), for another independent sample are also given in Table 12.2. Ordinarily, if all items in a scale could be considered to be measuring a

Table 12.2   Correlations between the Subtle and Obvious Scores on Five MMPI Scales Based on Two Independent Samples

	No. of Items		Correlations	
	Subtle	Obvious	$r_{SO}{}^a$	$r_{SO}{}^b$
D	20	40	−0.20	−0.22
Hy	28	32	−0.46	−0.41
Ma	23	23	0.24	0.17
Pa	17	23	0.10	−0.18
Pd	22	28	0.04	−0.12

[a]From Weiner (1948).
[b]From Gocka, Holloway, and Bigger (1962).

common trait, one would expect that if the items in the scale were divided into two sets and scores on the two sets were correlated, the resulting correlation would be positive and relatively high. Clearly, this is not the case with the subtle and obvious scales. Whatever is being measured by the subtle items in one of these scales is not highly related to what is being measured by the obvious items in the same scale.

12.5   Intercorrelations of the Obvious Scales

The intercorrelations between the obvious scales are shown in Table 12.3. The entries above the diagonal are the correlations reported by Weiner (1948) and the entries below the diagonal are those reported by Gocka,

Table 12.3   Intercorrelations of the Five Obvious Scales for Two Independent Samples. Correlations above the Diagonal Are from Weiner (1948) and Those below the Diagonal Are from Gocka, Holloway, and Bigger (1962)

	D-O	Hy-O	Ma-O	Pa-O	Pd-O
D-O	—	0.78	0.51	0.61	0.68
Hy-O	0.87	—	0.45	0.58	0.61
Ma-O	0.54	0.59	—	0.56	0.61
Pa-O	0.58	0.57	0.69	—	0.64
Pd-O	0.74	0.67	0.65	0.73	—

Holloway, and Bigger (1962). Despite the fact that these obvious scales represent selections of items from scales designed to measure different traits, it seems evident that they have more in common with each other than they have with their corresponding sets of subtle items supposedly relevant to each of the five traits.

12.6   Nature of Subtle and Obvious Items

Hanley (1956) has suggested that a subtle item might be one with a relatively neutral SDSV. Such items might be those for which it would be relatively difficult to judge which response is indicative of an emotional disturbance. In addition, Edwards (1957a) has suggested that a subtle item in an MMPI clinical scale might be one for which the trait response is an SD response. For example, in the clinical scales of the MMPI a high score would generally be considered as indicating a high degree of a trait that is itself regarded as socially undesirable. To obtain a high score on a scale of this kind an individual must, in general, have a relatively low rate of SD responding. If subtle items are present in the clinical scales, these statements may be of such a nature that an SD response is itself scored as indicating the presence of an undesirable trait. Thus, a subtle item in the *D* scale might be either an item with a relatively neutral SDSV or it might be one to which the SD response is scored as indicating an undesirable trait.

If an item is judged as obvious, then it seems reasonable to believe that it would have an SDSV that deviates from the neutral point on the social desirability continuum or falls outside the neutral interval. Because the traits measured by the five MMPI scales would themselves be judged as socially undesirable, the keying of the obvious items should also be, in general, equivalent to the SUD keying of the items. If this hypothesis is true, then most of the items in the obvious scales should be keyed for SUD responses and scores on these scales should be negatively correlated with individual differences in rates of SD responding as measured by an *SD* scale.

We have previously shown that as the proportion of neutral items in an MMPI scale increases, the correlation of the scale with individual differences in rates of SD responding decreases. Thus, if subtle items are relatively neutral items, then subtle scales should have relatively low correlations with the *SD* scale. On the other hand, if subtle items also consist of those items which are keyed for SD responses, then to the degree to which a scale contains subtle items of this kind, scores on the scale should correlate positively with scores on the *SD* scale.[1]

12.7   Correlations of Subtle and Obvious Scales with the *SD* Scale

Table 12.4 gives the correlations between the total scores, the obvious scores, and the subtle scores on the five MMPI scales with scores on the 39-item MMPI *SD* scale. We note that in all cases, the scores on obvious scales have higher negative correlations with scores on the *SD* scale than

[1]Rosen (1956) gave the MMPI under standard instructions and also under instructions to give SD responses. For the five obvious and the five subtle scales he reports *t* tests of the significance of the difference between the means under the two sets of instructions. The *t* tests were made separately for males and females. In all ten of the *t* tests for the difference between the means on the obvious scales, a significantly *lower* mean was obtained under instructions to give SD responses. For the ten *t* tests involving the means on the subtle scales, seven of the means were significantly *higher* under SD instructions. These results are in accord with the above discussion regarding the nature of the items in the obvious and subtle scales.

Table 12.4   Correlations of Total, Obvious, and Subtle
Scales with the SD Scale[a]

| | Correlations with SD Scale | | |
Scales	Total	Obvious	Subtle
D	−0.69	−0.78	0.33
Hy	−0.28	−0.71	0.54
Ma	−0.08	−0.53	0.40
Pa	−0.52	−0.72	0.06
Pd	−0.67	−0.85	0.27

[a]From an unpublished study by Fordyce and Rozynko
(1957) and cited in Edwards (1957a).

do the scores on the total scales. If the SDSVs of the items in each of the
obvious scales are examined in relation to the keying of the items in the
scale, it is found that almost without exception the trait-keyed responses to
the obvious items are also SUD responses.

Ma-O has the smallest negative correlation with the *SD* scale. Of the 23
items in the *Ma-O* scale, two are keyed for SD responses and 21 for SUD
responses, but seven of the items in this scale also have SDSVs falling in
the neutral interval. None of the other obvious scales has more than two
items with SDSVs in the neutral interval.

We note also that the five subtle scales all have positive correlations
with the *SD* scale, although one of the correlations, that for *Pa-S*, is only
0.06. An examination of the items in the *Pa-S* scale shows that ten of the
items are keyed for SD responses and seven for SUD responses. Thus, this
scale has a fair degree of balance in its SD-SUD keying. Furthermore,
five of the items in *Pa-S* have SDSVs falling within the neutral interval,
4.5 to 5.5, on the social desirability continuum. *Pd-S*, which has a correlation
of 0.27 with the *SD* scale, has seven items keyed for SD responses and
five keyed for SUD responses. Of the items in *Pd-S*, eight have SDSVs
falling in the neutral interval. Finally, *D-S*, which correlates 0.33 with the
SD scale, has 12 items keyed for SD responses and eight keyed for SUD
responses. Of the 20 items in the *D-S* scale, four have SDSVs falling within
the neutral interval.

The relatively low correlations of *Pa-S*, *Pd-S*, and *D-S* with the *SD*
scale can be accounted for by the fact that these scales have some degree
of balance in their SD and SUD keying and also by the fact that they tend
to have a fair number of items with neutral SDSVs.

12.8   Intercorrelations of the Subtle Scales

Table 12.5 shows the intercorrelations of the subtle scales. The values above the diagonal are those reported by Weiner (1948) and those below the diagonal are those reported by Gocka, Holloway, and Bigger (1962).

Table 12.5   Intercorrelations of the Five Subtle Scales for Two Independent Samples. Correlations above the Diagonal Are from Weiner (1948) and Those below the Diagonal Are from Gocka, Holloway, and Bigger (1962)

	D-S	Hy-S	Ma-S	Pa-S	Pd-S
D-S	—	0.51	−0.17	0.45	0.19
Hy-S	0.59	—	−0.06	0.59	0.36
Ma-S	−0.34	−0.04	—	−0.17	0.22
Pa-S	0.29	0.44	−0.19	—	0.14
Pd-S	0.35	0.50	0.13	0.20	—

The intercorrelations of the subtle scales are, in general, considerably lower than the intercorrelations of the obvious scales. This is not unexpected in terms of the discussion above regarding the nature of the items in subtle scales.

12.9   K-R 21 Values of the Total, Obvious, and Subtle Scales

In view of the correlation coefficients obtained between obvious scores and subtle scores on the *D*, *Hy*, *Pd*, *Pa*, and *Ma* scales, it is to be expected that the K-R 21 lower-bound estimates of internal consistency of total scores on these scales would not be very high. Based on a sample of 150 male students, the K-R 21 values of the five scales were found to be 0.48, 0.30, 0.57, 0.03, and 0.38, respectively.

Because the obvious scales are based on items keyed primarily for SUD responses, the K-R 21 values for these scales should be higher than those obtained for the total scores. When the subtle items are removed and scores are based only on the obvious items, the corresponding K-R 21 values of *D-O*, *Hy-O*, *Pd-O*, *Pa-O*, and *Ma-O* for the same sample are 0.91, 0.88, 0.69, 0.53, and 0.47, respectively. In every case, the K-R 21 values are higher for the obvious scales which have fewer items than for the longer total scales and, in some cases, strikingly so.

Because of the nature of the items and the keying of the items in the subtle scales, the K-R 21 values for these scales should not be as high as those obtained for the obvious scales. For the subtle scales, *D-S*, *Hy-S*, *Pd-S*, *Pa-S*, and *Ma-S*, the K-R 21 values are 0.23, 0.59, 0.33, 0.21, and 0.16, respectively.

12.10   Welsh's *A* and *R* Scales

Welsh (1956) constructed two scales, *A* and *R*, which are marker scales for the first and second principal components when MMPI scales are factor-analyzed. All but one of the items in the *A* scale are keyed for SUD responses, and this scale typically has a high loading opposite in sign to that of the *SD* scale on the first principal component. The *R* scale has a fair degree of balance in its SD-SUD keying and usually has its highest loading on the second principal component.

Because almost all of the items in the *A* scale are keyed for SUD responses, the trait keying is confounded with the SUD keying. Similarly, because all of the items in the *R* scale are keyed for False responses, scores on this scale have also been interpreted as possibly measuring acquiescent tendencies. There is considerable evidence, cited previously, that the second principal-component factor of the MMPI can be interpreted as measuring individual differences in rates of True responding to personality items.

12.11   Block's First Factor Scale: *ER-S*

Block (1965) has also developed two scales specifically designed to measure the first and second principal components of the MMPI scales. The first factor scale, which he calls an Ego-Resiliency Scale (*ER-S*), was developed by selecting individuals with high and low scores on the first MMPI factor and comparing their responses on MMPI items. Items which differentiated between the two groups were selected for the *ER-S*.

If Block had selected either those items which provided the *best* differentiation between his high- and low-scoring groups or *all* items which differentiated at some defined significance level, he would have obtained a scale in which the items were predominantly keyed for SD responses. Instead, Block attempted to develop the *ER-S* in such a way that scores on the scale could not be interpreted in terms of SD or acquiescent tendencies. He believed that this could be accomplished if the items in the *ER-S* were relatively neutral in their SDSVs and if, at the same time, half of the items were keyed for SD and half for SUD responses, and half were keyed for True and half for False responses. It is only reasonable to believe that in attempting to obtain a balance in the SD-SUD and True-False keying of the items in the *ER-S*, Block was forced to reject MMPI items which are, in fact, better measures of the first factor than some of the items he selected for inclusion in the *ER-S*. We shall see later some of the consequences of this item selection procedure.

Although the *ER-S*, as thus developed, was believed by Block to be a scale which would have a high loading on the first MMPI factor, it is curious that Block (1965) does not report a single factor analysis of MMPI scales in which the *ER-S* was included. There are many other factor analyses of MMPI scales reported in his book, but not one of these includes the *ER-S*.

Block's argument that the *ER-S* should have a high loading on the first principal component is based primarily on the correlations of the *ER-S* with the *SD* scale. These correlations, as reported by Block, for the four samples *not* used in selecting the items included in the *ER-S* are 0.64, 0.67, 0.66, and 0.59. Although these correlations are of a magnitude such as to indicate that the *ER-S* has approximately 36 to 45 percent of its variance in common with the *SD* scale there are, as we have previously shown, over 100 MMPI scales that have absolute correlations of 0.70 or higher with the *SD* scale. Any one of these MMPI scales is presumably a better measure of whatever it is that the *SD* scale and the first principal component measure than the *ER-S*. Only a few of these scales were intentionally designed to measure the first factor of the MMPI. One of these was the *A* scale but, as we have pointed out, the *A* scale has almost all of its items keyed for SUD responses.

Consider another aspect of the *ER-S*. For the four samples not used in selecting the items in the *ER-S*, the K-R 20 values of the scale are 0.67, 0.56, 0.67, and 0.61.[2] In an earlier chapter we gave a formula that can be used to determine the average intercorrelation of the items in a scale for a given value of r_{kk} and the number of items in the scale. For the $k = 40$ items in the *ER-S*, the average item intercorrelation, based on the four r_{kk} values, is somewhere between 0.03 and 0.05.

Presumably, if the items in a scale have been selected to measure a single common trait, one would expect the r_{kk} value of the scale to be higher than the values reported by Block for the *ER-S*. Given the fact that Block found 355 of the MMPI items to differentiate between high and low scorers on the first factor at the 0.05 level of significance, it would have been possible to construct a 40-item scale with a considerably higher r_{kk} value than that found for the *ER-S*. It is a reasonable hypothesis that in his attempt to obtain a balance in the SD-SUD keying of the items in the

[2]The corresponding K-R 20 values of the *SD* scale for these same four samples, as reported by Block (1965, p. 93), are 0.89, 0.79, 0.76, and 0.81, respectively.

ER-S, Block was willing to accept items that contributed relatively little to the internal consistency of the scale.

Consider still another property of the *ER-S*. Scores on the False keyed items in the *ER-S* are reported by Block (1965, p. 94) to correlate 0.50, 0.59, 0.56, and 0.38 with scores on the *SD* scale. These values may be compared with the correlations of total scores on the *ER-S* with the *SD* scale of 0.64, 0.67, 0.66, and 0.59, for the same four samples. Assuming that the average correlation of total scores on the *ER-S* with the *SD* scale is approximately 0.65, this means that approximately $(0.65)^2 = 0.42$ of the variance in the scores on the *SD* scale can be accounted for by total scores on the *ER-S*. Again, assuming that the average correlation of scores on the False keyed items in the *ER-S* with the *SD* scale is approximately 0.55, this means that the False scores alone account for approximately $(0.55)^2 = 0.30$ of the variance in the SD scores.

In another sample, Edwards (1968) found that total scores on the *ER-S* correlated 0.65 with scores on the *SD* scale.[3] The False scores correlated 0.58 with scores on the *SD* scale and the True scores correlated 0.42 with scores on the *SD* scale. When scores on the False keyed items of the *ER-S* were correlated with scores on the True keyed items, the resulting correlation coefficient was 0.21. For two 20-item scales, both purportedly measuring the same trait, a correlation of only 0.21 is rather unusual. For example, the True and False keyed scores on the *ER-S* have only approximately $(0.21)^2 = 0.04$ of their variance in common. Obviously, whatever it is that scores on the True keyed items of the *ER-S* are measuring, this trait has relatively little in common with that measured by scores on the False keyed items.[4]

For the scores on the False items the standard deviation was 3.17 and the standard deviation of scores on the True keyed items was 2.58. Given these two standard deviations and the correlation of 0.21 between scores on the False and True keyed scales, it is possible to calculate the average of the covariances of the True keyed items with the False keyed items. The average value of the 400 item covariances is only 0.0043. This finding strongly suggests that either many of the True-False item covariances are negative or that a very large number are close to zero, or that both of these conditions are present.

On the basis of the results cited above, it is a reasonable hypothesis that, as a consequence of his attempt to obtain a balance in the True-False and SD-SUD keying of the items in the *ER-S*, Block was forced to select items that are possibly better measures of factors other than the first

---

[3]From an unpublished study by Edwards (1968).
[4]For a further discussion of the nature of the True keyed items in the *ER-S*, see Jackson (1967a).

MMPI principal component. In other words, if the *ER-S* is included in a factor analysis with various other scales, we may expect to find that the *ER-S* has loadings on factors other than the first principal component. As we shall show later this is, in fact, the case.

12.12 Block's Second Factor Scale: *EC-5*

The second factor scale developed by Block was designated as *EC-5*. The *R* scale of the MMPI, which typically has a relatively high loading on the second factor, has been interpreted as possibly measuring the tendency to acquiescence or dissent because all of the items in the *R* scale are keyed False. The *EC-5* scale attempted to rule out an acquiescence interpretation by having an equal number of items keyed True and False. The *EC-5* scale consists of 32 items and the correlations of the *EC-5* scale with the *R* scale, as reported by Block (1965), for the four samples *not* used in developing the scale are 0.47, 0.12, 0.65, and 0.40. These correlations with the *R* scale cannot be considered as impressive and as indicating that the *EC-5* scale is measuring the same trait as the *R* scale.

12.13 Rosen's Scales

Rosen (1962) used five different groups of patients to develop five MMPI scales designed to differentiate between each of the patient groups and patients in general. These five scales were called Conversion Reaction (*Cr*), Paranoid Schizophrenia (*Pz*), Depressive Reaction (*Dr*), Anxiety Reaction (*Ar*), and Somatization Reaction (*Sm*). Although Rosen does not report the correlations of these scales with the *SD* scale, he does give the correlations of the scales with the *Pt* scale, which correlates about −0.84 with the *SD* scale. The correlations of *Cr*, *Pz*, *Dr*, *Ar*, and *Sm* with the *Pt* scale are −0.91, 0.65, −0.41, 0.45, and −0.72, respectively.

12.14 Some Other Factor Scales

Comrey (1957a, 1957b, 1957c, 1958a, 1958b, 1958c, 1958d, 1958e, 1958f) and Comrey and Marggraff (1958) have factor-analyzed the items in various MMPI scales. If the results of these item factor analyses of the MMPI scales were used to select those items in each scale which had relatively high loadings on the first factor, these revised MMPI scales should, in general, have higher negative or positive correlations with the *SD* scale than the original versions.[5]

A case in point is Dempsey's revision of the Depression scale, discussed earlier in the chapter. Dempsey, it will be recalled, succeeded in improving the unidimensionality of the Depression scale by eliminating those items which did not relate to the major dimension in his analysis. The resulting D_{30} scale was shown to have a higher negative correlation with the *SD* scale than the original *D* scale.

12.15   Tryon's Scales

More ambitious attempts to revise the MMPI have been undertaken by Tryon, Stein, and Chu (Stein, 1968) and Wiggins (1966). Tryon's objective was to group the MMPI items into clusters, such that the items within each cluster correlated positively with each other. Those MMPI items which shared no substantial common variance with other items were eliminated. As a result of various analyses, Tryon obtained seven clusters or scales involving 192 of the original MMPI items. The seven scales are described as: Introversion (*I*), Body Symptoms (*B*), Suspicion and Mistrust (*S*), Depression (*D*), Resentment (*R*), Autism (*A*), and Tension (*T*). Each of these seven scales has a relatively high internal consistency coefficient, but the method of clustering the MMPI items used by Tryon does not ensure that scores on the seven scales will be independent. The seven scales do not, in other words, represent seven orthogonal factors.

To determine whether Tryon's seven cluster scales represent the same two first principal components as those obtained when the standard MMPI scales are factor-analyzed, scores on the cluster scales along with scores on the *SD*, *R*, and *L* scales were intercorrelated and factor-analyzed by the method of principal components.[6] As has been shown previously, the *SD* scale typically has a high loading on the first MMPI principal component and the *R* scale has a high loading on the second component.

---

[5]Comrey used the complete centroid method of factoring and employed a Varimax rotation. An examination of the items which Comrey reports as having large loadings on the first factor in his analyses shows that in each case the items are consistently keyed for SUD responses. There are only two exceptions: MMPI Items 302 and 323 in *Pt* and *Sc*, respectively, are keyed for SD responses. The SDSVs of these two items are 7.04 and 5.10, respectively.

[6]The study described is based on a sample of 150 male students and is from an unpublished paper by Edwards (1968). Two published replications, one involving a sample of 468 male students (Edwards, Klockars, and Abbott, 1970) and the other a sample of 310 male adults (Edwards, Abbott, and Klockars, 1970) report results that are comparable to those shown in Table 12.6.

The unrotated loadings of the ten scales on the first three principal-component factors are given in Table 12.6. The first principal component accounts for 48 percent of the total variance, the second for 13 percent of

Table 12.6   Factor Loadings of Tryon's Seven Cluster Scales and Three Marker Scales: *SD*, *L*, and *R*[a]

		Factors		
Scales	I	II	III	h^2
I	0.52	0.46	−0.56	0.81
B	0.64	0.31	0.27	0.57
S	0.72	−0.21	0.23	0.62
D	0.84	0.20	−0.06	0.75
R[b]	0.75	−0.24	−0.12	0.64
A	0.76	−0.13	0.20	0.64
T	0.80	0.12	0.21	0.71
SD	−0.90	−0.21	0.01	0.85
L	−0.45	0.48	0.51	0.69
R[c]	−0.33	0.76	−0.05	0.69

[a] From an unpublished study by Edwards (1968).
[b] Tryon's *R* scale.
[c] The MMPI *R* scale.

the total variance, and the third for 8 percent of the total variance. It may be noted that the *SD* scale has its usual high loading on the first principal component and that the *R* scale has a relatively high loading on the second principal component. Five of Tryon's seven cluster scales have loadings of 0.72 or higher on the first principal component.

12.16   Wiggins' Scales

Another attempt to regroup the items in the MMPI was made by Wiggins (1966). Wiggins started his research with the original 26 content categories of the MMPI items as given by Hathaway and McKinley (1951). For example, there are nine items in the MMPI that were classified by Hathaway and McKinley as dealing with general health, eleven items that were classified as relating to the cranial nerves, eleven items that were classified as relating to the gastrointestinal system, and so on. Wiggins obtained scores for each of the 26 content categories. These scores were then inter-correlated and factor-analyzed. Using the results of this analysis, the content categories were revised by combining several categories into one, reassigning items from one category to another, eliminating some of the original categories, and re-keying some of the items within categories. Further analyses were then done with the revised content scales and finally 13 content scales were developed. These scales are described as: Social Maladjustment (*SOC*), Depression (*DEP*), Feminine Interests (*FEM*), Poor Morale (*MOR*), Religious Fundamentalism (*REL*), Authority Conflict (*AUT*), Psychoticism (*PSY*), Organic Symptoms (*ORG*), Family Problems (*FAM*), Manifest Hostility (*HOS*), Phobias (*PHO*), Hypomania (*HYP*), and Poor Health (*HEA*).

12.17 Factor Loadings of Block's *ER-S*

Wiggins reports two factor analyses, one for males and one for females, involving his 13 scales and six marker scales. The *SD* scale, unfortunately, was not included as a marker for the first factor, but the *A* scale, which typically has a high loading of the opposite sign on a common factor with the *SD* scale, was included. Because Wiggins believed that the *ER-S* would provide a measure of the first principal component that could not be interpreted as measuring individual differences in rates of SD responding, the *ER-S*, fortunately, was included as a marker variable for the first factor. Five principal-component factors were extracted in each analysis and the factor loadings were rotated by means of an orthogonal Varimax rotation.

For the female analysis, the *A* scale had a loading of 0.80 on the first rotated principal component. In the male analysis the loading was 0.85. Of interest are the factor loadings of the *ER-S* on the same factor on which the *A* scale has its highest loading. The loading of *ER-S* on the first rotated factor was −0.57 in the female analysis and −0.69 in the male analysis.

For the female sample, the *ER-S* had a loading of −0.42 on a factor marked by the *R* scale with a loading of −0.83, and a loading of −0.37 on a factor marked by Wiggins' *ORG* scale with a loading of 0.82. For the male sample, the *ER-S* also had a loading of −0.34 on a factor in common with Wiggins' *ORG* scale.[7]

In Chapter 8 we reported the results of a principal-component factor analysis by Edwards and Walsh (1964b) of 31 scales. In this analysis, the *ER-S* was included along with seven other scales specifically designed to measure the tendency to give SD responses. Six factors were extracted which accounted for approximately 73 percent of the total variance. The six factors were rotated orthogonally using a normal Varimax rotation. The

[7]Wiggins does not report factor loadings with absolute values less than 0.33.

normalized factor loadings of the scales on the six factors are given in Table 8.2. Below we reproduce the *normalized* loadings of the *ER-S* on the six factors:

	I′	II′	III′	IV′	V′	VI′	h^2
ER-S	−0.45	−0.24	−0.52	0.07	−0.23	−0.64	0.72

If you will refer back to Table 8.2 you will find that the first rotated factor is marked by the various *SD* scales, the second rotated factor by various scales designed to measure acquiescent tendencies, the third rotated factor by the MMPI *Lie* scale and the Marlowe-Crowne scale which was modeled after the *Lie* scale, the fourth rotated factor by scales with items with neutral SDSVs, the fifth rotated factor by two hostility scales, and the sixth rotated factor by Eysenck's *Extroversion* scale.

It is obvious that the *ER-S* cannot be considered to be a good measure of the first rotated factor on which the various *SD* scales all have their highest loadings. The denormalized loading of the *ER-S* on the first rotated factor is $-0.45\sqrt{0.72} = -0.38$. Thus approximately $(-0.38)^2 = 0.14$ of the total variance on the *ER-S* can be accounted for by the first rotated factor.

Chapter 13

Q-Sorts
and Rating Scales[1]

13.1 The Nature of a Q-Sort

In a Q-sort, as described by Stephenson (1953), individuals are asked to describe themselves by sorting personality statements into a set of successive categories or intervals, ranging from the least descriptive to the most descriptive. The number of statements that the individual can place in each interval is fixed in such a way that the resulting frequency distribution is somewhat normal in form. Weights or scores are assigned to each of the successive intervals and consequently to the statements within the interval. If 11 intervals are used, for example, the statements placed in the least descriptive category would be assigned weights of 1 and those in the most descriptive category weights of 11, the other nine intervals being assigned the successive integers between 1 and 11.

13.2 Structured and Unstructured Samples

Stephenson has described the use of "structured" and "unstructured" samples of statements in Q-sorts. By "unstructured sample" he means a set of statements which have not been subdivided in any way into smaller

---

[1]Some of the material in this chapter is based on a previously published article by Edwards and Horst (1953).

subsets. Thus a set of items in a personality inventory, designed to yield but a single score, might be taken as an example of an unstructured sample. By a "structured sample" Stephenson means that the sample includes at least two kinds of items with an equal number of each kind. For example, if we had 50 items designed to measure dominance and 50 items designed to measure submission, we would have the simplest kind of structured sample.

More complex structured samples of statements may be constructed. For example, a set of 96 statements might be first subdivided into sets of 48 items each, according to whether the items are believed to measure dependency or independency. Assume that within each set of 48 items it is possible to form two sets of 24 items each, according to whether the items are believed to measure behavior or feelings. Such a set of statements would correspond, in analysis of variance terms, to a 2×2 factorial design.

13.3 Composite Q-Sorts

For either structured or unstructured samples of items we have a score for each of the statements for each of the individuals involved. For unstructured samples, the analysis of the data is often carried out by correlating the scores assigned to the items with a *composite Q-sort*, i.e., one which is established by having a group of judges sort a set of items in terms of a given trait or attribute. Suppose, for example, that psychiatrists are given a set of statements and asked to sort them in such a way as to describe the personality of a psychoneurotic. If there is agreement among the psychiatrists, their Q-sorts will be positively correlated. The average rating can then be obtained for each statement and these averages can be used to obtain a new or composite Q-sort. The composite is called a *criterion* or *defining Q-sort*. If individuals are then asked to Q-sort the same statements in self-description, each of the individual Q-sorts can be correlated with the composite. The correlation coefficient between an individual's Q-sort and a criterion Q-sort can be regarded as a score, indicating the degree to which the individual possesses the trait or attribute defined by the composite.

If a Q-sort consists of a structured sample, as for example where the items have been classified as measuring dependency and independency, then it is possible to obtain a score for each of the two categories. The score on dependency would simply consist of the sum of the weights assigned to each of the dependency items. Similarly, the score on independency would be obtained by summing the weights assigned to each of the independency items.

13.4   Correlation between Mean Ratings and SDSVs

When individuals are asked to describe themselves by answering True or False to personality statements, the proportion answering each item True is the mean for the item. These item means have been shown to be linearly related to the SDSVs of the items. In a Q-sort the mean for a given item is simply the sum of the weights assigned to the item divided by the total number of individuals. It is a reasonable hypothesis that the mean ratings of items in Q-sorts are also linearly related to the SDSVs of the items.

A study designed to test this hypothesis has been reported by Edwards (1955). The Q-sort consisted of 135 statements for which the SDSVs were available. A group of 50 male and 50 female students described themselves by sorting the statements into eleven categories with frequencies of 5, 7, 8, 14, 20, 27, 20, 14, 8, 7, and 5 statements in the successive categories. A weight of 11 was assigned to the statements in the most descriptive category and a weight of 1 to those in the least descriptive, the other integers between 1 and 11 being assigned to the statements in the categories between the two extremes.

For each group the mean rating assigned to each statement in the Q-sorts was obtained and these means were then correlated with the SDSVs of the statements. The product-moment correlation between these two variables for the group of males was 0.84 and for the group of females the correlation was 0.87. These correlations are of approximately the same magnitude as those reported previously between $P(T)$ and SDSV.

13.5   The Kogan, Quinn, Ax, and Ripley Study

Kogan, Quinn, Ax, and Ripley (1957) constructed a Q-sort consisting of statements believed to be related to 25 personality variables. Each variable in the Q-sort was represented by several statements and, instead of dealing with the individual statements, they analyzed their data in terms of the scores for each of the 25 variables.

A small group of clinical psychologists and psychiatrists sorted the statements following a quasinormal distribution in terms of social desirability. An average weight was obtained from these sorts to represent the SDSVs of each of the 25 variables. A second Q-sort was also obtained from the same group of judges under the instructions to sort the statements in terms of sickness-health. These sorts provided an average value for each of the 25 variables with respect to a dimension of sickness-health.

Let us now see what happens when this same Q-sort is used for purposes of self-description and for assessing others. Two groups of individuals were involved. One group consisted of 24 male patients, diagnosed as psychoneurotic, at a VA hospital. The control group consisted of 24 male college students who were paid to participate in the study. Each individual in the two groups made a self-assessment with the Q-sort. The individuals in both groups were then put through an hour-long stress interview conducted by a psychiatrist. Upon completion of the stress interview, the psychiatrist described each individual in terms of the Q-sort. A third Q-sort assessment was made for each individual by another psychiatrist on the basis of case history reports, a psychiatric interview, and other information available to him.

For each group of individuals the mean Q-score was obtained for each of the 25 personality variables for each of the three assessments, and these means were then correlated with the social desirability and sickness-health values for the variables. Table 13.1 gives these correlations. It is clear that

Table 13.1   Correlations between Means of Q-Sort Variables and Social Desirability and Sickness-Health Values of the Variables[a]

Nature of Q-sort	Patients		Controls	
	SDSV	Health	SDSV	Health
Self-sort	0.67	0.59	0.85	0.90
Stress psychiatrist	−0.45	−0.53	0.76	0.81
Work-up psychiatrist	−0.54	−0.58	0.53	0.65

[a]From Kogan, Ax, Quinn, and Ripley (1957).

the mean scores under self-description for both patient and control groups are positively correlated with the mean scores for sickness-health and also for social desirability. The average self-sort for the patient group is, however, somewhat less related to social desirability and sickness-health than that for the control group. Note also the negative correlations between the psychiatrists' assessments and social desirability for the patient group. The patients are described primarily in terms of variables that are regarded as socially undesirable or as indicating sickness when assessed by the psychiatrists. The interpretation of the correlations shown in Table 13.1 is, unfortunately, complicated by the fact that the assessors were aware of whether each subject was a member of the patient or control group.

When the sickness-health values of the 25 variables were correlated with the social desirability values, the product-moment correlation was found to be 0.89. In view of the magnitude of this correlation, it is interesting to speculate on the relationship between clinical notions of disturbed, sick, and psychoneurotic personalities and the socially undesirable personality. Two additional studies bear on this point.

13.6 Correlations between Composites of Adjustment and Social Desirability

Weiner, Blumberg, Segman, and Cooper (1959) had a group of clinical psychologists Q-sort 100 personality statements in a way in which they believed a well-adjusted person would. Another group of clinical psychologists sorted the same statements in terms of social desirability. For each statement the mean rating was obtained under each set of instructions. The correlation between the two sets of means was 0.88.

In another study, Edwards (1965c) had a group of nine college students Q-sort the items in the California Q-set. The average rating assigned to each statement by these students was used to obtain a composite or defining Q-sort of social desirability. A composite or defining Q-sort of the optimally adjusted personality, based on the Q-sorts of clinical psychologists in terms of the California Q-set, has been reported by Block (1961). The social desirability composite, based on the judgments of the college students, was then correlated with the optimally adjusted composite, based on the judgments of clinical psychologists. The product-moment correlation between these two composites was 0.88.

13.7 SD Responding in Q-Sorts

When individuals are asked to describe themselves by answering personality statements True or False, it has been shown that there are reliable individual differences in rates of SD responding. On the basis of evidence previously presented, it seems reasonable that individuals with high rates of SD responding would be more likely to assign statements with high SDSVs to the more descriptive categories and the statements with low SDSVs to the less descriptive categories when they are asked to describe themselves in terms of a Q-sort. If the SDSVs of the statements in the Q-sort are known, then it would be possible to correlate each individual's self-descriptive Q-sort with a composite Q-sort defined by the SDSVs of the statements. Individual differences in these correlation coefficients might be regarded as scores corresponding to individual differences in rates of SD responding.

Now suppose that the same set of statements has been used to obtain various other composite Q-sorts corresponding to a number of different traits or characteristics. Presumably, composites could be obtained defining such traits as emotional instability, anxiety, extroversion, and so on. The correlations between individual Q-sorts and these composites would represent scores in much the same manner as scores on a True-False personality scale designed to measure the same traits.

Consider a specific example. If a composite Q-sort is obtained to define the trait of anxiety, then it seems reasonable to believe that the items placed in the more descriptive categories would be those with low SDSVs and those in the less descriptive categories would be those with high SDSVs. If an individual's Q-sort is negatively correlated with this composite, then he has placed the items with high SDSVs in the more descriptive categories and the items with low SDSVs in the less descriptive categories. If this same individual's Q-sort were correlated with the social desirability composite, the resulting correlation coefficient would be positive. These two correlation coefficients correspond to scores, one for anxiety and one for social desirability. If a large number of individuals have described themselves in terms of the Q-sort, the correlation coefficient between the two sets of scores could be obtained. This correlation coefficient would be similar to a correlation coefficient between scores on a personality scale designed to measure anxiety and on a scale designed to measure individual differences in rates of SD responding.

The fact that Q-sorts, instead of personality scales, may be used to obtain measures of individual differences in traits in no way precludes the possibility that scores based on Q-sorts may be related to individual differences in the tendency to give SD responses.

If we wish to minimize the influence of SD tendencies in Q-sorts, one way in which this might be accomplished would be to include in the Q-sort only those statements that have comparable SDSVs. If each of the statements has approximately the same SDSV, then the placement of the statements in the successive categories in self-description should be independent of individual differences in SD responding.

13.8   Q-Sorts of Structured Samples with Balanced SDSVs

Another possible solution, for structured samples, would be to construct a Q-sort in which the SDSVs of the statements are balanced with respect to the variable of primary interest. This procedure, although not controlling for individual differences in SD tendencies, would at least enable the investigator to determine which individuals were most influenced by the tendency to give SD responses.

Consider, for example, a Q-sort developed by Fordyce (1953) and Lamphere (1953). They were interested in selecting a group of statements designed to measure dependency and another group of statements designed to measure independency. By putting together in a single set an equal number of dependency and independency statements, they hoped to be able to determine whether individuals using Q-sort descriptions would characterize themselves primarily as dependent or independent. Preliminary investigation indicated, however, that the statements relating to independency tended, in general, to be judged as more socially desirable than the statements relating to dependency.

We might assume that, in the population of statements relating to dependency and independency, the distributions of SDSVs are as shown in Figure 13.1. Disregarding the SDSVs, a sample of k_1 statements is taken

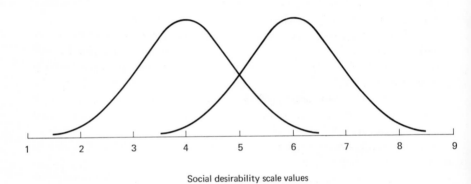

1   2   3   4   5   6   7   8   9

Social desirability scale values

Figure 13.1 Theoretical distributions of social desirability scale values of items relating to dependency and independency. From Edwards and Horst (1953).

to represent dependency and another sample of k_2 statements is taken to represent independency. Individuals are then asked to describe themselves by a Q-sort of the $k = k_1 + k_2$ statements.

We now apply analysis of variance techniques to the Q-sorts of individuals. If an individual has a mean on the independency items that is significantly higher than the mean on the dependency items, then we would not know whether this was a result of a strong trait of independency, the result of strong SD tendencies, or a result of both. In analysis of variance terms, SD responses and the trait responses are confounded.

Now consider a structured sample where the SDSVs of the items have been balanced with respect to the trait of interest. We assume, for example, that the SDSVs have been obtained for the items and that for each of the items in the independency set there is a corresponding item in the dependency set with approximately the same SDSV. The distribution of SDSVs in the two sets of items will then be comparable. We may arbitrarily classify these items that are above the median in terms of SDSVs as "socially desirable" items and those that are below the median as "socially undesirable" items. We thus have, in analysis of variance terms, a 2×2 factorial design.

Individuals are now asked to describe themselves by Q-sorting this set of items. The analysis of variance of the Q-sorts for each individual would take the following form:

Source of variation	d.f.
Dependency-independency	1
Social desirability-undesirability	1
Interaction	1
Replication	k-4

It is clear from the above summary of the analysis of variance that differentiation of the dependency-independency effect is possible. We can also determine whether an individual describes himself primarily in terms of the social desirability-undesirability variable, rather than in terms of the dependency-independency variable. If an individual selects those items with high SDSVs as being more descriptive of himself than those with low SDSVs, then the mean square for the social desirability-undesirability effect will be large and that for the dependency-independency effect will be small. On the other hand, a large mean square for the dependency-independency effect will result in a small mean square for the social desirability-undesirability effect. Thus, individuals with a significant dependency-independency mean square and a nonsignificant social desirability-undesirability mean square will be those who have responded to the items primarily in terms of the trait of interest.

13.9   Social Desirability and Self-Assessments by Means of Rating Scales

Asking an individual to describe himself in terms of a Q-sort is similar to presenting an individual with a set of statements and asking him to rate each statement on a 9- or 11-point rating scale in terms of the degree to which he believes the statements describe him. The difference, of course, is that in the latter case the individual is free to assign any number on the scale to as many statements as he chooses. In a Q-sort the number of statements that can be assigned a given rating is fixed.

Thus, if an individual is asked to sort statements into 11 or some other number of categories in self-description without restriction as to how many statements can be placed in a given category, this would be the same as if the individual had been asked to rate himself on an 11-point scale with respect to each statement. This form of self-description was used in a study by

Wright (1957). He gave 140 statements to a group of 127 college students. Approximately half the students were males and half females. He asked the students to rate the degree to which each statement characterized them on a 9-point scale. For each of the statements he found the mean rating assigned in self-description. These means were then correlated with the SDSVs of the statements. The correlation between the two variables for this sample was 0.88.

It would have been possible for Wright to have obtained the correlation between each individual's self-ratings and the SDSVs of the statements. Individual differences in these correlation coefficients might then be regarded as corresponding to individual differences in rates of SD responding.

13.10   Hillmer's Study

In the self-ratings obtained by Wright there was, of course, variability in the ratings assigned to a given statement by the individuals describing themselves. Some individuals might assign a rating of 7, others a rating of 6, and others some other value to the same statement. It occurred to Hillmer (1958) that knowledge of the distributions of ratings for each statement could be used in such a way as to provide an item format that would successfully minimize the relationship between the ratings assigned to the items in self-description and the SDSVs of the items.

For example, suppose that the median of the distribution of ratings in self-description were obtained for each statement. This would be the point on the rating scale at which 50 percent of the individuals assigned a higher rating and 50 percent a lower rating. Assume that the median fell someplace on the rating scale between the two descriptive categories "Very good description of me" and "Quite a good description of me." If a new group of individuals were presented with this statement and asked to choose between these two descriptive categories, Hillmer reasoned that aproximately 50 percent should choose one of the descriptive categories and approximately 50 percent the other.

Of course, the median rating seldom falls exactly between two adjacent categories. However, Hillmer developed a two-choice questionnaire, the alternatives being the two rating scale categories that most nearly divided the distribution of self-ratings into equal halves. For example, Wright's data showed that for one item 0.412 of the subjects rated the item in the category "Very good" or higher and 0.588 of the subjects rated the item in the category "Quite good" or lower. In Hillmer's two-choice questionnaire, these were the two alternatives presented to the subjects with respect to this item.

One might expect that in a new group approximately 0.412 of the subjects would choose the "Very good" alternative and approximately 0.588 would choose the "Quite good" alternative. For this particular item, however, 0.736 of the subjects chose the "Very good" category in describing themselves. When the proportion of individuals choosing the higher rating category for each item was plotted against the SDSVs of the items, the plot was linear. The correlation coefficient between these proportions and the SDSVs of the items was 0.87 for a sample of 227 subjects. This correlation coefficient is exactly the same as the correlation coefficient between $P(T)$ and SDSV for the same set of items when they are administered in a True-False format. Apparently, Hillmer's subjects regarded the higher rating category as corresponding to a True response to the item and the lower rating category as corresponding to a False response.

Chapter 14

SD Responding
and Other Personality Inventories

14.1 Introduction

Several approaches are possible to the development of personality scales which would be relatively uncorrelated with individual differences in rates of SD responding. One, following the suggestion of Weiner (1948) and Hanley (1956), would be to attempt to develop scales in which the items are primarily of the subtle or neutral type with respect to social desirability. We have shown, for example, that MMPI subtle scales tend to have relatively low correlations with the *SD* scale. We have also shown that the correlations of MMPI scales with the *SD* scale tend to decrease as the proportion of neutral items in the scale increases. Another possibility would be to attempt to develop scales which have a fair degree of balance in their SD-SUD keying. Scales of this kind also tend to have relatively low correlations with the *SD* scale. It is unfortunately the case, however, at least with respect to MMPI scales, that if a scale has either a large proportion of neutral items or a high degree of balance in its SD-SUD keying, then it also tends to have a relatively low degree of internal consistency.

14.2 Forced-Choice Scales: The EPPS

Another approach to developing scales which will be relatively un-correlated with individual differences in rates of SD responding is to use a *forced-choice format* for the items in a scale. One example of the forced-choice format is the Edwards Personality Preference Schedule (EPPS). In this inventory the items are paired on the basis of their SDSVs. The statements appearing in the inventory, for example, were first scaled for social desirability and then paired in terms of their SDSVs. For each pair of statements, the individual is asked to choose that member of the pair that he believes is the more descriptive of himself.

The notion underlying the forced-choice item format is that if two statements have approximately the same SDSVs, then this will decrease the probability that the choice of one of the two statements will be influenced by SD tendencies. If this is in fact the case, then the choice made between a pair of statements may be more trait-relevant.

As we have pointed out previously, scores on the complete set of 15 EPPS scales are ipsative. Because the sum of the 15 scores for each individual is equal to the same number, 210, this, in turn, means that scores on one of the scales are completely determined by the scores on the other 14 scales. For example, if we sum the scores on any 14 scales, then the score on the remaining scale is fixed and can be determined by subtracting the sum of the 14 scores from 210.

Ordinarily, if we intercorrelate and factor-analyze by the method of principal components a set of nonipsative scales, the number of principal-component factors required to account for all of the variance in the scales will be equal to k, the number of scales. Of course, as we have seen, the later principal components will ordinarily account for a relatively small proportion of the total variance. However, if scores on the 15 EPPS scales were intercorrelated and factor-analyzed, it would be impossible to obtain as many as 15 principal-component factors. It would require no more than 14 principal-component factors to account for all of the variance in the 15 EPPS scales, simply because scores on one of the scales are completely determined by scores on the other 14 scales. If any one of the 15 EPPS scales is eliminated, that is, if the scores on one of the scales are discarded, then the scores on the remaining 14 scales will not be ipsative.

14.3   Correlation between the Proportion Choosing the A Statement and the Difference between the SDSVs of the A and B Statements in the EPPS

There are 210 pairs of statements in the EPPS. One of the statements in each pair is referred to as the A statement and the other as the B statement. The intraclass correlation between the SDSVs of these AB pairs of statements is 0.85.[1] This correlation indicates that, although the matching of the

[1]In some cases a paired set of values can be regarded as both the ordered pair (X, Y) and the ordered pair (Y, X). The intraclass correlation is the correlation coefficient obtained when each pair of values is treated as (X, Y) and also as (Y, X).

statements with respect to SDSVs is fairly good, it is not perfect.[2] The distribution of the pairs of statements according to their scale separations or differences in SDSVs is such that for 160 or approximately 76 percent of the 210 pairs the difference in the SDSVs of the statements is within the range 0.0 to 0.5 of a scale unit.[3] In the remaining 50 pairs, either the SDSV of the A statement exceeds that of the B statement by 0.5 of a scale unit, or the SDSV of the B statement exceeds that of the A statement by 0.5 of a scale unit.

From the original normative group of 1509 individuals administered the EPPS, a serial sample of 81 males and 79 females was drawn. For this sample the proportion choosing the A statement in each of the 210 AB pairs was found. In Figure 14.1 the probability of an A choice is plotted against the scale separations of the statements, A − B. The product-moment correlation between the probability of an A choice and the scale separation between the A and B statements is 0.40.

That some degree of correlation would be found between the probability of an A choice and the scale separation of the A and B statements is to be expected for several reasons. In the first place, the pairs of statements are not perfectly equated for SDSVs, since the intraclass correlation between these paired values is 0.85 rather than 1.00. In the second place, approximately 50 of the 210 pairs of statements have scale separations greater than 0.5 of a unit on the social desirability continuum. This amount of scale separation may be sufficiently above threshold to permit discrimination. Thus responses to these 50 pairs of statements may be more influenced by SD tendencies than the responses to the remaining 160 pairs of statements where the scale separations are less than 0.5 of a unit. We can see this quite clearly when we compare the points at the extreme right and extreme left in Figure 14.1. When the A statement has a markedly higher SDSV than the B statement, the number of individuals choosing the A statement tends to exceed 50 percent. When the A statement has a markedly lower SDSV than the B statement, the number of individuals choosing the A statement tends to be less than 50 percent. Within the central range, the probability of an A choice bears little or no relationship to the scale separation of the A and B statements.

Some indication of the stability of the correlation of 0.40 between the probability of an A choice and the scale separation, A − B, is provided

---

[2]The SDSVs of the items in the EPPS were obtained using a scaling technique known as the *method of successive intervals*. A discussion of this scaling method can be found in Edwards (1957), Guilford (1954), and Torgerson (1958). There is ample evidence to show that scale values obtained by the method of successive intervals are highly and positively correlated with those obtained by methods described previously.

[3]There are 225 pairs of statements in the EPPS, but 15 of these are duplicates and are not used in obtaining scores on the EPPS scales.

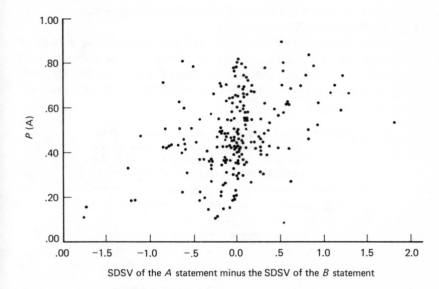

Figure 14.1 Probability of an *A* choice in each of the *AB* pairs of statements in the EPPS as related to the difference in the social desirability scale values of the paired statements. From Edwards (1957a).

by Wright (1957). He gave the EPPS to a sample of 134 students and found, for this sample, the probability of an *A* choice for each of the 210 pairs of statements. The correlation between the probability of an *A* choice and the scale separation of the pairs of statements was 0.45 for this sample.

In another repetition of this research, Klett (1957a) rescaled the items in the EPPS for social desirability using a group of high school students to obtain the SDSVs of the items. When the scale separations of the pairs of statements were based on the SDSVs of the high school students, Klett found that the correlation between the probability of an *A* choice and the scale separations of the paired statements was 0.51 for the high school students.

14.4 SD Responding and the EPPS

It has been found in several studies that two items which have approximately the same SDSVs when rated on a 9-point rating scale may be judged to have different SDSVs when paired and when individuals are asked to make a pair-comparison judgment of which item is more socially desirable. Thus, even though most of the paired statements in the EPPS have roughly equivalent SDSVs, responses to the paired statements may still be related to individual differences in SD responding.

In a study by Kelleher (1957), the EPPS and a 40-item *SD* scale were given to a group of 101 males and a group of 101 females.[4] For each group he computed the point biserial correlation between scores on the *SD* scale and each of the 210 pairs of statements in the EPPS. Table 14.1 gives the

Table 14.1   Distribution of Absolute Values of Point Biserial Coefficients between Scores on the *SD* Scale and Responses to the Items in the EPPS for 101 Females and 101 Males[a]

Point Biserial $\lvert r \rvert$	Females f	Males f
0.40–0.49	1	
0.30–0.39	5	3
0.20–0.29	24	22
0.10–0.19	72	60
0.00–0.09	108	125

[a]From Kelleher (1957).

distributions of the absolute values of the 210 point biserial coefficients for the group of males and the group of females. For slightly over one-half of the items, the point biserial coefficients fall in the interval 0.00 to 0.09 for both males and females. The remaining items all have absolute point biserial coefficients equal to or greater than 0.10.

To determine the degree to which individuals were consistently choosing the statement in each pair with the higher SDSV, Kelleher obtained a score for each individual in his two groups which was simply the number of times the individual chose the statement with the higher SDSV in each of the pairs of statements. Presumably, if an individual was consistently making his choice in each of the pairs in terms of the differences in the SDSVs of the items in a pair, then a high score should be associated with a high score on the *SD* scale. The correlation between these EPPS *SD* scores and those on the *SD* scale, however, was only 0.02 for the females and 0.17 for the males.

The major consideration with respect to the EPPS scales, however, is the degree to which scores on these scales are correlated with individual differences in rates of SD responding. Table 14.2 gives the correlations

[4]The *SD* scale used by Kelleher was the 39-item MMPI *SD* scale plus one additional item.

Table 14.2   Correlations of EPPS Scales with
Two *SD* Scales

	Correlations with *SD* Scales	
EPPS Scales	39-Item[a]	79-Item[b]
Ach	−0.05	0.09
Def	0.09	0.09
Ord	−0.01	0.19
Exh	0.08	−0.08
Aut	−0.07	−0.17
Aff	0.10	−0.02
Int	0.16	0.06
Suc	−0.17	−0.32
Dom	0.30	−0.02
Aba	−0.35	−0.14
Nur	0.02	−0.08
Chg	0.11	0.08
End	0.05	0.32
Het	0.01	0.07
Agg	−0.15	−0.10

[a]From an unpublished study by Edwards,
Klockars, and Abbott (1969).
[b]From Edwards (1959).

between scores on the 15 EPPS scales and individual differences in rates
of SD responding for two different samples of college students. One
sample consisted of 106 students and for this sample individual differences
in rates of SD responding were measured by a 79-item MMPI *SD* scale.
Almost all of the correlations of the EPPS scales with this *SD* scale tend to
be relatively low. The other sample consisted of 286 students and for this
sample individual differences in rates of SD responding were measured by
the 39-item MMPI *SD* scale. For this sample the correlations of the EPPS
scales with individual differences in rates of SD responding are also quite
low.

14.5   No-Choice Responses
and the Average of the Paired SDSVs in the EPPS

One of the difficulties with the EPPS is that some individuals find being
forced to choose between two statements that are fairly comparable
with respect to their SDSVs is a disagreeable and sometimes frustrating

experience. This is particularly true with respect to those pairs of statements in which the SDSVs are relatively undesirable. A study by Edwards and Diers (1962a) illustrates this point.

Individuals were administered the EPPS under modified instructions in which they were informed that they could omit answers to those items for which they found the choice too difficult. For each of the 210 pairs of items, the proportion failing to make a choice was obtained. Figure 14.2 shows these proportions plotted against the average of the SDSVs of the two items in each pair. It is clear from Figure 14.2 that the probability of a choice

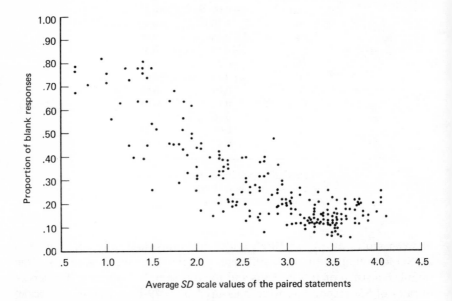

Average *SD* scale values of the paired statements

Figure 14.2   The proportion of no-choice responses for each of the 210 paired statements in the EPPS plotted against the average of the social desirability scales values of the paired statements. From Edwards and Diers (1962a).

not being made to a pair of items decreases as the SDSVs of the two statements become more socially desirable. The most difficult choices are obviously those involving a pair of statements with relatively low SDSVs.

14.6   Regression Lines of $P(T)$ on SDSV for High- and Low-Scoring Groups on the *SD* Scale

Another approach to the development of scales that might have relatively low correlations with the *SD* scale is suggested by the results of several studies in which the regression lines of $P(T)$ on SDSV were found separately for high- and low-scoring groups on the *SD* scale (Edwards and Walker, 1962; Edwards and Diers, 1963; Edwards, Gocka, and Holloway, 1964). The intersection of these two regression lines is at approximately 5.8 on the social desirability continuum. This is the point at which the predicted probability of a True response for the low-scoring and high-scoring groups on the *SD* scale is the same for both groups. These two regression lines are shown in Figure 14.3.

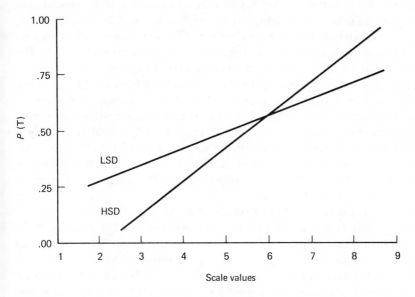

Figure 14.3   Regression lines of *P*(T) on SDSV for high- and low-scoring groups on the 39-item MMPI *SD* scale. From Edwards (1964b).

The neutral interval on a 9-point rating scale is somewhat arbitrarily defined as ranging from 4.5 up to 5.5 and the neutral point as falling at 5.0. If, on the other hand, the intersection of the regression lines of *P*(T) on SDSV for high- and low-scoring individuals on the *SD* scale intersect at approximately 5.8, then some of the statements made in earlier chapters need qualification. The evidence cited previously indicated that as the proportion of neutral items in an MMPI scale increases, the correlation of the scale with the *SD* scale decreases. But, if all of the neutral items in a scale are keyed True, then we might expect the scale to have a low negative correlation with the *SD* scale because, for items within this interval, low-scoring individuals have a higher probability of a True response than high-scoring individuals.

There is considerable evidence (Crowder, 1962; Diers, 1964; Edwards, 1963; Edwards and Diers, 1963; Edwards and Walsh, 1964b) to show that, in general, scales consisting of items with neutral SDSVs keyed True are, in fact, negatively correlated with scores on the *SD* scale. The magnitude of the correlation might be expected to depend on how the items are distributed in the neutral interval. If the items are concentrated at the lower end, 4.5, of the neutral interval, then the correlation would be expected to be higher than if the items were concentrated at the upper end, 5.5, of the neutral interval because, as Figure 14.3 shows, the two regression lines are closer together at 5.5 than at 4.5. A study by Edwards and Diers (1963) confirms this hypothesis. They found that a True-keyed scale consisting of items with SDSVs greater than 5.0 but less than 6.0 (with an average SDSV of approximately 5.4) had a smaller negative correlation with scores on the *SD* scale than a scale consisting of True-keyed items with SDSVs less than 5.0 but greater than 4.0 (the average value being approximately 4.6).

If the point of intersection between the regression lines of *P*(T) on SDSV for a group of high- and a group of low-scoring individuals on the *SD* scale is at approximately 5.8 on the social desirability continuum, then a scale consisting of items with SDSVs close to 5.8 should have only a relatively low correlation with scores on the *SD* scale. A 40-item True-keyed scale with an average item SDSV for males of 5.9 was found by Edwards and Diers (1963) to correlate only 0.09 with scores on the *SD* scale for a sample of 110 males.

In a repetition of the above research with the MMPI, Edwards, Gocka, and Holloway (1964) found that for male VA patients the point of intersection of the two regression lines was at approximately 6.0 on the social desirability continuum. They then selected a set of 40 MMPI items with SDSVs close to 6.0 and correlated True scores on this scale with scores on the *SD* scale. For a sample of 220 male VA patients the resulting correlation coefficient was 0.09.

An examination of the two regression lines in Figure 14.3 shows that the spread between the two lines is greater at the socially undesirable end of the continuum than at the socially desirable end. This, in turn, suggests that scales containing primarily items with extreme socially undesirable scale values, and in which the items are consistently keyed for True or for False responses, would be expected to have higher correlations with the *SD* scale than scales containing primarily items with socially desirable scale values and in which the items are consistently keyed for either True or for False responses.

14.7   The EPI Scales

In the development of the Edwards Personality Inventory (EPI), a systematic attempt was made to minimize the correlations between scales in the inventory and the *SD* scale. Figure 14.3 suggests, for example, that if a scale contained items fairly evenly distributed over the interval 4.0 to 8.0, and if the items in the scale were primarily keyed for True responses, then scores on this scale might be expected to have relatively low correlations with scores on the *SD* scale.

Table 14.3 shows the distribution of the SDSVs of the items in the EPI and we see that most of the items have SDSVs that fall in the interval 4.0 to 8.0 on the social desirability continuum and, in addition, most of

Table 14.3   Distribution of SDSVs of the Items in the EPI and the True and False Keying of the Items[a]

Scale Values	Keying		
	True *f*	False *f*	Combined *f*
8–9	8		8
7–8	237	16	253
6–7	291	27	318
5–6	211	27	238
4–5	155	59	214
3–4	258	71	329
2–3	80	9	89
1–2	2		2

[a]From Edwards (1966c).

the items are keyed for True responses. It may also be noted that only 91 of the items have SDSVs less than 3.0 and 75 of these items are in Booklets II and IV. These 75 items, in turn, are primarily concentrated in Scale K (Feels Misunderstood) of Booklet II and Scale A (Self-Critical) of Booklet IV. These two scales were retained in the EPI despite the fact that they were expected to have relatively high negative correlations with the *SD* scale. They were retained because the scales seemed to have a homogeneous content representing two important normal personality traits. Several other scales were also included in the EPI for the same reason, even though it was expected that these scales would also be correlated with the *SD* scale.

There were other related attempts to minimize the correlations between the EPI scales and the *SD* scale, and these are described by Edwards (1966c). Of major interest, however, is the degree to which these efforts were successful. Table 14.4 shows the distribution of the absolute values of the correlations of the EPI scales with the *SD* scale, as based on a sample of 286 students. The three scales with the largest absolute correlations with the *SD* scale are Scale A (Anxious About His Performance) in Booklet II, Scale K (Feels Misunderstood) in Booklet II, and Scale A (Self-Critical) in

Table 14.4   Distribution of the Absolute
Values of the Correlations
of the EPI Scales with the
SD Scale[a]

$|r|$	f
0.60–0.69	1
0.50–0.59	2
0.40–0.49	5
0.30–0.39	4
0.20–0.29	9
0.10–0.19	16
0.00–0.09	16

[a]From an unpublished study by
Edwards, Klockars, and Abbott (1969).

Booklet IV. These three correlation coefficients are -0.50, -0.52, and -0.60, respectively. Most of the other scales in the EPI have relatively low correlations with the SD scale.

14.8   The PRF Scales

The PRF scales, like those in the EPPS and EPI, are rational scales and they were also developed with the objective of minimizing the correlations between scores on the scales with individual differences in rates of SD responding. A discussion of the methods used in developing the PRF scales is given by Jackson (1967c).

The correlations of the PRF scales with the 39-item MMPI SD scale are not known. However, Jackson (1967c) does report the correlations of the PRF scales with his Dy, or Desirability, scale. Table 14.5 shows the distribution of the absolute values of the correlations of the PRF scales with the PRF measure of desirability, based on a sample of 1029 males, as reported by Jackson. If the Dy scale of the PRF is itself highly and positively correlated with the 39-item MMPI SD scale, then we can also assume that the PRF scales are relatively uncorrelated with individual differences in rates of SD responding as measured by the MMPI SD scale.

14.9   First and Second Factor Loadings of the CPI and 16 PF Scales

In a previous chapter we showed the distribution of the absolute values of the correlations of MMPI scales with the 39-item MMPI SD scale. It

Table 14.5 Distribution of the Absolute Values of the Correlations of the PRF Scales with the PRF *Dy* Scale[a]

$|r|$	f
0.40–0.49	3
0.30–0.39	4
0.20–0.29	7
0.10–0.19	2
0.00–0.09	5

[a]From Jackson (1967c).

was also shown that when MMPI scales were intercorrelated and factor-analyzed by the method of principal components, the first factor was marked by the MMPI *SD* scale and the second by the MMPI *R* scale. To complete the record, we now consider the correlations of the CPI and 16 PF scales with the *SD* scale and also the first and second factor loadings of these scales.

In developing the CPI and the 16 PF scales no systematic effort was made to minimize the correlations of the scales with individual differences in rates of SD responding. Table 14.6 shows the distribution of the absolute values of the correlations of the CPI and 16 PF scales with the MMPI *SD* scale. The correlation coefficients are based on a sample of 286 students.

Table 14.6 Distribution of the Absolute Values of the Correlations of CPI and 16 PF Scales with the *SD* Scale[a]

$|r|$	CPI Scales f	16 PF Scales f
0.70–0.79	1	
0.60–0.69	1	1
0.50–0.59	4	2
0.40–0.49	4	1
0.30–0.39	4	0
0.20–0.29	2	3
0.10–0.19	1	5
0.00–0.09	1	4

[a]From an unpublished study by Edwards, Klockars, and Abbott (1969).

The CPI scales were intercorrelated and factor-analyzed by the method of principal components. Included in the factor analysis were the *SD* and *R* scales which have been found to mark the first two principal-component factors when MMPI scales are factor-analyzed. The first unrotated principal-component factor accounted for approximately 29 percent of the total variance and the *SD* scale had a loading of 0.81 on this factor. Seven of the CPI scales had loadings equal to or greater than 0.60 on the first factor: *Cs* (0.61), *Wb* (0.79), *Sc* (0.63), *To* (0.80), *Gi* (0.70), *Ac* (0.76), and *Ie* (0.75). The second principal component accounted for approximately 15 percent of the total variance, and the loading of the *R* scale on this factor was 0.70. Five CPI scales had absolute loadings equal to or greater than 0.60 on the second factor: *Do* (−0.60), *Sy* (−0.68), *Sp* (−0.66), *Sa* (−0.71), and *Sc* (0.65).

The 16 PF scales were also intercorrelated and factor-analyzed by the method of principal components. Included in the factor analysis were the *SD* and *R* scales. For the 16 PF scales, the first unrotated principal component accounted for approximately 21 percent of the total variance and the loading of the *SD* scale on this factor was 0.72. The 16 PF scales with absolute loadings equal to or greater than 0.60 on the first factor were: *C* (0.74), *O* (−0.61), and Q_4 (−0.73). The second principal component accounted for approximately 14 percent of the total variance and the *R* scale had a loading of −0.62 on the second factor. The 16 PF scales with absolute loadings equal to or greater than 0.60 on the second factor were: *F*(0.65) and Q_2 (−0.64).

Chapter 15

Impression Management

15.1 Responses to Items in Achievement and Aptitude Tests

When an individual takes an achievement or aptitude test, he is usually aware of the fact that there is but one correct or right answer to each item in the test. Presumably, most individuals in taking a test of this kind are motivated to do well, and the scores on the test may be regarded as reasonably accurate measures of individual differences in the ability measured by the test. The individual taking an ability test can, of course, fail to give the correct answer to an item even when he knows it and will thus obtain a lower score than if he had been motivated to do well. He can, in other words, fake a bad or low score on the test, but he cannot fake a good or high score on the test.

Thus, a genius may, if so motivated, portray himself as a moron on a standardized intelligence test, but no moron has as yet succeeded in portraying himself as a genius on an intelligence test, regardless of how strongly motivated he may have been to do so. Conscious or intentional faking on intelligence and aptitude tests can occur in one direction only.

15.2 Responses to Items in Personality Scales

In the case of a personality scale, the situation is quite different. The only "correct" answer to an item in a personality scale is the one that accurately describes the individual. Thus, for some individuals the correct answer is

True and for other individuals the correct answer is False. The response scored in a personality scale is the trait or keyed response and this response, unlike the scored response to an ability item, cannot be regarded as the correct response for all individuals.

The individual responding to the items in a personality scale is undoubtedly aware that the person administering the scale is going to give consideration in some manner or other to his responses, but he is also undoubtedly aware that it would be extremely difficult, if not impossible, for anyone to establish whether the responses he gives in self-description are accurate or inaccurate. If motivated to do so, he can give whatever responses he chooses to the items and without regard to whether the responses are accurate or inaccurate.

If a personality item has an extremely high SDSV, the individual may be aware that by responding True to the item he is saying something good or socially desirable about himself and that if he responds False to the item he is denying that a socially desirable statement describes him. Similarly, he may be aware that a True response to an item with an extremely low SDSV will be regarded as indicating that he is saying something bad or socially undesirable about himself and that a False response will be regarded as a denial of a socially undesirable characteristic.

15.3   Meaning of Impression Management

In their discussion of the K scale of the MMPI, Meehl and Hathaway (1946) have observed that one of the most important defects of personality scales is their susceptibility to "faking," that is, to motivation on the part of some individuals to create either a favorable or unfavorable impression of themselves. We shall refer to all such conscious, deliberate, and intentional falsification of responses to personality items as attempts at *impression management*.

To state that an individual can, if motivated to do so, intentionally falsify responses to personality items does not, of course, establish that any given response has, in fact, been intentionally falsified. It is also conceivable that an individual may unconsciously falsify responses to personality items, but this form of self-deception would be even more difficult to prove than a deliberate attempt at impression management. We shall restrict the term impression management, therefore, to *conscious* and *intentional falsification* of responses.

15.4   Faking Good and Faking Bad

We have pointed out that an individual's responses to items may be "falsified" in such a way that he obtains either a higher or a lower score on a particular scale than he would if his responses were completely accurate. Thus, we may describe an individual as either faking good or faking bad. Faking good refers to the attempt to create a favorable impression by falsifying responses to personality items. If an individual attempts to fake good and is successful, then we may expect him to obtain a higher score on a scale than he otherwise would, if the trait measured by the scale is itself a socially desirable one. On scales measuring socially undesirable traits, a successful attempt to fake good should result in a lower score than would otherwise be obtained by the individual.

Faking bad, on the other hand, refers to motivation to create an unfavorable impression. Thus the influence of faking bad on personality scales should be just the opposite of faking good. Faking bad may occur in situations where an individual is under the impression that portraying himself in terms of socially undesirable characteristics may work to his advantage. For example, an individual may hope that he will be discharged from the army if he can respond to the items in an inventory in such a way as to give the impression that he is psychoneurotic or emotionally unstable. Thus he may attempt to falsify his responses and to answer the items in terms of his conception of how disturbed individuals might answer them. To fake bad in some situations may be of importance, but it does not seem that this form of impression management would be as prevalent as that to fake good.

15.5   Research Studies of Impression Management

The procedure frequently used in research studies of impression management is to have individuals take a personality inventory under standard instructions for self-descriptions and then to obtain a second record from the same individuals under special instructions to fake their responses. In some cases the special instructions have involved telling the individuals to answer the items as they would if they were applying for a particular job. In others the special instructions have involved telling the individuals to answer the items in such a way as to create a good impression or to give SD responses to the items. In still other studies the special instructions have involved telling the individuals to create a bad impression or to give SUD responses to the items.

In these studies of faking, assuming that the individuals involved actually attempt to comply with the special instructions given to them, what can we expect to find with regard to the mean score on a scale? If the special instructions are to fake good or to give SD responses, then the mean score should approach the number of items in the scale keyed for SD responses. Because there are individual differences in the judged social desirability of personality statements, all individuals will not necessarily give the same response to each statement and this should be particularly true with respect to items with neutral or moderately desirable and undesirable SDSVs. Still, it is a reasonable hypothesis that the mean score on the scale should be close to the number of items keyed for SD responses. Similarly, if the special instructions are to fake bad or to give SUD responses, we might expect the mean score on the scale to approach the number of items keyed for SUD responses. Both of these hypotheses have been confirmed in a study by Edwards and Diers (1962b).

If the items in a scale have a specific content such that each item is relevant to a common trait and if individuals are instructed to fake a high or low score on the scale, it seems reasonable to expect that this can be done, if they are able to recognize the keyed responses to the items. If this is the case, then the mean score under special instructions will be shifted and the distribution of the scores may be expected to be skewed. But what would this prove other than the fact that individuals can obtain different scores under instructions to fake their responses? The fact that scores may be faked under specific instructions to do so provides no information whatsoever as to which individuals, if any, are motivated by impression management under standard instructions and to what degree. Nor does the fact that scores may be shifted under special instruction in any way call into question the accuracy of scores obtained under standard instructions.

If individuals are given an inventory containing a number of scales and are specifically instructed to fake scores on one particular scale, the task may be somewhat more difficult. To the degree to which individuals are able to judge which items are relevant to the particular trait, the mean score on the scale may be changed. But again, these results simply indicate the degree to which individuals are able to recognize the relevant items and also the keyed responses to the items. No information is provided by the results of these studies regarding those individuals motivated by impression management under standard instructions.

More general instructions, such as to fake good or to create a favorable impression on an inventory containing many scales, cannot be expected to have much influence on items with extreme SDSVs. If an item has a high SDSV, then the proportion of individuals answering True to the item under standard instructions will also be quite high and at best this proportion can, under the special instructions, be increased only slightly. The same considerations apply to items with low SDSVs where the proportion of False responses under standard instructions is high.

For neutral items and items with moderately desirable and undesirable scale values, the proportion of individuals answering True or False to items under standard instructions tends to be more evenly balanced. For items of this kind there is, therefore, a greater possibility of large shifts in the proportion answering True or False under specific instructions to fake good. But we also know that there are individual differences in the judged desirability of items and that if an item has a neutral or moderately desirable scale value, then some individuals will judge this item to fall to the right of the neutral point and others will judge it to fall to the left of the neutral point. If individuals have been instructed to fake good, then those individuals who perceive the item as falling above the neutral point may be expected to answer the item True, but those individuals who perceive the item as falling below the neutral point may be expected to answer the item False. Such individual differences in the perceived desirability of an item will not result in a uniform shift in a consistent direction on the part of all individuals responding to the items under the special instructions to fake good.

To the degree to which individuals can accurately judge the SDSVs of the items and to the degree to which there is an imbalance in the SD-SUD keying of the items in the various scales included in an inventory, the mean scores on the scales may be expected to change under specific instructions to fake good. For example, if all of the items in a scale in an inventory are keyed for trait and SD responses, then all individuals who accurately judge the SDSVs of the items and, in turn, give the SD responses to the items, should obtain a score under the special instructions that is equal to the number of items in the scale. As a result the mean score on the scale should be increased. But if the scale contains a considerable number of items with neutral or moderately desirable or undesirable scale values, then the shift in the mean score under the special instructions to fake good may not be as great as would be the case if the items were more extreme in their SDSVs. If a scale contains a balance in its SD-SUD keying, then instructions to fake good should result in a mean score on the scale that is approximately equal to one-half the number of items in the scale.

The interesting fact is that regardless of the degree to which scores are altered under special instructions, these results provide no information whatsoever regarding motivation to impression management under standard instructions.

15.6   The *F* Scale of the MMPI

There have been several attempts to devise rational and empirical scales that might be related to individual differences in impression management. The *F* scale of the MMPI is a rational scale in which all of the items are keyed for responses given by less than 10 percent of normals. Thus a normal individual who obtains a high score on the *F* scale under standard instructions might conceivably be regarded as one motivated to create an unfavorable impression.

15.7   Wiggins' Dissimulation Scale: *Sd*

An empirical dissimulation scale for motivation to create a favorable impression has been developed by Wiggins (1959). Wiggins gave the MMPI under standard instructions to one group and under instructions to answer in a socially desirable direction to another group. For each of the MMPI items he found the proportion responding True under standard and under the special instructions. Those items for which the two proportions differed significantly were selected for inclusion in his Sd scale.

Because we have found that the proportion of True responses is linearly related to the SDSVs of personality items, those items with extremely high SDSVs have a high probability of being answered True under standard instructions and those with extremely low SDSVs have a low probability of being answered True under standard instructions. It is unlikely, therefore, that very many MMPI items could be found at the two extremes of the social desirability continuum for which the proportions answering True under standard and under the special instructions would differ significantly. The most likely candidates would be those items with neutral or with moderately desirable or undesirable scale values and, indeed, this is the case with the items in Wiggins' Sd scale.

The items in the Sd scale are keyed in the direction of the shift in response under instructions to fake good. For example, one of the items in the Sd scale is "I do not like everyone I know" (SDSV = 5.11). Under fake good instructions the proportion answering this item True is significantly smaller than the proportion answering True under standard instructions. The item is, therefore, keyed for a False response. Another item is "I do not always tell the truth" (SDSV = 3.08). Under fake good instructions the proportion answering this item True is less than under standard instructions and the item is keyed for a False response. An example of a True-keyed item is "I would like to be a singer" (SDSV = 5.84). Under special instructions to fake good, the proportion answering this item True is significantly greater than under standard instructions and the item is, therefore, keyed for a True response.

Because the keying of the items in the Sd scale is based on deliberate and intentional responses designed to create a favorable impression, high scores on this scale under standard instructions indicate a pattern of responses to the items that is similar to that obtained under special instructions to fake good. A high score, in other words, *may* be a sign of a deliberate attempt at favorable impression management.

When one examines the content of the items in the Sd scale, it is apparent that there are two small clusters of items, one having to do with the liking of various occupations and recreational activities and the other with religion and religious activities. A few of the items in the Sd scale also appear in the *Lie* scale of the MMPI. The other items have no obvious relevance to each other. It is not surprising, therefore, that under standard instructions the Sd scale tends to have a relatively low r_{kk} value. For example, in one study the K-R 21 lower-bound estimate of r_{kk} was only 0.41 (Edwards, 1963).

15.8   Impression Management
and Individual Differences in Rates of SD Responding

It is important to differentiate between attempts at impression management and individual differences in rates of SD responding. Impression management refers to a deliberate and conscious attempt on the part of an individual to give responses that he believes will create the impression he has in mind. An applicant for a sales position is motivated by impression management when he responds to the items in an inventory in such a way that he hopes to create the impression of being one who has the traits he judges to be desirable in a salesman, and his responses to the items cannot be regarded as providing a measure of his usual rate of SD responding. His rate of SD responding under these test conditions may increase, decrease, or remain the same, depending on the impression he is attempting to create.

Scores on impression management scales, such as the *Sd* scale and the *Lie* scale of the MMPI, have only small positive correlations with individual differences in rates of SD responding. When impression management scales are included in factor analyses with *SD* scales and various other personality scales, it is found that the impression management scales have relatively high loadings on a common factor, but relatively low loadings on the same factor on which the *SD* scales have relatively high loadings. Impression management scales, in other words, are not accurate measures of individual differences in rates of SD responding.

15.9   Meaning of High Scores on the *Sd* Scale

We have said that high scores on the *Sd* and other impression management scales *may* indicate strong motivation toward impression management, but it does not follow that all high scores on these scales are simply the result of impression management. Two individuals may each obtain a high score on the *Sd* scale, one because of his motivation toward impression management and the other because he believes the responses he has given to the items do, in fact, provide an accurate description of him. There *are* individuals who "like to hunt" and who "like to fish," who "like everyone they know," who "daydream very little," who are "good mixers," who do "go to church almost every week," who "never worry about their looks," who are "embarrassed by dirty stories," and so on. Such individuals can in all honesty obtain a high score on the *Sd* scale, and there is no way to differentiate between these individuals and those who obtain high scores on the *Sd* scale because of motivation toward impression management. It must be kept in mind that, in general, the keyed responses to the items in the *Sd* scale are not improbable responses but only those responses which were increased or decreased significantly under specific instruction to create a favorable impression.

15.10   Impression Management and Lie Scales

The sophisticated individual attempting impression management will not necessarily be trapped by items, such as those in the *Lie* scale, designed to indicate tendencies to prevaricate. He will recognize that the majority of normal individuals will answer True to the item "I gossip a little at times" and he will also answer this item True, knowing that a False (and keyed) response to this item may be regarded as a sign that he is motivated toward impression management. He will also recognize that a True response to the statement, "I have never told a lie," may itself be indicative of a tendency to prevaricate and accordingly respond False.

15.11   Individual Differences in Impression Management

How an individual motivated toward impression management responds to the items in a personality inventory obviously depends on the impression that he is trying to create. He may believe that it is more desirable to be extroverted than introverted but that too much extroversion is also undesirable. If the inventory contains a scale designed to measure extroversion-introversion and if an individual is successful in recognizing the items in this scale and the possible keyed responses to the items, he will attempt to falsify his responses to these items in such a way as to obtain a score that is above average — but not too far above average. Another individual, of course, may believe that it is more desirable to be somewhat introverted and will attempt to respond to the items in such a way as to obtain a below average score on the same scale.

15.12   Impression Management and Scores on Trait Scales

We have said that there is no way to differentiate between those individuals who obtain high scores on the *Sd* scale because of impression management and those who obtain high scores because they have answered the items accurately. Similarly, there is no way in which to differentiate between those individuals who obtain high (or low) scores on personality scales designed to measure specific traits because of impression management and those who obtain high (or low) scores because they have accurately described themselves. An individual motivated toward impression management, if successful, can obtain either a high or a low score on a scale designed to measure the trait of dominance, just as other individuals can obtain high (or low) scores because they have answered the items accurately.

One could take the extreme position and regard scores on any scale as simply resulting from individual differences in motivation toward impression management with respect to the particular trait being measured by the scale. If this were true, however, and if a scale has a relatively high r_{kk} value, there would have to be consistent, reliable individual differences with respect to impression management that are related to the responses to the items in the scale. When one considers some of the factors involved in successful impression management, it is difficult to believe that reliable individual differences in scores on trait scales could simply result from reliable individual differences in impression management.

The individual motivated toward impression management must consider the impression he wishes to create, the possible traits measured by the various scales in an inventory, the particular items included in these scales, and the keyed responses to these items. In addition, if he believes that either extremely high or extremely low scores on a scale are to be avoided, but that a score slightly above or slightly below average is desirable, then he must also attempt to guess the mean score on the scale. If he has decided that a score slightly above average is desirable and if he overestimates the mean score on the scale, then his attempts at impression management may result in a considerably higher score relative to the mean than he anticipated. The problems that individuals motivated toward impression management must face in responding to items in personality inventories are not inconsiderable, if they are to be successful. To believe that each different score on a personality scale simply results from individual differences in impression management does not seem at all reasonable.

The test-retest coefficients of personality scales are often sufficiently high so that each individual can be said to obtain approximately the same score on both administrations. Again, it is difficult to believe that individuals could be so consistent and reliable in their motivations toward impression management as to be able to obtain comparable scores on the two different occasions.

Chapter 16

Adjustment
and Social Desirability

16.1   Cultural Norms of Social Desirability

In every society an effort is made to teach children those standards of conduct and behavior that society considers "good" and "bad," or socially desirable and socially undesirable. Children are rewarded for acts that are believed to be desirable and are punished for those that are believed to be undesirable. It seems reasonable to believe that by early adolescence, if not before, almost all children will have acquired a fairly good understanding of what is desirable and undesirable within the framework of their particular culture. Evidence has been presented, for example, to show that, on the average, children's judgments of social desirability of personality statements are highly correlated with the SDSVs of the statements based on the judgments of adults.

It has also been shown that individual ratings of social desirability of personality statements by college students are, in general, substantially correlated with the normative ratings or SDSVs of the same statements. These results also indicate that individuals do tend to acquire or learn the cultural norms of what is desirable and undesirable in the way of personality traits and characteristics.

It would be erroneous to conclude that simply because an individual has learned the cultural norms of social desirability, he will necessarily behave in accordance with them. Almost all college students will agree that cheating on examinations is undesirable, including those students who sometimes engage in this behavior. Similarly, if one regards the correlation coefficient between an individual's ratings of social desirability and the SDSVs of personality statements as an index of the degree to which he has learned the cultural norms of social desirability, then the evidence is quite clear that those individuals who know the cultural norms do not necessarily describe themselves in terms of them. As we have shown, individual differences in rates of SD responding have little or no relationship to the correlations between individual ratings of social desirability and the SDSVs of personality statements.

In measuring individual differences in rates of SD responding, the SD response to a personality item has been defined in terms of the SDSV of the item. We have also shown, however, that when the SD response to an item was defined for each individual in terms of his own individual ratings of social desirability, rates of SD responding based on these individual notions of social desirability were highly correlated with rates based on SD responses defined in terms of the SDSVs of the items.

16.2   A Substantive Interpretation of the MMPI *SD* Scale

We have argued that individual differences in rates of SD responding represent a reliable personality trait and that *rational SD* scales can be developed to measure this trait without regard to the substantive content of the items in the scales, other than as this content determines the SDSVs of the items. Block (1965), however, has argued for a substantive interpretation of scores on the 39-item MMPI *SD* scale. He states that an examination of the items in the *SD* scale reveals to him that the items have a substantive content and appear to be related to a trait that he calls "ego-resiliency." Ego-resiliency is also the trait that Block believes is measured by the first MMPI factor. It is one thing, of course, to assign a trait name or label to a scale by a study of the content of the items in the scale and quite another thing to demonstrate the construct validity of this interpretation.

It will be recalled that a number of rational *SD* scales were constructed from a pool of 2824 items. The items in each of these scales were selected solely on the basis of their SDSVs and without regard to the substantive content of the items. When these *SD* scales were included in a factor analysis with the MMPI *SD* scale, it was found that they all had loadings on a common factor. If Block is correct in his argument that the items in the MMPI *SD* scale have a substantive content relevant to ego-resiliency, then presumably this would also be true of the items in each of these other *SD* scales.

LUTHER THEOLOGICAL SEMINARY
LIBRARY
ST. PAUL, MINNESOTA

16.3   MMPI Items Related to the First MMPI Factor

Block (1965) selected a group of 95 high scorers and a group of 97 low scorers on the first MMPI factor. Responses of these two groups were then compared on each of the MMPI items. A total of 355 or 63 percent of the MMPI items were found to differentiate between the two groups at the 0.05 level of significance. This empirical approach to finding those items relevant to the first MMPI factor does not alone have any bearing on the interpretation of the first factor. Presumably, after the fact, Block might be able to satisfy himself that each of these items also has a substantive content relevant to his conception of ego-resiliency.

If one interprets the first MMPI factor as measuring individual differences in rates of SD responding, then it is possible to predict something about the nature of the MMPI items which will differentiate between high and low scorers *prior* to the empirical findings. The *SD* scale which has been interpreted as measuring individual differences in rates of SD responding has a high loading on the MMPI first factor. We have previously shown that the regression lines of $P(T)$ on SDSV for high and low scorers on the *SD* scale have different slopes and that the greatest differences in $P(T)$ for the two groups are with respect to those items that fall toward the two extremes of the social desirability continuum.

Thus, if high scorers on the first MMPI factor consist of individuals with high rates of SD responding and low scorers consist of individuals with low rates of SD responding, then the majority of items that differentiate between high and low scorers should be those with SDSVs toward the two extremes. This is, in fact, the case. Block (1965, p. 86) reports that "the vast preponderance of the differentiating items" are those at one extreme or the other of the social desirability continuum. If these items were consistently keyed for ego-resiliency responses, then, in general, they would also be keyed for SD responses. Thus, Block's empirical results could have been predicted prior to study and in terms of the SDSVs of the MMPI items.

16.4   Q-Sort Descriptions of High
and Low Scorers on the First MMPI Factor

The high and low scorers on the first MMPI factor in Block's study were actually drawn from five different samples. The individuals in these samples had been observed in various contexts by psychologists and/or psychiatrists who recorded their impressions of each individual in terms of a Q-sort. The items in these Q-sorts, unfortunately, were not the same from sample to sample. There are other unfortunate aspects of this study. The context and nature of the observations were not constant for all samples nor were the observers the same for all samples. Despite these limitations, Block proceeded to *t* test all of the items in each Q-sort for each sample to find those items which differentiated between the high and low scorers. After a study of the content of these differentiating items, Block again arrived at a substantive or content interpretation of them: they are all relevant to ego-resiliency.

But another interpretation is also possible. For four of his five samples, each high scorer and each low scorer was interviewed. The interviews were conducted by psychologists and/or psychiatrists. We are not told the nature of these interviews, but presumably because the interviewer knew he was going to be required to provide a Q-sort of the personality of the subjects, relatively little time was spent in a discussion of the weather. It is not unreasonable to believe, therefore, that the interviewer's questions were directed toward discovering something about the personalities of the subjects.

If an individual tends to give SD responses to questions and statements in a personality inventory, why should he not also do so when he is asked similar kinds of questions in an interview? If an individual describes himself primarily in terms of socially desirable statements in an interview, he is likely to create a favorable impression on the interviewer and, in turn, be described by the interviewer in terms of socially desirable statements. On the other hand, if an individual describes himself primarily in terms of socially undesirable statements in an interview, he is likely to impress the interviewer unfavorably and might be described, in turn, by means of socially undesirable statements.

An examination of the Q-sort items that were significantly more characteristic of the high scorers on the first MMPI factor shows that almost without exception they would be judged to have socially desirable scale values. Similarly, the Q-sort items that were found to be more characteristic of the low scorers are, also almost without exception, items that would be judged to have socially undesirable scale values. There is nothing in these findings by Block that is inconsistent with the interpretation of high scores on the first MMPI factor as representing high rates of SD responding and low scores as representing low rates of SD responding. The case for an ego-resiliency interpretation of the first MMPI factor is surely not established by this research.

16.5   Construct Validity of *SD* Scales

SD scales designed to measure individual differences in SD responding are rational scales and, as we have pointed out previously, for rational scales there seldom exists an external criterion that can be regarded as accurately measuring the trait which the rational scale is designed to measure. Instead, rational scales are ordinarily validated by hypothesis testing and research.

In the preceding chapters of this book, we have developed a considerable number of hypotheses based on the interpretation of scores on *SD* scales as measuring individual differences in rates of SD responding, and we have reported the results obtained when these hypotheses were submitted to empirical test. We suggest that the reader reconsider these hypotheses and determine for himself whether they could have been developed in terms of a construct of ego-resiliency.

16.6 Group Differences in SDSVs

When personality statements are rated for social desirability by two different groups of judges, it has been found that the SDSVs based on the judgments of the two groups are highly and positively correlated. A high positive correlation between two sets of SDSVs indicates that, in general, the ordering of the items in terms of their SDSVs in one set is very similar to the ordering of the items in terms of their SDSVs in the other set. It does not mean that the paired SDSVs in the two sets are precisely the same. Thus, if a large number of personality statements have been rated for social desirability by two groups, and if the SDSVs of the two groups are compared item by item, there will undoubtedly be some items for which the SDSVs differ significantly. An early study by Klett (1957b) bears out this point.

Klett obtained ratings of social desirability of the items in the EPPS from a group of 118 manifestly disturbed patients in a Veterans Administration Hospital. The correlation between the SDSVs based on the judgments of the patients and those of college students was 0.88. The items in the EPPS, however, can be subdivided into 15 subsets corresponding to the 15 traits supposedly measured by the EPPS. For each of these subsets, Klett compared the difference in the mean SDSVs of the items for the two groups. He found that items relating to Deference, Order, and Aggression were judged as more socially desirable by patients than by college students and that items relating to Affiliation, Intraception, and Change were judged as more socially undesirable by patients than by college students. On the remaining subsets, the mean SDSV for patients did not differ significantly from the mean for college students.

16.7 Block's Notion of the "Equivalence" of Two Concepts

In another study, Block (1962) used *t* tests to evaluate the significance of the difference between the Q-values assigned to 100 statements when they were sorted for social desirability and for adjustment. The data he analyzed were obtained in a Q-study, described previously, by Weiner, Blumberg, Segman, and Cooper (1959). These investigators asked a group of 28 clinical psychologists to Q-sort a set of 100 items in the way they believed a well-adjusted person would sort them. Another group of 16 clinical psychologists Q-sorted the same statements in terms of their conceptions of how people in general would sort them with respect to social desirability. The items were Q-sorted into nine categories with the first category representing social desirability and adjustment and the ninth category social undesirability and maladjustment. The correlation between the mean Q-values of the statements under the two sets of instructions was 0.88.

Block found that 25 of the 100 items had significantly different Q-values when sorted for social desirability and for adjustment. On the basis of these results, he concludes that the concepts of adjustment and social desirability can not be considered as *equivalent*. A correlation of 0.88 between the scale values of the 100 items when rated for adjustment and for social desirability, however, is only slightly lower than the correlation typically found when two groups of judges rate the same set of statements for the same concept of social desirability. If the number of statements is large and if *t* tests are used to evaluate the significance of the difference between the SDSVs of the items for the two groups, there will also be some items for which the SDSVs differ significantly. Similarly, if two groups of clinical psychologists were to rate the same set of statements for the *single* concept of adjustment, there would be items for which the scale values differ significantly between the two groups. If one were to accept Block's argument, then one would also have to conclude that the concept of adjustment could never be equivalent to itself.

16.8   Degree to which Two Concepts Are Similar in Meaning

We need not, however, be concerned with the conditions under which one concept can be considered equivalent to itself or to another concept. Instead, we take the position that the degree to which a given concept, such as social desirability, is *similar in meaning* for two groups is indexed by the magnitude of the correlation coefficient between the SDSVs of the items based on the judgments of the two groups. The evidence presented in previous chapters shows quite clearly that the concept of social desirability is very similar in meaning for diverse groups.

Similarly, adjustment and social desirability may not be equivalent concepts, in Block's terms, but in view of the magnitude of the correlation coefficient between the scale values of items when rated for social desirability and for adjustment, the concepts of social desirability and adjustment are definitely quite similar in meaning.

There is evidence that Block, on other occasions, is not overly concerned about whether or not a concept may be considered equivalent to itself. In a publication describing his California Q-set, Block (1961) reports on several composite or defining Q-sorts. Each of these composite Q-sorts was obtained by averaging the individual Q-sorts of a group of nine clinical psychologists. If another group of clinical psychologists were asked to Q-sort the same items for the same concepts used by Block in obtaining his composites, items would be found for which the Q-values would differ significantly from those obtained by Block. Apparently then, the concepts of the optimally adjusted personality, the male paranoid, and the female hysteric, represented by the composite Q-sorts reported by Block, have no generality beyond the limited group of clinical psychologists who participated in his research.

Furthermore, it is entirely reasonable to believe that the individual Q-sorts of the nine clinical psychologists were not identical with each other. As a matter of fact, the average intercorrelations of the Q-sorts for the optimally adjusted personality, the male paranoid, and the female hysteric were 0.78, 0.55, and 0.51, respectively. If different judges assign different ratings to the same statements when rating the same concept, then can one consider the concept to be "equivalent" for all judges? In averaging the ratings of the nine clinicians to obtain a composite, Block must have believed the concept to be sufficiently *similar in meaning* for the clinicians that the averaging process would make sense. If these average ratings defining Block's composites are also substantially correlated with the average ratings assigned to the same statements by another group of clinicians, this result may also be regarded as indicating that the concepts defined by these composites are very similar in meaning for both groups of clinicians.

16.9   Scale Values Based on Q-Sorts and Free-Choice Scales

There are several other points that need to be considered with respect to Block's (1962) study. The Q-sort procedure used to obtain the scale values of items will ordinarily force some items to have higher or lower scale values than they might have if scaled on a free-choice rating scale. Suppose, for example, that there are ten items in a set to which a judge would assign a rating of 1 if he were free to do so. If the Q-sort permits the placement of only five items in the 1 category, then five of the items must, of necessity, receive a higher rating in the Q-sort than if they were rated on a free-choice scale. Similarly, if there are only two items that would be assigned a rating of 1, if the judge were free to do so, he must, of necessity, rate some items lower in the Q-sort than he otherwise would. If differences in scale values of items based on the judgments of two different groups are to be compared, it would appear more reasonable to have the items rated on a free-choice scale rather than in terms of the forced-choice Q-sort.

Another point regards the instructions given to the clinical psychologists who Q-sorted the items with respect to social desirability. Note that they were *not* instructed to sort them in terms of how socially desirable or socially undesirable *they* believed the items to be, but rather to sort them in terms of their conceptions of how people in general would sort them. The task set for the clinicians, in other words, was one of predicting how people in general would judge the items rather than one in which they were to evaluate the items in terms of their own standards of social desirability. We have no assurance that the scale values of the items would be the same under both sets of instructions. Consequently, we have no way of knowing whether the items for which Block found significant differences in scale values would also be those for which significant differences would be found if they had been Q-sorted under the simple instructions to sort them in terms of how socially desirable or undesirable the clinicians themselves believed them to be.

16.10   Adjustment and *SD* Scales

Suppose that the 25 items for which Block found the social desirability and adjustment scale values to differ significantly were used to form a scale to measure adjustment. All items with adjustment scale values on one side of 5.0, the so-called neutral point, would be keyed True, and all those with scale values on the other side of the neutral point would be keyed False. In terms of the Q-sort, all items on one side of the neutral point represent items which, on the average, were judged to represent adjustment, whereas those on the other side were those judged to represent maladjustment. Then an individual with a high score on this scale would be one who attributes to himself characteristics regarded as indicating adjustment by clinical psychologists and who denies those characteristics regarded as indicating maladjustment.

It is interesting to note that if these same 25 items were keyed for SD responses in terms of their Q-sort values for social desirability, 23 of the 25 items would be keyed in exactly the same direction. There are only two items in the set of 25 which have scale values on opposite sides of the neutral point when scaled for social desirability and when scaled for adjustment. One of the items was "I am critical of people," which had a scale value of 4.75 for adjustment and a scale value of 5.63 for social desirability. The other item was "I am impulsive" with a scale value of 4.69 for social desirability and a scale value of 5.39 for adjustment. The keying of these 25 items for adjustment and for social desirability would be almost completely confounded.

16.11   Individual Differences
in Healthy, Normal, Adjustive, and SD Responding

If a large number of personality items are scaled for health-sickness, or for adjustment-maladjustment, or for normality-abnormality by psychiatrists or clinical psychologists, the scale values of the items under any of these instructions will be found to be highly correlated with the scale values of the items when they are rated for social desirability by individuals who are not psychiatrists or clinical psychologists. The SDSVs of items have been used to define SD responses to the items. The scale values of the items when rated for normality-abnormality could also be used to define a "normal" response to the items. And similarly, it would be possible to define an "adjustive" response to an item, or a "healthy" response to an item.

In view of the relatively high correlation between the scale values of personality items when scaled in terms of any of the above dimensions, it is to be expected that for most items the normal, adjusted, and healthy response would be the same as the SD response. We have described *SD* scales in which all of the items are keyed for SD responses in terms of the SDSVs of the item and we have described scores on these scales as measuring individual differences in rates of SD responding. Thus individual differences in rates of normal, healthy, and adjustive responding, if not equivalent to individual differences in rates of SD responding, would be expected to be highly correlated with them.

16.12   The Need for Trait Scales Uncorrelated
with Rates of SD Responding

To state that individual differences in rates of SD responding may be expected, in general, to be positively correlated with individual differences in adjustive responding does not deny the possibility that a subtle adjustment scale might be developed. Scores on this scale might be uncorrelated with individual differences in rates of SD responding. If we wish to distinguish between the traits of adjustment and SD responding, then it will be necessary to develop scales that can be regarded as measuring adjustment and on which scores are relatively uncorrelated with scores on *SD* scales.

The discussion above applies, of course, to personality traits other than adjustment. There is no good reason why psychologists and other research workers should continue to develop new personality scales and to assign different trait names to these scales, only to find that scores on the various scales are, in turn, highly correlated with individual differences in rates of SD responding. Of much greater importance and significance would be the development of scales with sound psychometric properties and on which scores are relatively uncorrelated with individual differences in rates of SD responding.

Chapter 17

Trait
and Evaluative Consistency
in Self-Description[1]

17.1 Introduction

In a study described previously, Edwards and Walsh (1963a) divided
MMPI scales into two parts: those items keyed for SD responses and those
keyed for SUD responses. To determine the intensity of the SD and SUD
keying of each part of these scales, the SDSVs of the items keyed False were
reflected. The sum of the reflected and unreflected SDSVs were then
obtained for each part scale and this sum was divided by the number of items
in the scale to obtain an average index of intensity for each scale. The scales
were then intercorrelated and factor-analyzed. The correlation between the
signed loadings of the scales on the first principal component and the
average index of intensity of the scales was 0.88.

When each scale consists of a single item keyed True, the intensity of
the SD or SUD keying of the item is simply the SDSV of the item. In
other words, if there are no False-keyed items, there is no need to reflect
the SDSVs of the items in order to obtain the intensity index. For example,
an item with an SDSV of 7.0 keyed True is assumed to represent a greater
intensity of social desirability than an item keyed True for which the SDSV is
6.0. Similarly, if an item has an SDSV of 2.0 and is keyed True, it is assumed

[1]The material in this chapter is substantially the same as that in a previously published
article by Edwards (1969).

234

that this item has a greater intensity of social undesirability than an item with an SDSV of 3.0 which is also keyed True.

Let the score on a single item scale be 1 if answered True and 0 if answered False. For any given set of items it is possible to obtain the intercorrelation matrix of the item responses and to factor-analyze this matrix. If the results of the Edwards and Walsh study are applicable to single item scales, then the loadings of the items on the first principal component should be linearly related to the SDSVs of the item.

The 90 trait terms listed in Table 17.1 may be considered a set of 90 items to be answered True if a subject believes the term is descriptive of him and False if he does not. Note, however, that the 90 terms have been arranged in

Table 17.1 Sets of Trait Terms and Their Evaluative Ratings[a]

Set No.		Sets of Four		
		Temperament		
1	+0.9	Cautious	+1.1	Bold
	−1.1	Timid	−1.2	Rash
2	+1.7	Self-Controlled	+1.1	Uninhibited
	−1.4	Inhibited	−0.3	Impulsive
3	+1.3	Serious	+1.5	Gay
	−1.6	Grim	−1.2	Frivolous
4	+2.0	Alert	+1.8	Relaxed
	−1.1	Tense	−1.7	Lethargic
5	+0.8	Committed	+2.5	Open-Minded
	−2.4	Fanatical	−0.8	Noncommital
6	+1.3	Steady	+1.6	Flexible
	−2.1	Inflexible	−1.5	Vacillating
7	+2.0	Modest	+1.3	Confident
	−1.1	Self-Disparaging	−2.0	Conceited
		Social		
8	+0.9	Thrifty	+1.8	Generous
	−2.0	Stingy	−0.8	Extravagant
9	+0.5	Skeptical	+1.1	Trusting
	−1.4	Distrustful	−1.4	Gullible
10	+1.3	Selective	+2.5	Tolerant
	−0.5	Choosy	−1.4	Undiscriminating
11	+1.3	Firm	+0.9	Lenient
	−1.4	Severe	−0.9	Lax
12	+1.3	Discreet	+1.8	Frank
	−1.2	Secretive	−1.4	Indiscreet
13	+2.0	Individualistic	+1.6	Cooperative
	−2.0	Uncooperative	−1.6	Conforming

Table 17.1   Sets of Trait Terms and Their Evaluative Ratings[a]—*Continued*

Set No.		Sets of Four		

Ideas and Ability

14	+0.9	Pragmatic	+1.5	Idealistic
	−0.6	Opportunistic	−1.2	Unrealistic
15	+1.6	Cultivated	+2.1	Natural
	−2.2	Artificial	−0.7	Naive

		Sets of Three		

Temperament

16	+1.8	Thorough		
	−1.5	Fussy	−1.4	Careless
17	+1.3	Moral		
	−1.6	Self-Righteous	−1.6	Immoral
18	+1.8	Curious		
	−1.7	Nosy	−1.5	Uninquisitive

Social

19	+1.0	Forceful		
	−2.0	Domineering	−1.4	Submissive
20	+1.7	Peaceful		
	−1.2	Passive	−2.0	Belligerent
21	+1.6	Polite		
	−1.5	Ingratiating	−2.2	Rude

Ideas and ability

22	+2.6	Intelligent		
	−0.7	Crafty	−1.7	Stupid
23	+1.9	Foresighted		
	−1.3	Scheming	−1.5	Short-Sighted
24	+1.6	Meditative		
	−0.9	Brooding	−1.6	Unmeditative
25	+1.8	Witty		
	−0.8	Sarcastic	−2.1	Humorless

[a]The evaluative ratings are those given by Peabody (1967). Twenty judges rated the terms on a "favorable-unfavorable" scale and 20 rated the terms on a "desirable-undesirable" scale. In both cases the rating scale was from +3 to −3. The ratings are the means for the 40 judges.

15 sets of four terms and ten sets of three terms. The terms within each set were intended by Peabody (1967) to represent a common bipolar trait. In the first set, for example, "cautious" and "timid" were assumed to represent

one pole of a common trait and "bold" and "rash" the opposite pole. Furthermore, one of the two terms at each pole was intended to be positive or to have a socially desirable scale value and the other to be negative or to have a socially undesirable scale value. The *deviation* SDSVs listed in Table 17.1 are those reported by Peabody, who had the traits rated on a scale ranging from −3 to +3, with 0 defined as the neutral point.

17.2   Type I Correlation Coefficients

Within each set of four terms it is possible to calculate two correlation coefficients between two terms that are opposite in descriptive similarity and also opposite in evaluative sign. For example, for the first set, these correlation coefficients would be those between "cautious-rash" and "bold-timid." Similarly, each set of three terms results in one correlation coefficient of the kind described. We shall refer to these correlation coefficients as *Type I coefficients*.

For Type I coefficients, the trait consistent responses to the two terms are completely confounded with SD responses to the terms, as shown in Table 17.2. For example, if a subject answers True to "cautious," then

Table 17.2   **Trait Consistent and SD Consistent Patterns of Response to Pairs of Trait Terms in the First Set and Predicted Signs of the Correlation Coefficient between the Paired Terms**[a]

Trait Pairs	Consistent Trait Patterns	Sign of r	Consistent SD Patterns	Sign of r	Type of r
Cautious-Rash	TF and FT	−	TF and FT	−	I
Bold-Timid	TF and FT	−	TF and FT	−	I
Cautious-Bold	TF and FT	−	TT and FF	+	II
Timid-Rash	TF and FT	−	FF and TT	+	II
Cautious-Timid	TT and FF	+	TF and FT	−	III
Bold-Rash	TT and FF	+	TF and FT	−	III

[a]From Edwards (1969).

he should answer False to "rash" and both of these responses are SD responses. Similarly, if a subject answers True to "rash," then he should answer False to "cautious" and both of these responses are SUD responses. Both trait and SD consistencies in responding should, in this instance, result in negative values for Type I coefficients.

17.3   Type II Correlation Coefficients

Within each set of four terms it is also possible to calculate two correlation coefficients between two terms that are opposite in descriptive similarity but such that the evaluative signs of the two terms are either both plus or both minus. For example, in the first set, these two correlation coefficients would be those between "cautious-bold" and between "timid-rash." Another ten such correlation coefficients can be calculated for each set of three terms. We shall refer to correlation coefficients of the kind described as *Type II coefficients*.

For Type II coefficients, if the primary determiner of responses to the paired terms is trait consistency, then the dominant response patterns should be TF and FT, as shown in Table 17.2, and the Type II coefficients should be negative. On the other hand, if subjects tend to respond to these pairs of traits in terms of either SD or SUD consistencies, then the dominant response patterns should be TT and FF, as shown in Table 17.2, and the Type II correlations should be positive.

17.4   Type III Correlation Coefficients

Within each set of four terms two correlation coefficients can be calculated between traits that are descriptively similar but which are opposite in evaluative sign. For example, in the first set these two correlation coefficients would be those between "cautious-timid" and between "bold-rash." Similarly, each set of three terms results in one such correlation coefficient. We shall refer to correlation coefficients of the kind described as *Type III coefficients*.

If subjects give trait consistent responses, then the dominant response patterns for Type III coefficients should be TT and FF, as shown in Table 17.2, and the Type III coefficients should be positive. But if subjects tend to respond to these pairs of traits in terms of either SD or SUD consistencies, then the dominant patterns of response should be TF and FT and, as indicated in Table 17.2, the Type III coefficients should be negative.

The 90 trait terms thus provide an interesting set for investigating consistencies in "evaluative" or social desirability responding in self-description and also consistencies in trait responding.

17.5   The Correlation between $P(T)$ and SDSV for the 90 Traits

Social desirability ratings of the 90 traits were made by a group of 88 male and 126 female students on a 9-point rating scale. The traits were not presented to the judges in the same order in which they are listed in Tables

17.1 and 17.4. Instead, each of the 90 traits was typed on a 3 × 5 card and the cards were thoroughly and independently shuffled by two individuals to arrange them in random order. The traits were then printed in this random order in a booklet consisting of four pages. The first three pages of the booklet each contained 25 traits and the last page 15 traits. The judges were told that if they did not know the meaning of a given trait they should mark it with an X and not to assign a rating to it. Of the 90 traits, five were marked with an X by 16 or more of the combined group of 214 judges. These traits are listed in Table 17.3, which also shows the percentage of the judging group that did not assign a rating to them.

Table 17.3   Proportion of the $N = 214$ Judges Not Rating Five Terms and Proportion of $N = 307$ Subjects Not Answering the Same Five Terms[a]

	Ratings	Self-Description
Pragmatic	0.150	0.362
Self-Disparaging	0.145	0.371
Lethargic	0.079	0.283
Ingratiating	0.168	0.417
Vacillating	0.136	0.401

[a]From Edwards (1969).

SDSVs of the traits were determined separately for male and female judges, using only those judges who assigned a rating to the trait. The correlation between the male and female SDSVs was 0.986. For the male judges, the mean SDSV was 4.87 and the standard deviation of the SDSVs was 1.48. The corresponding values for the female judges were 4.79 and 1.81.

A simple unweighted mean of the male and female SDSVs was obtained for each trait and these are the SDSVs used in the present study. The SDSVs for each trait are given in Table 17.4. The correlation between these SDSVs and those obtained by Peabody and listed in Table 17.1 is 0.96.

The 90 traits were given to another group of 127 male and 180 female students. These students were asked to describe themselves in terms of traits by marking the trait True if they believed it accurately described them and False if they did not. The same random order of presentation of the traits used in obtaining social desirability ratings was used in obtaining self-descriptions. The subjects were also told that if they did not know the meaning of a given trait they were to mark it with an X and not to answer it True or False. The five traits with the largest number of X responses were the same as those which were most often not rated by judges in obtaining

Table 17.4   SDSVs of 90 Trait Terms and Loadings of the Terms on the First
Principal Component[a]

Trait No.	Trait	SDSV	Evaluative Sign	Factor Loading
1	Cautious	5.58	+	0.15
2	Bold	6.42	+	0.02
3	Timid	3.45	−	−0.29
4	Rash	3.60	−	−0.33
5	Self-Controlled	6.98	+	0.41
6	Uninhibited	5.88	+	0.01
7	Inhibited	3.67	−	−0.25
8	Impulsive	5.30	+	−0.21
9	Serious	5.92	+	0.01
10	Gay	6.57	+	0.23
11	Grim	3.01	−	−0.45
12	Frivolous	4.10	−	−0.21
13	Alert	7.14	+	0.34
14	Relaxed	6.60	+	0.44
15	Tense	3.44	−	−0.41
16	Lethargic	3.04	−	−0.37
17	Committed	5.98	+	0.19
18	Open-Minded	8.12	+	0.22
19	Fanatical	2.96	−	−0.36
20	Noncommittal	3.88	−	−0.34
21	Steady	6.55	+	0.40
22	Flexible	6.90	+	0.42
23	Inflexible	2.90	−	−0.51
24	Vacillating	4.13	−	−0.23
25	Modest	5.56	+	0.25
26	Confident	7.08	+	0.34
27	Self-Disparaging	3.70	−	−0.36
28	Conceited	2.92	−	−0.35
29	Thrifty	5.79	+	0.09
30	Generous	7.18	+	0.18
31	Stingy	2.84	−	−0.44
32	Extravagant	4.44	−	−0.25
33	Skeptical	5.07	+	−0.30
34	Trusting	7.00	+	0.38
35	Distrustful	2.72	−	−0.49
36	Gullible	3.62	−	−0.11
37	Selective	5.94	+	0.10
38	Tolerant	7.56	+	0.48
39	Choosy	4.34	−	−0.11
40	Undiscriminating	4.20	−	0.03

Table 17.4   SDSVs of 90 Trait Terms and Loadings of the Terms on the First
Principal Component[a]—*Continued*

Trait No.	Trait	SDSV	Evaluative Sign	Factor Loading
41	Firm	6.55	+	0.29
42	Lenient	5.77	+	0.25
43	Severe	3.05	−	−0.35
44	Lax	3.92	−	−0.30
45	Discreet	6.23	+	0.28
46	Frank	6.07	+	0.15
47	Secretive	3.96	−	−0.37
48	Indiscreet	3.42	−	−0.30
49	Individualistic	7.62	+	0.22
50	Cooperative	6.81	+	0.46
51	Uncooperative	2.71	−	−0.50
52	Conforming	4.48	−	0.06
53	Pragmatic	5.01	+	−0.09
54	Idealistic	6.56	+	−0.04
55	Opportunistic	4.59	−	0.05
56	Unrealistic	3.20	−	−0.22
57	Cultivated	6.46	+	0.16
58	Natural	6.81	+	0.37
59	Artificial	2.54	−	−0.59
60	Naive	3.78	−	−0.16
61	Thorough	6.48	+	0.27
62	Careless	3.40	−	−0.53
63	Fussy	3.70	−	−0.12
64	Moral	6.44	+	0.36
65	Immoral	2.89	−	−0.39
66	Self-Righteous	3.08	−	−0.12
67	Curious	7.33	+	0.25
68	Uninquisitive	2.86	−	−0.18
69	Nosy	2.94	−	−0.28
70	Forceful	5.52	+	−0.02
71	Submissive	4.03	−	−0.17
72	Domineering	3.16	−	−0.18
73	Peaceful	6.89	+	0.33
74	Belligerent	2.69	−	−0.37
75	Passive	3.69	−	−0.18
76	Polite	6.73	+	0.16
77	Rude	2.69	−	−0.39
78	Ingratiating	4.10	−	−0.22

Table 17.4   SDSVs of 90 Trait Terms and Loadings of the Terms on the First
Principal Component[a]—*Continued*

Trait No.	Trait	SDSV	Evaluative Sign	Factor Loading
79	Intelligent	7.60	+	0.20
80	Stupid	2.24	−	−0.45
81	Crafty	4.78	−	0.01
82	Foresighted	6.77	+	0.46
83	Short-Sighted	3.20	−	−0.54
84	Scheming	3.32	−	−0.18
85	Meditative	6.07	+	0.09
86	Unmeditative	3.52	−	−0.11
87	Brooding	3.42	−	−0.50
88	Witty	6.70	+	0.01
89	Humorless	3.02	−	−0.41
90	Sarcastic	3.95	−	−0.26

[a]From Edwards (1969).

the SDSVs of the traits. Table 17.3 shows the percentage of the combined group of 307 subjects who failed to answer each of the five traits.

There is no reason to believe that the students who rated the traits for social desirability were any more knowledgeable about the meaning of the traits than those who described themselves. Yet, in every case, the percentage of students not answering a trait in self-description is considerably larger than the percentage of students not rating the trait. It should be emphasized that both the ratings and self-descriptions were done anonymously. The obvious implication is that more students tend to be cautious when asked to make a judgment about themselves than when they are asked to make a judgment that has no self-reference.

For each trait, the percentage was obtained of the combined group of subjects responding True to the trait. These percentages are based on the responses of only those subjects who indicated that they knew the meaning of the trait by answering it either True or False. Each of these percentages may be regarded as an estimate of the probability that a given trait will be answered True in self-description by those subjects who believe they understand the meaning of the trait.

Figure 17.1 shows the relationship between $P(T)$ for each of the 90 traits and the SDSVs of the traits. It is obvious that $P(T)$ tends to increase with the SDSVs of the traits. The product-moment correlation between $P(T)$ and SDSV is 0.92 and is fairly typical of the correlations previously reported between these two variables.

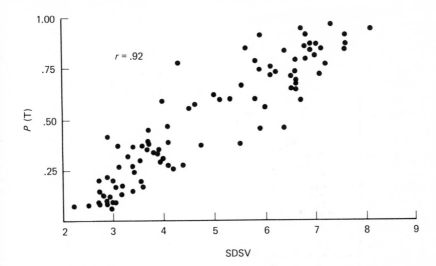

Figure 17.1 The relationship between $P(T)$ and SDSV for the 90 trait terms. From Edwards (1969).

17.6 The Correlation between the First Factor Loadings and the SDSVs of the Traits

The keyed response to each trait was taken as True and assigned a score of 1 and a False response was assigned a score of 0. Intercorrelations were then obtained between each of the 90 traits, the correlations in all cases being based on the responses of only those subjects who had indicated they knew the meaning of the traits by marking them either True or False.

The 90 × 90 correlation matrix was then factor-analyzed by the method of principal components. Table 17.4 gives the unrotated factor loadings of the traits on the first principal component.[2]

In Figure 17.2 the unrotated loadings of the traits on the first principal component are plotted against the SDSVs of the traits. Those traits with low or socially undesirable scale values tend to have relatively high negative loadings, whereas those traits with high or socially desirable scale values tend to have relatively high positive loadings. The product-moment correlation between the SDSVs and the unrotated first factor loadings of the traits is 0.90. Thus, the signed first factor loadings of these single item scales are linearly related to the intensity or SDSVs of the scales, a finding that is consistent with the results obtained by Edwards and Walsh.

Table 17.4 gives the evaluative sign of each trait, the sign being regarded

[2]The first principal component accounted for 0.093 of the total variance.

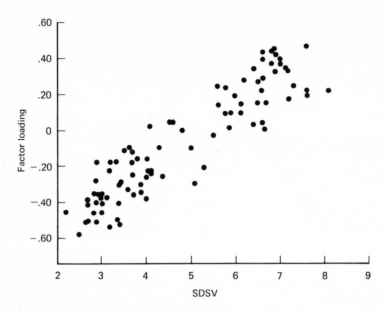

Figure 17.2   The relationship between the first factor loadings of the 90 trait terms and the SDSVs of the terms. From Edwards (1969).

as positive if the trait has an SDSV > 5.0 or as negative if the trait has an SDSV < 5.0. It may be noted that the signed loadings of the traits on the first principal component tend to alternate systematically in accordance with the evaluative signs of the trait. This finding is in accord with an interpretation of the first principal component as an SD-SUD factor.

17.7   Mean Values of the Type I, II, and III Correlation Coefficients

The frequency distribution of the 40 Type I correlation coefficients is given in column (1) of Table 17.5. As pointed out previously and as shown in Table 17.2, trait consistencies and SD consistencies are completely confounded in Type I correlation coefficients, and both trait and SD consistencies should result in negative values for Type I coefficients. The average value of the Type I coefficients is −0.24 and only four of the 40 coefficients are positive.

With respect to Type II coefficients, trait consistencies should result in negative and SD tendencies in positive correlation coefficients. The frequency distribution of the 40 Type II coefficients is given in column (2) of Table 17.5. It may be noted that 22 of the coefficients are positive and 18 are negative and that the average value is −0.01. This finding offers no con-

Table 17.5 Frequency Distributions of Correlation Coefficients for Pairs of Traits[a]

r	(1) f	(2) f	(3) f	(4) f	(5) f	(6) f
0.35			1		2	
0.30			1	2	4	
0.25				1	11	
0.20			2	5	15	
0.15			2	6	15	
0.10		6	10	9	13	
0.05		6	7	4	5	3
0.00	4	10	4	5	1	5
−0.00	2	5	5	2		7
−0.05	4	4	5			7
−0.10	3	5	3	1		13
−0.15	6	3		1		5
−0.20	4					5
−0.25	3	1				1
−0.30	3					2
−0.35	2					1
−0.40	2					
−0.45	2					
−0.50	1					
−0.55	3					
−0.60	1					
n	40	40	40	36	66	49
$\overline{X}$	−0.24	−0.01	0.06	0.12	0.19	−0.10
σ	0.18	0.09	0.11	0.11	0.08	0.15

(1) Pairs of traits opposite in descriptive similarity and opposite in evaluative sign.
(2) Pairs of traits opposite in descriptive similarity but with the same evaluative sign.
(3) Pairs of traits with descriptive similarity but opposite in evaluative sign.
(4) Pairs of traits from different sets and presumably different traits but with SDSVs equal to or greater than 7.0.
(5) Pairs of traits from different sets and presumably different traits but with SDSVs less than 3.0.
(6) Pairs of traits from different sets and presumably different traits but with opposite evaluative signs.

[a]From Edwards (1969).

vincing evidence that trait consistencies, in general, dominate SD consistencies or vice versa.

For Type III coefficients, SD consistencies should result in negative values and trait consistencies in positive values. The frequency distribution of the 40 Type III coefficients is given in column (3) of Table 17.5. The average value of the Type III coefficients is only 0.06, with 13 of the 40 coefficients being negative.

A reasonable hypothesis as to why the average value of the Type III coefficients is only 0.06 is that a considerable number of the subjects gave consistent SD or SUD responses to the paired terms. For these subjects the response patterns would be either TF or FT. If these response patterns occur with any degree of frequency, the trait consistent response patterns, TT and FF, will be reduced accordingly. Thus, consistent SD or SUD responses would tend to lower the correlation between the paired terms. Note, for example, that when trait consistent and SD consistent tendencies operate in the same direction, as in the case of Type I coefficients, the average correlation between the paired terms is −0.24.

17.8   Correlations between Items from Different Sets

There are nine trait terms with SDSVs equal to or greater than 7.0 and such that each of the terms is from a different set. Thus:

Trait No.	Trait	Set	SDSV
13	Alert	4	7.14
18	Open-Minded	5	8.12
26	Confident	7	7.08
30	Generous	8	7.18
34	Trusting	9	7.00
38	Tolerant	10	7.56
49	Individualistic	13	7.62
67	Curious	18	7.33
79	Intelligent	22	7.60

The fact that these traits were classified in different sets by Peabody, and that the terms within a given set are presumably related to a common attribute, would seem to imply that these nine traits should be less highly related than the trait terms within a given set. Calculating the correlation coefficient between each pair of the nine traits, we obtain 36 correlation coefficients. If SD consistencies are operating then, in general, the average value of the 36 coefficients should be positive. The distribution of the 36 correlation coefficients is shown in column (4) of Table 17.5, the average value being 0.12. This average is higher than the average value, 0.06, between pairs of traits with descriptive similarity but with opposed evaluative signs.

A dynamically oriented trait psychologist could undoubtedly offer a plausible explanation of why the nine traits tend to be positively inter-correlated. If the nine traits are regarded as a single scale in which the True response to each trait is the keyed response, then high scorers on this scale might be described as "well adjusted," as having a high degree of "ego-resiliency," and as being relatively free from "anxiety," and the like. All of these dynamic descriptions, however, are themselves socially desirable descriptions and, in essence, the high scorer on this scale would be one who tends to give SD responses in self-description.

If we select terms with SDSVs less than 3.0 and such that each term is from a different set, we have the following:

Trait No.	Trait	Set	SDSV
19	Fanatical	5	2.96
23	Inflexible	6	2.90
28	Conceited	7	2.92
31	Stingy	8	2.84
35	Distrustful	9	2.72
51	Uncooperative	13	2.71
59	Artificial	15	2.54
65	Immoral	17	2.89
69	Nosy	18	2.94
74	Belligerent	20	2.69
77	Rude	21	2.69
80	Stupid	22	2.24

Again, because these trait terms are from different sets, it might be assumed that they have less in common than the terms within a given set. Regardless of the differences in the traits, if SD consistencies are primary, then the average correlation between these pairs of terms should be positive. The distribution of the 66 correlation coefficients is shown in column (5) of Table 17.5 and the average value is 0.19. Again we note that this value is higher than the average value, 0.06, between traits with descriptive simi-larity but with opposite evaluative signs.

If we eliminate "generous" and "trusting" with positive evaluative signs and "uncooperative," "fanatical," "stupid," "nosy," and "conceited" with negative signs, we have a group of seven traits with positive signs and another group of seven traits with negative signs and such that no trait with a positive sign is from the same set as a trait with a negative sign. If SD consistencies are operating, then the average correlation between terms in these two groups should be negative. The distribution of the 49 correlation coefficients is shown in column (6) of Table 17.5. The average value is −0.10.

17.9   The Peabody Study

The 90 traits investigated in this study are the same as those used in a study by Peabody (1967). In the present study the objective was to investi- gate trait and SD consistencies when subjects are asked to describe them- selves by answering True or False to items or trait terms. In the Peabody study, however, the subjects were told that another person possessed a given trait and they were then asked to judge how likely it was that he possessed one of two other traits. For example, the subjects were told that another person was accurately described by "cautious" and were then asked to judge whether the same person was more likely to be "timid" or "bold." For 70 critical judgments in which a given trait was to be judged on a bipolar scale of two other terms from the same set so that descriptive and evaluative similarity opposed each other, as when "cautious" is to be judged on the scale "timid-bold," Peabody found that the *mean* ratings were all in the direction of descriptive similarity and away from evaluative similarity. He regards this finding as evidence that when subjects are confronted directly with a choice between descriptive similarity and evaluative similarity that descriptive similarity is decisive over evaluative similarity.

It may be noted, however, that Peabody's method of data collection is essentially a forced-choice technique. For example, the subjects are told that another person is "cautious" and now must choose between "timid" and "bold." It seems not at all unreasonable if a choice must be made between "timid" and "bold" that subjects would in general favor "timid" over "bold," simply because "timid" is closer in *meaning* to "cautious" than it is to "bold." On the other hand, the True-False format used in the present study permits a subject to answer True to "cautious" without the necessity of also answering True to "timid."

Rather than concluding that descriptive similarity is decisive over evaluative similarity, one might interpret Peabody's results as indicating that if subjects are given one word or term and then forced to choose between two other terms (one of which is similar in meaning and one of which is opposite in meaning) they will in general favor the word which is similar in meaning. It does not follow that simply because subjects believe "stingy" to be more similar in meaning to "thrifty" than "generous" that these two traits are necessarily related in the real world of people. That they are not for the subjects involved in the present study is shown by the fact that the correlation between "thrifty-stingy" is −0.02.

References

Block, J. *The Q-sort method in personality assessment and psychiatric research.* Springfield, Ill.: Charles C. Thomas, 1961.

Block, J. Some differences between the concepts of social desirability and adjustment. *Journal of Consulting Psychology,* 1962, **26**, 527–530.

Block, J. *The challenge of response sets.* New York: Appleton-Century-Crofts, 1965.

Block, J. Remarks on Jackson's "Review" of Block's *Challenge of response sets. Educational and Psychological Measurement,* 1967, **27**, 499–502.

Boe, E. E., Gocka, E. F., and Kogan, W. S. A factor analysis of individual social desirability scale values. *Multivariate Behavioral Research,* 1966, **1**, 287–292.

Boe, E. E., and Kogan, W. S. Social desirability response set in the individual. *Journal of Consulting Psychology,* 1963, **27**, 369.

Buros, O. K. (Ed.) *The sixth mental measurements yearbook.* Highland Park, New Jersey: Gryphon Press, 1965.

Chu, Chen-Lin. *Object cluster analysis of the MMPI.* (Unpublished doctoral dissertation, University of California, Berkeley, 1966).

Comrey, A. L. A factor analysis of items on the MMPI hypochondriasis scale. *Educational and Psychological Measurement,* 1957a, **17**, 568–577.

Comrey, A. L. A factor analysis of items on the MMPI depression scale. *Educational and Psychological Measurement,* 1957b, **17**, 578–585.

Comrey, A. L. A factor analysis of items on the MMPI hysteria scale. *Educational and Psychological Measurement,* 1957c, **17**, 586–592.

249

Comrey, A. L. A factor analysis of items on the F scale of the MMPI. *Educational and Psychological Measurement*, 1958a, **18**, 621–632.

Comrey, A. L. A factor analysis of items on the K scale of the MMPI. *Educational and Psychological Measurement*, 1958b, **18**, 633–639.

Comrey, A. L. A factor analysis of items on the MMPI hypomania scale. *Educational and Psychological Measurement*, 1958c, **18**, 313–323.

Comrey, A. L. A factor analysis of items on the MMPI paranoia scale. *Educational and Psychological Measurement*, 1958d, **18**, 99–107.

Comrey, A. L. A factor analysis of items on the MMPI psychasthenia scale. *Educational and Psychological Measurement*, 1958e, **18**, 292–300.

Comrey, A. L. A factor analysis of items on the MMPI psychopathic deviate scale. *Educational and Psychological Measurement*, 1958f, **18**, 91–98.

Comrey, A. L., and Marggraff, W. M. A factor analysis of items on the MMPI schizophrenia scale. *Educational and Psychological Measurement*, 1958, **18**, 301–311.

Couch, A., and Keniston, K. Yeasayers and naysayers: Agreeing response set as a personality variable. *Journal of Abnormal and Social Psychology*, 1960, **60**, 150–174.

Cowen, E. L. The social desirability of trait descriptive terms: Preliminary norms and sex differences. *Journal of Social Psychology*, 1961, **53**, 225–233.

Cowen, E. L., Davol, S. H., Reimanis, G., and Stiller, A. The social desirability of trait-descriptive terms: Two geriatric samples. *Journal of Social Psychology*, 1962, **56**, 217–225.

Cowen, E. L., and Frankel, G. The social desirability of trait-descriptive terms: Applications to a French sample. *Journal of Social Psychology*, 1964, **63**, 233–239.

Cowen, E. L., Staiman, M. G., and Wolitzky, D. L. The social desirability of trait descriptive terms: Applications to a schizophrenic sample. *Journal of Social Psychology*, 1961, **54**, 37–45.

Cowen, E. L., and Stricker, G. The social desirability of trait descriptive terms: A sample of sexual offenders. *Journal of Social Psychology*, 1963, **59**, 307–315.

Cowen, E. L., and Tongas, P. The social desirability of trait descriptive terms: Applications to a self-concept inventory. *Journal of Consulting Psychology*, 1959, **23**, 361–365.

Cronbach, L. J. Response sets and test validity. *Educational and Psychological Measurement*, 1946, **6**, 475–494.

Crowder, P. *An empirical investigation of the effects of varying initial rates of true responses on subsequent rates.* (Unpublished master's thesis, University of Washington, 1962).

Crowne, D. P., and Marlowe, D. A new scale of social desirability independent of psychopathology. *Journal of Consulting Psychology*, 1960, **24**, 349–354.

Cruse, D. B. Socially desirable responses in relation to grade level. *Child Development*, 1963, **34**, 777–789.

Cruse, D. B. Social desirability scale values of personal concepts. *Journal of Applied Psychology*, 1965, **49**, 342–344.

Cruse, D. B. Socially desirable responses at ages 3 through 6. *Child Development*, 1966, **37**, 909–916.

Dahlstrom, W. G., and Welsh, G. S. *An MMPI handbook.* Minneapolis: University of Minnesota Press, 1960.

Dempsey, P. A unidimensional depression scale for the MMPI. *Journal of Consulting Psychology*, 1964, **28**, 364–370.

Diers, C. J. Social desirability and acquiescence in response to personality items. *Journal of Consulting Psychology*, 1964, **28**, 71–77.

Edwards, A. L. The relationship between the judged desirability of a trait and the probability that the trait will be endorsed. *Journal of Applied Psychology*, 1953, **37**, 90–93.

Edwards, A. L. Social desirability and Q-sorts. *Journal of Consulting Psychology*, 1955, **19**, 462.

Edwards, A. L. *The social desirability variable in personality assessment and research.* New York: Holt, Rinehart and Winston, 1957a.

Edwards, A. L. *Techniques of attitude scale construction.* New York: Appleton-Century-Crofts, 1957b.

Edwards, A. L. Social desirability and probability of endorsement of items in the Interpersonal Check List. *Journal of Abnormal and Social Psychology*, 1957c, **55**, 394–395.

Edwards, A. L. *Manual for the Edwards Personal Preference Schedule.* (Rev. ed.) New York: Psychological Corporation, 1959.

Edwards, A. L. Social desirability or acquiescence in the MMPI? A case study with the *SD* scale. *Journal of Abnormal and Social Psychology*, 1961, **63**, 351–359.

Edwards, A. L. Social desirability and expected means on MMPI scales. *Educational and Psychological Measurement*, 1962, **22**, 71–76.

Edwards, A. L. A factor analysis of experimental social desirability and response set scales. *Journal of Applied Psychology*, 1963, **47**, 308–316.

Edwards, A. L. Prediction of mean scores on MMPI scales. *Journal of Consulting Psychology*, 1964a, **28**, 183–185.

Edwards, A. L. The assessment of human motives by means of personality scales. In D. Levine (Ed.), *Nebraska symposium on motivation.* Lincoln: University of Nebraska Press, 1964b, Pp. 135–162.

Edwards, A. L. Measurement of individual differences in ratings of social desirability and in the tendency to give socially desirable responses. *Journal of Experimental Research in Personality*, 1965a, **1**, 91–98.

Edwards, A. L. Correlation of a "unidimensional depression scale for the MMPI" with the *SD* scale. *Journal of Consulting Psychology*, 1965b, **29**, 271–273.

Edwards, A. L. Review of J. Block, *The California Q-set: A Q-sort for personality assessment and psychiatric research.* In O. K. Buros (Ed.), *The sixth mental measurements yearbook.* Highland Park, New Jersey: Gryphon, 1965c. Pp. 170–171.

Edwards, A. L. Relationship between probability of endorsement and social desirability scale value for a set of 2,824 personality statements. *Journal of Applied Psychology,* 1966a, **50,** 238–239.

Edwards, A. L. A comparison of 57 MMPI scales and 57 experimental scales matched with the MMPI scales in terms of item social desirability scale values and probabilities of endorsement. *Educational and Psychological Measurement,* 1966b, **26,** 15–27.

Edwards, A. L. *Manual for the Edwards Personality Inventory.* Chicago: Science Research Associates, 1966c.

Edwards, A. L. The social desirability variable: A broad statement. In I. A. Berg (Ed.), *Response set in personality assessment.* Chicago: Aldine, 1967a. Pp. 32–47.

Edwards, A. L. The social desirability variable: A review of the evidence. In I. A. Berg (Ed.), *Response set in personality assessment.* Chicago: Aldine, 1967b. Pp. 48–70.

Edwards, A. L. Trait and evaluative consistency in self-description. *Educational and Psychological Measurement,* 1969, **29,** 737–752.

Edwards, A. L., and Abbott, R. D. Further evidence regarding the R scale of the MMPI as a measure of acquiescence. *Psychological Report,* 1969, **24,** 903–906.

Edwards, A. L., Abbott, R. D., and Klockars, A. J. A replication and a reply to Stein. *Multivariate Behavioral Research,* 1970, in press.

Edwards, A. L., and Diers, C. J. Social desirability and conflict. *Journal of Social Psychology,* 1962a, **58,** 349–356.

Edwards, A. L., and Diers, C. J. Social desirability and the factorial interpretation of the MMPI. *Educational and Psychological Measurement,* 1962b, **22,** 501–509.

Edwards, A. L., and Diers, C. J. Neutral items as a measure of acquiescence. *Educational and Psychological Measurement,* 1963, **23,** 687–698.

Edwards, A. L., Diers, C. J., and Walker, J. N. Response sets and factor loadings on sixty-one personality scales. *Journal of Applied Psychology,* 1962, **46,** 220–225.

Edwards, A. L., Gocka, E. F., and Holloway, H. The development of an MMPI acquiescence scale. *Journal of Clinical Psychology,* 1964, **20,** 148–150.

Edwards, A. L., and Heathers, L. B. The first factor of the MMPI: Social desirability or ego strength? *Journal of Consulting Psychology,* 1962, **26,** 99–100.

Edwards, A. L., and Horst, P. Social desirability as a variable in Q technique studies. *Educational and Psychological Measurement*, 1953, **13**, 620–625.

Edwards, A. L., Klockars, A. J., and Abbott, R. D. Social desirability and the TSC MMPI scales. *Multivariate Behavioral Research*, 1970, in press.

Edwards, A. L., and Walker, J. N. Relationship between probability of item endorsement and social desirability scale value for high and low groups on Edwards' *SD* scale. *Journal of Abnormal and Social Psychology*, 1962, **64**, 458–460.

Edwards, A. L., and Walsh, J. A. The relationship between the intensity of the social desirability keying of a scale and the correlation of the scale with Edwards' *SD* scale and the first factor loading of the scale. *Journal of Clinical Psychology*, 1963a, **19**, 200–203.

Edwards, A. L., and Walsh, J. A. Relationships between various psychometric properties of personality items. *Educational and Psychological Measurement*, 1963b, **23**, 227–238.

Edwards, A. L., and Walsh, J. A. A factor analysis of ? scores. *Journal of Abnormal and Social Psychology*, 1964a, **69**, 558–563.

Edwards, A. L., and Walsh, J. A. Response sets in standard and experimental personality scales. *American Educational Research Journal*, 1964b, **1**, 52–61.

Edwards, A. L., Walsh, J. A., and Diers, C. J. The relationship between social desirability and internal consistency of personality scales. *Journal of Applied Psychology*, 1963, **47**, 255–259.

Fordyce, W. E. *Applications of a scale of dependency to concepts of self, ideal-self, mother and father.* (Unpublished doctoral dissertation, University of Washington, 1953).

Fordyce, W. E., and Rozynko, V. Unpublished paper cited in A. L. Edwards, *The social desirability variable in personality assessment and research*. New York: Holt, Rinehart and Winston, 1957.

Fricke, B. G. Response set as a suppressor variable in the OAIS and MMPI. *Journal of Consulting Psychology*, 1956, **20**, 161–169.

Fricke, B. G. A response bias (*B*) scale for the MMPI. *Journal of Counseling Psychology*, 1957, **4**, 149–153.

Fujita, B. Applicability of the Edwards Personal Preference Schedule to Nisei. *Psychological Reports*, 1957, **3**, 518–519.

Gocka, E. F., Holloway, H., and Bigger, C. Technical Report No. 3. Research Service, Veterans Administration Hospital. American Lake, Washington, 1962.

Goldberg, L. R. Test-retest item statistics for the Edwards Personal Preference Schedule. *ORI Research Monograph*, 1963, **3**, (3). Eugene: Oregon Research Institute.

Goldberg, L. R., and Rorer, L. G. Test-retest item statistics for original and reversed MMPI items. *ORI Research Monograph*, 1963, **3**, (1). Eugene: Oregon Research Institute.

Goldberg, L. R., and Rorer, L. G. Test-retest item statistics for the California Psychological Inventory. *ORI Research Monograph*, 1964, **4**, (1). Eugene: Oregon Research Institute.

Gough, H. G. An interpreter's syllabus for the California Psychological Inventory. In P. McReynolds (Ed.), *Advances in psychological assessment*, Volume I. Palo Alto, California: Science and Behavior Books, 1968.

Green, B. F. Attitude measurement. In G. Lindzey (Ed.), *Handbook of social psychology*. Volume I. *Theory and method*. Cambridge, Massachusetts: Addison-Wesley, 1954. Pp. 335–469.

Guilford, J. P. *Psychometric methods*. (2nd ed.) New York: McGraw-Hill, 1954.

Hanley, C. Social desirability and responses to items from three MMPI scales: *D*, *Sc*, and *K*. *Journal of Applied Psychology*, 1956, **40**, 324–328.

Hanley, C. Social desirability and response bias in the MMPI. *Journal of Consulting Psychology*, 1961, **25**, 13–20.

Hathaway, S. R., and McKinley, J. C. *Manual for the Minnesota Multiphasic Personality Inventory*. New York: Psychological Corporation, 1951.

Heineman, C. E. Unpublished paper cited in W. G. Dahlstrom and G. S. Welsh, *An MMPI handbook*. Minneapolis: University of Minnesota Press, 1960.

Heineman, P. O., and Cowen, E. L. The social desirability of trait descriptive terms: A mentally deficient sample. *American Journal of Mental Deficiency*, 1965, **70**, 57–62.

Hillmer, M. L., Jr. *Social desirability in a two-choice personality scale*. (Unpublished master's thesis, University of Washington, 1958).

Horst, P. *Factor analysis of data matrices*. New York: Holt, Rinehart and Winston, 1965.

Humphreys, L. G. The fleeting nature of the prediction of college academic success. *Journal of Educational Psychology*, 1968, **59**, 375–380.

Iwawaki, S., and Cowen, E. L. The social desirability of trait-descriptive terms: Applications to a Japanese sample. *Journal of Social Psychology*, 1964, **63**, 199–205.

Iwawaki, S., Fukuhara, M., and Hidano, T. Probability of endorsement of items in the Yatabe-Guilford Personality Inventory: Replications. *Psychological Reports*, 1966, **19**, 249–250.

Iwawaki, S., Okuno, S., and Cowen, E. L. The social desirability of trait-descriptive terms: Sex and cultural differences based on a Japanese arts college sample. *Tohoku Psychologica Folia Tomas*, 1965, **24**, 56–64.

Jackson, D. N. Review of J. Block, *The challenge of response sets. Educational and Psychological Measurement*, 1967a, **27**, 207–219.

Jackson, D. N. Balanced scales, item overlap, and the stables of Augeas. *Educational and Psychological Measurement*, 1967b, **27**, 502–507.

Jackson, D. N. *Manual for the Personality Research Form*. Research Bulletin No. 43. London, Canada: University of Western Ontario, 1967c.

Jackson, D. N., and Messick, S. Content and style in personality assessment. *Psychological Bulletin*, 1958, **55**, 243–252.

Jackson, D. N., and Messick, S. Acquiescence and desirability as response determinants on the MMPI. *Educational and Psychological Measurement*, 1961, **21**, 771–790.

Jackson, D. N., and Messick, S. Response styles on the MMPI: Comparison of clinical and normal samples. *Journal of Abnormal and Social Psychology*, 1962, **65**, 285–299.

Kaiser, H. F. The varimax criterion for analytic rotation in factor analysis. *Psychometrika*, 1958, **23**, 187–200.

Kaiser, H. F. Computer program for varimax rotation in factor analysis. *Educational and Psychological Measurement*, 1959, **19**, 313–420.

Kassebaum, G. G., Couch, A. S., and Slater, P. E. The factorial dimensions of the MMPI. *Journal of Consulting Psychology*, 1959, **23**, 226–236.

Kelleher, D. *The construction of a measure of test-taking attitude on the Edwards Personal Preference Schedule*. (Unpublished master's thesis, University of Washington, 1957).

Kenny, D. T. The influence of social desirability on discrepancy measures between real self and ideal self. *Journal of Consulting Psychology*, 1956, **20**, 315–318.

Klett, C. J. The stability of the social desirability scale values in the Edwards Personal Preference Schedule. *Journal of Consulting Psychology*, 1957a, **21**, 183–185.

Klett, C. J. The social desirability stereotype in a hospital population. *Journal of Consulting Psychology*, 1957b, **21**, 419–421.

Klett, C. J., and Yaukey, D. W. A cross-cultural comparison of judgments of social desirability. *Journal of Social Psychology*, 1959, **49**, 19–26.

Klieger, D. M., and Walsh, J. A. A pictorial technique for obtaining social desirability ratings from young children. *Psychological Reports*, 1967, **20**, 295–304.

Kogan, W. S., Quinn, R., Ax, A. F., and Ripley, H. S. Some methodological problems in the quantification of clinical assessments by Q array. *Journal of Consulting Psychology*, 1957, **21**, 57–62.

Lamphere, A. V. *The relationship between dependency factors and goal-setting behavior in duodenal ulcer patients*. (Unpublished doctoral dissertation, University of Washington, 1953.)

Lövaas, O. I. Social desirability ratings of personality variables by Norwegian and American college students. *Journal of Abnormal and Social Psychology*, 1958, **57**, 124–125.

McGee, R. K. The relationship between response style and personality variables: I. The measurement of response acquiescence. *Journal of Abnormal and Social Psychology*, 1962, **64**, 229–233.

McReynolds, P. (Ed.) *Advances in psychological assessment*. Volume I. Palo Alto, California: Science and Behavior Books, 1968.

Meehl, P. E., and Hathaway, S. R. The K factor as a suppressor variable in the Minnesota Multiphasic Personality Inventory. *Journal of Applied Psychology*, 1946, **30**, 525–564.

Mees, H. L., Gocka, E. F., and Holloway, H. Social desirability scale values for California Psychological Inventory items. *Psychological Reports, Monograph Supplement*, 1964, **15**, 147–158.

Messick, S. Dimensions of social desirability. *Journal of Consulting Psychology*, 1960, **24**, 279–287.

Messick, S., and Jackson, D. N. Desirability scale values and dispersions for MMPI items. *Psychological Reports*, 1961a, **8**, 409–414.

Messick, S., and Jackson, D. N. Acquiescence and the factorial interpretation of the MMPI. *Psychological Bulletin*, 1961b, **58**, 299–304.

Peabody, D. Trait inferences: Evaluative and descriptive aspects. *Journal of Personality and Social Psychology*, 1967, **7**, Monograph Supplement 4.

Rosen, A. Development of MMPI scales based on a reference group of psychiatric patients. *Psychological Monographs*, 1962, **76**, No. 8.

Rosen, E. Self-appraisal, personal desirability, and perceived social desirability of personality traits. *Journal of Abnormal and Social Psychology*, 1956, **52**, 151–158.

Slater, P. E. Unpublished paper, cited in S. Messick and D. N. Jackson, Acquiescence and the factorial interpretation of the MMPI. *Psychological Bulletin*, 1961, **58**, 299–304.

Sperber, Z. and Spanner, M. Social desirability, psychopathology, and item endorsement. *Journal of General Psychology*, 1962, **67**, 105–112.

Stein, K. B. The TSC Scales: The outcome of a cluster analysis of the 550 MMPI items. In P. McReynolds (Ed.), *Advances in psychological assessment*. Volume I. Palo Alto, California: Science and Behavior Books, 1968.

Stephenson, W. *The study of behavior*. Chicago: University of Chicago Press, 1953.

Stiller, A., Schwartz, H. A., and Cowen, E. L. The social desirability of trait-descriptive terms among high-school students. *Child Development*, 1965, **36**, 981–1002.

Taylor, J. B. Social desirability and MMPI performance: The individual case. *Journal of Consulting Psychology*, 1959, **23**, 514–517.

Thurstone, L. L. *Multiple factor analysis*. Chicago: University of Chicago Press, 1947.

Torgerson, W. S. *Theory and methods of scaling*. New York: Wiley, 1958.

Tryon, R. C., Stein, K. B., and Chu, Chen-Lin. Unpublished paper cited in K. B. Stein, The TSC Scales: The outcome of a cluster analysis of 550 MMPI items. In P. McReynolds (Ed.), *Advances in psychological assessment*. Volume I. Palo Alto, California: Science and Behavior Books, 1968.

Weiner, D. N. Subtle and obvious keys for the MMPI. *Journal of Consulting Psychology*, 1948, **12**, 164–170.

Weiner, M., Blumberg, A., Segman, S., and Cooper, A. Judgment of adjustment by psychologists, psychiatric social workers, and college students, and its relationship to social desirability. *Journal of Abnormal and Social Psychology*, 1959, **59**, 315–321.

Welsh, G. S. Factor dimensions A and R. In G. S. Welsh and W. G. Dahlstrom (Eds.), *Basic readings on the MMPI in psychology and medicine*. Minneapolis: University of Minnesota Press, 1956.

Wiggins, J. S. Interrelationships among MMPI measures of dissimulation under standard and social desirability instructions. *Journal of Consulting Psychology*, 1959, **23**, 419–427.

Wiggins, J. S. Strategic, method, and stylistic variance in the MMPI. *Psychological Bulletin*, 1962, **59**, 224–242.

Wiggins, J. S. Substantive dimensions of self-report in the MMPI item pool. *Psychological Monographs*, 1966, **80**, No. 22.

Wright, C. E. *Relations between normative and ipsative measures of personality*. (Unpublished doctoral dissertation, University of Washington, 1957).

Zax, M., Cowen, E. L., Budin, W., and Biggs, C. F. The social desirability of trait descriptive terms: Applications to an alcoholic sample. *Journal of Social Psychology*, 1962, **56**, 21–27.

Zax, M., Cowen, E. L., and Peter, Sister Mary. A comparative study of novice nuns and college females using the response set approach. *Journal of Abnormal and Social Psychology*, 1963, **66**, 369–375.

Appendix

Table I   The SDSVs of the *AB* Pairs of Statements in the EPPS and the Proportion of Males and Females Choosing the *A* Statement[a]

Item	SDSV A	SDSV B	P(A) M	P(A) F	Item	SDSV A	SDSV B	P(A) M	P(A) F
1	3.96	4.07	0.48	0.57	44	1.41	1.05	0.39	0.67
2	3.34	3.46	0.29	0.33	45	0.68	1.88	0.07	0.25
3	3.56	3.48	0.25	0.59	46	3.48	3.50[b]	0.48	0.20
4	2.84	2.30	0.63	0.59	47	2.49	2.59[b]	0.48	0.42
5	3.57	3.38	0.37	0.44	48	3.30	2.98[b]	0.29	0.25
6	2.91	3.19	0.74	0.66	49	1.47	1.30[b]	0.83	0.70
7	3.64	3.15	0.88	0.77	50	1.39	1.56[b]	0.48	0.20
8	3.30	3.19	0.86	0.69	51	4.07	3.84	0.52	0.42
9	2.45	2.49	0.80	0.79	52	3.34	3.40	0.26	0.11
10	1.84	2.49	0.42	0.45	53	3.56	3.47	0.42	0.22
11	3.48	3.38	0.71	0.50	54	2.57	2.61	0.26	0.09
12	3.34	3.30	0.42	0.34	55	3.60	3.68	0.75	0.63
13	3.64	3.36	0.68	0.67	56	2.79	2.79	0.71	0.39
14	2.57	2.54	0.85	0.74	57	2.30	2.21	0.40	0.32
15	3.44	3.36	0.75	0.63	58	3.38	3.66	0.16	0.08
16	2.79	2.84	0.91	0.80	59	2.45	2.66	0.51	0.58
17	2.30	1.75	0.49	0.60	60	3.44	3.76	0.35	0.20
18	1.88	2.57	0.43	0.34	61	3.38	3.46	0.62	0.58
19	1.97	1.66	0.47	0.31	62	3.15	3.12	0.40	0.44
20	1.39	1.47	0.66	0.40	63	3.30	3.24	0.45	0.53
21	3.61	3.57	0.82	0.63	64	2.03	2.69	0.66	0.72
22	3.17	3.42	0.42	0.56	65	2.02	2.70	0.47	0.50
23	3.28	3.44	0.36	0.43	66	3.46	3.41	0.59	0.48
24	1.41	1.39	0.42	0.44	67	3.17	3.28	0.17	0.19
25	0.64	0.68	0.64	0.54	68	3.36	3.62	0.17	0.18
26	3.80	3.80	0.55	0.36	69	1.75	1.87	0.48	0.75
27	3.19	3.25	0.18	0.12	70	1.77	1.97	0.71	0.67
28	3.56	3.59	0.32	0.29	71	2.30	2.15	0.29	0.33
29	2.84	2.99	0.57	0.34	72	1.70	1.17	0.60	0.76
30	3.57	3.53	0.47	0.27	73	1.88	0.64	0.58	0.62
31	2.91	3.08	0.40	0.39	74	1.41	1.42	0.54	0.60
32	3.09	3.11	0.29	0.29	75	0.68	0.60	0.42	0.55
33	2.54	2.88	0.24	0.20	76	4.14	4.07	0.73	0.90
34	3.07	3.00	0.62	0.55	77	3.22	3.38	0.36	0.39
35	3.42	3.22	0.55	0.49	78	3.63	3.80	0.15	0.20
36	3.61	3.63	0.55	0.33	79	2.80	2.79	0.42	0.58
37	3.58	3.54	0.75	0.63	80	2.98[b]	2.91	0.54	0.67
38	1.88	1.87	0.59	0.55	81	3.90	3.58	0.43	0.57
39	1.66	1.71	0.73	0.68	82	3.00	3.15	0.73	0.59
40	1.84	2.72	0.40	0.33	83	3.00	3.09	0.44	0.55
41	2.30	2.30	0.35	0.38	84	2.30	1.70	0.61	0.69
42	1.70	1.87	0.36	0.49	85	2.67[b]	2.30	0.58	0.63
43	3.28	2.80	0.22	0.28	86	3.53	3.56	0.55	0.76

Table I   The SDSVs of the *AB* Pairs of Statements in the EPPS and the Proportion of Males and Females Choosing the *A* Statement[a]—Continued

Item	SDSV		P(A)		Item	SDSV		P(A)	
	A	B	M	F		A	B	M	F
87	3.11	3.30	0.74	0.79	130	2.77[b]	2.77	0.53	0.46
88	3.54	3.38	0.61	0.70	131	3.48	3.40	0.61	0.52
89	2.74	3.28	0.86	0.69	132	2.71	2.74	0.34	0.31
90	2.77[b]	1.88	0.73	0.64	133	3.00	3.68	0.33	0.31
91	3.25	3.07	0.74	0.78	134	2.97	3.64	0.45	0.34
92	2.71	2.03	0.69	0.83	135	2.64[b]	2.66	0.36	0.42
93	1.71	1.75	0.23	0.53	136	3.90	3.80	0.54	0.68
94	1.05	1.66	0.40	0.15	137	2.63	2.64	0.45	0.54
95	1.56[b]	1.47	0.51	0.71	138	2.76	2.92	0.34	0.37
96	3.48	3.60	0.67	0.76	139	2.74	2.70	0.78	0.68
97	2.88	2.02	0.79	0.82	140	2.67[b]	2.69	0.42	0.55
98	1.87	1.84	0.51	0.62	141	4.14	3.66	0.36	0.46
99	1.87	1.77	0.66	0.58	142	2.38	2.12	0.39	0.63
100	1.30[b]	0.68	0.23	0.34	143	2.77	2.89	0.35	0.75
101	3.80	3.80	0.61	0.47	144	1.91	3.65	0.23	0.08
102	3.27	3.59	0.60	0.60	145	2.05[b]	1.97	0.48	0.76
103	3.76	3.90	0.43	0.35	146	2.99	1.81	0.58	0.83
104	2.97	2.99	0.91	0.70	147	2.38	2.15	0.45	0.59
105	3.50[b]	3.25	0.42	0.44	148	1.71	0.60	0.62	0.70
106	3.53	3.27	0.55	0.70	149	1.05	1.07	0.46	0.36
107	3.09	3.11	0.34	0.30	150	1.30[b]	1.36	0.18	0.42
108	2.76	3.08	0.41	0.37	151	3.96	4.07	0.51	0.68
109	1.91	2.38	0.49	0.31	152	3.66	3.61	0.42	0.70
110	2.64[b]	2.63	0.38	0.43	153	3.46	3.46	0.36	0.43
111	3.80	3.76	0.57	0.69	154	3.66	3.80	0.35	0.55
112	3.08	2.77	0.56	0.50	155	1.81	2.30	0.48	0.38
113	1.88	1.87	0.71	0.56	156	3.47	3.58	0.47	0.61
114	1.88	2.76	0.82	0.57	157	3.64	3.15	0.83	0.80
115	2.59[b]	2.72	0.46	0.48	158	2.92	3.17	0.54	0.31
116	3.48	2.97	0.53	0.69	159	2.88	3.09	0.47	0.27
117	2.71	1.82	0.39	0.56	160	1.07	1.70	0.34	0.31
118	2.72	1.91	0.33	0.58	161	3.40	3.56	0.52	0.82
119	1.41	1.05	0.43	0.65	162	3.68	3.56	0.71	0.74
120	1.56[b]	1.87	0.33	0.63	163	3.64	3.36	0.78	0.70
121	3.99	3.50[b]	0.94	0.85	164	3.28	3.30	0.69	0.80
122	2.63	2.05[b]	0.51	0.41	165	1.42	2.54	0.49	0.42
123	1.87	2.65[b]	0.53	0.32	166	2.77	3.07	0.36	0.49
124	1.82	2.05[b]	0.62	0.49	167	2.74	2.03	0.62	0.81
125	1.39	1.56[b]	0.57	0.24	168	2.69	2.45	0.41	0.24
126	3.99	3.96	0.42	0.38	169	1.97	1.66	0.32	0.24
127	2.63	3.28	0.37	0.27	170	0.60	1.41	0.34	0.37
128	3.76	3.80	0.23	0.21	171	3.28	3.60	0.37	0.62
129	2.80	3.28	0.62	0.43	172	2.79	2.02	0.71	0.82

Table I   The SDSVs of the *AB* Pairs of Statements in the EPPS and the Proportion of Males and Females Choosing the *A* Statement[a]—Continued

Item	SDSV A	SDSV B	P(A) M	P(A) F	Item	SDSV A	SDSV B	P(A) M	P(A) F
173	3.12	3.42	0.19	0.29	200	0.60	1.30[b]	0.65	0.57
174	2.12	1.77	0.48	0.53	201	4.07	3.84	0.65	0.53
175	0.64	0.68	0.61	0.52	202	3.76	3.80	0.54	0.57
176	3.96	4.14	0.49	0.38	203	3.80	3.84	0.45	0.26
177	3.76	3.80	0.54	0.48	204	3.65	3.68	0.76	0.77
178	3.80	3.99	0.20	0.21	205	2.15	2.61	0.28	0.11
179	3.66	3.59	0.75	0.63	206	3.80	3.66	0.43	0.44
180	2.15	2.99	0.66	0.36	207	2.30	2.21	0.47	0.33
181	3.40	3.22	0.60	0.68	208	3.46	3.64	0.36	0.31
182	2.79	3.00	0.33	0.56	209	3.41	3.40	0.65	0.57
183	2.92	3.11	0.32	0.30	210	1.36	2.21	0.55	0.22
184	2.88	2.88	0.55	0.20	211	3.84	3.64	0.43	0.58
185	0.60	2.38	0.20	0.15	212	2.66	2.70	0.63	0.69
186	3.68	3.63	0.46	0.43	213	3.30	3.24	0.48	0.59
187	3.40	3.00	0.71	0.60	214	3.62	3.12	0.78	0.83
188	3.24	3.54	0.48	0.30	215	1.42	2.64	0.22	0.22
189	3.28	2.77	0.81	0.72	216	3.47	3.65	0.33	0.33
190	1.17	1.71	0.65	0.38	217	3.68	3.41	0.39	0.65
191	2.77	2.74	0.21	0.49	218	3.24	3.62	0.29	0.14
192	2.74	2.30	0.58	0.66	219	1.75	1.87	0.55	0.70
193	3.64	1.82	0.48	0.66	220	0.60	1.87	0.28	0.43
194	2.12	1.88	0.33	0.40	221	2.61	1.81	0.80	0.97
195	0.64	1.05	0.34	0.45	222	2.21	1.17	0.57	0.86
196	2.77	2.98[b]	0.37	0.39	223	2.64	1.36	0.72	0.81
197	2.66	2.67[b]	0.67	0.63	224	1.87	1.07	0.56	0.41
198	2.69	2.77[b]	0.36	0.44	225	0.68	0.60	0.46	0.56
199	1.97	2.59[b]	0.58	0.31					

[a]The SDSVs are based on a scaling method known as the method of successive intervals. The judges consisted of 86 men and 66 women. The SDSVs with a superscript *b* have been estimated from the regression line of SDSV on P(A). For further details, see Edwards (1953). Items 1, 7, 13, 19, 25, 101, 107, 113, 119, 125, 201, 207, 213, 219, and 225 are duplicate items and are not scored.

The values of P(A) are based on a sample of 95 male and 108 female students at the University of Oregon. They are reproduced by permission from Lewis R. Goldberg: Test-retest item statistics for the Edwards Personal Preference Schedule, *ORI Research Monograph*, 1963, **3**, No. 3. Eugene: Oregon Research Institute.

Table II   The SDSVs of the CPI Items and the Proportion of Males and Females Responding
True to Each Item[a]

Item	SDSV	P(T) M	P(T) F	Item	SDSV	P(T) M	P(T) F
1	7.15	0.72	0.83	44	3.15	0.73	0.44
2	2.80	0.01	0.04	45	7.30	0.65	0.56
3	7.10	0.33	0.45	46	6.80	0.43	0.69
4	4.15	0.75	0.70	47	5.25	0.15	0.05
5	4.50	0.15	0.13	48	3.00	0.56	0.44
6	7.95	0.91	0.80	49	2.10	0.33	0.10
7	3.90	0.16	0.31	50	6.05	0.86	0.81
8	5.35	0.58	0.69	51	7.20	0.75	0.80
9	3.70	0.06	0.00	52	6.70	0.45	0.44
10	3.50	0.97	0.94	53	5.70	0.74	0.65
11	3.05	0.16	0.19	54	3.30	0.33	0.20
12	3.40	0.27	0.22	55	3.90	0.54	0.62
13	3.65	0.26	0.34	56	5.20	0.63	0.54
14	5.70	0.12	0.12	57	4.75	0.48	0.55
15	2.85	0.07	0.06	58	4.40	0.58	0.69
16	2.25	0.03	0.03	59	5.00	0.56	0.50
17	5.40	0.12	0.19	60	4.55	0.42	0.19
18	5.20	0.47	0.55	61	7.40	0.89	0.96
19	5.30	0.28	0.10	62	5.65	0.77	0.71
20	5.35	0.33	0.31	63	6.45	0.42	0.24
21	7.60	0.91	0.86	64	3.95	0.04	0.06
22	4.60	0.71	0.69	65	4.90	0.18	0.25
23	5.10	0.22	0.22	66	4.10	0.91	0.93
24	7.85	0.74	0.76	67	5.75	0.28	0.18
25	4.70	0.39	0.37	68	5.10	0.11	0.42
26	3.30	0.48	0.38	69	5.85	0.35	0.56
27	3.15	0.16	0.13	70	3.15	0.34	0.60
28	5.10	0.04	0.51	71	4.40	0.27	0.46
29	2.80	0.18	0.14	72	5.05	0.07	0.67
30	3.50	0.81	0.96	73	2.75	0.12	0.06
31	3.65	0.21	0.31	74	4.05	0.20	0.27
32	4.55	0.31	0.41	75	2.60	0.12	0.04
33	4.55	0.16	0.20	76	3.25	0.23	0.22
34	4.80	0.91	0.88	77	5.25	0.82	0.73
35	5.35	0.32	0.63	78	4.15	0.71	0.68
36	2.75	0.05	0.06	79	4.20	0.12	0.21
37	5.80	0.31	0.52	80	4.75	0.88	0.81
38	3.95	0.36	0.30	81	3.10	0.53	0.41
39	4.40	0.63	0.54	82	4.50	0.26	0.07
40	4.05	0.37	0.66	83	3.85	0.31	0.18
41	4.65	0.32	0.25	84	6.00	0.56	0.69
42	4.15	0.81	0.81	85	4.60	0.42	0.45
43	2.55	0.13	0.11	86	5.35	0.55	0.45

Table II   The SDSVs of the CPI Items and the Proportion of Males and Females Responding
True to Each Item[a]—Continued

		P(T)				P(T)	
Item	SDSV	M	F	Item	SDSV	M	F
87	5.40	0.81	0.36	130	6.35	0.53	0.72
88	6.25	0.76	0.88	131	7.05	0.77	0.82
89	3.30	0.08	0.08	132	3.65	0.22	0.24
90	2.00	0.01	0.00	133	6.20	0.65	0.53
91	3.45	0.49	0.51	134	4.20	0.34	0.39
92	3.90	0.26	0.41	135	6.95	0.40	0.31
93	2.75	0.11	0.13	136	3.15	0.16	0.09
94	2.55	0.08	0.08	137	4.40	0.26	0.23
95	6.85	0.60	0.48	138	5.85	0.87	0.84
96	7.60	0.77	0.87	139	2.90	0.56	0.43
97	6.55	0.45	0.53	140	6.75	0.62	0.69
98	5.45	0.34	0.36	141	5.15	0.59	0.53
99	3.70	0.25	0.25	142	3.55	0.69	0.61
100	5.40	0.76	0.54	143	4.55	0.44	0.44
101	3.10	0.61	0.60	144	3.70	0.24	0.48
102	4.10	0.47	0.50	145	2.65	0.20	0.35
103	6.05	0.46	0.56	146	5.85	0.76	0.90
104	6.20	0.87	0.78	147	3.85	0.54	0.62
105	4.15	0.39	0.43	148	4.40	0.59	0.26
106	4.45	0.58	0.56	149	7.35	0.42	0.32
107	5.85	0.87	0.85	150	4.55	0.59	0.68
108	6.85	0.68	0.56	151	3.85	0.28	0.29
109	4.50	0.75	0.80	152	6.95	0.61	0.66
110	5.60	0.48	0.69	153	4.15	0.66	0.69
111	3.75	0.27	0.23	154	5.25	0.38	0.69
112	6.50	0.58	0.76	155	4.70	0.52	0.32
113	3.80	0.12	0.16	156	3.45	0.15	0.08
114	2.80	0.47	0.12	157	4.15	0.15	0.12
115	4.60	0.31	0.45	158	3.55	0.24	0.22
116	5.35	0.82	0.88	159	3.75	0.39	0.42
117	3.05	0.32	0.19	160	6.20	0.46	0.63
118	7.05	0.94	0.85	161	3.35	0.48	0.49
119	4.20	0.26	0.22	162	7.20	0.86	0.92
120	2.85	0.93	0.81	163	6.90	0.79	0.83
121	4.00	0.21	0.22	164	3.70	0.14	0.15
122	6.15	0.51	0.71	165	6.40	0.64	0.65
123	5.95	0.40	0.34	166	6.85	0.54	0.56
124	3.80	0.44	0.31	167	6.40	0.39	0.47
125	5.35	0.80	0.73	168	7.85	0.53	0.56
126	6.60	0.83	0.56	169	4.55	0.38	0.34
127	7.85	0.65	0.72	170	3.95	0.48	0.53
128	5.05	0.41	0.31	171	4.05	0.14	0.04
129	5.25	0.68	0.27	172	5.45	0.59	0.50

Table II The SDVSs of the CPI Items and the Proportion of Males and Females Responding
True to Each Item[a]—Continued

| Item | SDSV | P(T) | | Item | SDSV | P(T) | |
		M	F			M	F
173	4.40	0.42	0.38	216	5.05	0.74	0.85
174	7.35	0.24	0.25	217	5.20	0.05	0.25
175	3.10	0.19	0.17	218	6.55	0.56	0.78
176	4.05	0.29	0.26	219	3.25	0.35	0.23
177	3.00	0.01	0.00	220	3.75	0.12	0.07
178	2.70	0.20	0.10	221	7.20	0.77	0.90
179	5.55	0.54	0.52	222	6.45	0.38	0.40
180	6.65	0.85	0.86	223	6.40	0.23	0.34
181	7.90	0.43	0.68	224	7.00	0.86	0.80
182	5.10	0.35	0.39	225	3.90	0.57	0.36
183	2.55	0.15	0.10	226	4.55	0.54	0.46
184	3.70	0.19	0.10	227	3.60	0.32	0.26
185	3.65	0.52	0.52	228	6.10	0.68	0.62
186	4.15	0.48	0.44	229	5.35	0.69	0.55
187	3.90	0.38	0.50	230	7.05	0.65	0.75
188	4.75	0.34	0.23	231	3.90	0.52	0.45
189	2.60	0.09	0.02	232	3.30	0.22	0.46
190	3.00	0.07	0.06	233	3.05	0.16	0.10
191	3.15	0.60	0.73	234	5.40	0.38	0.31
192	3.95	0.34	0.44	235	7.30	0.78	0.68
193	6.95	0.69	0.81	236	3.10	0.11	0.16
194	4.35	0.39	0.38	237	3.30	0.09	0.13
195	7.00	0.29	0.31	238	3.80	0.81	0.78
196	4.35	0.29	0.03	239	6.55	0.42	0.37
197	4.90	0.98	0.94	240	6.15	0.02	0.36
198	6.65	0.67	0.71	241	4.80	0.39	0.47
199	5.45	0.27	0.05	242	6.95	0.56	0.56
200	7.30	0.83	0.74	243	4.05	0.51	0.49
201	3.40	0.18	0.25	244	5.50	0.18	0.46
202	6.40	0.62	0.49	245	7.50	0.85	0.92
203	3.10	0.71	0.68	246	7.05	0.75	0.74
204	7.05	0.45	0.49	247	3.95	0.45	0.28
205	4.25	0.32	0.24	248	3.70	0.52	0.44
206	3.90	0.16	0.15	249	5.10	0.43	0.13
207	3.30	0.59	0.55	250	3.95	0.51	0.39
208	4.80	0.61	0.58	251	4.55	0.37	0.47
209	4.00	0.40	0.37	252	3.70	0.34	0.48
210	5.90	0.68	0.22	253	3.95	0.62	0.57
211	6.30	0.58	0.50	254	6.80	0.05	0.09
212	7.90	0.56	0.88	255	5.05	0.28	0.31
213	7.80	0.81	0.86	256	6.70	0.78	0.64
214	3.40	0.39	0.08	257	3.65	0.32	0.31
215	5.85	0.18	0.05	258	3.90	0.35	0.42

Table II The SDSVs of the CPI Items and the Proportion of Males and Females Responding True to Each Item[a]—Continued

Item	SDSV	P(T)		Item	SDSV	P(T)	
		M	F			M	F
259	7.55	0.97	0.95	302	2.80	0.39	0.30
260	7.85	0.71	0.72	303	5.10	0.31	0.39
261	2.80	0.12	0.06	304	6.80	0.77	0.84
262	3.65	0.73	0.75	305	6.40	0.78	0.83
263	7.00	0.56	0.54	306	3.65	0.04	0.11
264	6.00	0.78	0.83	307	2.35	0.14	0.09
265	4.50	0.17	0.44	308	3.55	0.07	0.05
266	3.25	0.36	0.29	309	3.00	0.17	0.32
267	3.75	0.21	0.16	310	4.85	0.72	0.72
268	4.40	0.74	0.74	311	2.45	0.05	0.05
269	6.60	0.74	0.65	312	7.55	0.93	0.95
270	2.90	0.11	0.11	313	5.70	0.69	0.70
271	5.10	0.14	0.14	314	5.40	0.55	0.58
272	4.50	0.31	0.56	315	3.10	0.07	0.08
273	3.40	0.14	0.19	316	7.30	0.97	0.89
274	4.95	0.07	0.02	317	6.85	0.91	0.94
275	3.60	0.68	0.64	318	5.05	0.25	0.18
276	7.00	0.74	0.69	319	7.15	0.37	0.48
277	6.40	0.73	0.69	320	5.90	0.51	0.44
278	7.90	0.39	0.58	321	3.35	0.04	0.08
279	4.65	0.67	0.72	322	6.75	0.94	0.98
280	7.50	0.93	0.88	323	7.20	0.47	0.70
281	3.40	0.09	0.07	324	1.65	0.03	0.00
282	3.50	0.62	0.67	325	3.55	0.15	0.17
283	6.40	0.74	0.56	326	5.40	0.82	0.86
284	3.85	0.39	0.34	327	3.00	0.18	0.11
285	3.30	0.31	0.33	328	6.50	0.58	0.61
286	5.10	0.13	0.31	329	4.70	0.55	0.45
287	6.00	0.44	0.58	330	3.30	0.01	0.00
288	2.75	0.17	0.02	331	2.60	0.37	0.37
289	4.10	0.79	0.88	332	2.30	0.03	0.02
290	7.55	0.81	0.94	333	7.75	0.86	0.93
291	4.65	0.28	0.16	334	4.55	0.54	0.71
292	6.35	0.64	0.71	335	3.30	0.47	0.65
293	3.50	0.36	0.44	336	3.85	0.55	0.56
294	3.65	0.18	0.15	337	3.30	0.01	0.06
295	6.25	0.40	0.52	338	3.30	0.03	0.01
296	5.70	0.31	0.39	339	1.75	0.16	0.05
297	2.90	0.34	0.30	340	4.55	0.13	0.10
298	3.95	0.25	0.37	341	3.20	0.07	0.10
299	2.30	0.12	0.04	342	3.40	0.97	0.93
300	4.55	0.52	0.45	343	7.50	0.98	0.99
301	3.40	0.05	0.36	344	4.40	0.38	0.53

Table II   The SDSVs of the CPI Items and the Proportion of Males and Females Responding True to Each Item[a]—Continued

Item	SDSV	P(T) M	P(T) F	Item	SDSV	P(T) M	P(T) F
345	3.40	0.13	0.05	388	3.35	0.60	0.59
346	5.40	0.46	0.63	389	5.95	0.55	0.58
347	7.30	0.18	0.26	390	2.90	0.14	0.02
348	6.10	0.80	0.87	391	6.75	0.23	0.40
349	1.80	0.04	0.03	392	5.90	0.32	0.29
350	1.95	0.02	0.02	393	2.05	0.24	0.12
351	3.95	0.46	0.56	394	5.80	0.32	0.39
352	2.65	0.00	0.03	395	5.90	0.73	0.81
353	2.90	0.08	0.08	396	3.70	0.44	0.42
354	6.65	0.55	0.38	397	5.20	0.33	0.35
355	6.45	0.38	0.24	398	2.65	0.00	0.00
356	4.95	0.42	0.58	399	3.40	0.47	0.45
357	4.95	0.27	0.22	400	6.05	0.43	0.39
358	4.25	0.23	0.25	401	2.50	0.01	0.01
359	6.00	0.44	0.39	402	2.75	0.00	0.04
360	2.50	0.03	0.02	403	6.15	0.36	0.31
361	6.80	0.69	0.77	404	5.65	0.13	0.26
362	5.20	0.83	0.81	405	2.95	0.14	0.13
363	4.35	0.38	0.36	406	2.65	0.14	0.04
364	3.85	0.21	0.15	407	6.50	0.87	0.85
365	2.10	0.02	0.00	408	7.10	0.31	0.33
366	4.35	0.03	0.03	409	5.10	0.32	0.31
367	7.65	0.48	0.51	410	7.15	0.96	0.94
368	6.40	0.87	0.93	411	3.80	0.09	0.03
369	3.40	0.16	0.19	412	5.85	0.69	0.67
370	4.70	0.09	0.19	413	5.75	0.94	0.94
371	6.90	0.69	0.77	414	5.15	0.94	0.93
372	3.15	0.07	0.09	415	3.50	0.14	0.16
373	4.50	0.77	0.76	416	3.50	0.22	0.14
374	2.30	0.02	0.03	417	3.05	0.13	0.03
375	2.90	0.54	0.45	418	3.50	0.19	0.23
376	5.90	0.56	0.56	419	2.65	0.09	0.10
377	5.35	0.54	0.44	420	2.60	0.49	0.31
378	2.80	0.04	0.06	421	3.00	0.16	0.05
379	3.80	0.33	0.38	422	2.50	0.07	0.29
380	7.60	0.64	0.67	423	2.55	0.00	0.03
381	4.05	0.02	0.01	424	5.60	0.34	0.51
382	6.30	0.73	0.56	425	4.65	0.20	0.25
383	4.65	0.23	0.20	426	4.50	0.82	0.71
384	1.80	0.01	0.02	427	4.75	0.89	0.83
385	3.35	0.08	0.17	428	4.10	0.20	0.17
386	4.70	0.43	0.51	429	3.70	0.27	0.38
387	5.15	0.55	0.65	430	3.60	0.12	0.19

Table II   The SDSVs of the CPI Items and the Proportion of Males and Females Responding True to Each Item[a]—Continued

Item	SDSV	P(T) M	P(T) F	Item	SDSV	P(T) M	P(T) F
431	2.70	0.17	0.04	456	3.55	0.33	0.34
432	5.25	0.89	0.84	457	2.35	0.05	0.04
433	6.60	0.83	0.87	458	4.65	0.48	0.48
434	4.70	0.08	0.12	459	3.00	0.06	0.06
435	4.50	0.12	0.14	460	4.55	0.18	0.17
436	2.90	0.11	0.03	461	4.25	0.15	0.17
437	3.15	0.01	0.01	462	3.35	0.15	0.20
438	3.15	0.03	0.01	463	3.80	0.41	0.36
439	7.65	0.64	0.58	464	6.15	0.92	0.91
440	5.05	0.96	0.96	465	4.05	0.27	0.28
441	3.90	0.13	0.24	466	4.75	0.33	0.62
442	5.35	0.57	0.54	467	2.60	0.33	0.33
443	5.00	0.67	0.87	468	3.90	0.40	0.22
444	3.20	0.14	0.17	469	3.80	0.21	0.19
445	7.60	0.97	0.96	470	4.65	0.47	0.44
446	5.55	0.96	0.93	471	5.05	0.40	0.48
447	7.70	0.95	0.98	472	7.35	0.82	0.81
448	6.90	0.29	0.35	473	6.55	0.32	0.26
449	3.15	0.00	0.02	474	3.75	0.44	0.39
450	4.40	0.42	0.36	475	6.35	0.92	0.94
451	6.80	0.67	0.78	476	3.65	0.21	0.34
452	4.15	0.36	0.46	477	3.95	0.13	0.31
453	4.25	0.22	0.30	478	4.95	0.45	0.53
454	3.55	0.05	0.08	479	3.95	0.21	0.19
455	3.45	0.01	0.04	480	4.20	0.05	0.54

[a]The SDSVs of the CPI items are based on a sample of 59 male and 68 female college students. They are reproduced from Hayden L. Mees, Edward F. Gocka, and Hildegund Holloway: Social desirability scale values for California Psychological Inventory Items, *Psychological Reports, Monograph Supplement*, 1964, **15,** 147–158, by permission of the authors and publisher. The authors report SDSVs separately for males and females. The values given in this table are the unweighted means of the male and female values.

The P(T)s of the items are based on a sample of 95 male and 108 female students at the University of Oregon. They are reproduced, by permission, from Lewis R. Goldberg and Leonard G. Rorer: Test-retest item statistics for the California Psychological Inventory, *ORI Research Monograph*, 1964, **4,** No. 1. Eugene: Oregon Research Institute.

Table III The SDSVs of the MMPI Items and the Proportion of Males and Females Responding True to Each Item[a]

Item	SDSV	P(T) M	P(T) F	Item	SDSV	P(T) M	P(T) F
1	5.48	0.65	0.16	44	2.44	0.04	0.06
2	6.78	0.96	0.94	45	3.02	0.82	0.74
3	7.75	0.46	0.45	46	6.34	0.88	0.79
4	4.62	0.07	0.25	47	3.65	0.02	0.05
5	4.34	0.31	0.33	48	2.80	0.00	0.01
6	4.84	0.61	0.42	49	1.48	0.01	0.04
7	5.98	0.89	0.58	50	2.45	0.01	0.07
8	8.28	0.93	0.95	51	6.26	0.92	0.93
9	6.81	0.94	0.97	52	2.56	0.18	0.14
10	2.94	0.00	0.06	53	2.38	0.03	0.03
11	3.08	0.06	0.05	54	6.90	0.91	0.97
12	5.77	0.68	0.67	55	6.42	0.87	0.85
13	3.25	0.24	0.37	56	3.67	0.16	0.01
14	2.26	0.08	0.06	57	7.15	0.74	0.72
15	3.71	0.42	0.49	58	4.78	0.32	0.30
16	1.55	0.01	0.00	59	4.63	0.62	0.44
17	7.72	0.91	0.92	60	5.10	0.97	0.99
18	5.68	0.91	0.85	61	3.39	0.12	0.04
19	3.95	0.38	0.32	62	3.86	0.16	0.28
20	6.86	0.78	0.96	63	5.83	0.89	0.86
21	3.97	0.38	0.48	64	4.41	0.47	0.34
22	3.23	0.07	0.19	65	8.21	0.88	0.93
23	1.80	0.01	0.00	66	2.93	0.13	0.11
24	2.54	0.05	0.04	67	4.13	0.39	0.30
25	5.78	0.52	0.49	68	5.64	0.85	0.87
26	4.24	0.38	0.39	69	1.11	0.05	0.11
27	2.23	0.05	0.04	70	4.87	0.35	0.69
28	2.64	0.23	0.10	71	4.84	0.73	0.80
29	3.02	0.12	0.04	72	3.25	0.13	0.03
30	5.10	0.92	0.93	73	4.19	0.25	0.23
31	3.22	0.03	0.13	74	4.57	0.04	0.55
32	3.12	0.26	0.30	75	5.83	0.94	0.95
33	5.28	0.24	0.23	76	3.07	0.08	0.04
34	2.95	0.05	0.10	77	5.00	0.31	0.81
35	1.69	0.00	0.01	78	6.08	0.45	0.73
36	5.29	0.60	0.73	79	6.46	0.51	0.29
37	7.49	0.85	0.93	80	3.61	0.48	0.32
38	3.85	0.58	0.31	81	5.62	0.62	0.40
39	3.85	0.52	0.38	82	3.53	0.17	0.25
40	3.42	0.18	0.14	83	7.87	0.96	0.96
41	2.89	0.40	0.39	84	4.43	0.31	0.22
42	3.86	0.03	0.07	85	1.58	0.01	0.01
43	2.85	0.09	0.05	86	2.58	0.26	0.31

Table III The SDSVs of the MMPI Items and the Proportion of Males and Females Responding True to Each Item[a]—Continued

		P(T)				P(T)	
Item	SDSV	M	F	Item	SDSV	M	F
87	5.25	0.12	0.41	130	6.33	0.84	0.81
88	7.73	0.97	0.98	131	5.62	0.64	0.75
89	4.84	0.31	0.27	132	5.85	0.12	0.56
90	4.52	0.99	0.97	133	6.45	0.68	0.89
91	5.19	0.53	0.35	134	5.51	0.88	0.89
92	5.39	0.04	0.38	135	4.19	0.67	0.43
93	3.82	0.47	0.33	136	4.12	0.32	0.20
94	3.48	0.21	0.20	137	7.10	0.87	0.82
95	7.15	0.35	0.44	138	3.66	0.23	0.44
96	7.30	0.83	0.73	139	1.97	0.12	0.08
97	3.75	0.41	0.31	140	6.50	0.56	0.69
98	5.41	0.53	0.49	141	5.21	0.69	0.68
99	6.11	0.71	0.66	142	3.82	0.45	0.50
100	4.59	0.64	0.76	143	5.79	0.33	0.39
101	4.85	0.58	0.27	144	5.34	0.23	0.06
102	4.99	0.69	0.69	145	3.62	0.47	0.09
103	5.73	0.93	0.94	146	4.60	0.13	0.11
104	2.11	0.07	0.04	147	3.68	0.32	0.30
105	4.58	0.91	0.89	148	3.81	0.22	0.20
106	2.90	0.13	0.06	149	4.95	0.08	0.68
107	7.95	0.92	0.96	150	6.46	0.97	0.93
108	3.52	0.07	0.05	151	1.88	0.00	0.00
109	4.10	0.56	0.74	152	6.36	0.63	0.57
110	2.42	0.02	0.05	153	7.46	0.99	0.92
111	5.00	0.18	0.31	154	7.40	0.97	0.97
112	7.50	0.77	0.62	155	6.08	0.71	0.56
113	8.01	1.00	1.00	156	2.83	0.12	0.07
114	3.10	0.03	0.02	157	3.53	0.09	0.12
115	6.70	0.68	0.77	158	3.41	0.03	0.37
116	4.74	0.32	0.30	159	3.48	0.06	0.14
117	4.16	0.38	0.38	160	7.42	0.64	0.50
118	4.23	0.25	0.10	161	3.85	0.06	0.09
119	5.45	0.76	0.70	162	4.10	0.33	0.27
120	4.58	0.87	0.82	163	6.88	0.76	0.61
121	2.21	0.01	0.01	164	7.62	0.86	0.81
122	6.09	0.93	0.85	165	5.21	0.61	0.69
123	2.60	0.01	0.01	166	4.00	0.32	0.50
124	3.64	0.56	0.40	167	3.34	0.20	0.16
125	2.91	0.04	0.03	168	1.77	0.02	0.05
126	5.94	0.49	0.72	169	6.87	0.95	0.94
127	4.25	0.49	0.64	170	4.87	0.25	0.05
128	6.22	0.83	0.64	171	3.89	0.29	0.33
129	4.48	0.41	0.48	172	4.28	0.35	0.53

Table III The SDSVs of the MMPI Items and the Proportion of Males and Females Responding True to Each Item[a] — Continued

Item	SDSV	P(T) M	P(T) F	Item	SDSV	P(T) M	P(T) F
173	7.39	0.87	0.94	216	2.10	0.08	0.11
174	6.43	0.80	0.70	217	3.60	0.62	0.61
175	6.41	0.97	0.89	218	2.11	0.07	0.00
176	6.04	0.69	0.53	219	5.58	0.44	0.12
177	8.32	0.95	0.96	220	8.73	0.97	0.96
178	7.33	0.95	0.94	221	6.51	0.80	0.65
179	3.61	0.23	0.13	222	4.66	0.52	0.34
180	3.46	0.28	0.33	223	6.04	0.68	0.19
181	5.41	0.81	0.69	224	3.73	0.12	0.10
182	1.89	0.03	0.06	225	4.54	0.92	0.98
183	4.40	0.40	0.31	226	3.97	0.39	0.43
184	2.51	0.01	0.01	227	3.65	0.12	0.14
185	6.76	0.97	0.93	228	6.49	0.64	0.70
186	3.55	0.22	0.23	229	6.50	0.46	0.50
187	6.38	0.95	0.91	230	6.28	0.76	0.75
188	6.76	0.54	0.48	231	5.50	0.69	0.54
189	2.87	0.04	0.05	232	5.70	0.22	0.16
190	6.49	0.92	0.73	233	4.18	0.43	0.30
191	3.96	0.34	0.36	234	4.47	0.37	0.31
192	6.74	0.96	0.89	235	5.19	0.62	0.48
193	6.67	0.73	0.78	236	3.02	0.14	0.07
194	2.41	0.00	0.04	237	4.55	0.54	0.52
195	5.07	0.91	0.92	238	4.02	0.41	0.52
196	7.59	0.98	1.00	239	4.17	0.52	0.40
197	2.87	0.01	0.00	240	4.57	0.08	0.06
198	5.60	0.49	0.44	241	4.26	0.26	0.21
199	7.04	0.86	0.87	242	5.82	0.77	0.76
200	2.79	0.01	0.01	243	6.59	0.91	0.93
201	5.47	0.41	0.47	244	4.08	0.27	0.18
202	2.14	0.00	0.00	245	3.43	0.08	0.06
203	5.60	0.18	0.56	246	3.54	0.03	0.08
204	5.80	0.19	0.31	247	2.81	0.04	0.06
205	1.99	0.04	0.00	248	6.17	0.53	0.65
206	5.48	0.20	0.21	249	5.64	0.42	0.43
207	7.59	0.95	0.90	250	3.77	0.35	0.19
208	5.70	0.67	0.74	251	2.76	0.08	0.01
209	2.92	0.04	0.01	252	2.65	0.07	0.04
210	3.31	0.00	0.02	253	5.18	0.81	0.84
211	3.12	0.00	0.01	254	4.72	0.54	0.43
212	3.12	0.03	0.06	255	3.67	0.58	0.61
213	3.00	0.03	0.06	256	3.15	0.02	0.05
214	6.06	0.38	0.35	257	7.00	0.95	0.89
215	2.54	0.23	0.19	258	8.42	0.86	0.94

Table III   The SDSVs of the MMPI Items and the Proportion of Males and Females
Responding True to Each Item[a]—Continued

| | | P(T) | | | | P(T) | |
Item	SDSV	M	F	Item	SDSV	M	F
259	3.74	0.34	0.31	302	7.04	0.87	0.92
260	3.90	0.18	0.17	303	3.28	0.15	0.11
261	5.21	0.14	0.38	304	3.60	0.34	0.41
262	6.03	0.59	0.49	305	2.98	0.15	0.18
263	4.02	0.17	0.19	306	5.10	0.95	0.95
264	5.92	0.31	0.12	307	3.29	0.31	0.33
265	3.40	0.23	0.11	308	3.98	0.40	0.50
266	4.69	0.27	0.40	309	6.72	0.85	0.91
267	3.77	0.25	0.24	310	7.13	0.78	0.95
268	6.17	0.69	0.84	311	3.65	0.57	0.32
269	3.02	0.08	0.05	312	2.64	0.05	0.03
270	4.48	0.59	0.56	313	4.80	0.34	0.39
271	3.57	0.21	0.16	314	3.99	0.39	0.36
272	7.13	0.95	0.96	315	2.35	0.01	0.01
273	3.08	0.03	0.01	316	3.45	0.47	0.38
274	6.94	0.68	0.59	317	4.07	0.31	0.35
275	1.86	0.01	0.00	318	7.74	0.93	0.92
276	8.21	0.95	0.95	319	3.52	0.32	0.16
277	4.35	0.56	0.52	320	4.05	0.24	0.14
278	3.92	0.45	0.54	321	3.96	0.29	0.57
279	4.75	0.05	0.05	322	4.25	0.42	0.35
280	3.53	0.15	0.10	323	5.10	0.25	0.25
281	5.78	0.88	0.87	324	3.13	0.14	0.20
282	3.54	0.23	0.41	325	3.59	0.14	0.18
283	6.21	0.71	0.31	326	3.22	0.09	0.14
284	2.99	0.23	0.12	327	5.11	0.68	0.66
285	5.88	0.97	0.95	328	3.26	0.29	0.24
286	3.53	0.02	0.06	329	4.71	0.46	0.31
287	6.00	0.42	0.56	330	6.59	0.87	0.85
288	2.70	0.00	0.00	331	2.34	0.00	0.01
289	5.21	0.59	0.66	332	3.65	0.05	0.15
290	3.93	0.25	0.38	333	2.70	0.03	0.05
291	2.78	0.01	0.03	334	3.69	0.17	0.11
292	3.19	0.42	0.30	335	3.13	0.21	0.18
293	2.63	0.05	0.00	336	3.10	0.38	0.33
294	7.10	0.56	0.91	337	3.40	0.29	0.23
295	5.80	0.60	0.74	338	3.01	0.11	0.08
296	6.64	0.67	0.77	339	1.19	0.01	0.01
297	4.54	0.28	0.17	340	4.56	0.53	0.65
298	3.58	0.37	0.19	341	4.46	0.04	0.03
299	5.23	0.36	0.33	342	3.03	0.07	0.19
300	4.55	0.55	0.14	343	4.26	0.18	0.19
301	2.92	0.08	0.08	344	3.02	0.17	0.22

Table III   The SDSVs of the MMPI Items and the Proportion of Males and Females
Responding True to Each Item[a]—Continued

Item	SDSV	P(T) M	P(T) F	Item	SDSV	P(T) M	P(T) F
345	3.55	0.06	0.14	388	3.15	0.08	0.29
346	4.22	0.11	0.24	389	3.23	0.23	0.22
347	6.47	0.93	0.97	390	5.00	0.46	0.41
348	4.56	0.34	0.38	391	6.96	0.58	0.79
349	3.78	0.14	0.09	392	3.56	0.01	0.08
350	2.91	0.04	0.11	393	1.59	0.02	0.04
351	2.80	0.01	0.02	394	5.77	0.63	0.58
352	3.28	0.20	0.29	395	3.75	0.12	0.13
353	6.92	0.69	0.58	396	3.49	0.32	0.25
354	3.24	0.01	0.07	397	3.30	0.37	0.40
355	1.66	0.08	0.06	398	3.81	0.25	0.23
356	3.58	0.28	0.29	399	6.77	0.77	0.76
357	2.95	0.36	0.44	400	6.13	0.46	0.32
358	3.40	0.16	0.06	401	6.93	0.77	0.71
359	3.80	0.25	0.37	402	5.07	0.28	0.34
360	2.71	0.01	0.01	403	7.10	0.89	0.94
361	3.34	0.27	0.40	404	4.34	0.28	0.26
362	3.66	0.32	0.37	405	6.33	0.94	0.97
363	3.12	0.05	0.08	406	4.61	0.34	0.20
364	2.40	0.02	0.01	407	6.86	0.83	0.75
365	3.42	0.04	0.06	408	4.62	0.64	0.77
366	3.07	0.13	0.09	409	4.43	0.58	0.72
367	5.94	0.87	0.65	410	4.79	0.56	0.38
368	4.40	0.27	0.36	411	3.24	0.17	0.17
369	5.45	0.53	0.52	412	7.09	0.88	0.60
370	5.79	0.61	0.70	413	4.31	0.18	0.16
371	6.26	0.66	0.70	414	3.17	0.26	0.28
372	5.91	0.74	0.67	415	6.03	0.67	0.50
373	5.61	0.34	0.22	416	4.22	0.48	0.62
374	4.44	0.72	0.80	417	4.80	0.29	0.12
375	3.74	0.11	0.18	418	2.99	0.24	0.31
376	6.60	0.91	0.94	419	3.93	0.05	0.02
377	3.23	0.25	0.18	420	4.88	0.08	0.07
378	4.68	0.55	0.41	421	4.11	0.27	0.44
379	6.30	0.66	0.67	422	3.26	0.08	0.13
380	5.99	0.80	0.72	423	6.21	0.76	0.46
381	3.63	0.12	0.08	424	4.22	0.22	0.26
382	5.19	0.31	0.44	425	4.89	0.41	0.51
383	4.14	0.49	0.41	426	4.77	0.57	0.22
384	4.05	0.34	0.31	427	4.43	0.08	0.44
385	3.88	0.03	0.20	428	6.28	0.55	0.54
386	4.34	0.39	0.31	429	6.41	0.56	0.63
387	3.77	0.25	0.15	430	7.50	1.00	0.92

Table III   The SDSVs of the MMPI Items and the Proportion of Males and Females
Responding True to Each Item[a]—Continued

Item	SDSV	P(T) M	P(T) F	Item	SDSV	P(T) M	P(T) F
431	3.68	0.31	0.24	474	5.62	0.77	0.71
432	5.82	0.39	0.31	475	3.88	0.59	0.58
433	3.62	0.09	0.21	476	2.94	0.03	0.03
434	5.24	0.59	0.17	477	5.16	0.62	0.52
435	5.13	0.16	0.21	478	4.57	0.76	0.72
436	4.33	0.78	0.59	479	7.08	0.92	0.87
437	3.77	0.45	0.44	480	3.48	0.09	0.28
438	3.85	0.54	0.41	481	4.17	0.71	0.72
439	4.16	0.46	0.64	482	5.80	0.60	0.59
440	6.23	0.78	0.83	483	6.13	0.66	0.74
441	5.33	0.47	0.66	484	3.83	0.24	0.15
442	3.85	0.48	0.51	485	3.85	0.38	0.28
443	3.62	0.20	0.28	486	6.46	0.95	0.85
444	4.24	0.19	0.29	487	2.68	0.13	0.19
445	6.43	0.91	0.89	488	6.67	0.38	0.59
446	5.17	0.69	0.41	489	4.77	0.47	0.41
447	5.09	0.55	0.30	490	6.29	0.12	0.08
448	3.43	0.11	0.15	491	3.79	0.16	0.20
449	7.09	0.79	0.87	492	4.41	0.15	0.38
450	6.79	0.69	0.80	493	6.20	0.65	0.56
451	6.71	0.81	0.81	494	3.29	0.02	0.13
452	3.64	0.46	0.19	495	6.00	0.76	0.58
453	4.12	0.32	0.23	496	5.84	0.84	0.79
454	4.13	0.23	0.23	497	6.72	0.97	0.90
455	4.63	0.25	0.25	498	6.44	0.44	0.29
456	3.70	0.13	0.12	499	4.58	0.63	0.69
457	3.00	0.05	0.04	500	4.84	0.42	0.39
458	5.05	0.21	0.20	501	6.31	0.61	0.61
459	2.84	0.13	0.04	502	6.41	0.85	0.75
460	6.04	0.88	0.96	503	4.79	0.42	0.40
461	6.12	0.33	0.23	504	4.49	0.32	0.19
462	6.22	0.92	0.95	505	5.18	0.24	0.25
463	5.47	0.41	0.94	506	3.68	0.26	0.27
464	5.50	0.95	0.95	507	3.68	0.29	0.24
465	5.19	0.64	0.59	508	6.07	0.97	0.97
466	6.65	0.84	0.78	509	3.57	0.19	0.21
467	4.61	0.08	0.20	510	3.41	0.05	0.14
468	5.63	0.51	0.60	511	3.64	0.15	0.19
469	3.91	0.11	0.11	512	2.08	0.08	0.04
470	2.95	0.02	0.09	513	4.95	0.71	0.71
471	3.46	0.11	0.02	514	2.99	0.12	0.03
472	3.80	0.25	0.38	515	6.82	0.96	0.95
473	3.31	0.13	0.08	516	4.52	0.42	0.59

Table III   The SDSVs of the MMPI Items and the Proportion of Males and Females
Responding True to Each Item[a]—Continued

| Item | SDSV | P(T) | | Item | SDSV | P(T) | |
		M	F			M	F
517	2.40	0.01	0.07	542	5.76	0.82	0.87
518	4.11	0.22	0.31	543	2.87	0.01	0.02
519	2.48	0.03	0.01	544	3.11	0.32	0.41
520	6.61	0.77	0.72	545	4.15	0.22	0.31
521	6.85	0.77	0.65	546	6.15	0.66	0.66
522	5.82	0.66	0.30	547	7.18	0.82	0.86
523	5.68	0.57	0.35	548	4.84	0.13	0.32
524	5.58	0.87	0.93	549	2.97	0.15	0.20
525	4.04	0.33	0.49	550	5.41	0.42	0.22
526	2.12	0.01	0.01	551	4.32	0.32	0.47
527	7.29	0.81	0.74	552	6.24	0.74	0.55
528	5.79	0.89	0.63	553	3.40	0.04	0.06
529	6.08	0.83	0.94	554	5.91	0.39	0.73
530	4.18	0.15	0.35	555	2.95	0.15	0.26
531	3.41	0.18	0.20	556	7.13	0.72	0.82
532	5.85	0.95	0.88	557	5.38	0.02	0.45
533	5.68	0.81	0.83	558	3.93	0.52	0.64
534	6.41	0.62	0.52	559	3.63	0.05	0.19
535	3.89	0.03	0.02	560	3.68	0.20	0.23
536	4.57	0.53	0.35	561	6.31	0.62	0.68
537	5.56	0.64	0.26	562	5.73	0.55	0.57
538	4.99	0.04	0.38	563	5.93	0.81	0.31
539	6.02	0.95	0.69	564	3.66	0.35	0.43
540	6.81	0.98	0.96	565	2.45	0.09	0.08
541	4.64	0.09	0.10	566	5.45	0.55	0.81

[a]The SDSVs of the MMPI items are based on a sample of 83 male and 88 female students
at Pennsylvania State University. They are reproduced from Samuel Messick and Douglas
N. Jackson: Desirability scale values and dispersions for MMPI items, *Psychological Reports*,
1961a, **8**, 409–414, by permission of the authors and publisher.

The P(T)s of the items are based on a sample of 95 male and 105 female students at the
University of Oregon. They are reproduced, by permission, from Lewis R. Goldberg and
Leonard G. Rorer: Test-retest item statistics for original and reversed MMPI items, *ORI
Research Monograph*, 1963, **3**, No. 1. Eugene: Oregon Research Institute.

Table IV The SDSVs of the EPI Items in Booklet IA and the Proportion of Males and Females Responding True to Each Item[a]

Item	SDSV	P(T) M	P(T) F	Item	SDSV	P(T) M	P(T) F
1	7.06	0.42	0.43	44	3.70	0.14	0.20
2	5.31	0.78	0.84	45	6.28	0.64	0.73
3	4.04	0.20	0.12	46	6.19	0.77	0.77
4	6.90	0.68	0.69	47	6.53	0.61	0.88
5	6.04	0.41	0.41	48	5.38	0.80	0.60
6	4.68	0.39	0.48	49	7.16	0.59	0.63
7	7.40	0.93	0.91	50	7.58	0.70	0.62
8	7.21	0.68	0.70	51	7.10	0.79	0.66
9	6.12	0.75	0.81	52	5.39	0.48	0.65
10	5.61	0.57	0.65	53	7.68	0.87	0.85
11	6.17	0.37	0.44	54	4.21	0.19	0.12
12	6.50	0.77	0.77	55	7.31	0.93	0.94
13	4.01	0.38	0.36	56	6.76	0.90	0.86
14	6.14	0.53	0.63	57	0.00	0.00	0.00
15	7.68	0.53	0.67	58	6.37	0.65	0.39
16	6.63	0.38	0.42	59	6.14	0.89	0.94
17	4.04	0.50	0.34	60	6.36	0.60	0.65
18	7.44	0.79	0.82	61	6.47	0.83	0.70
19	7.24	0.74	0.57	62	7.70	0.95	0.85
20	5.99	0.54	0.42	63	6.92	0.82	0.78
21	4.84	0.46	0.35	64	6.54	0.67	0.88
22	6.71	0.81	0.64	65	6.16	0.34	0.63
23	7.08	0.82	0.87	66	5.50	0.36	0.34
24	5.87	0.44	0.49	67	5.90	0.85	0.79
25	5.07	0.30	0.32	68	4.87	0.49	0.50
26	0.00	0.00	0.00	69	7.22	0.86	0.88
27	5.56	0.88	0.85	70	5.91	0.83	0.68
28	5.44	0.74	0.77	71	4.81	0.70	0.37
29	4.20	0.22	0.23	72	5.27	0.61	0.77
30	4.98	0.30	0.53	73	6.31	0.79	0.88
31	3.67	0.34	0.41	74	5.98	0.82	0.80
32	6.90	0.56	0.72	75	3.65	0.47	0.45
33	5.88	0.55	0.77	76	7.07	0.75	0.81
34	6.12	0.69	0.37	77	4.56	0.33	0.35
35	3.97	0.24	0.21	78	6.33	0.59	0.44
36	8.28	0.78	0.77	79	3.88	0.46	0.40
37	3.79	0.36	0.29	80	6.74	0.53	0.51
38	4.53	0.18	0.31	81	5.59	0.59	0.46
39	6.80	0.82	0.83	82	6.66	0.91	0.87
40	5.38	0.59	0.67	83	3.61	0.14	0.23
41	5.27	0.47	0.51	84	7.25	0.91	0.92
42	4.51	0.20	0.17	85	6.46	0.84	0.92
43	6.32	0.76	0.81	86	6.62	0.86	0.85

Table IV   The SDSVs of the EPI Items in Booklet IA and the Proportion of Males and Females Responding True to Each Item[a]—Continued

Item	SDSV	P(T) M	P(T) F	Item	SDSV	P(T) M	P(T) F
87	4.97	0.74	0.68	130	4.83	0.39	0.44
88	0.00	0.00	0.00	131	7.75	0.92	0.85
89	4.31	0.51	0.39	132	5.62	0.44	0.23
90	6.45	0.84	0.86	133	5.56	0.84	0.68
91	5.79	0.37	0.42	134	4.95	0.70	0.63
92	5.17	0.49	0.40	135	6.26	0.59	0.63
93	3.35	0.20	0.24	136	6.54	0.84	0.82
94	7.27	0.54	0.66	137	3.05	0.14	0.08
95	7.04	0.82	0.86	138	6.16	0.62	0.60
96	6.16	0.65	0.86	139	5.97	0.40	0.40
97	4.06	0.67	0.62	140	4.65	0.25	0.15
98	7.43	0.82	0.81	141	5.91	0.87	0.84
99	4.07	0.38	0.41	142	7.20	0.57	0.61
100	6.98	0.93	0.93	143	5.82	0.73	0.72
101	7.65	0.84	0.81	144	7.80	0.92	0.94
102	3.48	0.34	0.18	145	5.13	0.43	0.55
103	6.85	0.85	0.86	146	3.97	0.24	0.35
104	6.99	0.59	0.65	147	7.53	0.88	0.91
105	6.85	0.86	0.87	148	7.47	0.94	0.96
106	3.34	0.39	0.19	149	5.24	0.20	0.24
107	6.92	0.64	0.61	150	0.00	0.00	0.00
108	6.67	0.74	0.81	151	4.04	0.22	0.17
109	6.00	0.42	0.25	152	6.48	0.73	0.83
110	5.11	0.70	0.54	153	7.02	0.64	0.75
111	2.73	0.22	0.13	154	7.23	0.70	0.61
112	7.18	0.66	0.52	155	3.41	0.10	0.26
113	6.97	0.89	0.86	156	6.80	0.64	0.66
114	3.73	0.28	0.27	157	6.55	0.84	0.93
115	4.73	0.39	0.56	158	5.45	0.38	0.38
116	5.31	0.75	0.68	159	4.80	0.82	0.82
117	5.45	0.16	0.36	160	4.36	0.34	0.35
118	6.73	0.92	0.94	161	6.23	0.77	0.75
119	0.00	0.00	0.00	162	6.22	0.85	0.84
120	3.19	0.18	0.21	163	7.23	0.64	0.49
121	6.83	0.87	0.86	164	4.73	0.53	0.43
122	7.27	0.56	0.61	165	6.18	0.78	0.83
123	6.10	0.63	0.38	166	5.56	0.61	0.66
124	7.57	0.95	0.95	167	6.77	0.83	0.86
125	5.74	0.35	0.35	168	5.37	0.38	0.25
126	7.33	0.80	0.92	169	7.13	0.71	0.75
127	5.93	0.43	0.57	170	7.55	0.87	0.88
128	3.23	0.22	0.13	171	5.83	0.44	0.40
129	7.10	0.60	0.59	172	4.56	0.14	0.22

Table IV The SDSVs of the EPI Items in Booklet IA and the Proportion of Males and Females Responding True to Each Item[a]—Continued

Item	SDSV	P(T) M	P(T) F	Item	SDSV	P(T) M	P(T) F
173	5.44	0.24	0.22	216	5.58	0.46	0.41
174	5.18	0.81	0.58	217	7.14	0.88	0.86
175	4.37	0.17	0.39	218	5.54	0.31	0.30
176	5.34	0.71	0.71	219	6.03	0.60	0.59
177	6.39	0.63	0.59	220	6.99	0.21	0.22
178	7.48	0.90	0.95	221	5.57	0.61	0.71
179	6.68	0.87	0.90	222	3.98	0.46	0.47
180	7.24	0.74	0.64	223	4.68	0.55	0.46
181	5.88	0.91	0.94	224	5.40	0.50	0.33
182	3.20	0.16	0.13	225	5.76	0.75	0.63
183	5.76	0.62	0.82	226	6.35	0.91	0.95
184	7.74	0.84	0.91	227	6.92	0.80	0.73
185	5.91	0.54	0.38	228	7.61	0.72	0.81
186	7.20	0.54	0.48	229	5.65	0.25	0.27
187	6.08	0.67	0.80	230	4.70	0.40	0.39
188	5.70	0.64	0.66	231	4.83	0.34	0.28
189	7.68	0.92	0.93	232	4.78	0.25	0.34
190	3.04	0.23	0.10	233	4.12	0.17	0.11
191	7.14	0.59	0.73	234	5.15	0.48	0.65
192	4.62	0.42	0.39	235	5.90	0.52	0.47
193	6.96	0.95	0.87	236	5.39	0.48	0.26
194	4.94	0.56	0.34	237	7.46	0.84	0.69
195	6.65	0.94	0.95	238	5.11	0.55	0.62
196	6.43	0.54	0.59	239	7.56	0.92	0.95
197	4.58	0.51	0.31	240	5.23	0.67	0.59
198	6.72	0.73	0.60	241	6.92	0.44	0.54
199	6.51	0.65	0.59	242	3.77	0.32	0.29
200	6.63	0.79	0.81	243	4.07	0.09	0.04
201	6.75	0.74	0.81	244	5.39	0.83	0.63
202	5.91	0.37	0.31	245	7.08	0.87	0.90
203	5.07	0.45	0.29	246	7.31	0.86	0.93
204	7.76	0.87	0.86	247	5.72	0.57	0.69
205	7.61	0.72	0.69	248	7.20	0.58	0.56
206	4.02	0.06	0.10	249	6.59	0.64	0.71
207	5.32	0.55	0.52	250	6.99	0.80	0.79
208	7.91	0.77	0.86	251	4.66	0.40	0.53
209	6.21	0.65	0.67	252	4.97	0.31	0.40
210	7.65	0.75	0.79	253	6.26	0.58	0.45
211	5.65	0.75	0.68	254	4.57	0.30	0.22
212	5.10	0.40	0.35	255	6.35	0.67	0.43
213	4.52	0.27	0.23	256	5.92	0.71	0.40
214	5.19	0.50	0.49	257	4.75	0.59	0.40
215	6.40	0.69	0.55	258	4.04	0.24	0.22

Table IV   The SDSVs of the EPI Items in Booklet IA and the Proportion of Males and Females Responding True to Each Item[a]—Continued

Item	SDSV	P(T)		Item	SDSV	P(T)	
		M	F			M	F
259	6.54	0.40	0.50	280	6.67	0.68	0.60
260	6.67	0.79	0.77	281	6.15	0.74	0.73
261	3.41	0.29	0.15	282	4.02	0.29	0.18
262	6.78	0.84	0.86	283	4.45	0.54	0.48
263	3.63	0.34	0.38	284	6.05	0.80	0.84
264	6.27	0.44	0.40	285	4.26	0.42	0.43
265	5.19	0.49	0.42	286	7.06	0.90	0.82
266	7.03	0.63	0.51	287	6.25	0.71	0.61
267	6.03	0.62	0.55	288	5.12	0.80	0.73
268	3.79	0.09	0.08	289	6.37	0.79	0.84
269	3.72	0.17	0.16	290	7.00	0.74	0.58
270	5.51	0.60	0.53	291	3.84	0.37	0.27
271	4.22	0.47	0.36	292	3.99	0.30	0.15
272	4.74	0.62	0.49	293	6.41	0.66	0.66
273	5.75	0.83	0.88	294	7.36	0.79	0.74
274	5.74	0.65	0.78	295	6.23	0.55	0.62
275	4.44	0.29	0.38	296	5.33	0.31	0.53
276	5.71	0.87	0.82	297	6.95	0.53	0.49
277	4.62	0.35	0.36	298	7.43	0.91	0.77
278	8.37	0.39	0.52	299	6.34	0.71	0.64
279	6.90	0.94	0.92	300	5.58	0.71	0.68

[a]Items 26, 57, 88, 119 and 150 are not scored in Booklet IA.

Table V   The SDSVs of the EPI Items in Booklet IB and the Proportion of Males and Females Responding True to Each Item[a]

		P(T)				P(T)	
Item	SDSV	M	F	Item	SDSV	M	F
1	6.94	0.44	0.44	44	3.64	0.19	0.17
2	5.96	0.86	0.83	45	5.87	0.77	0.76
3	6.77	0.28	0.31	46	6.97	0.74	0.76
4	5.65	0.64	0.49	47	5.97	0.37	0.52
5	6.76	0.53	0.47	48	6.52	0.79	0.66
6	4.79	0.37	0.42	49	7.08	0.63	0.54
7	7.74	0.95	0.93	50	5.72	0.63	0.53
8	7.27	0.72	0.62	51	7.33	0.75	0.60
9	6.48	0.79	0.74	52	5.43	0.49	0.67
10	4.94	0.41	0.41	53	7.25	0.82	0.67
11	5.99	0.54	0.45	54	3.72	0.19	0.16
12	6.83	0.72	0.80	55	5.83	0.88	0.89
13	4.18	0.37	0.25	56	5.71	0.65	0.72
14	5.61	0.45	0.50	57	0.00	0.00	0.00
15	7.35	0.52	0.55	58	6.51	0.54	0.38
16	6.13	0.28	0.41	59	6.64	0.86	0.95
17	4.93	0.58	0.49	60	5.87	0.72	0.79
18	7.40	0.87	0.88	61	7.58	0.83	0.77
19	6.80	0.74	0.61	62	7.63	0.94	0.89
20	5.82	0.56	0.57	63	7.07	0.83	0.89
21	4.91	0.51	0.48	64	5.87	0.58	0.72
22	7.60	0.91	0.89	65	7.20	0.74	0.76
23	6.62	0.89	0.91	66	4.85	0.34	0.37
24	5.36	0.43	0.41	67	6.78	0.88	0.86
25	6.62	0.92	0.94	68	4.97	0.45	0.40
26	0.00	0.00	0.00	69	7.45	0.88	0.90
27	6.15	0.85	0.77	70	5.42	0.75	0.76
28	6.18	0.81	0.74	71	3.34	0.21	0.26
29	4.41	0.21	0.30	72	6.03	0.45	0.57
30	5.88	0.34	0.53	73	6.85	0.88	0.83
31	4.05	0.29	0.22	74	6.80	0.78	0.81
32	5.91	0.64	0.70	75	4.04	0.34	0.36
33	5.68	0.43	0.54	76	7.01	0.75	0.87
34	5.98	0.58	0.49	77	4.62	0.35	0.25
35	5.22	0.27	0.25	78	7.36	0.53	0.50
36	7.62	0.61	0.72	79	4.85	0.64	0.48
37	4.19	0.24	0.18	80	7.65	0.46	0.47
38	4.63	0.24	0.25	81	7.51	0.56	0.62
39	6.47	0.86	0.71	82	7.37	0.84	0.89
40	4.01	0.39	0.33	83	3.37	0.18	0.14
41	4.55	0.37	0.33	84	7.40	0.83	0.88
42	4.73	0.30	0.21	85	5.99	0.86	0.89
43	6.77	0.78	0.79	86	7.47	0.68	0.66

Table V   The SDSVs of the EPI Items in Booklet IB and the Proportion of Males and Females Responding True to Each Item[a]—Continued

Item	SDSV	P(T) M	P(T) F	Item	SDSV	P(T) M	P(T) F
87	6.67	0.89	0.93	130	3.95	0.33	0.29
88	0.00	0.00	0.00	131	6.78	0.88	0.84
89	6.08	0.54	0.47	132	6.71	0.39	0.27
90	6.97	0.85	0.84	133	6.16	0.79	0.62
91	5.28	0.32	0.31	134	5.14	0.66	0.68
92	5.39	0.55	0.59	135	6.24	0.71	0.79
93	3.76	0.22	0.29	136	7.17	0.74	0.84
94	7.56	0.64	0.71	137	3.11	0.11	0.12
95	7.21	0.91	0.90	138	6.20	0.80	0.73
96	6.22	0.74	0.87	139	6.43	0.43	0.44
97	5.62	0.77	0.58	140	4.77	0.34	0.24
98	7.24	0.78	0.64	141	5.55	0.65	0.57
99	3.75	0.33	0.41	142	7.21	0.46	0.50
100	7.28	0.94	0.87	143	5.77	0.79	0.66
101	7.74	0.84	0.82	144	7.47	0.93	0.89
102	4.12	0.44	0.36	145	5.31	0.54	0.56
103	6.06	0.69	0.68	146	3.62	0.14	0.14
104	7.23	0.57	0.57	147	7.23	0.91	0.92
105	6.78	0.88	0.86	148	7.37	0.88	0.96
106	6.18	0.24	0.22	149	6.41	0.79	0.78
107	6.83	0.53	0.54	150	0.00	0.00	0.00
108	7.12	0.77	0.85	151	3.29	0.25	0.19
109	4.64	0.32	0.31	152	5.66	0.76	0.80
110	5.44	0.83	0.65	153	7.18	0.79	0.85
111	3.12	0.29	0.23	154	6.03	0.60	0.42
112	7.14	0.53	0.49	155	3.90	0.13	0.12
113	6.47	0.89	0.81	156	6.64	0.66	0.65
114	3.82	0.24	0.30	157	6.81	0.71	0.83
115	4.94	0.67	0.58	158	6.41	0.35	0.21
116	5.91	0.74	0.69	159	5.20	0.74	0.72
117	5.73	0.31	0.22	160	4.54	0.34	0.29
118	7.05	0.93	0.96	161	6.88	0.83	0.83
119	0.00	0.00	0.00	162	7.04	0.83	0.81
120	3.53	0.17	0.25	163	7.77	0.70	0.53
121	7.08	0.86	0.87	164	5.96	0.79	0.63
122	6.93	0.54	0.54	165	5.84	0.84	0.93
123	6.57	0.66	0.49	166	7.28	0.67	0.64
124	7.82	0.87	0.76	167	6.54	0.87	0.80
125	5.48	0.42	0.43	168	3.66	0.41	0.31
126	6.55	0.80	0.88	169	6.77	0.75	0.85
127	5.80	0.54	0.45	170	5.18	0.72	0.72
128	2.77	0.27	0.13	171	6.36	0.44	0.42
129	7.46	0.69	0.57	172	5.41	0.23	0.35

Table V The SDSVs of the EPI Items in Booklet IB and the Proportion of Males and Females Responding True to Each Item[a]—Continued

Item	SDSV	P(T)		Item	SDSV	P(T)	
		M	F			M	F
173	3.25	0.16	0.13	216	6.56	0.54	0.53
174	5.37	0.74	0.69	217	6.88	0.76	0.67
175	3.94	0.19	0.18	218	6.03	0.48	0.50
176	4.78	0.68	0.76	219	7.34	0.64	0.76
177	7.02	0.34	0.32	220	5.54	0.34	0.32
178	6.67	0.92	0.95	221	6.93	0.73	0.62
179	6.12	0.83	0.85	222	3.86	0.49	0.44
180	6.54	0.95	0.88	223	5.44	0.43	0.55
181	6.85	0.89	0.94	224	6.01	0.66	0.35
182	3.81	0.15	0.07	225	4.68	0.73	0.53
183	5.88	0.68	0.84	226	5.24	0.26	0.42
184	7.74	0.81	0.91	227	6.48	0.78	0.80
185	5.26	0.41	0.49	228	5.47	0.70	0.80
186	7.24	0.62	0.48	229	5.88	0.27	0.29
187	7.62	0.67	0.68	230	3.90	0.20	0.24
188	5.38	0.56	0.60	231	3.78	0.15	0.14
189	6.52	0.91	0.88	232	7.98	0.34	0.33
190	3.27	0.22	0.13	233	4.12	0.24	0.10
191	6.93	0.74	0.68	234	6.42	0.82	0.83
192	4.17	0.31	0.31	235	5.83	0.82	0.67
193	6.75	0.90	0.88	236	5.98	0.36	0.24
194	4.53	0.44	0.36	237	7.52	0.85	0.83
195	5.34	0.24	0.23	238	6.65	0.64	0.71
196	4.86	0.44	0.41	239	7.01	0.95	0.85
197	5.97	0.39	0.45	240	6.32	0.58	0.61
198	6.16	0.67	0.69	241	6.23	0.67	0.68
199	4.41	0.70	0.58	242	3.88	0.65	0.25
200	5.95	0.80	0.71	243	4.00	0.12	0.05
201	6.87	0.70	0.75	244	6.35	0.68	0.62
202	5.96	0.44	0.36	245	6.22	0.86	0.92
203	4.02	0.34	0.33	246	7.43	0.86	0.94
204	7.66	0.83	0.86	247	6.91	0.50	0.77
205	7.65	0.73	0.67	248	6.52	0.64	0.67
206	4.14	0.10	0.18	249	6.40	0.65	0.57
207	4.94	0.54	0.63	250	4.86	0.72	0.72
208	6.63	0.84	0.76	251	4.83	0.42	0.57
209	5.61	0.55	0.54	252	4.63	0.39	0.42
210	6.70	0.73	0.85	253	5.53	0.62	0.53
211	5.68	0.58	0.46	254	4.74	0.44	0.38
212	5.08	0.40	0.36	255	6.64	0.57	0.54
213	4.46	0.16	0.15	256	5.48	0.64	0.49
214	4.38	0.50	0.35	257	5.65	0.65	0.57
215	6.83	0.59	0.62	258	4.43	0.19	0.20

Table V   The SDSVs of the EPI Items in Booklet IB and the Proportion of Males and Females Responding True to Each Item[a]—Continued

		P(T)				P(T)	
Item	SDSV	M	F	Item	SDSV	M	F
259	5.00	0.41	0.50	280	5.06	0.55	0.50
260	6.54	0.75	0.79	281	6.23	0.61	0.75
261	3.30	0.20	0.16	282	3.57	0.14	0.11
262	6.46	0.47	0.39	283	5.26	0.47	0.50
263	5.25	0.28	0.43	284	7.60	0.74	0.79
264	6.76	0.32	0.50	285	5.06	0.36	0.52
265	4.46	0.36	0.37	286	5.90	0.80	0.81
266	4.34	0.45	0.38	287	7.83	0.73	0.75
267	7.86	0.44	0.37	288	6.07	0.58	0.49
268	4.06	0.06	0.13	289	6.61	0.74	0.73
269	2.72	0.23	0.12	290	6.75	0.74	0.65
270	6.64	0.66	0.59	291	2.84	0.09	0.07
271	4.44	0.46	0.29	292	4.44	0.69	0.74
272	3.42	0.12	0.11	293	6.78	0.69	0.74
273	5.24	0.44	0.37	294	6.45	0.34	0.35
274	5.99	0.89	0.90	295	6.30	0.59	0.55
275	3.95	0.30	0.31	296	5.76	0.51	0.59
276	6.41	0.82	0.86	297	6.48	0.52	0.53
277	4.88	0.37	0.34	298	6.73	0.82	0.77
278	6.05	0.40	0.26	299	6.18	0.71	0.54
279	7.12	0.75	0.74	300	4.77	0.74	0.64

[a]Items 26, 57, 88, 119, and 150 are not scored in Booklet IB.

Table VI The SDSVs of the EPI Items in Booklet II and the Proportion of Males and Females Responding True to Each Item

Item	SDSV	P(T) M	P(T) F	Item	SDSV	P(T) M	P(T) F
1	6.48	0.75	0.84	44	4.77	0.28	0.13
2	3.36	0.24	0.26	45	7.60	0.84	0.89
3	3.08	0.16	0.12	46	3.01	0.21	0.14
4	5.90	0.70	0.75	47	3.13	0.32	0.25
5	6.07	0.87	0.80	48	2.93	0.17	0.13
6	4.38	0.29	0.22	49	7.61	0.83	0.90
7	3.12	0.07	0.11	50	6.06	0.63	0.75
8	7.56	0.84	0.91	51	3.36	0.25	0.25
9	3.35	0.31	0.38	52	3.41	0.08	0.08
10	3.62	0.24	0.26	53	3.86	0.34	0.45
11	2.92	0.10	0.10	54	7.23	0.91	0.84
12	7.33	0.85	0.90	55	7.56	0.92	0.88
13	3.12	0.14	0.22	56	3.27	0.24	0.31
14	3.66	0.19	0.16	57	5.08	0.33	0.36
15	3.77	0.46	0.21	58	2.54	0.08	0.04
16	2.83	0.15	0.06	59	5.15	0.46	0.60
17	2.93	0.06	0.09	60	3.68	0.66	0.66
18	7.40	0.87	0.85	61	2.73	0.22	0.14
19	4.21	0.58	0.37	62	5.48	0.53	0.28
20	4.26	0.50	0.46	63	2.26	0.12	0.06
21	2.30	0.09	0.04	64	2.95	0.08	0.05
22	3.42	0.39	0.40	65	2.32	0.17	0.04
23	3.53	0.12	0.04	66	4.34	0.45	0.48
24	2.90	0.14	0.15	67	3.93	0.19	0.26
25	2.93	0.16	0.15	68	6.70	0.87	0.90
26	3.53	0.11	0.12	69	3.26	0.14	0.07
27	3.04	0.17	0.05	70	4.86	0.31	0.30
28	5.08	0.25	0.45	71	3.28	0.14	0.25
29	3.58	0.29	0.27	72	3.88	0.44	0.43
30	3.60	0.21	0.22	73	3.06	0.22	0.13
31	4.81	0.37	0.30	74	5.23	0.41	0.25
32	3.59	0.34	0.27	75	3.76	0.17	0.22
33	3.56	0.22	0.20	76	6.24	0.50	0.54
34	7.01	0.45	0.49	77	3.31	0.22	0.16
35	5.34	0.29	0.39	78	2.66	0.06	0.04
36	3.58	0.12	0.12	79	3.03	0.38	0.28
37	2.53	0.06	0.04	80	6.46	0.62	0.50
38	2.81	0.06	0.05	81	4.10	0.10	0.15
39	3.57	0.17	0.13	82	3.19	0.24	0.10
40	3.27	0.18	0.18	83	7.39	0.70	0.87
41	3.15	0.06	0.14	84	4.58	0.48	0.67
42	2.96	0.40	0.31	85	6.91	0.69	0.68
43	5.01	0.24	0.22	86	5.84	0.35	0.31

Table VI   The SDSVs of the EPI Items in Booklet II and the Proportion of Males and
Females Responding True to Each Item—Continued

		P(T)				P(T)	
Item	SDSV	M	F	Item	SDSV	M	F
87	3.22	0.14	0.12	130	3.33	0.15	0.10
88	4.47	0.45	0.31	131	3.43	0.25	0.22
89	3.01	0.10	0.12	132	6.77	0.63	0.67
90	4.07	0.20	0.21	133	2.78	0.09	0.06
91	3.27	0.17	0.18	134	3.67	0.49	0.55
92	3.53	0.22	0.29	135	3.20	0.19	0.09
93	3.64	0.06	0.16	136	4.81	0.35	0.29
94	2.24	0.13	0.06	137	3.22	0.14	0.11
95	3.62	0.28	0.16	138	3.95	0.20	0.15
96	6.68	0.70	0.75	139	7.35	0.80	0.81
97	4.54	0.36	0.18	140	2.90	0.10	0.06
98	4.57	0.20	0.28	141	4.92	0.30	0.23
99	3.58	0.21	0.14	142	6.10	0.57	0.62
100	2.86	0.15	0.20	143	4.45	0.27	0.44
101	3.02	0.11	0.13	144	2.85	0.14	0.12
102	3.11	0.06	0.16	145	3.27	0.12	0.13
103	3.93	0.16	0.24	146	3.07	0.14	0.16
104	3.07	0.24	0.18	147	3.52	0.08	0.10
105	4.16	0.20	0.18	148	2.86	0.08	0.11
106	3.97	0.22	0.22	149	3.43	0.47	0.33
107	5.59	0.76	0.65	150	4.21	0.36	0.36
108	2.77	0.08	0.07	151	3.16	0.24	0.17
109	3.50	0.31	0.22	152	7.16	0.82	0.74
110	5.46	0.38	0.36	153	3.36	0.17	0.26
111	7.59	0.68	0.72	154	2.11	0.12	0.05
112	3.88	0.18	0.22	155	6.70	0.74	0.65
113	3.57	0.33	0.28	156	3.14	0.18	0.05
114	2.92	0.13	0.05	157	3.82	0.35	0.40
115	3.20	0.15	0.22	158	3.75	0.14	0.15
116	3.99	0.24	0.18	159	4.77	0.34	0.39
117	3.34	0.33	0.29	160	3.15	0.22	0.22
118	4.39	0.55	0.55	161	2.60	0.04	0.02
119	3.53	0.12	0.09	162	6.42	0.67	0.63
120	2.95	0.15	0.08	163	3.95	0.17	0.30
121	5.67	0.74	0.69	164	3.56	0.20	0.28
122	7.62	0.96	0.95	165	3.17	0.04	0.05
123	3.26	0.17	0.26	166	2.84	0.14	0.09
124	4.79	0.39	0.25	167	6.39	0.50	0.36
125	7.26	0.80	0.90	168	3.04	0.12	0.18
126	3.22	0.25	0.20	169	6.27	0.55	0.61
127	3.20	0.17	0.14	170	5.85	0.25	0.34
128	3.97	0.08	0.15	171	2.82	0.49	0.32
129	3.77	0.09	0.13	172	5.36	0.47	0.35

Table VI   The SDSVs of the EPI Items in Booklet II and the Proportion of Males and
Females Responding True to Each Item—Continued

Item	SDSV	P(T) M	F	Item	SDSV	P(T) M	F
173	6.74	0.65	0.64	216	3.92	0.33	0.42
174	5.63	0.75	0.56	217	4.46	0.22	0.15
175	4.14	0.42	0.32	218	2.90	0.11	0.11
176	3.35	0.14	0.09	219	5.23	0.25	0.30
177	4.00	0.47	0.66	220	4.00	0.66	0.47
178	3.86	0.39	0.13	221	4.11	0.39	0.28
179	2.90	0.15	0.17	222	4.60	0.36	0.40
180	3.00	0.08	0.19	223	2.27	0.08	0.06
181	3.97	0.19	0.13	224	7.16	0.80	0.78
182	3.27	0.40	0.40	225	6.30	0.48	0.39
183	6.31	0.75	0.75	226	4.01	0.53	0.64
184	4.21	0.28	0.29	227	3.66	0.29	0.31
185	3.62	0.25	0.18	228	3.32	0.24	0.20
186	6.10	0.84	0.70	229	5.28	0.79	0.61
187	2.13	0.05	0.01	230	3.19	0.09	0.14
188	3.56	0.27	0.34	231	6.12	0.63	0.60
189	3.05	0.12	0.04	232	2.82	0.05	0.11
190	3.95	0.19	0.21	233	2.86	0.15	0.05
191	4.48	0.14	0.20	234	3.11	0.47	0.43
192	3.80	0.22	0.16	235	7.38	0.88	0.88
193	2.65	0.09	0.06	236	6.00	0.84	0.72
194	6.31	0.26	0.30	237	2.86	0.16	0.13
195	5.15	0.55	0.54	238	2.45	0.16	0.11
196	3.20	0.22	0.18	239	2.47	0.06	0.06
197	3.56	0.35	0.26	240	4.43	0.31	0.22
198	3.82	0.22	0.14	241	3.41	0.20	0.21
199	3.44	0.09	0.18	242	2.75	0.13	0.05
200	3.84	0.14	0.10	243	3.17	0.39	0.30
201	3.46	0.19	0.25	244	2.77	0.12	0.10
202	2.43	0.20	0.08	245	7.68	0.77	0.74
203	7.94	0.94	0.95	246	2.58	0.08	0.05
204	6.91	0.78	0.70	247	3.40	0.12	0.17
205	6.87	0.94	0.86	248	4.70	0.27	0.13
206	3.74	0.31	0.26	249	3.48	0.26	0.14
207	3.84	0.47	0.32	250	3.25	0.15	0.13
208	3.97	0.34	0.28	251	5.81	0.77	0.93
209	5.98	0.43	0.35	252	4.61	0.50	0.44
210	3.16	0.09	0.14	253	4.41	0.25	0.28
211	7.65	0.84	0.82	254	3.40	0.24	0.11
212	3.16	0.11	0.10	255	3.62	0.40	0.33
213	3.90	0.25	0.27	256	3.58	0.31	0.22
214	6.90	0.84	0.71	257	4.22	0.43	0.44
215	3.28	0.21	0.23	258	3.53	0.41	0.43

Table VI The SDSVs of the EPI Items in Booklet II and the Proportion of Males and Females Responding True to Each Item—Continued

Item	SDSV	*P*(T) M	*P*(T) F	Item	SDSV	*P*(T) M	*P*(T) F
259	3.21	0.07	0.09	280	2.94	0.31	0.18
260	7.08	0.79	0.68	281	3.48	0.25	0.21
261	7.07	0.78	0.86	282	2.99	0.19	0.11
262	4.33	0.34	0.25	283	4.88	0.24	0.20
263	6.78	0.90	0.88	284	3.92	0.18	0.28
264	2.62	0.14	0.09	285	2.97	0.11	0.03
265	4.91	0.44	0.42	286	3.07	0.16	0.08
266	7.26	0.79	0.86	287	5.67	0.51	0.52
267	6.92	0.89	0.82	288	2.61	0.08	0.06
268	3.22	0.09	0.13	289	3.21	0.17	0.13
269	2.22	0.13	0.07	290	3.24	0.28	0.15
270	3.79	0.28	0.34	291	7.34	0.85	0.79
271	3.30	0.20	0.09	292	3.43	0.13	0.21
272	5.65	0.61	0.57	293	3.86	0.23	0.21
273	5.90	0.63	0.79	294	7.36	0.93	0.95
274	3.01	0.21	0.08	295	2.32	0.03	0.02
275	3.16	0.21	0.14	296	3.08	0.24	0.15
276	7.20	0.62	0.49	297	7.62	0.85	0.82
277	2.87	0.10	0.06	298	6.42	0.79	0.69
278	3.25	0.08	0.08	299	3.55	0.24	0.18
279	4.08	0.22	0.08	300	3.47	0.11	0.05

Table VII The SDSVs of the EPI Items in Booklet III and the Proportion of Males and Females Responding True to Each Item[a]

Item	SDSV	P(T) M	P(T) F	Item	SDSV	P(T) M	P(T) F
1	6.92	0.51	0.69	44	2.39	0.24	0.04
2	5.86	0.92	0.73	45	7.10	0.56	0.63
3	5.43	0.41	0.49	46	4.30	0.47	0.33
4	5.55	0.47	0.36	47	4.01	0.48	0.22
5	5.62	0.34	0.45	48	6.15	0.49	0.29
6	3.55	0.24	0.25	49	7.36	0.84	0.78
7	3.77	0.52	0.41	50	6.71	0.80	0.80
8	6.76	0.84	0.82	51	3.40	0.15	0.16
9	7.33	0.58	0.66	52	4.35	0.46	0.40
10	6.93	0.67	0.49	53	6.25	0.61	0.38
11	4.36	0.19	0.22	54	4.06	0.24	0.17
12	7.52	0.95	0.82	55	4.96	0.54	0.38
13	3.59	0.11	0.07	56	3.58	0.25	0.22
14	3.04	0.28	0.14	57	6.98	0.64	0.58
15	3.34	0.23	0.09	58	2.81	0.32	0.12
16	6.54	0.82	0.92	59	7.79	0.69	0.73
17	4.98	0.41	0.31	60	5.92	0.41	0.43
18	7.54	0.86	0.93	61	4.90	0.14	0.18
19	7.24	0.77	0.78	62	5.16	0.48	0.40
20	4.27	0.46	0.37	63	7.40	0.76	0.90
21	8.10	0.57	0.60	64	5.08	0.78	0.62
22	3.85	0.20	0.42	65	7.00	0.76	0.68
23	7.85	0.77	0.78	66	7.34	0.67	0.65
24	5.37	0.57	0.40	67	5.32	0.39	0.41
25	7.90	0.64	0.74	68	3.94	0.15	0.19
26	6.99	0.49	0.48	69	7.43	0.56	0.66
27	2.84	0.30	0.18	70	5.12	0.29	0.32
28	3.58	0.21	0.21	71	6.77	0.79	0.79
29	5.92	0.54	0.62	72	4.54	0.36	0.51
30	0.00	0.00	0.00	73	5.85	0.52	0.47
31	3.37	0.21	0.22	74	5.87	0.72	0.42
32	5.94	0.46	0.71	75	1.88	0.07	0.02
33	6.55	0.70	0.53	76	6.50	0.76	0.71
34	5.06	0.46	0.31	77	7.54	0.86	0.76
35	7.65	0.60	0.59	78	6.58	0.68	0.62
36	4.95	0.63	0.52	79	5.74	0.56	0.62
37	3.62	0.12	0.22	80	3.98	0.35	0.25
38	3.30	0.54	0.54	81	7.11	0.80	0.85
39	6.26	0.76	0.82	82	4.96	0.39	0.40
40	4.34	0.52	0.31	83	3.15	0.10	0.17
41	6.35	0.70	0.60	84	7.72	0.75	0.59
42	3.24	0.38	0.31	85	2.96	0.09	0.06
43	6.71	0.86	0.72	86	6.45	0.64	0.47

Table VII   The SDSVs of the EPI Items in Booklet III and the Proportion of Males and Females Responding True to Each Item[a]—Continued

Item	SDSV	P(T) M	P(T) F	Item	SDSV	P(T) M	P(T) F
87	7.85	0.85	0.90	130	3.55	0.13	0.28
88	7.25	0.79	0.65	131	7.55	0.68	0.75
89	3.24	0.39	0.29	132	6.47	0.75	0.86
90	7.62	0.64	0.80	133	5.30	0.24	0.20
91	6.19	0.74	0.73	134	7.01	0.53	0.60
92	6.75	0.64	0.65	135	7.38	0.83	0.78
93	6.61	0.83	0.86	136	4.75	0.34	0.14
94	6.94	0.60	0.80	137	4.58	0.50	0.31
95	5.70	0.47	0.43	138	3.30	0.40	0.26
96	6.85	0.64	0.65	139	3.50	0.15	0.12
97	3.13	0.26	0.16	140	6.31	0.76	0.61
98	5.37	0.34	0.32	141	5.84	0.58	0.66
99	6.59	0.45	0.25	142	7.56	0.72	0.80
100	3.66	0.29	0.19	143	7.39	0.86	0.75
101	5.76	0.35	0.35	144	4.02	0.57	0.97
102	7.75	0.80	0.84	145	7.31	0.46	0.32
103	4.19	0.38	0.38	146	8.00	0.75	0.59
104	7.93	0.71	0.82	147	3.94	0.65	0.49
105	6.82	0.86	0.71	148	4.33	0.24	0.41
106	2.80	0.10	0.03	149	7.48	0.88	0.89
107	7.37	0.33	0.42	150	3.48	0.12	0.16
108	3.06	0.22	0.17	151	3.46	0.32	0.25
109	6.34	0.76	0.75	152	7.23	0.72	0.57
110	4.61	0.19	0.13	153	6.99	0.74	0.49
111	7.40	0.72	0.81	154	4.53	0.44	0.39
112	6.84	0.81	0.84	155	4.36	0.40	0.36
113	4.53	0.54	0.43	156	7.00	0.64	0.90
114	3.32	0.34	0.27	157	6.40	0.80	0.80
115	7.02	0.70	0.66	158	7.01	0.56	0.54
116	6.48	0.81	0.79	159	4.50	0.35	0.22
117	6.37	0.70	0.48	160	5.51	0.55	0.31
118	3.24	0.24	0.19	161	4.12	0.24	0.33
119	6.17	0.65	0.56	162	3.59	0.22	0.22
120	2.16	0.12	0.01	163	5.87	0.64	0.61
121	5.68	0.41	0.42	164	7.58	0.84	0.92
122	5.91	0.72	0.38	165	7.74	0.90	0.90
123	5.83	0.72	0.48	166	8.07	0.87	0.94
124	7.54	0.63	0.74	167	5.59	0.35	0.15
125	5.92	0.61	0.94	168	4.57	0.59	0.53
126	5.34	0.86	0.77	169	3.72	0.37	0.27
127	6.14	0.66	0.70	170	4.35	0.40	0.31
128	8.05	0.83	0.88	171	7.47	0.79	0.81
129	6.08	0.44	0.45	172	4.07	0.23	0.13

Table VII   The SDSVs of the EPI Items in Booklet III and the Proportion of Males and Females Responding True to Each Item[a]—Continued

Item	SDSV	P(T) M	P(T) F	Item	SDSV	P(T) M	P(T) F
173	7.40	0.57	0.55	216	3.10	0.09	0.13
174	6.96	0.82	0.78	217	3.08	0.44	0.38
175	6.03	0.80	0.79	218	5.67	0.62	0.86
176	7.62	0.47	0.56	219	6.99	0.94	0.83
177	3.79	0.16	0.17	220	7.59	0.83	0.79
178	6.72	0.63	0.62	221	6.15	0.78	0.69
179	5.88	0.74	0.36	222	5.33	0.61	0.58
180	7.33	0.84	0.86	223	6.95	0.65	0.75
181	5.71	0.44	0.50	224	7.68	0.60	0.70
182	2.24	0.36	0.22	225	7.11	0.91	0.96
183	7.35	0.71	0.71	226	7.73	0.81	0.79
184	4.75	0.50	0.33	227	5.10	0.50	0.61
185	3.28	0.34	0.18	228	7.37	0.79	0.87
186	7.81	0.62	0.75	229	6.18	0.86	0.53
187	5.37	0.33	0.46	230	3.55	0.35	0.27
188	6.27	0.79	0.75	231	3.60	0.29	0.26
189	7.77	0.58	0.57	232	3.26	0.38	0.26
190	6.74	0.68	0.62	233	6.06	0.61	0.46
191	5.64	0.45	0.53	234	4.35	0.24	0.17
192	3.75	0.21	0.35	235	7.00	0.84	0.73
193	2.54	0.35	0.27	236	6.64	0.86	0.90
194	4.97	0.47	0.56	237	6.02	0.45	0.59
195	6.34	0.44	0.55	238	7.16	0.58	0.70
196	3.52	0.37	0.42	239	6.66	0.81	0.78
197	7.54	0.72	0.71	240	3.48	0.14	0.08
198	6.73	0.60	0.33	241	7.22	0.77	0.75
199	3.08	0.23	0.10	242	2.95	0.12	0.10
200	6.91	0.61	0.60	243	6.55	0.64	0.76
201	3.43	0.23	0.15	244	3.62	0.29	0.22
202	7.31	0.73	0.71	245	7.46	0.84	0.86
203	4.22	0.38	0.22	246	6.50	0.75	0.54
204	7.59	0.76	0.69	247	4.01	0.57	0.36
205	7.80	0.87	0.91	248	3.28	0.21	0.14
206	4.66	0.59	0.42	249	6.72	0.65	0.78
207	7.36	0.57	0.59	250	5.45	0.42	0.33
208	3.93	0.11	0.25	251	7.55	0.89	0.81
209	5.38	0.69	0.49	252	7.06	0.38	0.45
210	7.15	0.92	0.93	253	4.55	0.24	0.22
211	3.27	0.12	0.09	254	8.04	0.81	0.59
212	5.79	0.78	0.76	255	3.43	0.43	0.39
213	4.10	0.46	0.21	256	6.86	0.81	0.87
214	6.31	0.35	0.40	257	7.74	0.73	0.71
215	5.12	0.51	0.28	258	4.23	0.36	0.34

Table VII   The SDSVs of the EPI Items in Booklet III and the Proportion of Males and Females Responding True to Each Item[a]—Continued

Item	SDSV	P(T) M	P(T) F	Item	SDSV	P(T) M	P(T) F
259	7.26	0.44	0.46	280	4.96	0.59	0.55
260	6.42	0.91	0.82	281	5.78	0.62	0.44
261	2.39	0.07	0.04	282	5.60	0.58	0.30
262	7.76	0.60	0.86	283	6.97	0.86	0.81
263	4.10	0.31	0.26	284	5.77	0.39	0.50
264	5.67	0.29	0.16	285	4.15	0.17	0.28
265	6.08	0.45	0.40	286	2.25	0.28	0.21
266	7.30	0.54	0.47	287	6.76	0.86	0.90
267	6.63	0.82	0.86	288	7.65	0.64	0.68
268	5.23	0.88	0.85	289	6.76	0.74	0.64
269	7.52	0.55	0.71	290	4.90	0.27	0.27
270	3.63	0.08	0.12	291	7.16	0.84	0.73
271	5.21	0.50	0.29	292	1.91	0.11	0.02
272	4.70	0.37	0.39	293	3.15	0.52	0.38
273	6.13	0.89	0.68	294	2.91	0.11	0.12
274	6.91	0.55	0.61	295	5.88	0.71	0.63
275	2.58	0.36	0.28	296	5.47	0.53	0.32
276	7.33	0.72	0.71	297	3.62	0.27	0.22
277	5.98	0.75	0.66	298	5.94	0.54	0.68
278	3.21	0.34	0.13	299	4.11	0.44	0.30
279	4.20	0.24	0.22	300	8.02	0.18	0.38

[a]Item 30 is not scored in Booklet III.

Table VIII   The SDSVs of the EPI Items in Booklet IV and the Proportion of Males and Females Responding True to Each Item[a]

| | | *P*(T) | | | | *P*(T) | |
Item	SDSV	M	F	Item	SDSV	M	F
1	6.55	0.55	0.37	44	4.78	0.64	0.52
2	7.10	0.53	0.55	45	3.55	0.25	0.14
3	5.39	0.83	0.83	46	0.00	0.00	0.00
4	3.54	0.38	0.22	47	4.23	0.28	0.39
5	3.93	0.30	0.20	48	7.20	0.72	0.77
6	0.00	0.00	0.00	49	3.11	0.10	0.08
7	6.84	0.84	0.72	50	3.43	0.27	0.16
8	3.64	0.29	0.22	51	5.42	0.43	0.50
9	3.22	0.16	0.10	52	5.90	0.56	0.79
10	7.92	0.89	0.87	53	0.00	0.00	0.00
11	5.10	0.58	0.49	54	6.78	0.90	0.92
12	2.70	0.38	0.30	55	3.08	0.23	0.14
13	3.64	0.19	0.25	56	4.23	0.66	0.69
14	3.30	0.15	0.21	57	2.55	0.19	0.16
15	0.00	0.00	0.00	58	0.00	0.00	0.00
16	6.67	0.65	0.63	59	5.30	0.56	0.58
17	6.44	0.85	0.82	60	4.04	0.35	0.29
18	3.85	0.43	0.45	61	3.62	0.24	0.22
19	3.31	0.34	0.13	62	7.54	0.84	0.90
20	4.52	0.41	0.52	63	6.92	0.61	0.34
21	2.94	0.12	0.13	64	7.14	0.60	0.68
22	0.00	0.00	0.00	65	4.85	0.55	0.52
23	7.10	0.79	0.86	66	3.33	0.36	0.24
24	7.22	0.86	0.94	67	6.30	0.34	0.33
25	3.07	0.18	0.16	68	0.00	0.00	0.00
26	6.23	0.75	0.77	69	5.65	0.64	0.59
27	0.00	0.00	0.00	70	3.17	0.38	0.28
28	6.67	0.87	0.86	71	2.78	0.09	0.07
29	3.91	0.38	0.22	72	7.36	0.89	0.93
30	5.17	0.48	0.40	73	6.84	0.88	0.92
31	3.35	0.34	0.23	74	3.48	0.49	0.33
32	6.98	0.86	0.83	75	3.51	0.23	0.16
33	7.08	0.79	0.86	76	4.66	0.60	0.59
34	4.35	0.22	0.16	77	0.00	0.00	0.00
35	3.52	0.38	0.22	78	3.98	0.46	0.42
36	4.04	0.28	0.30	79	7.11	0.81	0.81
37	0.00	0.00	0.00	80	3.11	0.13	0.10
38	3.61	0.14	0.16	81	3.41	0.25	0.18
39	3.79	0.21	0.15	82	3.70	0.13	0.05
40	3.05	0.16	0.06	83	4.99	0.76	0.50
41	3.61	0.25	0.20	84	0.00	0.00	0.00
42	6.76	0.84	0.86	85	6.37	0.91	0.88
43	2.96	0.25	0.06	86	7.65	0.89	0.82

Table VIII   The SDSVs of the EPI Items in Booklet IV and the Proportion of Males and
Females Responding True to Each Item[a]—Continued

		P(T)				P(T)	
Item	SDSV	M	F	Item	SDSV	M	F
87	3.55	0.36	0.39	130	0.00	0.00	0.00
88	3.41	0.39	0.43	131	4.39	0.21	0.25
89	0.00	0.00	0.00	132	3.93	0.53	0.34
90	5.35	0.71	0.72	133	2.71	0.09	0.11
91	3.54	0.07	0.10	134	7.38	0.81	0.70
92	3.30	0.16	0.09	135	6.02	0.84	0.87
93	7.51	0.80	0.86	136	2.81	0.18	0.19
94	5.86	0.54	0.56	137	3.30	0.25	0.10
95	6.96	0.65	0.75	138	4.87	0.34	0.35
96	5.74	0.49	0.47	139	0.00	0.00	0.00
97	3.79	0.50	0.22	140	4.25	0.45	0.44
98	6.88	0.74	0.77	141	6.85	0.84	0.82
99	0.00	0.00	0.00	142	2.96	0.19	0.16
100	5.11	0.25	0.23	143	5.06	0.57	0.52
101	7.03	0.67	0.68	144	3.80	0.22	0.22
102	3.23	0.11	0.09	145	4.77	0.33	0.49
103	7.66	0.78	0.77	146	0.00	0.00	0.00
104	7.62	0.87	0.93	147	6.52	0.90	0.79
105	4.03	0.44	0.23	148	2.40	0.25	0.14
106	7.62	0.75	0.83	149	6.90	0.62	0.63
107	5.32	0.71	0.84	150	6.94	0.80	0.74
108	0.00	0.00	0.00	151	0.00	0.00	0.00
109	4.64	0.30	0.27	152	3.13	0.21	0.17
110	7.11	0.74	0.77	153	5.68	0.35	0.40
111	3.33	0.27	0.13	154	3.58	0.16	0.20
112	3.59	0.47	0.27	155	7.51	0.91	0.90
113	3.05	0.07	0.04	156	6.42	0.56	0.55
114	5.01	0.49	0.49	157	7.49	0.84	0.81
115	0.00	0.00	0.00	158	5.01	0.33	0.26
116	7.03	0.91	0.90	159	4.48	0.30	0.42
117	7.99	0.78	0.76	160	4.76	0.34	0.44
118	3.08	0.12	0.06	161	0.00	0.00	0.00
119	4.62	0.18	0.29	162	6.32	0.84	0.76
120	0.00	0.00	0.00	163	7.01	0.79	0.79
121	3.35	0.32	0.23	164	3.65	0.33	0.31
122	3.65	0.30	0.16	165	7.70	0.78	0.88
123	4.15	0.39	0.23	166	6.91	0.88	0.90
124	7.38	0.67	0.59	167	3.85	0.33	0.18
125	6.11	0.75	0.78	168	3.70	0.24	0.24
126	6.61	0.69	0.71	169	5.74	0.85	0.92
127	3.25	0.12	0.13	170	0.00	0.00	0.00
128	3.44	0.20	0.09	171	6.47	0.81	0.81
129	6.76	0.75	0.68	172	6.94	0.93	0.89

Table VIII   The SDSVs of the EPI Items in Booklet IV and the Proportion of Males and Females Responding True to Each Item[a]—Continued

		P(T)				P(T)	
Item	SDSV	M	F	Item	SDSV	M	F
173	3.45	0.24	0.15	216	3.72	0.23	0.13
174	2.84	0.41	0.35	217	7.73	0.89	0.87
175	4.39	0.39	0.28	218	6.30	0.64	0.49
176	3.79	0.14	0.09	219	7.35	0.60	0.70
177	0.00	0.00	0.00	220	3.30	0.24	0.22
178	7.15	0.75	0.67	221	2.98	0.42	0.30
179	2.63	0.31	0.18	222	3.95	0.46	0.31
180	2.96	0.13	0.10	223	0.00	0.00	0.00
181	7.27	0.54	0.64	224	4.01	0.14	0.08
182	0.00	0.00	0.00	225	3.47	0.28	0.31
183	3.32	0.29	0.21	226	2.38	0.14	0.11
184	2.95	0.18	0.09	227	6.97	0.69	0.61
185	3.95	0.26	0.21	228	6.88	0.84	0.86
186	7.76	0.78	0.86	229	3.42	0.35	0.19
187	6.92	0.68	0.47	230	4.45	0.34	0.35
188	7.02	0.37	0.54	231	3.99	0.09	0.04
189	6.24	0.61	0.69	232	0.00	0.00	0.00
190	4.14	0.40	0.23	233	4.40	0.24	0.42
191	3.82	0.26	0.25	234	7.25	0.77	0.83
192	0.00	0.00	0.00	235	3.47	0.22	0.15
193	3.72	0.25	0.22	236	3.08	0.32	0.25
194	3.66	0.39	0.31	237	6.59	0.54	0.67
195	2.64	0.15	0.07	238	3.40	0.07	0.22
196	7.60	0.86	0.92	239	0.00	0.00	0.00
197	6.18	0.91	0.91	240	6.19	0.81	0.79
198	2.51	0.20	0.05	241	4.13	0.39	0.33
199	3.70	0.14	0.13	242	2.88	0.20	0.20
200	4.53	0.19	0.13	243	7.32	0.72	0.77
201	0.00	0.00	0.00	244	0.00	0.00	0.00
202	5.57	0.67	0.75	245	3.58	0.18	0.12
203	7.43	0.80	0.75	246	3.27	0.14	0.13
204	2.81	0.15	0.07	247	3.91	0.24	0.22
205	4.70	0.51	0.33	248	7.72	0.80	0.76
206	3.39	0.05	0.08	249	6.21	0.34	0.23
207	3.45	0.32	0.20	250	6.73	0.57	0.55
208	0.00	0.00	0.00	251	5.40	0.61	0.59
209	6.86	0.85	0.89	252	3.73	0.43	0.27
210	7.16	0.91	0.96	253	4.35	0.24	0.44
211	4.55	0.67	0.66	254	0.00	0.00	0.00
212	7.32	0.90	0.91	255	7.06	0.69	0.53
213	0.00	0.00	0.00	256	4.42	0.44	0.41
214	3.48	0.41	0.38	257	2.66	0.21	0.16
215	3.83	0.14	0.19	258	7.46	0.82	0.90

Table VIII The SDSVs of the EPI Items in Booklet IV and the Proportion of Males and Females Responding True to Each Item[a]—Continued

Item	SDSV	P(T) M	P(T) F	Item	SDSV	P(T) M	P(T) F
259	6.90	0.84	0.91	280	6.92	0.49	0.26
260	3.24	0.51	0.51	281	6.62	0.51	0.57
261	3.73	0.19	0.21	282	3.22	0.12	0.12
262	5.92	0.44	0.40	283	4.83	0.44	0.23
263	0.00	0.00	0.00	284	3.59	0.23	0.14
264	3.59	0.29	0.29	285	0.00	0.00	0.00
265	7.06	0.58	0.72	286	3.77	0.28	0.26
266	3.40	0.48	0.49	287	5.46	0.60	0.62
267	2.88	0.24	0.11	288	2.76	0.08	0.06
268	3.70	0.10	0.12	289	5.35	0.51	0.63
269	4.36	0.41	0.44	290	6.51	0.80	0.87
270	0.00	0.00	0.00	291	3.95	0.51	0.27
271	5.76	0.66	0.68	292	7.51	0.66	0.69
272	4.05	0.34	0.44	293	3.68	0.44	0.52
273	3.53	0.29	0.14	294	0.00	0.00	0.00
274	5.70	0.73	0.69	295	6.45	0.34	0.31
275	0.00	0.00	0.00	296	6.48	0.17	0.38
276	3.59	0.39	0.31	297	3.61	0.24	0.15
277	6.80	0.71	0.82	298	6.05	0.44	0.47
278	3.39	0.09	0.09	299	5.43	0.64	0.68
279	7.93	0.66	0.73	300	4.91	0.24	0.16

[a]Items 151, 182, 213, 244, and 275 are not scored in Booklet IV. The other items in this booklet for which the SDSV is given as 0.00 are scored in Scale M but these items were not scaled for social desirability. For further details regarding the SDSVs of the EPI items, see Edwards (1966c).

Table IX The SDSVs of the PRF Items and the Proportion of Males and Females Responding True to Each Item[a]

Item	SDSV	P(T) M	P(T) F	Item	SDSV	P(T) M	P(T) F
1	6.39	0.46	0.54	44	2.50	0.13	0.09
2	7.90	0.94	0.96	45	6.53	0.56	0.58
3	2.48	0.11	0.06	46	5.94	0.85	0.83
4	3.49	0.68	0.48	47	3.31	0.18	0.16
5	3.30	0.18	0.21	48	3.48	0.51	0.28
6	5.18	0.83	0.85	49	4.23	0.35	0.51
7	4.62	0.47	0.43	50	6.10	0.81	0.89
8	5.50	0.57	0.67	51	3.97	0.44	0.44
9	6.05	0.59	0.51	52	4.41	0.46	0.56
10	3.68	0.35	0.21	53	4.51	0.64	0.54
11	6.73	0.69	0.66	54	3.82	0.42	0.35
12	3.66	0.31	0.36	55	5.07	0.73	0.75
13	7.22	0.95	0.96	56	5.04	0.45	0.34
14	3.21	0.12	0.07	57	4.38	0.72	0.79
15	5.67	0.51	0.59	58	3.74	0.24	0.10
16	3.51	0.11	0.08	59	5.40	0.57	0.37
17	6.24	0.92	0.99	60	2.69	0.07	0.06
18	6.76	0.75	0.83	61	6.49	0.94	0.98
19	4.35	0.31	0.18	62	6.31	0.82	0.94
20	2.92	0.08	0.07	63	4.76	0.53	0.38
21	4.67	0.01	0.05	64	3.31	0.11	0.11
22	8.07	0.87	0.92	65	3.76	0.02	0.04
23	3.80	0.19	0.07	66	7.24	0.78	0.75
24	2.66	0.03	0.04	67	4.18	0.59	0.40
25	7.19	0.91	0.93	68	3.28	0.28	0.17
26	5.79	0.40	0.56	69	7.89	0.89	0.93
27	6.53	0.92	0.91	70	4.09	0.39	0.43
28	3.58	0.10	0.04	71	6.17	0.66	0.63
29	6.10	0.78	0.84	72	3.77	0.21	0.12
30	4.91	0.64	0.55	73	5.21	0.66	0.60
31	4.18	0.24	0.41	74	5.09	0.63	0.61
32	6.83	0.89	0.91	75	4.21	0.31	0.42
33	3.73	0.07	0.22	76	6.63	0.40	0.50
34	4.76	0.47	0.41	77	4.97	0.25	0.40
35	3.63	0.33	0.28	78	4.68	0.31	0.56
36	6.88	0.69	0.67	79	4.44	0.31	0.33
37	3.66	0.32	0.22	80	6.98	0.87	0.87
38	6.83	0.77	0.74	81	4.36	0.46	0.46
39	3.33	0.12	0.07	82	6.55	0.76	0.70
40	3.83	0.18	0.19	83	3.30	0.06	0.06
41	6.97	0.88	0.84	84	4.76	0.39	0.37
42	7.12	0.93	0.92	85	6.32	0.56	0.56
43	7.14	0.95	0.97	86	6.97	0.57	0.54

Table IX   The SDSVs of the PRF Items and the Proportion of Males and Females
Responding True to Each Item[a]—Continued

		P(T)				P(T)	
Item	SDSV	M	F	Item	SDSV	M	F
87	5.70	0.01	0.07	130	7.24	0.88	0.92
88	3.55	0.07	0.09	131	2.98	0.05	0.05
89	4.93	0.46	0.45	132	3.35	0.23	0.17
90	7.03	0.59	0.56	133	2.92	0.17	0.21
91	3.00	0.14	0.09	134	6.07	0.73	0.65
92	3.39	0.31	0.19	135	3.30	0.24	0.17
93	4.13	0.32	0.32	136	4.33	0.61	0.66
94	6.52	0.87	0.90	137	6.35	0.55	0.66
95	3.74	0.28	0.31	138	6.55	0.77	0.74
96	5.71	0.52	0.71	139	4.05	0.36	0.28
97	6.86	0.63	0.50	140	5.45	0.61	0.67
98	3.90	0.40	0.39	141	5.53	0.52	0.49
99	5.24	0.50	0.54	142	4.24	0.31	0.34
100	5.68	0.61	0.52	143	5.08	0.48	0.51
101	5.72	0.65	0.70	144	4.92	0.74	0.60
102	3.86	0.22	0.19	145	3.86	0.55	0.58
103	5.78	0.39	0.45	146	3.19	0.15	0.09
104	4.05	0.14	0.11	147	6.59	0.69	0.63
105	6.29	0.83	0.97	148	4.33	0.35	0.28
106	5.92	0.76	0.64	149	6.72	0.88	0.95
107	5.27	0.59	0.39	150	5.23	0.56	0.43
108	3.12	0.13	0.07	151	5.28	0.54	0.42
109	7.14	0.98	1.00	152	3.70	0.12	0.06
110	6.98	0.94	0.88	153	3.64	0.01	0.00
111	4.81	0.58	0.56	154	6.90	0.88	0.89
112	3.20	0.38	0.27	155	5.69	0.55	0.54
113	7.56	0.83	0.88	156	3.62	0.38	0.35
114	5.36	0.55	0.51	157	7.16	0.87	0.74
115	6.84	0.62	0.58	158	6.94	0.71	0.72
116	5.04	0.24	0.14	159	5.82	0.89	0.76
117	6.27	0.58	0.42	160	3.87	0.09	0.12
118	4.88	0.53	0.44	161	4.20	0.42	0.38
119	4.88	0.29	0.46	162	4.16	0.43	0.41
120	6.13	0.75	0.63	163	4.79	0.28	0.53
121	4.05	0.44	0.36	164	6.44	0.72	0.72
122	4.50	0.28	0.48	165	4.25	0.44	0.41
123	5.63	0.40	0.39	166	4.15	0.32	0.39
124	6.93	0.55	0.61	167	5.04	0.37	0.37
125	4.27	0.37	0.33	168	6.12	0.61	0.66
126	4.80	0.59	0.57	169	4.86	0.41	0.43
127	3.46	0.14	0.06	170	5.24	0.73	0.67
128	4.42	0.31	0.27	171	4.32	0.06	0.10
129	5.91	0.80	0.84	172	4.73	0.52	0.46

Table IX   The SDSVs of the PRF Items and the Proportion of Males and Females
Responding True to Each Item[a]—Continued

| Item | SDSV | P(T) | | Item | SDSV | P(T) | |
		M	F			M	F
173	5.03	0.25	0.86	216	4.83	0.55	0.45
174	6.89	0.85	0.86	217	4.97	0.38	0.42
175	6.88	0.98	1.00	218	6.58	0.80	0.66
176	2.98	0.22	0.19	219	3.50	0.01	0.02
177	5.28	0.39	0.42	220	3.09	0.22	0.20
178	6.46	0.58	0.41	221	4.30	0.29	0.32
179	4.15	0.29	0.33	222	5.94	0.66	0.59
180	3.14	0.19	0.16	223	3.32	0.29	0.33
181	3.81	0.47	0.55	224	3.68	0.39	0.22
182	4.98	0.58	0.43	225	5.51	0.42	0.39
183	5.43	0.55	0.72	226	6.36	0.35	0.50
184	6.18	0.62	0.69	227	3.82	0.46	0.48
185	5.70	0.41	0.27	228	4.62	0.46	0.67
186	3.70	0.41	0.43	229	4.83	0.56	0.30
187	5.20	0.45	0.43	230	4.33	0.42	0.45
188	5.72	0.78	0.57	231	5.00	0.40	0.32
189	5.90	0.61	0.47	232	4.82	0.54	0.37
190	3.29	0.17	0.08	233	4.58	0.54	0.55
191	5.28	0.54	0.48	234	3.11	0.14	0.15
192	4.04	0.23	0.37	235	4.15	0.23	0.15
193	6.54	0.92	0.95	236	5.26	0.39	0.38
194	4.91	0.38	0.38	237	6.16	0.90	0.86
195	4.87	0.67	0.61	238	4.09	0.46	0.38
196	3.40	0.10	0.12	239	5.73	0.93	0.70
197	6.43	0.98	0.97	240	4.49	0.21	0.17
198	6.30	0.86	0.75	241	6.44	0.97	0.96
199	4.56	0.66	0.61	242	6.46	0.71	0.71
200	3.95	0.40	0.23	243	5.67	0.73	0.72
201	5.76	0.61	0.59	244	3.64	0.25	0.25
202	5.81	0.69	0.79	245	7.54	0.94	0.92
203	5.33	0.70	0.61	246	6.88	0.88	0.80
204	3.89	0.19	0.14	247	4.75	0.41	0.41
205	5.80	0.61	0.56	248	4.16	0.37	0.40
206	3.78	0.44	0.35	249	4.41	0.47	0.47
207	4.60	0.41	0.51	250	4.26	0.28	0.28
208	6.56	0.59	0.64	251	5.59	0.53	0.90
209	3.95	0.49	0.50	252	6.59	0.62	0.61
210	4.95	0.39	0.47	253	4.97	0.31	0.37
211	6.39	0.64	0.43	254	4.13	0.18	0.18
212	7.26	0.56	0.56	255	6.21	0.61	0.54
213	4.10	0.38	0.39	256	6.29	0.65	0.73
214	5.38	0.61	0.61	257	4.08	0.41	0.40
215	4.24	0.16	0.21	258	5.74	0.79	0.71

Table IX   The SDSVs of the PRF Items and the Proportion of Males and Females
Responding True to Each Item[a]—Continued

		P(F)				P(T)	
Item	SDSV	M	F	Item	SDSV	M	F
259	4.10	0.06	0.03	302	5.28	0.62	0.53
260	5.50	0.83	0.62	303	3.69	0.07	0.03
261	5.16	0.50	0.64	304	5.94	0.51	0.47
262	5.66	0.72	0.75	305	5.15	0.24	0.47
263	2.25	0.09	0.08	306	6.80	0.92	0.89
264	3.56	0.24	0.20	307	5.96	0.95	0.88
265	3.53	0.24	0.24	308	4.64	0.50	0.46
266	6.67	0.71	0.79	309	3.67	0.26	0.31
267	3.03	0.17	0.08	310	5.50	0.44	0.50
268	2.88	0.27	0.21	311	4.03	0.45	0.49
269	5.82	0.53	0.55	312	3.24	0.23	0.16
270	5.96	0.70	0.75	313	6.18	0.85	0.65
271	4.52	0.48	0.51	314	5.35	0.55	0.62
272	5.74	0.54	0.70	315	5.67	0.62	0.71
273	5.36	0.39	0.35	316	6.27	0.76	0.83
274	3.62	0.54	0.50	317	5.90	0.37	0.17
275	3.20	0.31	0.25	318	4.81	0.48	0.67
276	6.32	0.78	0.81	319	4.33	0.15	0.32
277	4.74	0.40	0.60	320	5.84	0.81	0.67
278	4.10	0.31	0.22	321	4.28	0.50	0.59
279	6.03	0.33	0.37	322	3.65	0.28	0.16
280	5.44	0.64	0.52	323	4.08	0.24	0.20
281	6.49	0.83	0.88	324	4.82	0.45	0.37
282	5.41	0.60	0.53	325	6.28	0.53	0.85
283	5.65	0.76	0.66	326	4.10	0.33	0.23
284	3.49	0.19	0.17	327	5.66	0.52	0.54
285	3.43	0.03	0.03	328	4.83	0.30	0.40
286	7.34	0.80	0.88	329	6.22	0.89	0.89
287	6.42	0.84	0.86	330	7.04	0.84	0.78
288	3.49	0.39	0.37	331	6.14	0.87	0.83
289	7.19	0.80	0.82	332	4.63	0.28	0.50
290	6.35	0.78	0.79	333	7.02	0.66	0.73
291	4.86	0.39	0.36	334	6.99	0.94	0.95
292	3.89	0.23	0.19	335	4.55	0.44	0.50
293	4.93	0.54	0.46	336	4.41	0.39	0.24
294	3.68	0.50	0.26	337	5.85	0.44	0.43
295	4.61	0.51	0.59	338	5.75	0.83	0.74
296	5.97	0.82	0.61	339	3.63	0.33	0.44
297	5.54	0.54	0.48	340	4.77	0.38	0.31
298	4.79	0.15	0.20	341	4.55	0.42	0.44
299	6.42	0.84	0.61	342	3.69	0.13	0.23
300	6.09	0.25	0.54	343	5.87	0.72	0.51
301	4.14	0.47	0.50	344	6.55	0.52	0.51

Table IX The SDSVs of the PRF Items and the Proportion of Males and Females
Responding True to Each Item[a] — Continued

| Item | SDSV | P(T) | | Item | SDSV | P(T) | |
		M	F			M	F
345	4.30	0.60	0.54	388	6.13	0.19	0.42
346	5.14	0.59	0.49	389	4.99	0.65	0.65
347	3.61	0.11	0.05	390	3.85	0.30	0.39
348	6.49	0.69	0.75	391	4.21	0.31	0.37
349	4.67	0.27	0.46	392	5.67	0.72	0.81
350	5.59	0.61	0.59	393	4.34	0.34	0.39
351	6.92	0.92	0.98	394	5.94	0.38	0.47
352	3.31	0.28	0.24	395	5.66	0.08	0.01
353	4.42	0.17	0.26	396	3.44	0.35	0.29
354	4.16	0.27	0.28	397	2.89	0.11	0.13
355	3.89	0.32	0.34	398	4.68	0.15	0.19
356	2.42	0.20	0.08	399	5.10	0.62	0.62
357	6.16	0.78	0.71	400	2.85	0.16	0.10
358	5.64	0.48	0.46	401	5.89	0.82	0.69
359	6.16	0.77	0.74	402	4.65	0.14	0.09
360	5.68	0.79	0.77	403	6.08	0.81	0.79
361	4.90	0.53	0.30	404	6.68	0.87	0.88
362	4.94	0.84	0.88	405	3.98	0.24	0.33
363	3.37	0.23	0.06	406	6.15	0.71	0.75
364	5.62	0.80	0.68	407	4.91	0.17	0.14
365	5.90	0.53	0.63	408	5.50	0.90	0.78
366	3.76	0.29	0.28	409	5.00	0.49	0.45
367	5.89	0.41	0.30	410	3.56	0.17	0.12
368	5.81	0.66	0.65	411	3.98	0.23	0.13
369	6.22	0.75	0.82	412	5.59	0.69	0.69
370	3.99	0.22	0.32	413	5.91	0.65	0.81
371	6.43	0.82	0.83	414	3.97	0.26	0.24
372	5.14	0.40	0.72	415	6.26	0.94	0.87
373	3.23	0.06	0.03	416	5.57	0.72	0.53
374	6.01	0.85	0.79	417	6.79	0.94	0.92
375	5.49	0.73	0.76	418	6.10	0.50	0.39
376	4.01	0.38	0.25	419	6.10	0.66	0.61
377	6.03	0.52	0.50	420	5.87	0.66	0.92
378	7.03	0.82	0.94	421	6.55	0.34	0.29
379	4.56	0.39	0.30	422	7.31	0.93	0.94
380	6.02	0.70	0.65	423	3.69	0.18	0.13
381	5.15	0.26	0.36	424	5.38	0.73	0.85
382	3.38	0.27	0.37	425	4.58	0.30	0.26
383	5.03	0.64	0.75	426	3.67	0.29	0.21
384	4.91	0.20	0.17	427	5.44	0.62	0.64
385	4.36	0.23	0.29	428	6.07	0.39	0.39
386	4.15	0.06	0.12	429	4.98	0.51	0.66
387	4.30	0.22	0.23	430	3.65	0.10	0.06

Table IX   The SDSVs of the PRF Items and the Proportion of Males and Females
Responding True to Each Item[a]—Continued

Item	SDSV	$P(T)$ M	$P(T)$ F	Item	SDSV	$P(T)$ M	$P(T)$ F
431	5.53	0.63	0.57	436	7.75	0.94	0.87
432	6.00	0.11	0.35	437	3.61	0.15	0.18
433	4.76	0.72	0.84	438	5.46	0.22	0.21
434	4.78	0.34	0.58	439	7.20	0.97	0.99
435	4.43	0.30	0.29	440	3.68	0.34	0.41

[a]The items in the PRF were rated for social desirability on a 9-point rating scale by 51 male and 49 female students. The mean SDSV of the items in the PRF for the males was 5.07 with a standard deviation of 1.13. For the females the corresponding values were 5.04 and 1.36. The correlation between the male and female SDSVs was 0.95. The SDSVs reported are for the combined group of 100 judges. A sample of 109 male and 109 female students completed the PRF in self-description. The $P(T)$s for males and females given in the table are based on this sample.

Name Index

Abbott, R. D., 160, 161, 162, 188, 207, 212, 213
Ax, A. F., 194, 195
Bigger, C., 180, 183
Biggs, C. F., 91
Block, J., 118, 150, 156, 184, 185, 186, 187, 196, 225, 226, 227, 228, 229, 230, 231
Blumberg, A., 196, 229
Boe, E. E., 98, 119, 120
Budin, W., 91
Buros, O. K., 52
Chu, Chen-Lin, 188
Comrey, A. L., 187, 188
Cooper, A., 196, 229
Couch, A., 135, 142, 143, 157
Cowen, E. L., 91, 92, 107
Cronbach, L. J., 158
Crowder, P., 157, 209
Crowne, D. P., 135
Cruse, D. B., 89, 91, 107
Dahlstrom, W. G., 56, 127, 145
Davol, S. H., 91
Dempsey, P., 177
Diers, C. J., 60, 128, 129, 130, 132, 135, 141, 142, 145, 146, 148, 157, 159, 208, 209, 210, 218
Edwards, A. L., 60, 88, 89, 90, 91, 92, 93, 94, 95, 106, 107, 109, 110, 111, 112, 113, 114, 115, 116, 117, 118, 120, 126, 128, 129, 130, 132, 134, 135, 138, 139, 140, 141, 142, 143, 144, 145, 146, 148, 151, 152, 153, 154, 156, 157, 159, 160, 161, 162, 167, 172, 173, 175, 180, 182, 186, 188, 189, 190, 192, 194, 196, 198, 204, 205, 207, 208, 209, 210, 211, 212, 213, 218, 220, 234, 237, 239, 242, 243, 244, 245
Fordyce, W. E., 182, 197
Frankel, G., 91, 92
Fricke, B. G., 142, 157
Fujita, B., 91
Fukuhara, M., 107
Gocka, E. F., 91, 98, 133, 180, 183, 209, 210
Goldberg, L. R., 139, 168, 173

Gough, H. G., 57
Green, B. F., 88
Guilford, J. P., 88, 204
Hanley, C., 107, 144, 148, 157, 180, 202
Hathaway, S. R., 189, 216
Heathers, L. B., 143
Heineman, C. E., 128, 145
Heineman, P. O., 91
Hidano, T., 107
Hillmer, M. L., Jr., 200
Holloway, H., 91, 180, 183, 209, 210
Horst, P., 192, 198
Humphreys, L. G., 37, 51
Iwawaki, S., 91, 92, 107
Jackson, D. N., 91, 128, 135, 139, 142, 143, 145, 146, 148, 150, 157, 168, 186, 212, 213
Kaiser, H. F., 81
Kassebaum, G. G., 143
Kelleher, D., 206
Keniston, K., 135, 142, 157
Kenny, D. T., 107
Klett, C. J., 91, 92, 205, 228
Klieger, D. M., 91
Klockars, A. J., 151, 152, 153, 154, 188, 207, 212, 213
Kogan, W. S., 98, 119, 120, 194, 195
Lamphere, A. V., 197
Lövaas, O. I., 92
Marggraff, W. M., 187
Marlowe, D., 135
McGee, R. K., 158
McKinley, J. C., 189
Meehl, P. E., 216
Mees, H. L., 91
Messick, S., 91, 99, 128, 135, 139, 142, 143, 145, 146, 148, 150, 157, 168
Okuno, S., 91
Peabody, D., 236, 248
Peter, Sister Mary, 91
Quinn, R., 194, 195
Reimanis, G., 91
Ripley, H. S., 194, 195
Rorer, L. G., 139, 168, 173
Rosen, A., 187

301

Subject Index